Plain Folk
of the South
Revisited

Plain Folk
of the South
Revisited

Edited by

SAMUEL C. HYDE, JR.

Louisiana State University Press • *Baton Rouge and London*

Copyright © 1997 by Louisiana State University Press
All rights reserved
Manufactured in the United States of America
First printing
06 05 04 03 02 01 00 99 98 97   5 4 3 2 1

Designer: Michele Myatt Quinn
Typeface: Adobe Goudy Old Style
Typesetter: Impressions Book and Journal Services, Inc.
Printer and binder: Thomson-Shore, Inc.

Library of Congress Cataloging in Publication Data

Plain folk of the South revisited / edited by Samuel C. Hyde, Jr.
    p.   cm.
    Based on a symposium held in spring 1996 at Southeastern Louisiana
University.
    Includes index.
    ISBN 0-8071-2200-9 (cloth : alk. paper)
    1. Southern States—Social life and customs—Congresses.
2. Southern States—Social conditions—Congresses.   3. Labor and
laboring classes—Southern States—History—Congresses.   4. Middle
class—Southern States—History—Congresses.   I. Hyde, Samuel C.,
1958–   .
F209.P57   1997
975—dc21   97-20625
                                                        CIP

CONTENTS

II
Social Groups and Attitudes

III
Plain-Folk Democracy and Its Limits

ACKNOWLEDGMENTS

During the three years it took to organize, host, and publish the papers of the Plain Folk of the South Symposium, numerous people and institutions provided invaluable assistance. Each of the contributors worked under pressing time constraints to expand our understanding of the plain folk, all the while maintaining the highest level of professionalism and cheerfully enduring my constant deadlines. A special word of thanks to John Boles, Brad Bond, and Jerah Johnson for their insightful criticism of the final product.

Raising funds to support historical conferences remains a constant challenge, but in this case we were particularly fortunate. The Dan Durham family, Hibernia National Bank, D. C. Heath College Publishing, and the Louisiana Endowment for the Humanities continued their traditional support of scholarly endeavors and made this symposium a reality through their generous contributions.

The staff at Louisiana State University Press epitomize the spirit of professionalism and scholarly achievement. Their consistent encouragement and diligent work ethic make the most demanding of tasks a pleasure. Special thanks to John Easterly, who guided the project from idea to book, and to Gerry Anders, who proved an excellent copy editor.

A list of persons who contributed to making this project a success would rival the length of the essays. A particular word of thanks, however, is due Randy Sanders and Shane Hodgson, who worked tirelessly in support of the symposium. Bill Cooper and Clarence Mohr gave kindly of their time and provided dutiful criticism of the project. Roman Heleniak remains the single person most responsible for this venture. His commitment to scholarly excellence, and his ability to make the impossible happen, ensured the success of the conference.

Finally, a word of thanks to Frank Owsley, whose contribution to southern history fifty years ago demonstrated a vitality among common southerners that has allowed us to discover more in the lives and the culture of the plain folk than even he could ever have imagined.

JOHN B. BOLES

FOREWORD: REVISITING THE PLAIN
FOLK OF THE SOUTH

In 1948 Frank L. Owsley, then a professor of history at Vanderbilt University, presented the Walter Lynwood Fleming Lectures at Louisiana State University. Dr. Owsley entitled his four lectures "Plain Folk of the Old South," and these expanded lectures, supplemented with a fifth, largely statistical chapter, were published the following year by LSU Press.[1] This book has arguably been the most influential of all those in the distinguished series, and has been subjected both to stringent criticism and to uncritical admiration.[2] Yet even the book's friends realize that the Owsley concept of the plain folk, or "yeoman farmers" as he often called them, has in its use by historians become slippery and ill defined. Often historians use the term *plain folk* as a synonym for non-slaveholders, but Owsley himself clearly included "small slaveholding farmers" among the plain folk.[3] To some degree Owsley's definition has only begged the question. Exactly who were the small slaveholding farmers—those owning only one or two slaves? those owning fewer than ten? A more precise definition of the plain folk needs to be formulated and agreed upon. Owsley's antebellum plain folk were all rural, but if we extend the concept beyond the Civil War, were there not town- and city-dwelling folk who were the social and cultural descendants of his plain folk? The term *plain folk* will probably remain grounded in class, but its temporal expansion requires elaboration beyond rural lifestyles.

1. Burl Noggle, *The Fleming Lectures, 1937–1990: A Historiographical Essay* (Baton Rouge, 1992), 15–16; Frank L. Owsley, *Plain Folk of the Old South* (rev. ed.; Baton Rouge, 1982).

2. The best introduction to the historiographical debates swirling around the book is Randolph B. Campbell, "Planters and Plain Folks: The Social Structure of the Antebellum South," in *Interpreting Southern History: Historiographical Essays in Honor of Sanford W. Higginbotham*, ed. John B. Boles and Evelyn Thomas Nolen (Baton Rouge, 1987), 48–77.

3. Owsley, *Plain Folk*, 7.

Even more troublesome than definitional imprecision is the extent to which historians have taken Owsley's already somewhat romanticized account of the yeoman farmers and portrayed them as salt-of-the-earth people, living in close, face-to-face communities, almost free of a competitive spirit, exchanging goods and services in a cashless society in which there appear to be no losers, no crime, no social pathology. A reverse image has also developed, in which the plain folk are portrayed as the surviving remnants of the ancient Celtic tribes of Europe, and as such, hopelessly lazy but happy, content to drink, fight, fornicate, curse, hunt, or anything else rather than till the soil. In a sense, Owsley's plain folk have suffered interpretative polarization, with the result that the term *plain folk* itself has become virtually useless, so simplified that it is now more a stereotype than a category for analysis. In short, there is a need to complexify the term, to show that the plain folk were more varied, more complex, than the popular usage suggests. It is precisely that task that these ten essays set out to do.

One of the many virtues of Owsley's original book was that it made historians aware that the southern white population consisted of more than planters and poor white trash; that is, the book was itself a work of complexification. But historians since have insufficiently taken up Owsley's implicit challenge to study the plain folk. We now are in the ironical situation of knowing far more about the slaves—and the elite white planter class—than we know about the majority population group of the Old South. At one time the excuse was that the plain folk did not leave the kind of written records the elite slaveholders did, and that is true; but consider the skill with which historians have combed through even less evidence about slaves and teased out of those sources a rich, acutely nuanced interpretation of slave culture, religion, family life, work routines, and so on. Women's historians are also demonstrating that it is possible to reconstruct the life and attitudes of people who a generation ago were mostly omitted from the history that was written. Perhaps the next great advance in the historiography of the South will be the discovery of the plain folk—men and women, rural and urban, agricultural and industrial, black and white, from colonial times to the present. A sprinkling of monographs and dissertations, many of them cited in the chapters in this book, shows that the work is under way. Here lies the great frontier in southern studies. We have already been taught, by the recent scholarship in black history and women's history, that sensitivity to race and gender significantly recasts our entire understanding of the past. Greater sensitivity to issues of class—specifically, recovering the history of the non-elites—promises the same interpretative riches.

The papers presented at the symposium on the plain folk organized by Samuel C. Hyde, Jr., and held at Southeastern Louisiana University, February 29–March 2, 1996, cumulatively had the implicit assignment of complexifying the concept of the plain folk, making it more inclusive in terms of race and gender and extending the interpretation from the antebellum period through the first third of the twentieth century. True to Owsley's original discussion, the participants in the symposium addressed such issues as how the plain folk made their living, the houses they dwelled in, some of their cultural artifacts. But in every instance the authors of the essays presented here pushed beyond the easy stereotype to show that there is more to the story than we first assumed. The general strategy is to begin with the traditional interpretation, then to show that it is too simple to explain the evidence, and finally to suggest a more complete, complicated interpretation. No attempt is made by any of the authors, or by the editor, to discover a general metatheory to explain everything (and often, thereby, nothing) about the South. Rather, the authors are filling in gaps, elaborating, examining new topics like the Sunday-school movement, reminding us that there were social groups like the free people of color that have tended to fall between the interpretative cracks.

The approach is diverse and the conclusions more so. At times the cultural creativity and eclecticism of the plain folk are praised, as in Bill Malone's insightful analysis of the origin of the music of the southern plain folk or in Jerah Johnson's musings about the origins of southern vernacular architecture; but then Sam Hyde discusses the proclivity of the plain folk in certain circumstances to sink into political depravity and violence, concluding in effect that some regions of the rural South were not ready for democracy. The symposium papers were neither uncritical nor patronizing toward the plain folk. This collection of articles contains new information, fresh interpretations, both confirmation of what we thought we knew and surprises. Like all such collections, the essays are uneven, and readers will disagree over which ones are the most convincing. Most readers will end the book thinking of other topics that should have been included. That is the best measure of the success of the symposium and the resulting book: the conference could be held annually for a

number of years and still not finish the task of exploring the role and contributions of the plain folk to the history of the South. As the modern
cliché puts it, this is a work in progress.

Various scholars and commentators have suggested either Anglo-Saxon
(specifically, Elizabethan English) or Celtic origins for southern music,
but Bill Malone, the preeminent authority in the field, shows persuasively
that the southern folk borrowed musical styles from many other sources as
well and made them their own. Music from Britain, from France, from
Hawaii, from Africa, from Mexico and Latin America, from vaudeville
and Tin Pan Alley, all entered into the blend; there were protest songs,
work songs, religious songs, bawdy songs; there was sentimental parlor
music and lively dancing tunes and the raucous music of honky-tonks.
The southern folk seldom knew or cared where musical forms, styles, and
idioms came from. If they liked the way it sounded, then it became part of
the mix they called their own. Even the author of "Dixie" was from the
North. Musical tastes transcended race as well as region, with Elvis Presley borrowing from black sources and Charlie Pride singing the songs of
Hank Williams. Southern plain folk loved the gospel music of Thomas A.
Dorsey and Albert E. Brumley, and most did not know that Dorsey was
black, Brumley white. What is commonly called country-western or hillbilly music is, as Malone has argued over the years, the music of the
southern folk. Its origins are diverse and its forms protean, and it has
spread across the world as one of the nation's premier cultural artifacts.

Jerah Johnson leads us through the debates over the origin of the log
cabin in both its simple form and its double form known as the dog-trot
house, and he rehearses the older debates about Swedish or German origins. He complexifies the issue by observing that the British had horizontal log structures too, and he shows that British craftsmen were certainly
familiar with the notching technique of fastening timbers together. Moreover, he shows that British barns were identical in style to the dog-trot
houses. In short, Johnson persuasively suggests that early American
builders had sources nearer to home than Scandinavia or Germany. Had
Johnson had more space, he might have discussed other characteristics of
southern vernacular architecture, such as use of the veranda or porch, the
so-called shotgun houses, and the raised houses of the Carolina and
Louisiana lowcountry, and pondered their provenance. In providing shel-
ter, as in music, southern folk builders borrowed from a number of

sources, and climate, terrain, and available materials—along with a variety of building traditions—were entered into the folk calculus that produced southern vernacular architecture.

One of the persisting oversimplifications about the southern plain folk is the idea that they were all subsistence farmers who, if they produced any cotton, were primarily safety-first farmers who emphasized foodstuffs and participated in the market economy only if they anticipated having surplus labor. Such subsistence farmers were allegedly anticommercial in orientation. Bradley G. Bond in his essay shows that the story was more complex than realized at first glance. The evidence indicates that many of the plain folk who moved into the piney-woods region of southern and eastern Mississippi, migrants too poor to purchase plots of even this inexpensive, relatively infertile land sufficient to allow dependence on grain, were quick to realize the commercial possibilities of livestock. The open range allowed the plain folk to develop sizable herds of cattle, and these cattle could be driven on hoof to market towns. Rather than grow enough grains to support their families, as the safety-first model would argue, these farmers put their efforts into maximizing their livestock herds, using the profits gained from the sale of their cattle to purchase grains and other foodstuffs. Only when the profits gained from this commercial livestock trade allowed them to purchase much larger plots of land did the plain folk in the piney woods begin a transition from commercial herding to cotton farming. Bond's work complements such studies as that of John C. Inscoe, who has shown that the farmers in the mountainous regions of North Carolina, rather than being isolated subsistence farmers removed from the market economy, were quick to seize opportunities to sell their surplus butter, apples, hay, and oats to planters in the lowcountry who maximized their cotton or rice production. Inscoe and others have also shown how important was the commercial production of hogs in the mountain region.[4] Bond's chapter, in combination with a number of recent articles, dissertations, and books, convincingly indicates that the older image of the self-sufficient yeoman farmer, removed from the world of commerce and the concept of profits, needs at least to be complemented with the image of the small farmer as a go-getter, quick to see an

4. See John Inscoe, *Mountain Masters, Slavery, and the Sectional Crisis in Western North Carolina* (Knoxville, 1989), 11–58, and Forrest McDonald and Grady McWhiney, "The Antebellum Southern Herdsman: A Reinterpretation," *Journal of Southern History,* XLI (May 1975), 147–66.

opportunity and even quicker to seize it. The concept of the lazy southerner *as a type* should be discarded. In similar fashion, we need to know
more about the southern artisanal class: how they worked and for whom,
and the extent of their self-consciousness as a distinct group with unique
interests.[5]

Some historians may have indiscriminately equated the terms *peonage*
and *sharecropping*, thereby exaggerating the extent to which propertyless
farmers, white and black, were tied to the land. J. William Harris reminds
us that although most farmers were constantly in debt, few were actually
tied to the land. His evidence, and that of dozens of memoirs[6] and even
such a familiar song as that of the boll weevil searching for a home,
speaks to the ability of most sharecroppers to move around at the end of
the crop year, searching—usually in futility—to find a better deal, hoping against hope to end the year out of debt and with perhaps a down
payment for land of their own. Landowners often had to compete with
one another for croppers. Historians also need to be more precise when
they discuss the variety of arrangements between landless farmers and the
landholders, for in addition to peonage, which was always rare and more
common in the early twentieth century than in the nineteenth, there
were several gradations of farming on shares (what proportion of the crop
the actual farm laborer retained depended on several factors) and tenant
farming as well.

One of the most exciting developments in southern history over the
last two decades has been the growth of women's history. In none of the
mainstream Protestant denominations were women able to be ministers
and preach, but as Sally McMillen demonstrates, women played leading
roles in the Sunday-school movement that swept across the South in the
decades after the Civil War. Here women could teach, organize, raise
funds, and help mold the youth of the South. Thousands of women found
in the Sunday school an outlet for their energy, their ability, and their
Christian zeal; the Sunday schools taught literacy, the Bible, morality. Often religious history has concentrated on ministers, sermons, and official
denominational issues. McMillen has redirected our attention to what

5. See the study by Michele Gillespie, *Fruits of Their Labor: White Artisans in Slaveholding Georgia, 1790–1860* (Athens, Ga., forthcoming).

6. A particular favorite of mine is William A. Owen, *This Stubborn Soil* (New York,
1966). For a black sharecropper's experience, see [Theodore Rosengarten], *All God's Dangers: The Life of Nate Shaw* (New York, 1974).

might be called domestic religion. The lessons these countless women taught, the moralistic, sentimental religion they espoused, greatly shaped southern culture. This was a religion marked not by theological sophistication but by piety, and male ministers and women Sunday-school teachers together shaped a southern folk religion that was low-church, emotional, moralistic, and more concerned with conversion and charity than with a prophetic critique of society. To a degree not often understood, women played a major role in creating and cultivating the southern evangelical tradition. We need to understand better if and how the predominance of women in most congregations shaped the ministerial style and sermon content of the male preachers. McMillen points the way toward a very fruitful line of inquiry.

Even though the general reading public—remembering from the novel *Gone with the Wind* that all nonplanters were the "trashy, no-good, low-down po'-w'ite Slatterys"[7]—often forgets that Gerald O'Hara was not born into the planter class, no scholar since Owsley's Fleming Lectures has been able to speak of antebellum southern whites as consisting of only planters and white trash. In like fashion, despite the work of such scholars as John Hope Franklin, Ira Berlin, and Michael P. Johnson and James L. Roark on free blacks, few readers who are not professional historians seem to know that there were blacks in the antebellum South who were not slaves.[8] Free blacks are an unusually complicated subject, and their situation in life depended greatly on region, time, economic opportunity, and the white patrons they were able to develop. Moreover, the assumption has long been that conditions in Louisiana, for reasons of its peculiar French and Spanish background, were significantly different from those elsewhere in the South. Gary B. Mills offers a very detailed analysis of free blacks in Alabama, with mostly implicit comparisons to Louisiana, to argue that the story of free blacks in Alabama—and presumably elsewhere—is far more complex, and less different from the situation in Louisiana, than previously thought. He offers persuasive evidence that we can not assume that the existence of laws circumscribing free blacks actually defined or described their lives. Over and over again

7. Margaret Mitchell, *Gone with the Wind* (New York, 1936), 416–17.

8. John Hope Franklin, *The Free Negro in North Carolina, 1790–1860* (Chapel Hill, 1943); Ira Berlin, *Slaves Without Masters: The Free Negro in the Antebellum South* (New York, 1974); Michael P. Johnson and James L. Roark, *Black Masters: A Free Family of Color in the Old South* (New York, 1984).

he shows free blacks owning property or testifying in court or remaining in a region after they were required by law to leave. Life as lived ranged far beyond what the law required, and habit, practice, and convenience often overruled legislative intentions. Mills's work shows how difficult it is to make generalizations about the lives of free blacks and is a perfect example of how the standard account needs to be complexified.

Grady McWhiney's chapter differs from the others in that he attempts not to make more complex, but rather to simplify, previous understandings of an issue. Specifically, he argues against the bipolar interpretation of the South into aristocratic Cavaliers and plain-folk crackers by urging us to consider Cracker not an economic condition but a culture. He then urges us to conflate both Cracker and Cavalier into one, essentially a culture of courage. It is true that the popular images of Cavalier and Cracker are more stereotypes than descriptions of reality, but in McWhiney's new formulation it seems to me that he neglects the role of religion—peculiar given his discussion of Confederate generals—and does not investigate the full cultural consequences of the concept of courage. Gerald F. Linderman has shown that the almost magical early belief in courage evolved during the course of the Civil War, and by the later stages of the conflict it no longer was assumed that raw courage would protect a soldier from death.[9] McWhiney also does not make clear if or how southern courage differed from that of northern soldiers. The whole question of cultural differences and perceptions, one region of the other,[10] calls for more scholarship, and McWhiney hints at the interpretative riches we might expect from that work. As McWhiney suggests, the premium put on honor extended beyond the planter class down to the yeomen farmers, and we need more research exploring how honor manifested itself in popular culture and how it was related to evangelical religion.[11]

It is evident to even the most casual student of history that the political culture of the South (indeed, the nation) changed between the Age of Jefferson and the Age of Jackson, and much more by the age of the twentieth-century mass politician. The decline of deference and the rise

9. Gerald F. Linderman, *Embattled Courage: The Experience of Combat in the American Civil War* (New York, 1987).

10. Here one thinks of Michael C. C. Adams' provocative study *Our Masters the Rebels: A Speculation on Union Military Failure in the East, 1861–1865* (Cambridge, Mass., 1978).

11. Compare Edward R. Crowther, "Holy Honor: Sacred and Secular in the Old South," *Journal of Southern History*, LVIII (November 1992), 619–36.

of democratic politics has long been an organizing theme of political history, but precisely the role of the plain folk in this process has not always
been clear. What did the plain folk believe and want? What were their
political concerns? Did they have a well-developed identity? How did
they triangulate between their status, the planter aristocracy, and the
slave population itself? Lacy K. Ford approaches these questions by
looking at what the spokesmen for the plain folk advocated at three
important state constitutional conventions—Virginia in 1829–1830,
Mississippi in 1832, and Tennessee in 1834. What he found resonates
throughout the political history of the next several decades, for the plain
folk argued for the equality of all white men, accepted the rule of the
majority, revealed antipathy toward every vestige of privilege and aristocracy, and insisted on defining political citizenship in terms of race and
gender rather than class. Such a set of values provided the ground rules
for much of antebellum politics, and these attitudes persisted for decades
into the twentieth century. The prospects for political and economic reform even in the late nineteenth century were limited by these deeply
embedded beliefs, and even the woman's suffrage movement in the early
twentieth century had to learn how to tack against these racial and gender concerns to achieve their goals.

For at least a generation historians have often interpreted southern
white politics, even the rise of the republican form of government, in the
context of the presence of slavery. The felt necessity of whites to maintain a kind of united front amidst the perceived threat of servile rebellion
contributed to the concept of white man's democracy—class divisions
were largely erased in the face of the potential of slave insurrection. In
fact, as William Cooper has shown, even the definition of white liberty
was tied up with the defense of black slavery.[12] Implicit in this analysis is
the potential for white factionalism once slavery ended and the need to
accept planter leadership evaporated. It is this fascinating topic that
Samuel Hyde examines in his chapter. A detailed investigation of the
Florida parishes of Louisiana forms the basis of his probe into the culture
of violence, political chaos, and exaggerated individualism that existed in
certain limited regions of the South, and he is careful to show that where
the conditions were right in states other than Louisiana, this descent into

12. William J. Cooper, Jr., *Liberty and Slavery: Southern Politics to 1860* (New York, 1983).

a political heart of darkness was possible. Political democracy depends on shared ideas, firm leadership, and a commitment to some sort of community, and where these were lacking, the southern plain folk could prove politically incorrigible. Hyde's chapter is a fresh, innovative analysis of southern social and political history and has to be taken into account by those who would uncritically romanticize the southern folk. Like all people, the plain folk had (and have) passions that must be restrained and rechanneled.

Michael L. Kurtz suggests one form this restraint and rechanneling took in the two decades on either side of 1900. A style of political leader arose, often described in condemnatory fashion as a demagogue, who used appeals of stark racism (and also class consciousness) to generate political support for policies that were frequently progressive. Kurtz reminds us of the derivation of the word *demagogue,* traces its decline to a pejorative term, and then shows that many such popular leaders appealed to the false interests of the plain folk to advance their legitimate interests. The result is a partial rehabilitation of several well-known political leaders, although in the case of Huey Long there has been a needed backlash against some of the more benign interpretations of his political practices and policies.[13] Kurtz points out how the vocabulary of race infused the political environment of the South, and by so doing he points toward another aspect of the South's history that could benefit by being complexified. We need to know more about the turn to harsher racism about 1890, we need to probe more the possibilities for biracial political reform, we need to understand more about the popular sources of racism during the decades following 1890.[14] Could a different kind of political leadership on the part of the regnant Democrats have tempered this nadir of race relations? What exactly were the parameters of race and reform, and is resort to race the only possible explanatory tool?

Complexification does not suggest that there is no place in southern history for large-scale generalizations. On the contrary, such generalizations provide the baseline against which deviation, special cases, regional variation, and the role of class, gender, and race are highlighted. Written

---

13. I refer, of course, to William Ivy Hair, *The Kingfish and His Realm: The Life and Times of Huey P. Long* (Baton Rouge, 1991), which corrects, in my view, the overly romanticized account by T. Harry Williams, *Huey Long* (New York, 1969).

14. See, for example, Gregg Cantrell and D. Scott Barton, "Texas Populists and the Failure of Biracial Politics," *Journal of Southern History,* LV (November 1989), 659–92.

history provides a dialogue between generalization and particularism, and both are seen more clearly when held in interpretative tension. The dynamics of relations between the classes, the races, and across gender all suggest that the past is more complex than is often represented. Methodologically innovative work and exciting new interpretations in one field or for one group open up questions for other related groups, and the synergistic effect of human attitudes and actions on others means that new interpretations of part of the past have broad analytical implications. The recent advances in understanding southern blacks and women lead us to reassess the lives of the plain folk, secure in our belief that advances in this topic will similarly impact the whole of southern history. Surely it is time to rid the term *plain folk* of the temporal implications of Owsley's work and to develop a definition that may be applied to non-elite southerners from the colonial period to the present. Such is the implicit recommendation of this book. The kinds of questions asked by the authors of the articles in this collection, and the varied answers they provide, should be of interest to everyone burdened by the pursuit of southern history.

Plain Folk
of the South
Revisited

SAMUEL C. HYDE, JR.

Introduction: Perspectives on the Common South

S outh-baiting," C. Vann Woodward once wrote, "became a northern
journalistic industry with fabulously rich resources to mine below the
Potomac." Participants in the bloodless sport reviled the white South for
its lynching, peonage, chain gangs, sharecropping, corrupt courts and politics, poverty, illiteracy, bigotry, and hookworm. Woodward noted the en-
durance of Yankee scorn for the South, adding that the ridicule often
manifested deep-rooted contempt for southerners and southern ways, a
contempt that originated in antebellum critiques of slavery and disdain
for poor whites.[1]

Many of the problems Woodward identified had long served as defining characteristics of the South and its seemingly peculiar inhabitants.
A tendency to focus on the unappealing qualities of the South, however,
proved as central to the historiography of the region as distinctive problems did to southern culture. During the late antebellum period numerous
northern and European adventurers toured the South, commenting on
the oddities of the region. Led by Frederick Law Olmsted, most of these
men concentrated on the evils of southern society, particularly the slave
system, and what they regarded as the "mean" quality of life confronting
the mass of southerners. Like Olmsted, many of these observers applied

---

1. C. Vann Woodward, Thinking Back: The Perils of Writing History (Baton Rouge,
1986), 15–17.

the standards of their own community to the southern interior, a fact that led historian Clement Eaton to conclude they "were looking for the picturesque and unusual, not the representative aspects of southern life."[2]

The strongest criticism invariably fell upon the common folk of the South. The Puritan work ethic, evident in many regions of the North, contrasted sharply with the perceived lifestyle of common southerners, subjecting the South's less fortunate to the most severe reproach. The Englishman, William Howard Russell, summarized this perception, describing the culture of the backcountry South as, at best, crude. Lucius V. Bierce, a youthful adventurer from Ohio, likewise regarded the southern countryside as "delightful but the people devilish." Many southern observers shared outsiders' disdain for the common folk. As early as 1728 the Virginia gentleman William Byrd described common farmers as "indolent wretches" who were ignorant, unsanitary, and "lazy as Indians." Similarly, Robert Patrick, an aspiring member of the planter class in East Feliciana Parish, Louisiana, described the common folk as virtually devoid of culture, and claimed that his family "had blessed little to do with them."[3]

A more sympathetic view of common southerners appeared in 1860 in Daniel R. Hundley's *Social Relations in Our Southern States*. Although Hundley acknowledged the existence of a lower class of whites whom he called "poor white trash," he argued that a productive middle class constituted the largest single group of southerners. As a native southerner Hundley disputed the prevailing perception of the common folk and encouraged a more positive reconsideration of southern society. Yet the significance of his work remained limited because it appeared on the eve of secession. As the bloody cost of the Civil War came home to Ameri-

2. Frederick Law Olmsted, *The Cotton Kingdom: A Traveller's Observations on Cotton and Slavery in the American States* (New York, 1953); William Howard Russell, *My Diary North and South* (New York, 1954); Clement Eaton, *The Growth of Southern Civilization, 1790–1860* (New York, 1961), 153.

3. Russell, *My Diary North and South*; George W. Knepper, ed., *Travels in the Southland, 1822–1823: The Journal of Lucius Verus Bierce* (Columbus, Ohio, 1966), 99; William Byrd, "A History of the Dividing Line," in *The Writings of Colonel William Byrd of Westover in Virginia, Esquire*, ed. John Spencer Bassett (New York, 1901), 44–45, 75–77; F. Jay Taylor, ed., *Reluctant Rebel: The Secret Diary of Robert Patrick, 1861–1865* (Baton Rouge, 1959), 9; George M. Weston, *The Poor Whites of the South* (Washington, D.C., 1856).

cans North and South, the image of ragged, semiliterate rebels that appeared regularly in *Harper's Weekly* and other northern journals came to dominate the popular impression of common southerners rather than Hundley's more constructive view.[4]

Critical, if not contemptuous, portrayals of average white southerners proved dominant throughout the late nineteenth and into the early twentieth century. Highly celebrated examples of backcountry lawlessness such as the legendary Hatfield-McCoy feud fueled the imaginations of scores of "yellow" journalists who concentrated more on images of armed, bearded hillbillies sporting jugs of moonshine than they did on historical accuracy. Transplanted northerners such as Albion Tourgée, along with dissenting southerners like George Washington Cable, furthered the stereotype of the indolent, bigoted southerner consumed by ignorance and enthusiastically receptive to a racial caste system that pitted poor whites and blacks against each other in a cruel competition for the scraps of an unjust society.[5]

Although much of the criticism was well deserved, it often evinced an absence of sympathetic understanding that bordered on vindictiveness. The various writings of H. L. Mencken epitomized the ridicule of southern society and culture. Though Mencken's motives are often interpreted as constructive, his description of the South as a "vast plain of mediocrity, stupidity, lethargy, almost of dead silence" and its people as "the most degraded race of human beings claiming an Anglo-Saxon origin that can be found on the face of the earth" certainly influenced the popular perception of the region. Mencken condemned the "barbaric" South for its failure to support art galleries, museums, theaters, musicians, and the like, as well as for its idolization of suspect champions from an era long past that had reduced the region to the "Sahara of the Bozart." His denunciations

---

4. Daniel R. Hundley, *Social Relations in Our Southern States* (New York, 1860); Stephen Ash, "Poor Whites in the Occupied South," *Journal of Southern History*, LVII (1991), 39–62. For a humorous description of antebellum southern society see Joseph G. Baldwin, *The Flush Times of Alabama and Mississippi* (New York, 1853).

5. Altina Waller, *Feud: Hatfields, McCoys, and Social Change in Appalachia, 1860–1900* (Chapel Hill, 1988), 1; Albion Tourgée, *A Fools Errand* (New York, 1880); George W. Cable, *The Silent South* (New York, 1885); William Alexander Percy, *Lanterns on the Levee: Recollections of a Planter's Son* (New York, 1941); Hodding Carter, *Southern Legacy* (Baton Rouge, 1950).

provoked a memorable response from a group of Vanderbilt University–based scholars who celebrated the South's agrarian tradition in *I'll Take My Stand*.[6]

Mencken's diatribes served as the quintessential model for dismissing southern culture, even though the South would continue to provide its detractors with abundant cause for reproach. The calls for social change that characterized early- and mid-twentieth-century America sustained the disparaging portrayal of the South and its people. William Alexander Percy, Hodding Carter, and other southerners added voices to the criticism of common southerners that were no less accusatory, particularly regarding plain whites' resistance to the long overdue struggle for black civil liberties, yet grounded in a hands-on awareness of the peculiarities of southern culture. By the mid-twentieth century, however, numerous studies had emerged that demonstrated the flaws inherent in a simplistic approach to understanding southern behavior. One of the most influential of such studies appeared in 1941 with Wilbur J. Cash's *Mind of the South*. Cash argued that far from yielding to simple explanations, white southerners commanded a complex culture. They were guilty of much insensitivity and criminal behavior in part due to outside forces over which they had little, if any, control, but also owing to the presence of an inherently violent cultural intolerance that consumed common southerners and retarded regional development. Although Cash did reassign some of the responsibility for the South's peculiar development, declaring the region "The Frontier the Yankee Made," he lamented the "Proto-Dorian Convention" and concomitant "savage ideal" that defined southern culture, a private hell that southerners had created for themselves sustained by bigotry, violence, and crassness.[7] Although Cash and others encouraged in-

6. For a good analysis of Mencken's writings and their impact, see Fred C. Hobson, Jr., *Serpent in Eden: H. L. Mencken and the South* (Chapel Hill, 1974), or Hobson's more recent *Mencken: A Life* (New York, 1994). W. L. Taitte, "Springtime in the Desert: The Fine Arts and Their Patronage in the Modern South," in *Dixie Dateline: A Journalistic Portrait of the Contemporary South*, ed. John B. Boles (Houston, 1983), 81–96, provides a good refutation of Mencken's characterization of the South as the "Sahara of the Bozart." See also Twelve Southerners, *I'll Take My Stand: The South and the Agrarian Tradition* (New York, 1930). For another less-than-flattering portrayal of common southerners, see Erskine Caldwell, *Tobacco Road* (New York, 1932).

7. Percy, *Lanterns on the Levee*; Carter, *Southern Legacy* and *So the Heffners Left McComb* (New York, 1965); Ben Robertson, *Red Hills and Cotton: An Upcountry Memory* (Columbia, 1960); Wilbur J. Cash, *The Mind of the South* (New York, 1941). For a detailed

creasing debate concerning the nature of southern society, it was left to historian Frank Owsley in 1949 to offer a reconsideration of common white southerners that directly challenged the prevailing historical stereotype. Owsley's assessment differed from earlier studies not only in its concentration on the positive qualities of southern culture, but also in its refutation of much conventional scholarship that depicted the common folk as virtually irrelevant if not nonexistent. The conventional view, championed forcefully by such early twentieth century historians as Ulrich B. Phillips, Lewis C. Gray, William E. Dodd, and others, depicted the antebellum South as dominated entirely by the planter elite, with the common people remaining peripheral to the region's economic and political development. Although acknowledging the relevance of the planters, Owsley, promoting his agrarian view and echoing Daniel Hundley, argued that a thriving middle class, the plain folk, represented the most significant group of southerners. His rejection of the notion of planter hegemony included a reappraisal of the culture of common southerners that, much as Hundley had done earlier, demonstrated the fallacy of applying distant cultural norms to the South. According to Owsley, Mencken's theaters and art remained as irrelevant to common southerners as they themselves did to Mencken. Owsley's plain folk had many redeeming traits and values, ranging from their hard work, farm ownership, and wholesome recreation to their spirit of cooperativeness. He advanced his defense of these people with census-return evidence that appeared to confirm the significance of common southerners. Moreover, far from an apology, Owsley's work demonstrated that he was clearly proud of the plain folk, a fact that also represented a departure from the past.[8]

In the wake of Owsley's contribution, numerous studies that both supported and challenged his findings appeared. Perhaps Owsley's greatest contribution was that his persistent promotion of the crucial role played

analysis of Cash's work, see Paul D. Escott, *W. J. Cash and the Minds of the South* (Baton Rouge, 1992). For a description of the common folk of the South that appeared in this era but focused exclusively on the Civil War years, see Bell Irvin Wiley, *The Plain People of the Confederacy* (Baton Rouge, 1944).

8. Ulrich B. Phillips, "The Origin and Growth of the Southern Black Belts," *American Historical Review*, XI (1906), 798–816; Lewis Cecil Gray, *History of Agriculture in the Southern United States to 1860* (2 vols.; Washington, D.C., 1933), I, 444–74, 532–37; William E. Dodd, *The Cotton Kingdom: A Chronicle of the Old South* (New Haven, 1920), 24–45; Frank L. Owsley, *Plain Folk of the Old South* (Baton Rouge, 1949).

by the plain folk encouraged a more balanced approach to southern history. No more were southern whites seen as either planter aristocrats or poor white trash. The great middle portion was clearly identified as the largest population group in the antebellum South. In short, although abundant surveys of the planter elite would continue to appear, the plain folk could never again be dismissed as uncivilized or relegated to an irrelevant role. The work of Grady McWhiney, Forrest McDonald, I. A. Newby, and others have further demonstrated the defining role played by the plain folk in southern society.[9]

In an effort to advance the more balanced approach to southern history begun by Owsley and his followers, in the spring of 1996 ten historians gathered at Southeastern Louisiana University to consider and expand on the existing scholarship focusing on the common people of the South. In the spirit of Owsley's contribution, the conference was titled the "Plain Folk of the South Symposium," and it concentrated on the common folk throughout the course of the nineteenth century up to the advent of modernity during the World War I era. Fully aware of the fun-

---

9. James C. Bonner, "Plantation and Farm: The Agricultural South," in *Writing Southern History: Essays in Historiography in Honor of Fletcher M. Green*, ed. Arthur Link and Rembert Patrick (Baton Rouge, 1965), 147–53, provides a good description of the debate. See also Grady McWhiney, *Cracker Culture: Celtic Ways in the Old South* (Tuscaloosa, 1988); Forrest McDonald and Grady McWhiney, "The Antebellum Southern Herdsman: A Reinterpretation," *Journal of Southern History*, XLI (1975), 147–66; Fabian Linden, "Economic Democracy in the Slave South: An Appraisal of Some Recent Views," *Journal of Negro History*, XXXI (1946), 140–89; Ralph Wooster, *The People in Power: Courthouse and Statehouse in the Lower South, 1850–1860* (Knoxville, 1969), and *Politicians, Planters, and Plain Folk: Courthouse and Statehouse in the Upper South, 1850–1860* (Knoxville, 1975); and J. William Harris, *Plain Folk and Gentry in a Slave Society: White Liberty and Black Slavery in Augusta's Hinterlands* (Middletown, Conn., 1985). For a good analysis of the debate concerning Owsley's work, see Donald L. Winters, "'Plain Folk' of the Old South Reexamined: Economic Democracy in Tennessee," *Journal of Southern History*, LIII (1987), 565–86. Despite the progress made toward a more comprehensive understanding of southern culture, the popular perception of the South often remains fixed on the less appealing aspects of southern society. A recent *Time* magazine article describing the 1996 Olympic Games at Atlanta openly encouraged the city to break with its cultural traditions and emerge as an international city devoid of its attachments to the past and unique southern flavor. The article seemed to imply that, excepting the sites and heroes associated with the civil rights movement, Atlanta—and by association the South—maintained little if anything in its history that commanded respect. See Pico Iyer, "Atlanta: A Host of Contradictions," *Time*, Special Olympic Edition, Summer 1996, p. 42.

damental changes southern society has experienced since Owsley's work first appeared, the conferees expanded the definition of plain folk beyond the white-only designation of earlier times to include common blacks and to incorporate a greater emphasis on women. Moreover, the perception of plain folk emerged as a synthesis of Owsley's middle class and other southerners who remained outside elite circles. The broader definition allowed for greater analysis of the diverse groups who have long been relegated to the back shelf of history in favor of the southern elite and their unwilling bondsmen.[10]

The first section of the book, entitled "Home, Labor, and Leisure," concentrates on distinctive aspects of plain-folk homelife and on the demands confronting southern laborers. In the first essay, Bill Malone examines the music of the plain folk. According to Malone, the neglect and misunderstanding of common southerners is nowhere more apparent than in the treatment of their music. The history of the plain folk, and especially their overwhelming support for slavery and the Confederacy, led scores of journalists, historians, and other commentators to dismiss their musicians as little more than "hillbilly rabble" or to assign credit for their musical accomplishments to an Anglo-Celtic or African tradition. Instead, Malone argues that the plain folks' music personifies their culture, defying comparisons with transplanted African or European traditions in part because of the constancy of the music's relationship with the poorer, backcountry element of the South, who through it achieved a dignity otherwise typically denied them. Much as the study of common southerners has moved beyond the dismissive criticism of Mencken and others to reveal a far more vibrant culture, so too plain-folk music has emerged, in Malone's view, as the virtual musical voice of America itself.[11]

10. For examples of the changing perception of the plain folk, see I. A. Newby, *Plain Folk in the New South: Social Change and Cultural Persistence, 1880–1915* (Baton Rouge, 1989); J. Wayne Flynt, *Dixie's Forgotten People: The Southern Poor Whites* (Bloomington, Ind., 1979); Keith L. Bryant, Jr., "The Role and Status of the Female Yeomanry in the Antebellum South: The Literary View," *Southern Quarterly*, XVIII (1980), 73–88; and Bill Cecil-Fronsman, *Common Whites: Class and Culture in Antebellum North Carolina* (Lexington, Ky., 1992).

11. For examples of critical commentaries on plain folk music, see Arthur Smith, "Hillbilly Folk Music," *Etude*, LI (1933), and Thomas D. Clark, *The Kentucky* (New York, 1942), 128.

Another area where a plain-folk tradition is often confused with transplanted European or wider American patterns involves backcountry architecture. Jerah Johnson's essay demonstrates that this understudied field
also embodies the popular willingness to dismiss the accomplishments of
the plain folk. Just as social historians have concentrated primarily on the
activities of the southern elite and their slaves, so architectural historians
have focused predominantly on the buildings associated with the great
plantations. To emphasize the dearth of research in the field, Johnson
demonstrates that even the vocabulary concerning southern architecture
remains largely unstandardized—in his view a serious oversight, since
vernacular architecture accounted for the building tradition of essentially
99 percent of the nineteenth century southern population. According to
Johnson, the paucity of research concerning plain-folk architecture has
led to a misunderstanding of its stylistic origins.

Existing research has assigned the source of plain-folk architecture to a
Fenno-Swedish tradition, transplanted Saxons in Pennsylvania, or Ger-
manic peoples from western Switzerland and the Black Forest region.
While admitting the limitations of hard evidence to support any theory,
Johnson proposes a reconsideration that attributes credit to colonial Virginia craftsmen. Rather than attempting to emulate an old-country style,
he suggests, plain-folk architecture—whether standard log cabin, dog-
trot, or other form—may have emerged from seventeenth-century innovations in British carpentry and cabinetmaking adapted to environmen-
tal demands and available materials. In essence, the architecture common
to the southern plain folk represented an indigenous development that
addressed the climatic demands of the South and highlighted the creativity and resourcefulness of common southerners.[12]

The third and fourth selections in Part I examine the role, or absence,
of the plain folk in the southern economy. To many observers, self-

12. Fiske Kimball, *Domestic Architecture of the American Colonies and of the Early Repub-
lic* (1922; rpr. New York, 1966); Henry C. Mercer, "The Origin of Log Houses in the
United States," *Old-Time New England*, XVIII (July 1927), 2–20; Thomas T. Waterman,
The Dwellings of Colonial America (Chapel Hill, 1950); Hugh Morrison, *Early American Ar-
chitecture, From the First Colonial Settlements to the National Period* (New York, 1952);
Thomas Jefferson Wertenbaker, *The Founding of American Civilization: The Middle Colonies*
(New York, 1938), 288–303; Terry G. Jordan, *Texas Log Buildings: A Folk Architecture*
(Austin, 1978); and Jordan, "Alpine, Alemanic, and American Log Architecture," *Annals
of the Association of American Geographers*, LXX (1980), 154–80.

sufficiency remained the defining cultural principle of backcountry yeoman farmers. In a direct challenge to this perception, Bradley Bond disputes the "myth" of self-sufficiency in the backcountry South long championed by historians such as Stephen Hahn. According to Bond, far from seeking the traditional yeoman lifestyle, thousands of backcountry folk, too poor to afford prime cotton lands, migrated to the piney woods of the southwestern frontier seeking not economic isolation or a mere subsistence but access to markets of their own choosing. Employing extensive census data to support his position, Bond contends that most piney-woods farmers on the old southwestern frontier avoided a survival-oriented "safety first" pattern of production, which would have evidenced a proclivity toward a hermetic existence, and instead moved to the newer lands of the southern backcountry to secure a place for themselves in the market economy. In short, the migration of southern farmers to the frontier region of the Old Southwest embodied not an effort to sustain an isolated lifestyle, but a progressive effort to improve their standard of living.[13]

In a similar challenge to an oft-cited perspective, J. William Harris questions the existence of peonage in the New South. According to one highly touted view, after the Civil War impoverished former slaves came to depend on landlords and country merchants to provide them food and supplies on credit. Southern states gave this system legal force by allowing creditors to place a lien on crops, thus guaranteeing their right to take the harvest to settle the sharecropper's debt and to seek legal action against those who could not pay in full. Creditors took advantage of the freed people by charging exceptionally high prices and interest rates that virtually ensured the sharecroppers would become caught in an increasing cycle of debt. Black farmers, reduced to a state of chronic debt peonage, faced imprisonment and forced labor unless they toiled the land according to the instructions of their creditors.

This view of the New South rural economy emerged in the late nineteenth century and continues to appear as a standard assumption in the works of some writers. The inclination to accept the existence of peonage

13. Steven Hahn, *The Roots of Southern Populism: Yeoman Farmers and the Transformation of the Georgia Upcountry, 1850–1890* (New York, 1983); Robert Gallman, "Self-Sufficiency in the Cotton Economy of the Antebellum South," *Agricultural History*, XLIX (1970), 5–23; William K. Hutchinson and Samuel K. Williamson, "The Self-Sufficiency of the Antebellum South: Estimates of the Food Supply," *Journal of Economic History*, XXXI (September 1971), 591–612.

is based on the pervasive presence of debt throughout the agricultural South, the concomitant necessity of credit, the expressed desire of the planter elite to limit labor mobility and the legal sanctions that supported their efforts, and finally, the extensive analysis of peonage conducted by Pete Daniel and other researchers. Although accepting the damaging effects of a cycle of credit and debt, Harris demonstrates that the system did not constitute a state of peonage. In other words, it is not enough to show that sharecroppers were poor and indebted; it is necessary to show also that they were tied to their plantations. According to Harris, it is debt bondage—not debt itself, which was pervasive among all classes of southerners in the postwar South—that creates peonage. He points to statistical evidence that demonstrates exceptional levels of mobility among black sharecroppers, concluding that New South peonage was at best rare, and occurred only under special circumstances. His analysis has led him to caution against haphazard usage of the term *peonage* when discussing conditions in the late-nineteenth-century South.[14]

The essays in Part II, entitled "Social Groups and Attitudes," concentrate on establishing parameters for identifying the plain folk in a modern sense. Frank Owsley's pathbreaking research forever dispelled the myth that the Old South lacked a thriving middle class, the same group he identified as the plain folk. Subsequent research has demonstrated that although battered by the Civil War and Reconstruction, a middle class endured amid the poverty characterizing the late-nineteenth-century South. The designation "plain folk," however, is more useful as an indicator of social and political status than of economic condition. Moreover, for the purposes of southern culture studies, simplified groupings of people enhance identification of the differing goals and aspirations that separated the haves and have-nots, the plain from the elite South. At its most fundamental level, southern society up to 1865 consisted of slaves, the rich and powerful, and those who remained free yet far less prominent socially, economically, or politically than their elite neighbors and kin. After 1865 the appearance of blacks as freed people complicated the picture, but they,

14. Pete Daniel, *The Shadow of Slavery: Peonage in the South, 1901–1969* (Urbana, 1972); Roger Ransom and Richard Sutch, "Debt Peonage in the Cotton South After the Civil War," *Journal of Economic History*, XXXII (1972), 641–69; Jonathan M. Wiener, "Class Structure and Economic Development in the American South, 1865–1955," *American Historical Review* LXXXIV (1979), 970–82.

too, clearly became a part of the common South. Many subgroups existed among common southerners, they all remained part of the plain folk. Recognizing the plain folk as all those "common" southerners who remained outside elite circles and bondage serves as the focus of Part II.

As late as the 1970s the term *southerner* was frequently employed to describe exclusively whites, and often only those southerners, primarily men, who supported the Confederacy and its legacy. More recently, our expanding awareness of the contributions others have made to southern society, despite the institutionalized repression many faced, has hastened the decline of such homogeneous impressions of the South. As noted, the term *plain folk* has frequently been employed in an equally exclusive manner, typically describing either the South's destitute poor or the male-dominated middle class while overlooking the roles of women and free blacks. The first two essays in this section illustrate the significance non-elite women and free blacks held for southern society and, most important, their contributions to the emergence of a distinctive plain-folk culture.

In the first selection, Sally McMillen examines the influence of the Sunday-school movement in shaping southern society, and especially the opportunities it created for women. The role of women within the various southern religious denominations has long been recognized, but McMillen demonstrates that Sunday schools created a variety of ways for women to promote their own talents, as well as assume responsibilities typically reserved for men. According to McMillen, in an effort to improve the moral and educational standing of future generations of southerners, women developed effective fundraising, literary, and administrative skills, all the while maintaining a uniquely southern style that rejected the more aggressive demands of their northern counterparts. The efforts of female Sunday-school teachers not only gave women a standing they had never previously enjoyed, but also improved the quality of life for many Sunday-school pupils by, at the very least, instilling in these southern children the knowledge that patience and discipline were virtues consistent with their way of life.

In the second essay, Gary Mills examines a frequently overlooked, yet important, component of the common South, the free people of color. Despite some notable studies, the southern free black population remains something of a mystery. Free blacks' African heritage necessarily excluded them from studies of common whites, and their freedom and comparatively advanced social status frequently limited their inclusion in African American studies. Mills, drawing on impressive research that has allowed him to identify virtually every free black person in Alabama prior to the Civil War, concludes that the ambiguity surrounding the free black population has led to a misunderstanding of the group's actual social status and relationship to common whites. In his comparative study of the free people of color in Alabama and Louisiana, Mills identifies a consistent pattern regarding their status. He agrees with earlier research that declared the free black population of Louisiana to be the Deep South's largest and most assertive group of free people of color. Yet he qualifies the perception of Louisiana as unique with regard to having a substantial population of free blacks. According to Mills, even in the face of increasingly restrictive laws during the course of the late antebellum period, free blacks thrived throughout most of the South. Simply put, where free blacks served an important economic role or possessed a needed skill, such as gunsmithing, or where they enjoyed the protection of powerful local whites or simply lived in quiet obscurity, the laws were ignored on a widespread basis.[15]

In describing this pattern, Mills identifies a softer, more sympathetic side of average white southerners than is often portrayed. Although white southerners remained responsible for the harsh reality of the slave system and the laws that restricted the rights of free blacks, many apparently tolerated free people of color, and some embraced them as significant contributors to southern society. Tolerance certainly does not qualify institutionalized racism, but it does allow a consideration of sensitivity, if not compassion, on the part of many among the plain folk.

No discussion of common southerners during the nineteenth century would be complete without mention of the thousands who filled the ranks of the Confederate army. Even before the close of hostilities, cries of "rich man's war, poor man's fight" were raised to describe the southern effort in the Civil War. Implied in this message was the belief, shared by many, that the war had been promoted by the rich while the poor did the fighting, suffering, and dying. Studies concentrating on disaffection

15. Ira Berlin, *Slaves Without Masters: The Free Negro in the Antebellum South* (New York, 1974); John Hope Franklin, *The Free Negro in North Carolina, 1790–1860* (Chapel Hill, 1943); David C. Rankin, *The Forgotten People: Free People of Color in New Orleans, 1850–1870* (Baltimore, 1976); H. E. Sterkx, *The Free Negro in Ante-Bellum Louisiana* (Rutherford, N.J., 1972).

within the Confederacy seem to support the view that a wide chasm separated the champions of secession from much of the army and civilian
population.[16] Although few would challenge the notion that differing in-
centives often encouraged the enlistment of rich and poor Confederates,
in the final essay in this section Grady McWhiney demonstrates that
among the fighting men a common spirit prevailed, one that indicates the
prevalence of an important cultural bond between plain folk and elite
southerners.[17]

Honor has long been identified as one of the defining characteristics of
southerners whether rich or poor. In his comprehensive study of southern
honor, Bertram Wyatt-Brown concluded that honor served as the principal determinant that bound southern society together and contributed to
the emergence of a distinctive southern identity.[18] McWhiney agrees,
noting that honor manifested itself most fundamentally as courage, and
that courage remained among the most cherished principles of southerners. Honor, and correspondingly courage, provided southerners of all classes
with a common identity and created the impetus to support a common
cause. McWhiney advances this line of reasoning by arguing that the
term *Cracker*, commonly applied to the plain folk, best defined the shared
values of a culture that demanded courage of its adherents; therefore,
he suggests, regardless of economic status virtually all southerners were
Crackers. In short, in McWhiney's view, the martial exploits of Confederate officers and their troops demonstrate that despite differing social and
economic backgrounds, the lines separating the plain from the elite South
were not as wide as they may seem.

Reconciling the contradictions inherent in plain folks' political behavior
and their perceptions of democracy, as evinced in their rhetorical allegiance to egalitarianism, offers historians a formidable challenge. The es-

16. Stephen Ambrose, "Yeoman Discontent in the Confederacy," *Civil War History*,
VIII (1962), 259–68; Paul D. Escott, *After Secession: Jefferson Davis and the Failure of Con-
federate Nationalism* (Baton Rouge, 1978); Marc Kruman, "Dissent in the Confederacy: The
North Carolina Experience," *Civil War History*, XXVII (1981), 293–313.

17. James McPherson, *What They Fought For, 1861–1865* (Baton Rouge, 1994).

18. Bertram Wyatt-Brown, *Honor and Violence in the Old South* (New York, 1986). For
additional descriptions of southern honor, see Edward Ayers, *Vengeance and Justice: Crime
and Punishment in the 19th-Century American South* (New York, 1984), and McWhiney,
Cracker Culture.

says included in Part III, entitled "Plain-Folk Democracy and Its Limits," seek to define the concept of democracy embraced by the common folk, to identify its parameters, and to explain its unusual manifestations.

The history of the nineteenth-century South, which includes slavery, restrictions on the suffrage, and circumscription of social and economic opportunity, demonstrates that American democracy was not monolithic. Although other regions of the nation suffered equally restrictive forms of democracy, the version that emerged in the South certainly constituted the most peculiar. Despite their fierce attachment to the republican prin-ciples that sustained democracy, common white southerners frequently surrendered political power to a self-serving elite and enthusiastically sup-ported a racial caste system that denied human dignity to a significant proportion of the southern population.[19]

In the late twentieth century, it is difficult to understand why the over-whelming majority of ordinary whites habitually relinquished political autonomy to powerful others and supported a system that denied the vote to black southerners. It is especially difficult to sympathize with dis-gruntled whites who wished to challenge the hegemonic control of poli-tics and government by elites but who failed to cast aside their racial chauvinism to unite with their natural allies—blacks. With the excep-tion of the Populists in a few states, plain folk proved unable and unwill-ing to escape the bonds of their *Herrenvolk* democracy. Their failure to do so exposes certain historical circumstances, in many ways unique to the plain folk, that shaped their values, culture, and sense of self. The plain folk remained a people who had rarely enjoyed political control over their own lives, had suffered greatly during the Civil War for a cause held in contempt by the victor, and had reaped few of the rewards of the slave system yet endured severe economic competition as a result of its col-lapse. The historical progression of the mass of common whites from proud farmers possessing qualified political influence in a slaveholding so-

19. For descriptions of the peculiar nature of southern democracy, see Eugene Genovese and Elizabeth Fox-Genovese, "Yeoman Farmers in a Slaveholder's Democracy," in *Fruits of Merchant Capital: Slavery and Bourgeois Property in the Rise and Expansion of Capitalism* (New York, 1983), 249–64; Michael Wayne, "An Old South Morality Play: Reconsidering the Social Underpinnings of the Pro-Slavery Ideology," *Journal of American History,* LXXVII (1990), 838–63; George Fredrickson, "Aristocracy and Democracy in the Southern Tradi-tion," in *The Southern Enigma: Essays on Race, Class, and Folk Culture,* ed. Walter J. Fraser, Jr., and Winfred B. Moore, Jr. (Westport, Conn., 1983).

ciety, to soldiers of a suspect cause, to defeated rebels in a region that offered little opportunity and where the federal government remained distant and unsympathetic, and finally, to the whipping boys of popular culture, demands reconsideration of the motivating forces that shaped their perception of democracy.

The violence that convulsed the South, the racism that consumed millions of its people and victimized millions of others, and the distinctive political aspirations of the people all remain among the most recognized aspects of southern culture and each contributed directly to the emergence of a peculiar form of democracy. To dismiss these realities of southern life as simply the products of ignorance and bigotry is to ignore the harsh historical truths that confronted the plain folk and helped to define them as a people. The essays in Part III concentrate primarily on the forces that determined the South's distinctive form of democracy, the nature of political appeals and the intentions of the men who presented them, and some of the implications of democracy's limitations.

Part of the problem associated with explaining the plain folks' perception of democracy involves the limited availability of primary evidence concerning their beliefs. In an effort to overcome this situation, Lacy K. Ford considers the views presented by the champions of the plain folk during the constitutional reform movements of the Jacksonian era in Virginia, Mississippi, and Tennessee. In doing so, Ford identifies a consistent pattern of support for egalitarian reforms that helped define the view of democracy common among the plain folk. In each state differing perceptions of republicanism separated conservatives from reform-minded egalitarians, allowing Ford to recognize four consistent principles embraced by the plain folk: equality among all white men; an affinity for the rule of the majority; hostility toward policies or institutions perceived as promoting aristocracies of wealth, privilege, or political preferment; and a determination to sharpen the racial and gender boundaries of popular republicanism. According to Ford, plain folk interest in obliterating class distinctions among whites matched their desire to limit the inclusion of nonwhite males.

In Ford's analysis, the plain-folk perspective that emerged in the Jacksonian era and contributed to defining the outlines of a new American democratic ideology involved associating independence with race. Their insistence on majority rule led the plain folk to demand that all white men enjoy the privilege of voting and the opportunity to govern. In short, rather than the earlier view of democracy that defined personal independence largely in economic terms, the view presented by the champions of the common folk declared citizenship, and all its rewards, a racial entitlement. The "us versus them" politics of racial exclusion, therefore, became the means by which common southerners promoted their demands for greater opportunity.

Plain folks' desire for expanded democratic privilege in no way reflected on their ability to govern. Quite the contrary, Thomas Jefferson's calls for an elite of the educated to maintain order and secure the republic appeared to warn of the conditions that confronted many regions of the late-nineteenth-century backcountry South. In the second essay in this section, my own research demonstrates that following the collapse of the antebellum power structure, some regions of the South descended into virtual anarchy.

Conditioned by the slaveholding elite to fear unseen enemies that threatened their liberty, many plain folk remained suspicious of government and of those who sought to enforce its policies. The presence of slavery served as a constant reminder that independence demanded constant vigilance, and the rhetoric of the antebellum elite, equating black bondage with white liberty, contributed to the emergence of a warped impression of individual rights that allowed for unqualified resistance to perceived agents of oppression. The war and Reconstruction intensified the contempt for authority in many regions and provided valuable lessons in the effectiveness of violence.

With the close of Reconstruction, some common southerners rejected not only the authority of the antebellum elite who had led them to ruin, but also that of the emerging business-oriented leaders of the New South, and instead embraced a backcountry code of justice that allowed for a maximum of personal independence in defiance of the established legal system. What resulted was a state of chronic anarchy that only the coordinated efforts of respected citizens, local peace officers, and state authority could contain. Ultimately, events in these regions demonstrated the necessity of strong leadership to maintain stability and a semblance of democracy. And, more important, they illustrate that the limitations of plain-folk democracy were not confined to racial and gender restrictions.

One group that championed the values of the plain folk in the late nineteenth and early twentieth centuries was the so-called New South demagogues. With the emergence of a new sense of racial justice in the mid-twentieth century, most of these eccentric politicians have been dismissed as race-baiting hatemongers who served little, if any, constructive purpose. In his essay, Michael Kurtz separates the race-conscious rhetoric from the liberal accomplishments and finds not only that the term *demagogue* poorly describes these men, but that they in many ways exemplified the contradiction central to common white southerners.

Few would argue that men such as Theodore Bilbo, Eugene Talmadge, James K. Vardaman, and others owed their political success to the vitriol of racial politics. Kurtz agrees that the contempt heaped upon these men in recent years for aggravating the charged racial climate of the South is well deserved. In his analysis of their political accomplishments, however, Kurtz uncovers a liberal tendency that brought much-needed reforms to the rural South, reforms such as roads and bridges, free textbooks for schoolchildren, and improved health care. Long neglected by the established political elite, the New South Demagogues assumed a language and appearance that appealed directly to the common folk and stirred their political consciousness into a potent political force. With their frequently outlandish behavior and attire, they tapped into the despondency of the disaffected white masses of the South to address legitimate grievances. According to Kurtz, these champions of the little guy did exactly what was necessary to get elected, and they then delivered on their promises, both evil and progressive.

I

Home, Labor, and Leisure

BILL C. MALONE

Neither Anglo-Saxon nor Celtic:
The Music of the Southern Plain Folk

One can scarcely conceive of American music in this century without thinking of the profound role played by southern-born white musicians. Beginning in the 1920s with Gene Austin, the pioneer pop crooner from Sherman, Texas, and Jimmie Rodgers, the yodeling ex-brakeman from Meridian, Mississippi, a continuing array of white southern musicians have participated prominently in the musical culture of America. A few of them, like Gene Autry, Bob Wills, Hank Williams, Bill Monroe, and Elvis Presley, have created major stylistic genres that are known around the world.

The burgeoning of country music in our own time, when entertainers like the Oklahoma superstars Garth Brooks and Reba McEntire achieve media recognition that rivals or surpasses that of performers in any other style of music, provides dramatic evidence of the appeal exhibited by southern-born musicians. A recent article in the *New Republic*, in fact, described country music as "the voice of America," and although the essayist noted that performers from the North and Canada now participate prominently in a musical genre that has become increasingly affluent and middle-class, it nevertheless seems significant that twenty-six of the thirty-one entertainers who are mentioned come from either the original Confederate states or from Oklahoma.[1]

---

1. Bruce Feiler, "Gone Country: The Voice of Suburban America," *New Republic*, February 5, 1996, pp. 19–24.

The prominence of these southern entertainers, most of whom have working-class backgrounds, seems all the more remarkable when we recall that the music of their ancestors was scarcely known, or valued, by Americans at large or by the southern elites until the years running roughly from 1910 to 1917. In contrast, the music of black southerners had moved long before that time, in various manifestations, into the consciousness of Americans everywhere and had even become a powerful presence in the popular culture of Great Britain. Whether displayed in the caricatured forms popularized by the blackface minstrels or the "coon" songs, or in the irresistible rhythms of black ragtime pianists, southern music seemed to be African American music. Speaking of still another southern black-derived musical form, Anton Dvorak, the Czech composer, who first heard such music after he came to the United States in 1892, argued that the Negro spirituals represented the very essence of the American soul.[2]

John Lomax's *Cowboy Songs and Other Frontier Ballads* (1910) and Cecil Sharp's *English Folk Songs from the Southern Appalachians* (1917) were the first significant collections of music that in any way reflected the culture of southern white folk.[3] These collections, however, touched only the geographic fringes of the South—the Appalachians on the east and the Texas Plains on the west—and they concentrated primarily on the music of those regions and only incidentally on the people who produced and preserved it. Lomax and Sharp were actually more inclusive in their treatment than most of the collectors who came immediately after them, and they did often identify their informants. Reading the commentary or headnotes that accompanied Sharp's selections, one would know, for example, that Jane Gentry of Hot Springs, North Carolina, supplied him with sixty-four items, his single largest cache of ballads.[4] As had been the fate of the Negro spirituals in the late nineteenth century, the Appalachian ballads and cowboy songs were first made available to a rather

2. For an overview of the musical contributions made by southerners, see Bill C. Malone, *Southern Music, American Music* (Lexington, Ky., 1979).

3. John A. Lomax, *Cowboy Songs and Other Frontier Ballads* (New York, 1910); Cecil J. Sharp and Olive Dame Campbell, *English Folk Songs from the Southern Appalachians* (New York, 1917).

4. Sharp and Campbell, *English Folk Songs*, xi. Betty Smith has written a good summary of Ms. Gentry's life and career in "Jane Gentry: A Singer Among Singers," *Tar Heel Junior Historian*, XXV (Winter, 1986), 11–14.

small and educated group of Americans, and in versions made palatable to middle-class tastes by the classical concert styles of musicians like Howard Brockway, Loraine Wyman, and John Jacob Niles who had been trained at the Julliard School of Music or other approved centers of high-art education. Confined to performances before women's clubs, music appreciation groups, college audiences, and other devotees of "serious music," this body of music reached the ears of few Americans, and in styles that were far removed from those heard in the communities where the songs had been collected.

Whether presented on the pages of a published song collection or in the repertoire of a concert musician, the music of the southern white folk seemed interesting but nevertheless in danger of extinction. Although Cecil Sharp asserted that he had found himself "in a community in which singing was as common and almost as universal a practice as speaking" and that he could get what he wanted from "pretty nearly every one . . . young and old," he still conveyed the impression that the best of their music would soon be gone, and that it was being replaced by inferior products of the street and music hall.[5] Collectors and concert musicians alike went about their work with a sense of urgency, feeling that the music and the culture that had sustained it were both dying.

While the archaicism of southern folk music was one source of its appeal, its identification with a presumed racially homogeneous culture was an additional attraction to those who saw America's own supposed racial purity disappearing in the years surrounding World War I. The southern mountains seemed to be one of the last remaining repositories of Anglo-Saxonism in the United States, a quality that stood out in bold relief when compared with the nation's large cities and their hordes of blacks and "new immigrants" who were already changing American culture in dramatic ways. The suggestion that the allegedly backward southern mountaineers were really "our contemporary ancestors," a group of people whose dialects and folkways presumably provided evidence of the nation's pure Anglo-Saxon origins, was not likely to effect any significant political changes in American life.[6] But it was a romantically appealing image and

5. Sharp and Campbell, *English Folk Songs*, viii.

6. The best discussion of the discovery of the southern Appalachians, and the consequent belief that they constituted a unique region of the United States, is Herbert D. Shapiro, *Appalachia on Our Mind: The Southern Mountains and Mountaineers in the American Consciousness, 1870–1920* (Chapel Hill, 1978).

a satisfying rationale for the preservation of the ballads and other remaining cultural artifacts of that society. The journalist William Aspenwall Bradley was so impressed by his sojourn in the southern mountains in 1915 and by the conservatism of life there as to remark that "wandering through the mountains, one now knew he might at any time meet a company of Robin Hood's men encamped in some sequestered cove."[7]

A few years later, two of the pioneer promoters of southern folk festivals, Jean Thomas and John Powell, continued to view southern folk arts as survivals of early English culture. The self-styled "traipsing woman," Jean Thomas, who was a longtime court reporter in the Kentucky hills and the founder of the Singin' Gatherin', even saw the ghost of Anne Boleyn lingering in the songs that had endured in the southern hills. Thomas built a cottage, the "Wee House in the Wood," whose gateway and entrance were "modeled after the cottage entrance of Anne Boleyn." Her rationale, she insisted, was that Boleyn "was the mother of Queen Elizabeth and because many of our Kentucky mountain ballads and folk dances date back to the time of Queen Elizabeth, this replica of the English cottage has been built to recreate the scene where our balladry was cradled." Powell, a nationally known classical pianist and composer from Richmond, Virginia, was not nearly so prone to flights of romantic fantasy as was Ms. Thomas, and he was one of the first collectors of southern folk music to argue that examples of such music survived outside the mountains and had in fact been preserved across class lines. Powell, though, was explicit in his assertions that southern balladry arose from an Anglo-Saxon past and that this purportedly superior racial component linked the upper-class southerner to his poor-white neighbors. He argued further that "our only hope as a nation lies in grafting the stock of our culture on the anglo-saxon root," and that "familiarity with this noble inheritance would revive and confirm in ourselves those traditions and feelings which are the crown of our race and assure to us as well that supreme glory, a nationhood unparalleled in the annals of all time."[8]

7. William A. Bradley, "Song-Ballets and Devil's Ditties," *Harper's Monthly*, May 1915, p. 905.

8. Jean Thomas, *Ballad Makin' in the Mountains of Kentucky* (New York, 1939), 266; John Powell, untitled article in *Etude*, XLV (May 1927), 349–50. David Whisnant describes such people as Thomas and Powell as "cultural interventionists" in his superb study *All That Is Native and Fine: The Politics of Culture in an American Region* (Chapel Hill, 1983).

Terms like *Anglo-Saxon* and *Elizabethan* appeared frequently in discussions of southern folk music despite the fact that the English were not alone in the settling of Appalachia or other regions of the South. Students of Appalachian balladry, who far outnumbered any other kind of folk-song specialists, seemed to assume that the mountains had been populated exclusively by Englishmen or that English-descended culture had overwhelmed that of every other group who came to the region. Cecil Sharp, for example, recognized the presence of Scotch-Irish and border elements in the southern hills but nevertheless entitled his epochal book *English Folk Songs from the Southern Appalachians*. The musical influence of the Scotch-Irish people, the largest group to settle the backcountry South, seldom received mention in any academic discussion of southern folk music until as late as the 1960s. My doctoral dissertation of 1965 described the music of the white South as "Anglo-Celtic" in an effort to suggest that the music of the region drew upon resources from all over the British Isles.[9] Some writers and academicians have since gone well beyond that assumption, though, and have argued that Celtic influences lie at the core of plain-folk music and such commercial descendants as country and Cajun. We have been assured on record-liner notes, in the public statements of a few country musicians, and in at least one book that Celtic musical traits/styles can easily be discerned in the playing and singing of southern country musicians. Buttressed by that faith, and emboldened perhaps by an enmity toward any and all things English, or perhaps by the desire to deny the prominence of black influence in country music, such observers imagine the strains of a Celtic bagpipe whenever they hear the drone of a country fiddle or banjo. They seek cultural legitimacy for modern country music by linking it to an ancient tradition, but instead obscure our understanding of it under a murky veil of romanticism.[10]

9. Billy Charles Malone, "A History of Commercial Country Music in the United States, 1920–1965" (Ph.D. dissertation, University of Texas, 1965).

10. Playing at a concert in Durham, North Carolina, on April 7, 1990, the old-time banjo player Dave Sturgill announced that he would play "Mississippi Sawyer" and said, "If you listen, you'll hear the sounds of the bagpipes." Historian Grady McWhiney has asserted that "even in the late twentieth century the continuity between the country music of Celts and Southerners is startling"; *Cracker Culture: Celtic Ways in the Old South* (Tuscaloosa, 1988), 120. In contrast, the leading scholar of ethnic music in the United States, Richard K. Spottswood, declared that "Irish music bears no relation to bluegrass and little more to

The narrow perspectives of the early collectors and concert interpreters inhibited an understanding of the total picture of plain-folk music. The music they valued, and which they adapted to the concert stage,
seemed to be an archaic expression of a stagnant or dying culture. By concentrating on a special type of balladry—the remnants of those English
and Scottish items canonized in the late nineteenth century by the Har-
vard scholar Francis James Child—they ignored the wide breadth of
southern folk music, and by emphasizing the secular material in the folk
songbag they underestimated the extent and influence of the religious
songs that lay at the heart of southern folk culture. Above all, they neglected the largest domain of plain-folk culture, that vast geographical interior of the South that lay between the Appalachian Mountains and the
Texas plains. Until the publication of G. P. Jackson's epochal *White Spirituals in the Southern Uplands* in 1933 and Arthur Palmer Hudson's *Folksongs of Mississippi and Their Background* in 1934, no book-length study of
the music of the interior South had appeared.[11] The commercial music
industry, of course, had been making such music available since the early
twenties in radio broadcasts and phonograph recordings, under such labels as "old-time," "old familiar," and "hillbilly."[12] This music, however,
did not conform very readily to the images of southern folk music conveyed earlier by the academic folklorists and concert interpreters. One
suspects that it was the taint of commercialism that did most to give academicians pause. True folk musicians, it was believed, were not concerned
about money, nor did they seek economic rewards for their art. Of course,
we really do not know what the academicians thought, since most of
them tended to ignore the music of the radio hillbillies. The pioneer
southern sociologist Howard Odum was one of the rare students of south-

---

southern country music as a whole"; Spottswood, *Bluegrass Unlimited,* May 1978, pp.
47–50. The British folksinger Ian Robb argued that "for many people, the term Celtic is
simply an ill-considered but convenient way to exclude English music. For them it is a geo-
political distinction, which outside of overtly anti-English songs has little to do with music"; Robb, "The British–North America Art," *Sing Out,* XL (May–June–July, 1995), 80.

    11. George Pullen Jackson, *White Spirituals in the Southern Uplands* (Chapel Hill, 1933);
Arthur Palmer Hudson, *Folksongs of Mississippi and Their Background* (Chapel Hill, 1936).

    12. For a general survey of the commercialization of southern white folk music, see Bill
C. Malone, *Country Music, USA* (1968; rev. ed. Austin, 1985), and Archie Green, "Hillbilly Music: Source and Symbol," *Journal of American Folklore,* LXXVIII (1965), 204–28.

ern life who bothered to look at the music distributed on phonograph recordings and to take it seriously as a source to the southern folk mind.[13] Probably more representative of the view of southern academicians was that of the historian Tom Clark, who while singing the praises of the frontier fiddlers of Kentucky could nevertheless refer to their commercial descendants as "the hillbilly rabble" of radio.[14]

It must be confessed that a handful of Yankees, and even a few sophisticated city entertainers, contributed to the making of the hillbilly music business, but most of the fiddlers, string bands, balladeers, and gospel singers who disseminated their art on radio broadcasts, phonograph recordings, and personal appearances came from the working-class South. And while their audience may have been diverse—extending in fact all the way to Australia and the frozen wilds of Alaska—its core came from what Arthur Smith, a cynical "dealer in sound-reproducing machines," described in 1933 as a "subterranean musical world" inhabited by "a great, unnumbered, inarticulate multitude" who were "interested, like children, in trains, wrecks, disasters, and crimes."[15] He of course was talking about the musical world of the southern plain folk.

Smith's condescending comments are not surprising. After all, he spoke of a culture that had never generated much sympathy or respect. Unlike the mountain South, this vast, interior South—the land of the plain folk—had supported slavery and the racial values that surrounded it and had contributed few soldiers to the Union army, thus eliciting little support from northern missionary or philanthropic groups. Long stigmatized as poor whites or rednecks, mainly by their more affluent neighbors, these people seemed never to have recovered from the war or from the

13. In *An American Epoch: Southern Portraiture in the National Picture* (New York, 1930), 201–203, Odum provided an extensive list of folk songs which came from both commercial and noncommercial sources, and he made no invidious distinctions between the two categories. His discussion of religious music (pp. 180–200) was exceptionally perceptive and sympathetic. Historian Daniel Joseph Singal, in *The War Within: From Victorian to Modernist Thought in the South, 1919–1945* (Chapel Hill, 1982), points to ambivalence in Odum and argues that he overlooked the "miseries of his own rural childhood" and tended to romanticize the people from whom he came, 139.

14. Thomas D. Clark provided excellent vignettes of folk fiddlers in his history of the Kentucky River, *The Kentucky* (New York, 1942), but he expressed contempt for commercial hillbilly fiddlers (p. 128).

15. Arthur Smith, "Hillbilly Folk Music," *Etude*, LI (1933), 154, 208.

economic dislocations that followed it. More important, they seemed to possess neither the ambition nor the skills to rise above economic distress, or the ability to overcome the catalog of well-publicized ills such as pellagra, hookworm, racial violence, religious bigotry, ignorance, and sharecropping that too often consumed their lives. They were responsible, it seemed, for the South's grossest political excesses and could therefore elicit the hatred of men like William Alexander Percy, the Mississippi Delta aristocrat who could say much later of his poor white neighbors, "I can forgive them as the Lord God forgives, but admire them, trust them, love them—never. At their door must be laid the disgraceful riots and lynchings gloated over and exaggerated by Negrophiles the world over."[16] Writing in 1917, the acerbic Baltimore journalist H. L. Mencken had bemoaned the collapse of the South's "great civilization," which had been despoiled by the "mob of peasants" who ascended in the wreckage left by the Civil War. The South had been inherited by "the poor white trash" in whose veins flowed "some of the worst blood of Western Europe."[17]

Musically, what had been the reality of life for those "lowly white folk" who lived in the "subterranean culture" described by Arthur Smith? He had been right about a few things. Contrary to romantic perceptions, the "lowly native white folk of the South" did not sing Stephen Foster songs, unless they were introduced to them in elementary-school songbooks. And they did like songs about disasters and outlaws. Those musical preferences were part of their British inheritance and were shared by their African American neighbors. Their culture, though, was considerably more complex than Smith, Mencken, or other critics suggested, and its reality was accurately summed up by neither its romancers nor its detractors. It was neither Anglo-Saxon nor Celtic, although elements from those traditions were present in its composite mixture. Southern folk culture and the music that emerged from it were anything but pure, and they certainly were not static. As blendings of cultures and influences, they represented a syncretic process that neither began nor ended when ethnic

16. William Alexander Percy, *Lanterns on the Levee: Recollections of a Planter's Son* (1941; rpr. Baton Rouge, 1973), 20.

17. H. L. Mencken, "Sahara of the Bozart," in *A Mencken Chrestomathy* (New York, 1920), rpr. in *The South Since Reconstruction*, ed. Thomas D. Clark (Indianapolis, 1973), 551, 554.

and racial cultures met in the colonial South; the process had begun on the borders of Great Britain and in West Africa, and it continued throughout the evolving social history of the South.[18]

Neither was the culture exclusively "folk," if one means by that a self-contained, socially ingrown society that drew exclusively upon its inherited cultural resources. This remarkably organic culture was built and preserved by a people who were sufficiently isolated and socially conservative to retain musical traits long after they had ceased to be fashionable elsewhere, but who were nevertheless remarkably receptive to new and externally originated musical influences, and prone to change them to fit their own tastes and styles. New songs and tunes were freely adopted, but styles of performance—which were deeply rooted in the culture of childhood—changed much more slowly. Cecil Sharp had noted in 1916 that when "the text of a modern street-song succeeds in penetrating into the mountains it is at once mated to a traditional tune."[19] Change nevertheless came both consciously and unconsciously.[20] Musical choices and styles of performance, as well as the definitions applied to songs, were shaped by the people's own aesthetic and moral criteria, at least until the early collectors, academicians, and commercial record producers suggested that some songs were more valuable than others. The early collectors sought surviving specimens of British material; the folk, in contrast,

18. For excellent discussions of the cultural, social, and ethnic intermingling that occurred in the British Isles prior to the settling of English North America, see Carl Bridenbaugh, *Vexed and Troubled Englishmen, 1590–1642* (New York, 1968), and David Hackett Fischer, *Albion's Seed: Four British Folkways in America* (New York, 1989). For discussions of similar interacting interrelationships in this country, see Mechal Sobel, *The World They Made Together: Black and White Values in Eighteenth-Century Virginia* (Princeton, 1987), and Alan Lomax, *The Folk Songs of North America* (New York, 1960).

19. No analysis has yet surpassed that of Alan Lomax, who discussed the conservatism of folk musical style in "Folk Song Style," *American Anthropologist*, LXI (1959), 927–55, but Roger Abrahams and George Foss have contributed a useful discussion in *Anglo-American Folksong Style* (Englewood Cliffs, N.J., 1968). Sharp's quote is in Sharp and Campbell, *English Folk Songs*, ix.

20. Phillips Barry, whose analyses were among the most commonsensical of earlier folklorists', declared that "when we say that tradition—with due stress on its diversification—makes the folksong what it is, we are simply stopping short of a more nearly ultimate statement: the individualism of the folksinger, both consciously and unconsciously exerted, makes the tradition what it is"; Barry, "American Folk Music," *Southern Folklore Quarterly*, I, 2 (1937), 30.

had embraced any kind of musical material that fitted their social and aesthetic needs.[21]

A large body of British-derived material *did* survive among the southern folk, most often in fragmentary form but sometimes in much lengthier versions. Before this music came to America it had already moved frequently across regional and social boundaries and had been circulated by both professional and folk performers.[22] It came to America in the possession of the original settlers and in the repertoires of professional entertainers who arrived in this country with circuses, puppet shows, equestrian shows, and dramatic troupes. Southern folk culture was overwhelmingly oral, but it was no more resistant to the printed or written preservation of songs and ballads than its British forebears had been. The British folk wrote favorite songs down and pasted the broadside sheets to the walls of inns, alehouses, homes, barns, and cowsheds.[23] None of the broadsides seems to have survived among southern rural families, but favorite songs were laboriously written down in English composition books, five-cent tablets, or on loose sheets of paper ("song ballets"), and song lyrics were clipped from magazines or newspapers and posted on the pages of some old schoolbook.[24] Singers generally tried to perform or preserve a song exactly as they had first learned it (a marked difference from the practice followed by African American singers), but alterations in tunes and lyrics inevitably occurred, largely through faulty recollection or the imperfect comprehension of a word or phrase, but sometimes through the conscious decision to "improve" a song, tune, or dance. This inherited material, which varied from place to place, existed comfortably alongside the newer songs and dances, with young people generally being the crucial agents of change.

21. It should be noted that the music chosen by folk entertainers has often included material shaped by the judgments and definitions of the folklorists and other collectors of music. "Pure" folk musicians (that is, those who performed at the festivals or other venues favored by the folklorists) and "commercial" musicians (hillbilly, country) have often chosen to do material favored or suggested by folklorists. Similarly, during the folk revival of the 1960s, country and bluegrass performers like Johnny Cash and the Stanley Brothers sometimes performed music learned from the urban revivalists.

22. See A. L. Lloyd, *Folk Song in England* (New York, 1967), *passim.*

23. *Ibid.*, 25–34.

24. I recall from personal experience that this practice remained strong at least into the 1940s. My mother clipped songs from the "Young People's Page" of the Dallas *Semi-Weekly Farm News* and pasted them to the pages of an old schoolbook.

One can never know precisely who the principal makers of music were in folk communities, why they made music, or what effects their songs or performances had on their listeners. Gender roles, for example, cannot be conclusively determined. Performance, however, was governed largely by the etiquette surrounding the social hierarchical structure. Public performance—before a group larger than one's family—tended to be male-dominated and oriented most often toward the playing of instruments or solo dancing. Solo vocal performance, on the other hand, may have been female-dominated, and it tended to occur at home or in some other private setting, during work or relaxation, and was rendered usually for one's own personal enjoyment or that of family or a small circle of friends. In short, most singing was not perceived as "performance" at all.

Surprisingly few references to singing appear in nineteenth-century accounts of plain-folk life, except for some generalized observations about camp-meeting choruses, singing school performances, play-party refrains, or the group singing done around Civil War battlefield campfires.[25] Solo singing—lullabies to children, the individualized expression of private anguish, loneliness, or happiness, or an act of friendship or love for family or friends—may have been too personal to share with the casual stranger or observer who passed through the community.[26] Women certainly played crucial roles in the shaping of children's musical tastes and singing styles, and they may have been the chief preservers of ballads and other types of songs. Emma Bell Miles spoke only of the mountain women whom she knew in southeastern Tennessee, but her observations probably ring true for poor rural women throughout the South. Comparing mountain women with their men, who had "the adventures of which future ballads will be sung," she said that "the woman belongs to the race, to the

25. See, for example, Joseph T. Durkin, ed., *John Dooley, Confederate Soldier: His War Journal* (Washington, D.C., 1945), which describes a Confederate soldier and ballad singer, Archibald Goven, who was clearly of poor-white extraction. Another Confederate soldier, James M. Williams, described "psalm singers" who made the night "hideous with their horrid nasal twang butchering bad music"; John Kent Folmar, ed., *From That Terrible Field: Civil War Letters of James M. Williams, Twenty-First Alabama Infantry Volunteers* (Tuscaloosa, 1981), 13. The distinguished historian of Confederate soldiers and other plain folk Bell Wiley said that soldiers gathered often about the campfires or in winter huts to sing songs like "Home Sweet Home" or "Lorena"; Bell Irvin Wiley, *The Plain People of the Confederacy* (Baton Rouge, 1944), 18.

26. This shyness or emotional reserve may explain the awkwardness sometimes displayed by the folk singer before the folk-song collector.

old people. . . . It is over the loom and the knitting that old ballads are dreamily, endlessly crooned."[27]

For both men and women, singing may often have been little more than a diversion or momentary release of emotional energy, or a means of soothing the spirits of a child. But the songs chosen, whether religious or secular, may have been vehicles for social expression or complaint.[28] For plain-folk women especially, singing, like the making of a quilt or the planting of a flower garden, could be a way of bringing a bit of beauty into a life that was often drab and colorless. In a patriarchal society that generally discouraged or repressed the articulation of private anguish, music also could exert a cathartic function, permitting the discharge of frustrations, pain, or rage. Alan Lomax argued that "the British folk songs most popular in the backwoods were not merely survivals from a body of lore handed on indiscriminately from overseas sources, but a selection from that lore of vehicles for fantasies, wishes, and norms of behavior which corresponded to the emotional needs of pioneer women in America. In fact, the universally popular ballads represented the deepest emotional preoccupations of women who lived within the patriarchal family system." Further evidence of the effects wrought by that system appear, he argued, "in the folklore of the Devil or the bogeyman," where "we can feel the bottomless fear aroused by ruthless, authoritarian father figures who have held women and children in thrall for centuries."[29] The bloody ballads and old lonesome tunes appealed across age and gender lines, and like the equally cherished violent fairy tales, they may have functioned as musical soap operas. Women, though, may have found a means to channel their aggression by singing about cruel mothers, hardhearted lovers, and spurned but murderous sweethearts.

27. Emma Bell Miles, *The Spirit of the Mountains* (1905; rpr. Knoxville, 1975), 68–69.

28. The lyric content of the songs favored by the southern folk in the eighteenth and nineteenth centuries remains one of the most neglected areas of folk-music scholarship. The execution of such a study is hampered by our inability to know precisely when, where, and by whom the songs were sung. Nevertheless, good beginnings have been made by Dickson Bruce, Jr., *And They All Sang Hallelujah: Plain-Folk Camp-Meeting Religion, 1800–1845* (Knoxville, 1974); Bruce Collins, *White Society in the Antebellum South* (London, 1985); and Bill Cecil-Fronsman, *Common Whites: Class and Culture in Antebellum North Carolina* (Lexington, Ky., 1992).

29. Alan Lomax, *Folk Songs of North America*, 169.

The old ballads may have provided valuable, if unconscious, links to an important but slowly receding past, and important vehicles for the discharge of repressed emotions, but religious music was far more important in shaping the content, values, and style of southern folk music.[30] Music accompanied the dissenting Protestant sects who settled the southern backcountry, and it played an indispensable role in the implantation of evangelical Christianity in the South. Baptists, Methodists, New Light Presbyterians, and German pietistic groups conquered the southern backcountry with a democratic message that promised salvation for those who believed and with a body of music that borrowed freely from the rhythms of that sinful world that the dissenters hoped to redeem. From at least as early as the First Great Awakening, in the 1740s, when radical Baptists and dissenting Anglicans threw down their challenge to the established church and ruling hierarchy of Virginia, music was an indispensable weapon in the evangelizing of the South, making the region the greatest stronghold of evangelical Protestantism in the United States and bequeathing to the plain folk a body of songs and performance styles that have affected every secular genre of southern music.[31]

Religious music became an integral part of southern life, a constant presence from infancy to death. A southerner can escape neither religion nor the music associated with it. Most people learned to sing, or were en-

30. One of the first scholars to recognize the cultural value of southern religious music was Howard W. Odum, who noted that such music "not only brought forth the sweep of social heritage and individual memories but touched deep the chords of old moralities and loyalties"; Odum, *An American Epoch: Southern Portraiture in the National Picture* (New York, 1930), 180.

31. Although neither scholar talks much about music, John Boles and Rhys Isaac have provided the best general and interpretive accounts of the Protestant evangelization of the South: Boles, *The Great Revival, 1787–1805: The Origins of the Southern Evangelical Mind* (Lexington, Ky., 1975), and Isaac, *The Transformation of Virginia, 1740–1790* (Chapel Hill, 1982). Studies of religious music are much more common, but unfortunately not all of them are published. See, for example, James C. Downey, "The Music of American Revivalism" (Ph.D. dissertation, Tulane University, 1969); Timothy Alan Smith, "The Southern Folk-Hymn, 1802–1860: A History and Musical Analysis, With Notes on Performance Practice" (M.M. thesis, California State University–Fullerton, 1981); Richard H. Hulan, "Camp-Meeting Spiritual Folksongs: Legacy of the 'Great Revival in the West'" (Ph.D. dissertation, University of Texas, 1978); Bruce, *They All Sang Hallelujah*; and Jackson, *White Spirituals*.

couraged to do so, in religious settings—in church, at revivals, or at singing conventions (the sites of the famous all-day-singing-with-dinner-on-the grounds)—and they learned the rudiments of harmony and the skill of reading music at church-sponsored singing schools and conventions where the shape-note method was taught, or by listening to the professional singers employed by the shape-note publishing houses.[32]

Southerners made their first contributions to the larger body of American music as early as 1805 when songs from the Kentucky camp meetings began to appear in pocket-sized songsters, and after 1813 when songs from those books reappeared in John Wyeth's *Repository of Sacred Music, Part Second,* a widely circulated northern songbook.[33] It is difficult to determine how early or to what extent southern singing styles affected those who heard them, but in the early contexts of the camp meetings and shape-note publishing houses we encounter some of the most vital ingredients that shaped and defined the music of the plain folk: the easy confluence of secular melodies and religious lyrics (a tradition inherited from their British ancestors), the borrowing of African American styles and rhythms, and the employment of commercial methods of dissemination. The large throngs who attended the Kentucky revivals of the early 1800s thundered out spirituals in melodies that often bespoke tavern or street origins, lent them an emotional vocal color that may have been borrowed from the African Americans who were in their midst, and prolonged them (and made them easier to memorize) with techniques that also may have been borrowed from Africans—refrains and choruses. The songs, or others like them that were alleged to be products of the camp meetings, then appeared in printed songsters or tunebooks, where they began their task of permanently influencing the religious music of both northerners and southerners.

The southern folk religious repertory in the nineteenth century was a melange of old and new traditions, inherited from Great Britain or newly molded in the environment of America. Some congregations sang only the unadorned and musically unaccompanied psalms, utilizing only a few time-tested melodies, employing the practice of "lining the hymn," eschewing

32. The seminal work on the shape-note tradition is Jackson, *White Spirituals.* It should be supplemented with Harry Eskew, "Shape-Note Hymnody in the Shenandoah Valley, 1816–1860" (Ph.D. dissertation, Tulane University, 1966), and Buell E. Cobb, Jr., *The Sacred Harp and Its Music* (Athens, Ga., 1978).

33. Hulan, "Camp-Meeting Spiritual Folksongs," xxv, 47–49, 91–93.

harmony, but embellishing the melody with odd vocal bendings and twists and extended notes that remained characteristic of southern backwoods singing. Long before the journey to America was made, British folk had contributed to the democratization of religious music by creating ballads that united popularly known melodies with spiritual or moralistic texts to describe the Christian's earthly travail or celebrate his joy, or warn the listener about the awful fate that awaited the transgressor. Plain-folk theology rejected the world and its vanity, but the folk could not forget, or resist the temptation to use, the secular tunes that had enriched their lives.

Coexisting with the psalms and folk spirituals, but soon supplanting them in the affections of the folk, were the newer composed hymns of Isaac Watts, Charles Wesley, and other professional composers, which spread with the revivals in the late eighteenth and early nineteenth centuries. Powered largely by the enthusiastic singing of the Methodists, who took them to every corner of the southern frontier, such hymns as "Amazing Grace" and "When I Can Read My Title Clear" moved into the repertoires of both white and black Christians. Laboring to make the songs even more singable, and striving to make them easier to learn, dissenting Protestants democratized the performance of this music even further by altering melodies and adding refrains and choruses. In the decades following the Civil War, a new variety of revival songs, described as "gospel" after 1875, entered the South in great numbers, accompanying the tours made by such popular evangelists and songleaders as Dwight Moody and Ira Sankey. In the South they became permanently enshrined in widely circulated songbooks. Written mostly by such northern songwriters as Philip Bliss, James McGranahan, and Charles Gabriel, these songs bore striking resemblance to the pop songs of the day with their sentimental imagery, evocations of pastoral simplicity, refrains, and singable melodies.[34] The alliance between pop and gospel only became stronger at the

---

34. There is no good, comprehensive history of nineteenth century gospel music, but the outlines of the story can be found in biographies of the revivalists and their musical accompanists and in a few reminiscences of the gospel composers: William G. McLoughlin, Jr., *Modern Revivalism* (New York, 1959), and *Billy Sunday Was His Real Name* (Chicago, 1955); James F. Findlay, Jr., *Dwight L. Moody, American Evangelist, 1837–1899* (Chicago, 1969); Kathleen Martha Minnix, "God's Comedian: The Life and Career of Evangelist Sam Jones" (Ph.D. dissertation, Georgia State University, 1986); Charles Gabriel, *Gospel Songs and Their Writers* (Chicago, 1913); and Phil Kerr, *Music in Evangelism* (Glendale, Calif., 1939).

end of the century when the emerging Pentecostal movement successfully adapted the "worldly" sounds of brass bands, ragtime pianos, and jazzlike syncopations into their music. Ironically, while southerners labored to rebuild their war-ravaged economy and struggled to preserve the conviction that God was still on their side despite the humiliation of defeat, they often retreated to "Beautiful Isle of Somewhere," "Shall We Gather at the River," "Will the Circle Be Unbroken," and other northern-composed gospel songs to find solace and reassurance in a time of spiritual and social malaise.

Religious music did not simply offer emotional release; it also brought the business of music to the South. Whether motivated by spiritual zeal or by capitalistic enterprise, music merchandisers contributed to southerners many of their most cherished songs while also promoting innovations in performance style. As new songs and styles emerged from the crucible of revivalism and from the sectarian competition that raged in the southern backcountry, singing-school teachers in the early 1800s came down out of Pennsylvania, through the Valley of Virginia, and into the lower South, holding ten-day schools where they taught the shape-note style of notation and the singing of four-part harmony. Publishers and songbooks representing the singing-school movement appeared as early as 1816 when Ananias Davisson published his *Kentucky Harmony,* one of the first "tunebooks" to appear in the South.[35] Often called "longboys" because their width exceeded their height, these cherished books became the nucleus of a regional publishing business that codified and circulated most of the South's religious music styles. Although the most famous books emerging from the tradition, *Southern Harmony* and *The Sacred Harp,* exemplified the four-note fasola system, a style that had been familiar to Shakespeare, the shape-note business adapted easily and quickly to the seven-note doremi fashion. Led by the Ruebush-Kieffer company, which began operations in a Virginia town appropriately named Singer's Glen, the shape-note publishing business soon after the Civil War sent teachers and songbooks to every section of the South and laid the groundwork for the flourishing southern gospel business of our own time.[36] The most enterprising leader of the Ruebush-Kieffer empire,

35. Rachel Augusta Harley, "Ananias Davisson: Southern Tunebook Compiler" (Ph.D. dissertation, University of Michigan, 1972).

36. The official journal of the Ruebush-Kieffer company, and the leading publicist of the doremi shape-note style, is discussed in Paul M. Hall, "The *Musical Million:* A Study

James D. Vaughan, from Lawrenceburg, Tennessee, ultimately made the most crucial innovations in the emerging gospel phenomenon. After the turn of the century he employed traveling quartets to popularize his songs and songbooks, and made these performers and his business even more widely known through pioneering phonograph records and radio broadcasts.[37] With good reason, the *Singing News*, the premier journal of what is now called "southern gospel music," carries Vaughan's photograph on its masthead.[38]

The early and continuing commercialization of southern religious music is a vivid reminder of the role played by popular culture and the marketplace in the lives of the southern folk. Songs, instrumental pieces, dances, instruments, comedy, and performance styles of popular or professional origin had moved constantly into the repertoires of the folk since long before they left the British Isles to begin new lives in the vastness of the southern frontier. The ultimate origins of the famous British ballads will never be known, but the most cherished of them all, "Barbara Allen," enjoyed a life in popular culture as early as 1666.[39]

In this country a wide array of traveling shows—equestrian, puppet, circus, dramatic, medicine, tent repertoire, blackface minstrel, and vaudeville—dispensed musical entertainment to city and village alike, while also constantly borrowing ideas from people in the hinterlands.[40] The

---

and Analysis of the Periodical Promoting Reading Music Through Shape-Notes in North America from 1870 to 1914" (D.M.A. dissertation, Catholic University of America, Washington, D.C., 1970). See also Grace I. Showalter, *The Music Books of Ruebush and Kieffer, 1866–1942* (Richmond, Va., 1975).

37. Jo Fleming, "James D. Vaughan, Music Publisher" (S.M.D. dissertation, Union Theological Seminary, 1972). Another influential alumnus of Ruebush-Kieffer is discussed by Joel Francis Reed in "Anthony J. Showalter (1858–1924): Southern Educator, Publisher, Composer" (Ed.D. dissertation, New Orleans Baptist Theological Seminary, 1975).

38. Published by Maurice Templeton, and edited by Jerry Kirksey, *Singing News* is a monthly publication located in Boone, North Carolina.

39. The famous English diarist Samuel Pepys heard the ballad sung by the actress Mrs. Knipp on January 1, 1666. We will probably never know how old the song was at the time she learned it, or how it came into her possession. *The Diary of Samuel Pepys*, ed. Robert Latham and William Matthews (11 vols.; Berkeley, 1970–83), Vol. VII, Pt. 1, p. 5.

40. I have written an extended discussion of the popular influence: "Popular Culture and the Music of the South," in Bill C. Malone, *Singing Cowboys and Musical Mountaineers: Southern Culture and the Roots of Country Music* (Athens, Ga., 1993), 43–69. I have also written on the most popular songwriter of the late nineteenth century, William S. Hays, who composed many songs that eventually moved into the folk and country music reper-

cultural interchange that marked this relationship between town and country makes it next to impossible to determine precisely the origins of pre-twentieth-century forms of music and the styles with which they were performed. Music and dance often traveled in a rather circular process of cultural transmission. A professional entertainer, for example, might pick up a catchy tune on the street, adapt it successfully into his stage act, and then reintroduce his altered version to the folk through his traveling show. Similarly, on an occasional jaunt into town, a country fiddler might learn a new tune from any number of sources, such as a circus brass band, a saloon piano player, a minstrel string band, or a phonograph recording displayed in a department store window. When the fiddler incorporated the tune into his own repertory, it began a new life as a "country" tune— that is, until some later professional entertainer "borrowed" it and rein-troduced it to a "popular" audience, or until some folklorist "discovered" the tune and published it as a "folk song"![41]

New musical ideas journeyed to the rural South as inseparable prod-ucts of the larger phenomenon of modernization. A powerful array of forces, including the Civil War, the expansion southward of the nation's railway system, and the steady growth of cities after the war, weakened the traditional hegemony of agriculture in the region, broadened the reach of the market system, and popularized the merchandise of the towns and the values of middle-class life.[42] As a colonial economy,

---

toires; "William S. Hays: The Bard of Kentucky," *Register of the Kentucky Historical Society*, XCIII (1995), 286–307.

41. There is no better example of this process than the history of the famous fiddle tune, "Listen to the Mockingbird." The Philadelphia songwriter Septimus Winner heard the tune being whistled by a black man, Richard Milburn, on a street near Winner's office sometime in the 1850s. Winner appropriated the tune, added sentimental lyrics about the death of a young maiden, and then saw it circulated widely throughout the United States by blackface minstrel troupes. The song became very popular in the South and is now known almost exclusively as a virtuoso fiddle piece in which fiddlers imitate birdcalls.

42. The market economy, of course, expanded into the southern backcountry at an ir-regular pace and at different periods of time. Steven Hahn provides a model for other po-tential students in his excellent case study of northern Georgia, *The Roots of Southern Popu-lism: Yeoman Farmers and the Transformation of the Georgia Upcountry, 1850–1890* (New York, 1983). Thomas D. Clark speaks of the emerging network of international credit that enveloped all rural southerners after the war in *Pills, Petticoats, and Plows: The Southern Country Store* (Norman, Okla., 1944). Edward L. Ayers provides a masterful survey of the entire South's integration into the national economy during the late nineteenth century in

the South had never had a popular culture that it could call its own. Even during the Civil War, when southerners consciously strove to produce an indigenous body of patriotic and nationalistic poetry, they more often embraced songs of northern vintage, such as "Lorena" and "Listen to the Mockingbird," and even adopted Ohio-born Dan Emmett's minstrel walkaround "Dixie" as their battle song.[43] The market/urban revolution of the late nineteenth century only increased the flow of songs, sheet music, instruments, and ultimately phonographs and phonograph recordings into the hinterlands of the South. When the commercialization of southern folk music began in the early 1920s, with the introduction of such music to a larger public through phonograph recordings and radio broadcasts, rural musicians already possessed a large body of music that came from the performances of blackface minstrels, tent performers, vaudeville entertainers, ragtime pianists, and other popular performers.[44] Songs of unabashed sentimentality, like "Little Rosewood Casket," "Put My Little Shoes Away," and "The Blind Child," coexisted happily with more lighthearted tunes like "Dill Pickle Rag" or bawdy saloon numbers

---

The Promise of the New South: Life After Reconstruction (New York, 1992). The industrialization of the South has been well discussed in a number of books, including David L. Carlton, *Mill and Town in South Carolina, 1880–1920* (Baton Rouge, 1980); Ronald D. Eller, *Miners, Millhands, and Mountaineers: Industrialization of the Appalachian South, 1880–1930* (Knoxville, 1982); Crandall Shiflett, *Coal Town: Life, Work, and Culture in Company Towns of Southern Appalachia, 1880–1960* (Knoxville, 1991); Jacqueline Hall et al., *Like a Family: The Making of a Southern Cotton Mill World* (Chapel Hill, 1987); and James C. Cobb, *Industrialization and Southern Society, 1877–1984* (Lexington, Ky., 1984). For a more extensive bibliography of industrialization, see the notes to Ayers, *Promise of the New South.* The other side of the coin, the disintegration of southern agriculture, has been discussed by many scholars, including Gilbert C. Fite, *Cotton Fields No More: Southern Agriculture, 1865–1980* (Lexington, Ky., 1984); Pete Daniel, *Breaking the Land: The Transformation of Cotton, Tobacco, and Rice Cultures Since 1880* (Urbana, Ill., 1985); and Jack Temple Kirby, *Rural Worlds Lost: The American South, 1920–1960* (Baton Rouge, 1987).

43. The South's struggle to create a body of music and poetry of its own can be seen in the plethora of paperback songsters produced during the war. The ones I have seen are located in the Harris Collection, Hay Library, Brown University, Providence, Rhode Island. Richard B. Harwell discusses the massive outpouring of southern songs during the Civil War in *Confederate Music* (Chapel Hill, 1950).

44. Evidence of early country music's debts to such performers is found in the valuable record collection *Minstrels and Tunesmiths: The Commercial Roots of Early Country Music,* JEMF recording 109, produced and edited by Norm Cohen, the most important student of folk music's indebtedness to the pop tradition.

like "Frankie and Johnny."[45] Even more significant, these songs moved, with little apparent sense of contradiction, into the repertories of rural performers alongside such venerable ballads as "Barbara Allen," "The House Carpenter," and "The Wife of Usher's Well."

Whatever their origin, the vocal songs, secular and religious, were clearly indispensable to the shaping of the total southern folk-song corpus, and they continued to appear, often in fragmentary or greatly altered form, in the repertories of the radio hillbillies of the post-1920s era. We need to recall, however, that it has been in the area of performance style that white southern folk have made their most vital contributions to the music of the world. The multiplicity of sounds that form the southern style and set it apart from other regional expressions were a product of the total southern experience, and they were forged in a culture of interrelating ethnic, racial, religious, and commercial involvement. The church was a powerful shaper of values and a bottomless fount of songs and vocal styles, all of which contributed to the tone and sound of southern music, but dance has functioned even more crucially in the formation of *performance* styles. In the arena of public dance, white folk musicians learned to work with each other and, above all, to play for and strive to please audiences outside of their immediate families. The quest for an expanding audience broadened the repertories of musicians, sharpened their skills, and ultimately took their music to performing venues far removed from the rural South.

It is no accident that most of the rural musicians who made phonograph recordings and radio broadcasts in the early twenties were solo fiddlers or members of string bands who were not known for their singing. Most of them were heirs to the venerable frolic tradition of rural America and the British Isles, a tradition of country dancing celebrating rural harvests, religious and patriotic holidays, and the events that accompanied life's most important passages.[46] Evangelical religion might encourage guilt about the bodily pleasures of the dance while also questioning the morality and social utility of musicians who would squander their God-given time

45. A major study of the sentimental songs that moved into the folk tradition is sorely needed. A useful beginning has been made by William C. Ellis, "The Sentimental Mother Song in American Country Music, 1923–1945" (Ph.D. dissertation, Ohio State University, 1978).

46. See chap. 1, "Southern Rural Music in the Nineteenth Century," in Malone, *Singing Cowboys and Musical Mountaineers*, for a more extended discussion of the frolic tradition.

in the pursuit of frivolity, but dancing remained a passion in the rural South among rich and poor and black and white. Although the image of the drunken fiddler, along with the British-born legend of the musician who had sold his soul to the devil, remained strong in southern folklore and fiction, the fiddler was more venerated than scorned by rural southern folk. Undoubtedly some fiddlers were mere wastrels, but they also included respected politicians, judges, lawyers, preachers, and planters, as well as solid workingmen of all gradations—yeomen farmers, poor whites, free blacks, slaves. The fiddler reigned supreme at country dances held in houses great and small, and in the humble cabins of the slaves, from the Chesapeake Bay to the plains of Texas.[47]

The frolic tradition reaffirms the essential eclecticism of southern rural culture, and the varied sources of its music. The first fiddlers in colonial America (and the first recorded arrival in the South is that of John Utie, who came to Virginia in 1621)[48] unquestionably brought styles and tunes born in the British Isles and Western Europe. But on the southern frontier or in the important cultural seedbed of Western Pennsylvania,[49] they and their descendants came into almost immediate contact with other musicians, including fiddlers, from Germany, France, Spain, and Africa. As the geographical South expanded from its original base in the Chesapeake Bay to the last frontier of Texas, plain-folk southerners preserved their love for fiddle music and transmitted it to their children and grandchildren. White southerners clearly learned from one another, but they remained acutely aware of the presence of two other important bodies of fiddlers in the nineteenth century—African Americans and professional blackface minstrels. From both groups they absorbed songs and styles, as well as precedents for string band music, including the use of the five-string banjo as both a percussive and melodic instrument. The union of

47. One of the first and best accounts of a southern country dance, and a suggestive statement about the wide range of people who were attracted to such affairs, is "The Dance," in Augustus Baldwin Longstreet, *Georgia Scenes* (1835; 2d ed. New York, 1859). For other references to frolics, see the notes to Malone, *Singing Cowboys and Musical Mountaineers*.

48. Earl V. Spielman, "Traditional North American Fiddling: A Methodology for the Historical and Comparative Analytical Style Study of Instrumental Musical Traditions" (Ph.D. dissertation, University of Wisconsin, 1975), 191.

49. Samuel Bayard, *Hill Country Tunes: Instrumental Folk Music of Southwestern Pennsylvania* (Philadelphia, 1944).

banjo and fiddle profoundly testified to the influence of commercial popular entertainment in the lives of the southern folk and was also powerfully emblematic of the fusion of African and European traits in their musical culture.[50]

Southern country fiddlers and the dancers for whom they played rejected no song or performance style that could successfully be transferred to the fiddle or adapted to the dance floor. Old World pieces of both folk and stage origin, such as "Soldier's Joy" and "Fisher's Hornpipe," and home-grown tunes with similarly clouded identities, such as "The Eighth of January," "The Arkansas Traveler," and "Durang's Hornpipe," competed for the affections of fiddlers with more recent tunes of minstrel, vaudeville, ragtime, and Tin Pan Alley origin such as "Listen to the Mockingbird," "Whistling Rufus," "Dill Pickle Rag," "Over the Waves," "Under the Double Eagle," "Ragtime Annie," and "Red Wing."[51]

The dances favored by southern country people displayed a similar history of cultural exchange across racial, ethnic, and social lines.[52] British settlers surely brought memories of Old World dances to the southern frontier, including not only those that had been passed from parents to

50. No topic of music scholarship has been more hotly contested than the question of how the African-derived five-string banjo and its styles moved into southern white folk culture. Robert Winans, for example, argues that professional white entertainers—the blackface minstrels—took the instrument and frailing techniques of performance into the southern hills: "The Folk, the Stage, and the Five-String Banjo in the Nineteenth Century," *Journal of American Folklore*, LXXIX (1976), 407–37. William Tallmadge and Cecelia Conway, on the other hand, believe that African Americans took the instrument and styles to the mountains: Tallmadge, "The Folk Banjo and Clawhammer Performance Practice in the Upper South: A Study of Origins," in *The Appalachian Experience: Proceedings of the Sixth Annual Studies Conference*, ed. Barry M. Buxton (Boone, N.C., 1983); Conway, *African Banjo Echoes in Appalachia: A Study of Folk Traditions* (Knoxville, 1995). Three good studies of blackface minstrelsy, each of which assay the complicated questions concerning the origins of minstrel music, are Robert C. Toll, *Blacking Up: The Minstrel Show in Nineteenth Century America* (New York, 1974); Hans Nathan, *Dan Emmett and the Rise of Early Negro Minstrelsy* (Norman, Okla., 1962); and Howard L. Sacks and Judith Rose Sacks, *Way Up North in Dixie: A Black Family's Claim to the Confederate Anthem* (Washington, D.C., 1993).

51. Gene Wiggins, "Popular Music and the Fiddler," *JEMF Quarterly*, XV, 55 (1979), 144–52.

52. Folk dancing has become a favored topic among people interested in old-time music, especially in the *Old-Time Herald*, edited by Alice Gerrard in Durham, North Carolina. The journal regularly carries a column called "The Dance Beat."

children, but also steps that had been learned from professional entertainers or that had even been imitations of courtly amusements. The group dances of the rural South, which usually included four or more couples, and which even some intensely religious people could tolerate because they involved no intimate frontal contact between dancers, were ultimately traceable to the interchange that went on between the upper-class English and French during the reign of King Charles II. Dances presumably of rural peasant English origin were taken to France in the 1660s, recodified in French instruction books and given French names (such as cotillion and quadrille), and then transported back to England—and to America—by French dance instructors or others who had learned from them. In the United States some of the French vocabulary of instruction was preserved, but improvising Americans abandoned the books and instead employed a caller (who was often the fiddler himself) who shouted the movements to the dancers as they went through their paces. "Square dancing" (so-called because four couples constituted a square) thus began its venerated and enduring history as the dance of rural America.[53]

Individual step dancing also came to the rural South in a number of guises that prevent an accurate attribution of origins. The dances came in the repertories of professional stage entertainers (who invariably included solo dancing as part of their musical, comedic, or dramatic routines), in the pedagogy of the dance instructors, and in the possession of humble immigrants who learned them from God only knows where. In the United States the old dances were further preserved and modified and new ones were introduced and popularized, particularly by African Americans and by the innovative and perambulating blackface minstrels. Terms like *clog*, *jig*, and *hornpipe*, which may have referred to precisely differentiated steps in the Old World, were generally used indiscriminately in this country to describe any kind of solo step dance. The dance variations intro-

53. Much of the interest in country dancing in the seventeenth century is ultimately traceable to John Playford's collection of 1651, *The English Dancing Master*. The book went through many editions and supplements. The best study of English rural dancing's transplantation in the United States is S. Foster Damon, "History of Square Dancing," *American Antiquarian Society Proceedings*, April 1952, pp. 63–98. It can be usefully supplemented by Richard Nevell, *A Time to Dance: American Country Dancing from Hornpipes to Hot Hash* (New York, 1977). The best survey of the play-party, the venerable tradition of children's game songs that often served as a substitute for dancing, is B. A. Botkin, *The American Play-Party Song* (1937; rpr. New York, 1963).

duced by professional entertainers, although eagerly embraced by rural
people, only complicate the task of dance historians. Whatever the source
or fate of these dances, they persistently powered variations among fiddlers
and other rural musicians who tailored their playing to fit the often-
intricate movements of the steps and who preserved the tunes long after
the dances themselves were forgotten. All country fiddlers today can play
versions of tunes such as "Sailor's Hornpipe," "Durang's Hornpipe," or
"Fisher's Hornpipe," but only rarely does one know that the term once
described a solo, quickstep dance that was performed by humble folk
throughout the British Isles and by professional entertainers there and in
the United States.[54]

When the components of its musical repertoire are reviewed, it becomes readily apparent that southern folk culture was neither homogeneous in its ethnic or racial composition nor static in its social development. This socially conservative culture, which changed slowly and often
with dogged resistance, was nevertheless remarkably receptive to new
and diverse musical ideas. By the end of the nineteenth century a broad
array of songs, tunes, dances, and performance styles was available to the
southern folk, often in substantially altered or modified forms. In assessing
its relationship or value to plain folk musical culture, the origin of this
musical material is irrelevant. If a song, dance, or style resonated successfully with the aesthetic and social needs of the folk, the material became
the property of the folk and was integrated into their culture.[55] Consequently, Old World ballads and dances coexisted amicably with northern-
composed gospel songs, Tin Pan Alley parlor songs, and minstrel jigs and

54. For discussions of the Old World origins of step dancing, see William Chappell,
Popular Music of the Olden Time (2 vols.; London, 1855), I; Vuillier Gaston, *A History of
Dancing* (New York, 1898); and Charles Baskervill, *The Elizabethan Jig* (Chicago, 1929).
There is as yet no comprehensive treatment of folk step-dance history in the United
States, but see the following: Marian Hannah Winter, "American Theatrical Dancing from
1750 to 1800," *Musical Quarterly*, XXIV (1938), 58–73; Alan S. Downer, ed., *The Memoir
of John Durang* (Pittsburgh, 1966); the notes in Malone, *Singing Cowboys and Musical
Mountaineers*; and various articles in the *Old-Time Herald*.

55. Lawrence Levine's arguments concerning slave culture are worth repeating here:
"We have only gradually come to recognize not merely the sheer complexity of origins but
also its irrelevancy for an understanding of consciousness. It is not necessary for a people to
originate or invent all or even most of the elements of their culture. It is necessary only that
these components become their own, embedded in their traditions, expressive of their world
view and lifestyle." Levine, *Black Culture and Black Consciousness* (New York, 1977), 24.

hornpipes. The European-derived fiddle preserved its dominance as a dance instrument, but by the end of the nineteenth century it had been joined in string bands by a variety of instruments that bespoke diverse ethnic and commercial origins—the African five-string banjo, the Spanish guitar, the Italian mandolin, the German harmonica and accordion, and the American-born autoharp, all of which were being made widely available by mail-order catalogs and other forms of commercial merchandising.[56]

Receptivity to musical innovation, of course, did not necessarily equate with social democracy or racial egalitarianism. The pre-twentieth-century South was a region plagued by the sins of racial injustice and economic inequality. Poor whites and blacks viewed each other with hostility even as they borrowed music from each other, and the social distance between rich and poor remained wide, and virtually impassable, even if musical styles sometimes crossed class barriers. Music could not empower the powerless, but it could give voice to the poor and lend dignity, self-respect, and emotional sustenance to their quest for survival. As the product of two centuries of migration across the southern frontier, and of successive and often traumatic adaptations to the changes that marked the transition from rural to urban-industrial life, the musical culture of the plain folk survived into the twentieth century to become both the enduring inspiration for those who value traditional music, and the generating nucleus of much of America's popular commercial music. Under such guises as country, cowboy, Cajun, gospel, rockabilly, and southern rock, the music of the plain folk has moved around the world and has become virtually the musical voice of America itself. But that is another story.[57]

56. The widespread popularity in the late-nineteenth-century South of Montgomery Ward, Sears, Roebuck, and other mail-order catalogs is documented in Ayers, *Promise of the New South*, 87–89. The role played by merchandising in making the autoharp a "folk" instrument is discussed by A. Doyle Moore, "The Autoharp: Its Origin and Development from a Popular to a Folk Instrument," in Harry Taussig, *Folk Style Autoharp* (New York, 1967), 10–20 [orig. publ. in *New York Folklore Quarterly*, XIX, 4 (December 1963)].

57. The general outlines of that story can be found in Malone, *Southern Music, American Music*. The book is currently undergoing revision.

Jerah Johnson

The Vernacular Architecture of the South: Log Buildings, Dog-Trot Houses, and English Barns

Study of the building traditions of southern plain folk, commonly called "southern vernacular architecture," has a number of problems associated with it, problems of such a special nature that they call for some comment at the outset. First, the term *vernacular architecture* itself can cause confusion, for as used in the United States it means something quite different from what it does abroad. In both instances, "vernacular architecture" means the common, everyday building traditions of the people—low-culture, homemade architecture, so to speak, as distinct from high-culture, designer-originated building traditions.[1] But outside the United States, the term is almost always used to mean the building traditions of a particular people, of a cultural or ethnic group, building traditions employed by the group wherever they may live, be it in their homeland or in areas into which they have migrated, however long ago. Bedouin tents, for example, are found wherever Bedouins are found, whether at the westernmost tip of Morocco or two thousand miles to the

1. Instead of the two-category schema used here, vernacular/designer, some writers have suggested a three-category schema, folk/vernacular/designer. Fortunately this needless complication has not been adopted by many scholars. See Milton B. Newton, Jr., *Louisiana: A Geographical Portrait* (2d ed.; Baton Rouge, 1987), 171. Because the audience for the present essay is expected to be largely historians rather than vernacular architecture specialists, technical terms have been avoided and familiar descriptive language, the language of historians, used instead.

east in Israel. Bedouins use a particular kind of black tent—Bedouin vernacular—and there are no variations by region or in tent types.

On the other hand, in the United States and to a very large degree in Canada, vernacular architecture is considered almost exclusively in terms of variations by geographical regions and in building types. There are, of course, obvious, good, and sound historical reasons why this is the case. Anglo North America was populated by a heterogeneous collection of peoples, who once having migrated here have continued for generations upon generations to move about the expanses of the continent in ever-more-fragmented groups.

All of these groups, as they moved, carried their traditions with them, at least fragments of their traditions. And *fragments* is the governing word, for the moves themselves, the new and often quite different environment, the passage of time as generations piled up, and particularly interaction and intermarriage with persons from different groups and different places, constantly eroded the original traditions or so infused them with elements from other traditions as to alter them substantially. That process, of course, has been commonly called "the American melting pot."

But it is important to keep in mind that of all of the elements that constitute an ethnic tradition, building practices erode far more rapidly and far more completely than any other single one. And for good reason. On the frontier, people made their own clothes at home, people cooked their traditional food at home, people played their own music at home, did their own dances at home, practiced their own religion or lack thereof at home, and spoke their own language or dialect. But very few people built their own houses, because very few could. Even in frontier societies, most people had to hire or trade with someone in the community with the know-how to build or oversee the building of a house for them.

Let us say, for example, that a new settler in Louisiana's Florida parishes in the 1830s went to his local know-how-to-build-a-house man, who came from, say, upcountry North Carolina, and told him he wanted a South Carolina lowcountry raised cottage like the one his grandfather had outside Charleston. The builder would not have known what the settler was talking about. The local builder knew how to build what he knew how to build and nothing else. The newcomer would have had to settle for an upcountry I-house, or maybe a dog-trot or maybe a saddle-bag house—whatever the builder knew how to build.

The point is that because of such realities, building traditions were far more fragmented and disjointed than any other element of ethnic tradition. Hence, no wonder that in Anglo North America, unlike the rest of the world, vernacular architecture cannot be categorized by ethnic group, but only by region and by type.[2]

Another problem encountered in the study of vernacular architecture is that of deciding where to draw the line between vernacular and designer architecture. That is to say, what is the dividing line between plain folk and fancy folk? It is a well-known fact to all southern historians, but one that bears repeating as a reminder, that so-called planters were in most cases simply frontier farmers who, by hook or crook, got rich. And just because they got rich, they did not necessarily change much. Their style of living did not change much, and their houses often did not change at all. The most famous planter's house in Georgia history was that of Governor George M. Troup, who along with members of the Georgia Triumvirate helped effect the Compromise of 1850, which averted the Civil War for ten years. Troup had been a major force in Georgia politics for nearly thirty years, from the early 1820s, and remained one until his death in 1856. The barbecues and dances Governor Troup gave at his plantation, Valle d'Aosta, or as it came to be spelled, Valdosta, which stood near the town of Dublin, made the residence—named for the Valley of Augustus in northern Italy—far and away the most celebrated in Georgia, with people all over the state vying for invitations to it. Valle d'Aosta, the most famous house in Georgia, was in fact a log dog-trot structure with clay chimneys. However rich, famous, and powerful Governor Troup had gotten, he never changed his original frontier house for a fancy new designer model the way many planters did.[3]

2. The unique problems encountered in the study of the vernacular architecture of Anglo North America recently came pointedly to the attention of Paul Oliver, ed., *Encyclopedia of Vernacular Architecture of the World* (3 vols.; Cambridge, Eng., 1997). He sought for North American contributors writing on vernacular architecture in ethnic categories but found none. Consequently he had to redesign the North American section of the *Encyclopedia* along regional and typological lines. The *Encyclopedia*, now the basic standard work on the subject in its global ramifications, uses the term *vernacular* to embrace the various kinds of buildings often termed folk, peasant, traditional, primitive, or indigenous architecture.

3. Lucian Lamar Knight, *Georgia's Landmarks, Memorials, and Legends* (2 vols.; Atlanta, 1913–14), II, 828, 888–89. Troup's Valdosta is not to be confused with the town of Valdosta in extreme south Georgia, which was established later and named for Troup's

Left front view of the overseer's house on the Mitchell Place, one of Georgia governor (1823–1827) George M. Troup's plantations. The boarded front shedroom was probably enclosed sometime after the original log house with its full-width porch was built. While on an inspection trip to this plantation in 1856, Troup fell ill and died in this house.

This and the following photographs were made in 1910 by Horace B. Folsom, editor and publisher of the Mount Vernon (Ga.) weekly newspaper the *Montgomery Monitor*. That year Folsom made a trek through Georgia's old Montgomery and Washington Counties taking notes and pictures. Subsequently many of his photographs were lost. But in the 1970s Albert Sidney Johnson of Decatur, Georgia, discovered four of Folsom's glass-plate negatives, showing the ruins of Troup's Valle d'Aosta or Valdosta Plantation and the overseers' houses on two of the other five nearby plantations Troup owned. The photographs, published here for the first time, are from those negatives. All are courtesy of Albert Sidney Johnson.

Right front view of the overseer's house on the Mitchell Place. Note the wood and stick chimney and the triangular wooden blocks serving as piers for the structures, seen most clearly beneath the detached log kitchen to the rear of the house.

Overseer's house on Rosemont in Treutlen County, Georgia, one of Governor Troup's six plantations. Note the mortises at the ends of the front sill; they originally received tenons on the side sills of an attached front porch. The small building at the rear is a later addition; originally a detached log kitchen stood a bit farther to the rear.

Ruins of a portion of Troup's residence, Valle d'Aosta or Valdosta Plantation, in Laurens County, Georgia. In 1854, Troup added this detached structure to his much older log dog-trot house for use as a reception room, effectively an office that doubled as a ballroom on social occasions. It was built of dovetailed, dressed logs that were plastered inside, and it featured a sandstone chimney.

If Valle d'Aosta is the most famous planter's house in Georgia history, the most famous house in Georgia fiction, indeed in southern fiction, or for that matter, in all American fiction—the House of Seven Gables notwithstanding—is *Gone with the Wind*'s Tara. And Tara—the Tara of the book, not the Tara of the film (Margaret Mitchell's letters go on and on for months complaining about what the movie makers had done to her Tara)—was no great, imposing, white-columned mansion, but an unpretentious and utterly unprepossessing simple, square, whitewashed brick house that Gerald O'Hara had struggled to build long before he got rich. Tara, like Valle d'Aosta, though the residence of a prosperous planter, was very much vernacular architecture.[4]

And there is another consideration: One often finds vernacular buildings and designer buildings literally conjoined. Designer houses, for example, not infrequently had porches, extra bedchambers, and (almost always) freestanding kitchens added by local builders. Or sometimes the original log house was simply built over and around—encased, as it were—by later, fancier, more "modern" designer work. Such additions and encasements complicate the problem of classification.

A more important problem arises from the fact that southern vernacular architecture remains an underdeveloped field of study. Not that it is particularly new—it is actually almost as old a field as southern history itself, for scholars started working in it in the 1920s, not long after serious modern study of southern history began. But scholars working in vernacular architecture were few in number, very few, and almost all were geographers, folklorists, or anthropologists. Few architectural historians dealt with the subject, for they focused on plantation manors and the great town houses of a few southern cities. And hardly any historians proper paid any attention at all to the subject. Either they did not feel competent to deal with it or they thought it trivial.

The result is that the scholarship is fragmented, hypothesis-based, theory-ridden, general-law-driven, still largely conjectural, and terribly confusing. Even the technical vocabulary remains largely unstandardized,

---

plantation. Little or no important work has been done on Troup in quite some time. The last major treatment was Porter L. Fortune, Jr., "George M. Troup: Leading States Right Advocate" (Ph.D. dissertation, University of North Carolina–Chapel Hill, 1949).

4. Richard Harwell, ed., *Margaret Mitchell's "Gone with the Wind" Letters, 1936–1949* (New York, 1976), 36, 105–106, 137, 249–50, 254, 358, 406–407; Darden Asbury Pyron, *Southern Daughter: The Life of Margaret Mitchell* (New York, 1991), 369–72, 390.

with writers often using highly individualized terminology. What one
writer calls a "two-crib barn" another writer calls a "three-bay barn"; various writers call the same notching technique by different names; and
definitions of geographical areas such as uplands and lowlands often vary
greatly.

Even so, the situation is improving. Increasing numbers of geographers,
folklorists, and anthropologists are continuing the work on vernacular architecture that their predecessors initiated seventy years ago. Recently
they have been joined by some architectural historians, by a number of
material culture specialists, and by even more historical archaeologists.
And historians of the South are beginning to take an interest.

But this new interest in vernacular architecture comes almost too late.
Had the interest developed in the 1950s or even the 1960s, scholars
would have had plenty of examples to study: old houses, barns, cribs, shelters, stables, smokehouses, meat blocks, fowl houses, outhouses, pens,
fences, dams, mills, sluices, church houses, and schoolhouses. During the
last thirty years, however, most such structures have disappeared. Many of
the houses were pulled down in the prosperous 1950s and replaced by
ranch-style bungalows, or burned down because of the undercircuited
wiring installed during the final stages of the federal Rural Electrification
Administration. In the 1960s and 1970s more houses, as well as churches
and schools, were abandoned as small farmers sold out to corporate agricultural endeavors and left for town and city jobs. Abandoned, the structures quickly rotted or even more quickly were eaten up by termites,
which in the old days had been kept in check, as were cockroaches, by
ever-present chickens, which were no more. And in the 1980s and early
1990s the new agriculture of irrigation, herbicides, plastic beds, and truck
farming made every foot of open ground usable. Consequently, most remaining structures, including dams, millraces, fences, and even the trees
and shrubs that marked old house sites were swept away to make room for
enlarged fields.

What the new agriculture and termites failed to get, the urbanization
of the countryside did: new or widened roads and networks of water and
sewerage pipelines that were laid to supply endless subdivisions, rural
shopping malls, and country trailer parks. Today *in situ* examples of vernacular architecture are hard to find. The best are in outdoor rural-life
museums, and although they offer something, they are not ideal for study
because each such museum tends to have only one example of each type

of structure: one dog-trot, one corncrib, one mule barn, one henhouse, one schoolhouse, one store, one doctor's office. Moreover, such museums are few and far between and most are quite small, often with only half a dozen or fewer structures.

Further, most surviving examples of vernacular buildings have been moved from their original sites and restored. This complicates, and in some cases precludes, study of some important aspects of the structures. Removal and restoration obliterate most or all evidence relative to the original use of individual rooms or portions of rooms. The removal from sites and the small number of examples also make impossible any meaningful comparisons of structures originally occupying a given area, comparisons that could have revealed a good deal about the local builders in the various locales. Even without removal, determining original owners, which is critical to dating a structure accurately, represents a major problem. Rarely do early conveyance records, when they exist at all, indicate the date a structure was built, if they even mention a structure. Moreover, early settlers were constantly buying, selling, or swapping parcels of land, not infrequently the same parcel, back and forth, which makes tracing a particular parcel back through even the most complete set of records a complex job.[5]

Despite the many problems, much has been done and much more remains to be done in the study of vernacular architecture. The most important, as well as the most ingenious and the most intriguing, southern vernacular construction method was building with logs. In this construction technique, logs were laid horizontally one atop another and locked at the corners with notches, in a fashion most easily visualized as a log cabin or as a child's Lincoln Log set. The locking notched corners are a critical qualification, for they distinguish this type of log construction from the quite different piece-on-piece construction, in which logs were shaped into timbers, laid horizontally, and joined by pegs, mortises, or groove-and-lip to sturdy upright corner posts. Piece-on-piece was a com-

5. Even in the areas of South with the shortest histories, such as southwest Georgia and most of Alabama, which were seized by Andrew Jackson from the Creek Nation in 1814 and effectively began to be settled only in the late 1820s and the 1830s, frequent buying, selling, and rebuying of the same parcel of land becomes a complex matter to trace. There are parcels of lands in Georgia's Brooks and Lowndes Counties, for example, that were owned by the same person upwards of half a dozen different times. In areas with longer histories, the matter can become even more complex.

mon method of building with logs in Canada, but rare in the United States and almost unknown in the South.

Notched-corner log construction was by no means uniquely southern. It was found to some degree from the Atlantic and Gulf coasts to as far north as Michigan, Wisconsin, and southern Ontario and as far west as the Rocky Mountains, the Pacific Northwest, and northern Mexico. But it held central importance in southern history because it was the most common and the most characteristic building technique used in the South. It accounted for an overwhelming percentage of all housing on the antebellum southern frontier. George Washington noted that when he made his tour of the southern states in 1791, except for the dwellings in some towns and a few plantation houses along the road between Charleston and Savannah, he saw virtually nothing but log houses with mud-and-stick chimneys from the time he left Virginia until he returned.[6] When Andrew Jackson, who himself was born in a log cabin on the Carolina frontier, bought the land that became his Hermitage Plantation outside Nashville in 1804, there were only four buildings on it, all log structures.[7] And it is important to remember that even in 1860, 70 or 80 percent of the South was still frontier. Indeed, as late as the opening of World War II, 5.4 percent of all farmhouses in the South were still log; in several counties the proportion exceeded 20 percent, and in at least one it stood at 42 percent.[8]

6. Donald Jackson and Dorothy Twohig, eds., *The Diaries of George Washington* (6 vols., Charlottesville, Va., 1976–79), VI, 158.

7. Stanley Horn, *The Hermitage: Home of Old Hickory* (1938; rpr. New York, 1950), 17, 138–39, 142–43. Alex W. Bealer and John O. Ellis, *The Log Cabin: Homes of the North American Wilderness* (Barre, Mass., 1978), 130–31, has fine photographs of the surviving two of the four log cabins originally on the Hermitage grounds. Indeed, all the photographs in this book are exceptional. Andrew Jackson lived in one of the log cabins until he built the Hermitage mansion in 1819. He afterward used the cabins as guesthouses, quartering there such notables as President James Monroe, Aaron Burr, Sam Houston, and the young Jefferson Davis.

8. U.S. Department of Agriculture, *Farm-Housing Survey*, Miscellaneous Publication No. 323 (Washington, D.C., March 1939), 5–6. The 5.4 percent adjusted figure includes West Virginia, Kentucky, and southern Illinois, and excludes southern Florida, southern Louisiana, and western Texas, areas that traditionally had few log structures. Virginia, with 14.5 percent had the highest incidence of log farmhouses in 1939 and Tennessee, with 9.3 percent, the second highest. Kentucky's Knott County had 26.8 percent, and West Virginia's Grant County had 20.4 percent. Amherst and Halifax Counties, both in the Virginia piedmont, had 19.8 and 42 percent, respectively.

Notched-log construction is ingenious, for it represents a unique construction technique: building with wood but without the need of any framing. Being able to omit framing not only saved enormous amounts of time and labor, but it also meant that even nails or pegs could be done without. Everything could be held together by weight and notches: the walls by locked corners, the roof by rafters notched on one end into the top wall log of the front and rear walls and on the other end into the ridgepole, and the roof covering—thatch, bark, boards, or shingles— held down by weight poles wedged into place. All one actually had to have was an ax. Building with notched logs was something like building with brick or stone, except far faster and easier. Brick had to be made and, like stone, required months of highly skilled labor to lay, some very special tools, and a great deal of strong mortar, things not easy to come by in frontier forests.[9]

And building with logs represents the most intriguing of all American construction techniques because notched, locking log corners did not exist in any building traditions of the British Isles. How, then, the great historical question became, and remains, did the British colonists of North America learn to construct such buildings? Did they learn it from the Indians? Almost certainly not, for no real evidence has turned up to point in that direction. Did they invent it? Simply think it up? Probably not. All, or almost all, the scholars who have worked on this problem during the past seventy years believe the British colonials did not develop notched-corner log construction on their own but learned it from other colonists in their midst who did have such construction techniques in their building traditions. These writers have developed three hypotheses.

In the 1920s a group of scholars, notably Fiske Kimball and Henry C. Mercer, postulated that it was the Swedish and Fenno-Swedish settlers of

9. Builders in fact virtually always had a considerable variety of tools. See Warren E. Roberts, "The Tools Used in Building Log Houses in Indiana," *Pioneer America*, IX (July 1977), 32–61, rpr. in *Common Places: Readings in American Vernacular Architecture*, ed. Dell Upton and John Michael Vlach (Athens, Ga., 1986), 182–203; Alex W. Bealer, *The Tools That Built America* (New York, 1980), 19–46, 112–200; Henry C. Mercer, *Ancient Carpenters' Tools* (Doylestown, Pa., 1929); Peter C. Marzio, "Carpentry in the Southern Colonies During the Eighteenth Century with Emphasis on Maryland and Virginia," in *Winterthur Portfolio VII*, ed. Ian M. G. Quimby (Charlottesville, Va., 1972), 229–50; Peter C. Welsh, *Woodworking Tools, 1600–1900*, Museum of History and Technology Paper 51 (Washington, D.C., 1966).

the Delaware Valley in the 1630s who introduced the notched technique, and from there it spread across the rest of America. By the time those scholars and their followers, many of whom were still writing in the 1960s, had finished, they had attributed to the Delaware Swedes and Finns not only notched-log construction, but also many, if not most, of the elements of midland and southern house types, floor plans, notching techniques, barns, cribs, smokehouses, and even rail fences.[10]

But the Scandinavianists did not have the field to themselves for long, for in 1938, Thomas Jefferson Wertenbaker kicked off an attack on them by suggesting that it was not from Scandinavia that log construction came, but from German Europe. Specifically, he said, it came from Saxony, brought, in the early eighteenth century, by the Moravian Brethren to Pennsylvania, from where the technique spread. Some of his followers, most famously Fred Kniffen and Henry Glassie, agreed that Pennsylvania Germans were the bringers, but not just those from Saxony. Many, they said, were Mennonites who came from neighboring Moravia proper, from Bohemia, and from Silesia. This school discounted the Delaware Swedes and Finns, pronouncing that they had in fact made no contribution.[11]

10. Fiske Kimball, *Domestic Architecture of the American Colonies and of the Early Republic* (1922; rpr. New York, 1966); Henry C. Mercer, "The Origin of Log Houses in the United States," *Old-Time New England,* XVIII (July 1927), 2–20, continued in XVIII (October 1927), 51–63; Thomas T. Waterman, *The Dwellings of Colonial America* (Chapel Hill, 1950); Hugh Morrison, *Early American Architecture, From the First Colonial Settlements to the National Period* (New York, 1952); Martin Wright, "The Antecedents of the Double-Pen House Type," *Annals of the Association of American Geographers,* XLVIII (1958), 109–17; Clinton A. Weslager, "Log Structures in New Sweden During the Seventeenth Century," *Delaware History,* V (September 1952), 77–95; Weslager, "The Excavation of a Colonial Log Cabin near Wilmington, Delaware," *Archeological Society of Delaware Bulletin,* XVI (April 1954), entire issue; Weslager, "Log Houses in Pennsylvania During the Seventeenth Century," *Pennsylvania History,* XXII (July 1955), 256–66; Weslager, "Log Houses in Virginia During the Seventeenth Century," *Archaeological Society of Virginia Quarterly Bulletin,* IX (1954), 2–8; Weslager, *The Log Cabin in America from Pioneer Days to the Present* (New Brunswick, N.J., 1969); Amandus Johnson, "Sweden Gave America the Rail Fence," *American Swedish Monthly,* June 1955, pp. 6–7, 29.

11. Thomas Jefferson Wertenbaker, *The Founding of American Civilization: The Middle Colonies* (New York, 1938), 288–303 [G. Edwin Brumbaugh, "Colonial Architecture of the Pennsylvania Germans," *Pennsylvania German Society Proceedings and Papers,* XLI (1933), Pt. 2, pp. 5–60, actually preceded Wertenbaker in crediting the Germans, but his obscure piece had nothing like the impact that Wertenbaker's did]. Fred B. Kniffen, "Folk Housing:

Still a third group of scholars in the 1960s, 1970s, and 1980s agreed that German Europe was the point of origin of American log construction. But the source was not the eastern areas of Saxony, Moravia, Bohemia, and Silesia, they insisted; it was the other side of Germany, the far western areas of Switzerland and the Black Forests of Baden and Württemberg along the Rhine. The Germanists, of whichever camp, Eastern or Western, pretty soon had attributed to German origin not only all log construction, but most midland and southern house types and barn types as well.[12]

The Germanists triumphed for a while, but the Swedes and Finns have lately made a major comeback, due largely to the work of Terry Jordan, Walter Prescott Webb Professor of Geography at the University of Texas. Jordan, interestingly enough, started as an advocate of the East German, Saxon, Bohemian, Moravian, and Silesian theory, to which he added the Czechoslovakian Sudeten hill country. But then, as a result of a series of field trips to Europe in the late 1970s and early 1980s, he changed his

Key to Diffusion," *Annals of the Association of American Geographers*, LV (1965), 549–77; Kniffen and Henry Glassie, "Building in Wood in the Eastern United States: A Time-Place Perspective," *Geographical Review*, LVI (1966), 40–66; Kniffen, "On Corner Timbering," *Pioneer America*, I (January 1969), 1–8; Henry Glassie, "The Appalachian Log Cabin," *Mountain Life and Work*, XXXIX (Winter, 1963), 5–14; Glassie, "The Old Barns of Appalachia," *Mountain Life and Work*, XL (Summer, 1965), 21–30; Glassie, "The Pennsylvania Barn in the South," *Pennsylvania Folklife*, XV (Winter, 1965–66), 8–19, continued in XV (Summer, 1966), 12–25; Glassie, *Pattern in the Material Folk Culture of the Eastern United States* (Philadelphia, 1968); Glassie, "The Types of the Southern Mountain Cabin" in *The Study of American Folklore: An Introduction*, ed. Jan H. Brunvand (New York, 1968), 338–70; Glassie, "A Central Chimney Continental Log House," *Pennsylvania Folklife*, XVIII (Winter, 1968–69), 32–39; Glassie, "The Double-Crib Barn in South-Central Pennsylvania," *Pioneer America*, I (January 1969), 9–16, continued in I (July 1969), 40–45, and in II (January 1970), 47–52, and II (July 1970), 23–34; Glassie, "Eighteenth-Century Cultural Process in Delaware Valley Folk Building," *Winterthur Portfolio VII*, 29–57, rpr. in *Common Places*, ed. Upton and Vlach, 394–425.

12. G. M. Ludwig, "The Influence of the Pennsylvania Dutch in the Middle West," *Pennsylvania German Folklore Society Publications*, X (1945), 71–83; Robert C. Bucher, "The Continental Log House," *Pennsylvania Folklife*, XII (Summer, 1962), 14–19; Bucher, "The Swiss Bank House in Pennsylvania," *Pennsylvania Folklife*, XVIII (Winter, 1968–69), 2–11; Amos Long, Jr., "Bank (Multi-Level) Structures in Rural Pennsylvania," *Pennsylvania Folklife*, XX (Winter, 1970–71), 31–39; Robert F. Ensminger, "A Comparative Study of Pennsylvania and Wisconsin Forebay Barns," *Pennsylvania Folklife*, XXXII (Spring, 1983), 98–114; Ensminger, "A Search for the Pennsylvania Barn," *Pennsylvania Folklife*, XXX (Winter, 1980–81), 50–70.

mind and began championing the almost discarded Fenno-Scandinavian hypothesis, albeit with the compromise of allowing that many barn types did come from Switzerland and the Black Forest areas. His old friends the East German Saxons, Bohemians, Moravians, Silesians, and Czechs he relegated to, at best, having given some reinforcement to the use of notched-log techniques introduced by the Scandinavians.[13]

That is where the matter stands today. Even with all the theorizing that has been done, there is one possibility that has been largely overlooked: that North American British colonists did not have to be taught notched-log construction by Finns, Swedes, or Germans, but developed it themselves, out of their own traditions.

Exploration of that possibility will require a careful look at two things. First, much more attention will need to be given to the number of log structures we know were built in very early seventeenth-century Virginia, including houses—vertical, post-in-ground construction, but nonetheless log—and to the many horizontal-log houses, churches, and prisons built in New England since the founding of Plymouth in 1620 and in such southern colonies as Maryland since at least 1663 and in North Carolina since at least 1680. And as those early log structures are more closely studied, it will be important to keep in mind that even though building tradition in Britain itself did not include notched interlocking corners, it did include horizontal as well as vertical shaped-timber and log construction of fortifications, palisades, walls, prisons, stockades, blockhouses, and market shelters.[14]

---

13. Terry G. Jordan, *Texas Log Buildings: A Folk Architecture* (Austin, 1978); Jordan, "Alpine, Alemanic, and American Log Architecture," *Annals of the Association of American Geographers*, LXX (1980), 154–80; Jordan, "A Reappraisal of Fenno-Scandian Antecedents for Midland American Log Construction," *Geographical Review*, LXXIII (1983), 58–94; Jordan, "Moravian, Schwenkfelder, and American Log Construction," *Pennsylvania Folklife*, XXXIII (Spring, 1984), 98–124; Jordan, *American Log Buildings: An Old World Heritage* (Chapel Hill, 1985), 7–13, which gives a good summary of the controversy over origins of log construction; Jordan and Matti Kaups, *The American Backwoods Frontier* (Baltimore, 1989). The latter two books represent prime examples of the theory-ridden and general-law-driven nature of much of the scholarship on vernacular architecture. Both books open with long sections devoted to establishing theoretical frameworks, then present data, and then close with sections showing how the data fit the framework.

14. The 1657 meetinghouse in Portsmouth, New Hampshire, for example, was a forty-foot-square blockhouse, the sides of which were "of Logs 9 Inches thick," and the 1659 meetinghouse in Norwalk, Connecticut, was "set upon posts in the ground 12 foot in

It is not enough for scholars, citing what they call the "general law of Absence of Innovation on Frontiers," simply to set aside all known examples of log construction by British colonists as unimportant and focus their attention exclusively on finding other possible explanations.[15]

Second, and more important, scholars will need to look very carefully at British colonial craftsmen, bearing in mind that the late sixteenth and early seventeenth centuries represented a period of intense experimentation and innovation in the craft of woodworking. Indeed, during the hundred years between the mid-sixteenth and the mid-seventeenth century,

---

length" and "10 foot distance from the ground," in the fashion of English market halls. Patricia Irvin Cooper, "Some Misconceptions in American Log-Building Studies," *Material Culture*, XXIII (Summer, 1991), 50–51, lists a number of seventeenth- and early-eighteenth-century British colonial log structures. See also Peter Benes and Philip D. Zimmerman, *New England Meeting House and Church* (Boston, 1979), 3–4; Antoinette F. Downing, *Early Homes of Rhode Island* (Richmond, Va., 1937); Anthony N. B. Garvan, *Architecture and Town Planning in Colonial Connecticut* (New Haven, 1951); Richard M. Candee, "A Documentary History of Plymouth Colony Architecture, 1620–1700," *Old-Time New England*, LIX (Winter, 1969), 59–71, continued in LIX (Spring, 1969), 105–11, and in LX (Fall, 1969), 37–53; Fraser D. Neiman, "Domestic Architecture at the Clifts Plantation: The Social Context of Early Virginia Building," *Northern Neck of Virginia Historical Magazine*, XXVIII (December 1978), 3096–3128, rpr. in *Common Places*, ed. Upton and Vlach, 292–314; William G. Hoskins, "The Rebuilding of Rural England, 1570–1640," *Past and Present*, November 1953, pp. 45–57; Hoskins, *The Making of the English Landscape* (1955; rpr. Harmondsworth, Eng., 1970); John W. Reps, *Tidewater Towns: City Planning in Colonial Virginia and Maryland* (Williamsburg, Va., 1972); Henry C. Forman, *Tidewater Maryland Architecture and Gardens* (New York, 1956), 120; Weslager, "Log Houses in Pennsylvania," 264; Weslager, "Log Houses in Maryland," 2–8; George C. Gregory, "Log Houses at Jamestown, 1607," *Virginia Magazine of History and Biography*, XLIV (October 1936), 287–95; and J. Frederick Kelly, "A Seventeenth-Century Connecticut Log House," *Old-Time New England*, XXXI (October 1940), 28–40. For a different view, see Harold R. Shurtleff, *The Log Cabin Myth: A Study of the Early Development of the English Colonists in North America* (1939; rpr. Gloucester, Mass., 1967).

15. Relative to the notion of a lack of innovation by American colonials, Wilbur Zelinsky, *The Cultural Geography of the United States* (1973; rev. ed. Englewood Cliffs, N.J., 1992), 83, is frequently cited: "Despite the stubborn romantic inclination to believe otherwise, the settlement frontier cannot be credited with the origination of any important inventions, material or otherwise." A typical example of setting aside British influence is Jordan, *Texas Log Buildings*, 23. After listing a number of examples of early-seventeenth-century British log buildings, he dismisses them: "In sum, some log buildings may have been present in various English colonies during the 1600s, but, if so, the log construction technique failed to spread to the English colonial population at large. The few scattered examples could not have served as the antecedent for the American log culture complex."

British craftsmen made more advances in woodworking than in the entirety of history before or after. It was during that hundred years or so that the more highly skilled joiners separated themselves from common carpenters and that the even more highly skilled cabinetmakers separated themselves from joiners. For example, one regularly and increasingly finds references to saddle notching on spars by ships' carpenters after 1512, to dovetailing by cabinetmakers after 1565, and to V-notching and square notching by carpenters after 1577.[16]

A close look at British colonial carpenters, joiners, and cabinetmakers—something no one investigating the origins of American log construction has done—may very well reveal that the early joiners took techniques they had learned from ships' carpenters and cabinetmakers and applied them to logs. By the time Jamestown was settled in 1607—and its early carpenters were ships' carpenters—dovetailing, V-notching, and square notching, all commonly used log-notching techniques, had been in everyday use in Britain half a century or more. And before the Finns and Swedes arrived in the Delaware Valley in the 1630s, British saddle-notching, the very most common method of locking log corners, was already well over a century old.

Almost as controversial as the origin of notched-log construction are the origins of southern plain folks' houses and barns. Of dwelling types, the dog-trot house is by far the most written about and the most controversial. The dog-trot house, although it occurred occasionally as far north as Pennsylvania, Ohio, Indiana, and Illinois and was seen here and there throughout the upland South, was the most common and most characteristic house type of the frontier, lower South coastal plain. Dog-trot houses dotted the landscape from Virginia through the Carolinas and Georgia, across Alabama, Mississippi, central and northern Louisiana (skipping

16. Stella Kramer, *The English Craft Guilds* (New York, 1967); A. H. Mackmurdo, ed., *Plain Crafts* (London, 1892); Barry Sanders, ed., *The Craftsman: An Anthology* (Santa Barbara, Calif., 1978); W. L. Goodman, *The History of Woodworking Tools* (London, 1964); Brock Jobe and Myrna Kaye, *New England Furniture: The Colonial Era* (Boston, 1984), 46–100; Percy Macquoid and Ralph Edwards, *The Dictionary of English Furniture* (3 vols.; 1924–27; rpr. Woodbridge, Eng., 1983), II, 125–33, 272–73; Cecil Alex Hewett, *The Development of Carpentry 1200–1700* (New York, 1969). The *Oxford English Dictionary* (12 vols. and Supplement, 3 vols.; 1933; rpr. Oxford, Eng., 1961) gives the earliest known occurrence in print of the terms for the various notching techniques. Unlike words invented by writers, such common terms appeared in print only after they had been in general use for quite some time, which means they were current long before the dates cited.

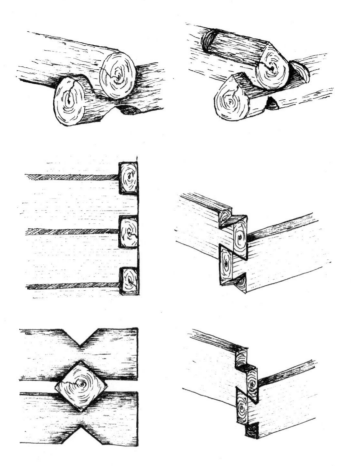

The six most common corner-notching techniques in American log construction. Clockwise from top left: saddle notching, V-notching, full dovetail notching, half dovetail notching, diamond notching, and square notching.
Drawings by Melissa Lindenmuth

the southern Louisiana French area that had its own architectural tradition), and east Texas.[17]

The dog-trot house was essentially two one-room log cabins placed
lineally, gable end to gable end, ten or so feet apart. The intervening
space was bridged over with a floor, and the whole complex covered by a
single roof, pitched to the front and rear and gabled on the ends. The
bridged-over space was thus formed into an incorporated, open passage-
way or hall, the dog-trot proper. Usually there was a chimney on each
gable end, an attached porch across the front, and one across the rear.
Each end of the rear porch was enclosed to form two shedrooms. The result was a four-room house with an open hallway running through it. To
the rear of the main house, and apart from it by several feet, was added
another detached, freestanding log unit, the kitchen and dining room.
That unit was usually connected to the dogtrot of the main house by a
narrow, runwaylike covered porch. Thus, the whole complex added up to
a six-room house.

The big question concerns the origin of the dog-trot design. There
have been several hypotheses advanced as answers. To a degree the hypotheses parallel the three schools of thought on the origins of American
log construction, but only to a degree. In most cases the several possibilities do not constitute such discrete, exclusive, or delimiting interpretations. Most writers, although they may favor a particular theory relative
to the origin of the dog-trot, are willing to admit some of the other possibilities. Consequently, most writers mention most of the possibilities.

By far the most exclusive are the scholars who see the origin of the
dog-trot in Swedish and Finnish Delaware. They point to the seventeenth-century paired cottages common to that area: two cottages built
close together and covered with a single roof, leaving a sort of walkway or

---

17. Dog-trot houses are also sometimes called dog-run, possum-trot, turkey-trot,
double-log, two-pens-and-a-passage, two-P, three-P, open-hall, hallway, double-pen-and-
passage, central-passage houses, or occasionally, and confusingly, double-pen or saddle-bag
houses. Preoccupation with origins of the dog-trot design unfortunately has diverted too
much attention from scholarly study of the southern house types that succeeded the dog-
trots. Raised cottages, bluffland houses, southern "I" houses, pyramidal houses, bungalows,
and sharecroppers' shacks remain understudied. And the very important raised, frame,
designer-built dog-trot houses with double-doors enclosing the trot, very common in the
nineteenth-century lower Atlantic and Gulf coastal plain, are largely unnoted and entirely
unstudied.

passage between them.[18] A few scholars not very convincingly suggested German origins, and a few others early speculated on West Indies, Caribbean, or even Huguenot influences, particularly on porches, piers, and detached kitchens.[19] Some writers even argued that the heat of southern summers gave rise to the open-hall design, only to be countered by the argument that if summers were hot, winters were cold, and the climate argument fell largely into abeyance.[20] That is unfortunate, for the hot climate of the lower South, although it certainly did not give rise to the design, made the openness of the dog-trot ideal for the coastal plain, which helps account for the house's preponderance there. Conversely, that very openness made the design less than ideal for cold mountainous areas, which partially accounts for the dog-trot's minor manifestation there.

Scholars have also argued that the dog-trot design was a frontiersman's primitive attempt to imitate English central-hall houses, which in their Georgian form were highly fashionable in the older tidewater sections of the colonial South.[21] This has become the most widely embraced, indeed

18. Weslager, *Log Cabin in America*, 73, 153; Martin Wright, "The Antecedents of the Double-Pen House Type," 113; Richard Hulan, "Middle Tennessee and the Dogtrot House," *Pioneer America*, VII (July 1975), 44–45; Hulan, "The Dog-trot House and Its Pennsylvania Connection," *Pennsylvania Folklore*, XXVI (Summer, 1977), 25–32; Eugene M. Wilson, "Some Similarities Between American and European Folk Houses," *Pioneer America*, III (July 1971), 11; Jordan, *Old World Heritage*, 66–71; 146–49, 162n67; Terry G. Jordan and Matti Kaups, "Folk Architecture in Cultural and Ecological Context," *Geographical Review*, LXXVII (1987), 52–75, which appears virtually unaltered as chap. 7 of Jordan and Kaups, *American Backwoods Frontier*, 179–210, wherein the authors give a good summary (pp. 193–208) of the dog-trot controversy and suggest pinpointing the origins of the American dog-trot in the Savo-Karelian colony in central Sweden.

19. Wilbur Zelinsky, "The Log House in Georgia," *Geographical Review*, XLIII (1953), 186, suggested German origin, and Glassie, "Appalachian Log Cabin," 14, argued that the dog-trot came from the German double-crib barn. Frances Benjamin Johnston and Thomas T. Waterman, *The Early Architecture of North Carolina: A Pictorial Survey* (Chapel Hill, 1941), 41–42, 178, suggested West Indian and Huguenot influence. See also Newton, *Louisiana*, 185.

20. Howard W. Marshall, "Dog Trot Comfort: A Note on Traditional Houses and Energy Efficiency," in *Program Book: Festival of American Folklore* (Washington, D.C., 1980), 29–31; Newton, *Louisiana*, 183; Diane Tebbetts, "Traditional Houses of Independence County, Arkansas," *Pioneer America*, X (June 1978), 52; Zelinsky, "Log Cabin in Georgia," 175.

21. Glassie, "Appalachian Log Cabin," 12; Glassie, *Patterns in the Material Folk Culture*, 96; Wright, "Antecedents of the Double-Pen House," 111; Wilson, "Some Similarities Be-

the almost universally accepted, theory. Which is puzzling, for there is not a shred of hard evidence for this explanation. Arguments for it are based solely on what anthropologists and cultural geographers call the "law of the Dominance of Contemporary Fashion." The weakness of the argument is obvious. Although frontiersmen surely were not altogether oblivious to fashion—no one is or ever has been, completely—they equally as surely had far more pressing and immediate concerns than fashion, particularly when, finding themselves in the frontier wilderness, it came to getting a roof over the heads of their families as quickly and as cheaply as possible.[22]

Dell Upton of UCLA, one of the most astute and commonsensical writers in the field today, has summarized the state of the scholarship on the origins of the dog-trot succinctly: "Unfortunately . . . study . . . has concentrated on the identification of typological examples, through often superficial field examination. No careful study of the physical histories of individual, closely dated examples, of archival sources, and of socioeconomic or room-use pattern has been made, nor has there been direct field study of . . . proposed precedents. Consequently, scholars do not know how old . . . types are or what their history in the region is."[23]

One reason for so many theories on the origin of the dog-trot is that basic to the question of *how* the dog-trot originated is the question of *where* it originated. That has to be settled before one can intelligently ask how or why. But for a long time the where was misplaced, and hence all the hows and whys were off base. Misled by the fact that extant examples of dog-trots occurred most frequently in the mountainous upland South, earlier writers jumped to the conclusion that the dog-trot was characteristic and hence indigenous to that area. Henry Glassie went so far as to identify its origin in eastern Tennessee in or around the year 1825. Obviously his date was wrong, for dissenting scholars quickly pointed out any number of dog-trots built well before that time not only farther west in

---

tween American and European Folk Houses," 8–12; Milton B. Newton, "Dogtrot House," 498–99, and Dell Upton, "Vernacular Architecture (Lowland South)," 110–12, both in *Encyclopedia of Southern Culture*, ed. Charles Reagan Wilson and William Ferris (Chapel Hill, 1989); Morrison, *Early American Architecture*, 169–70.

22. Kniffen, "Folk Housing," 558, as rpr. in *Common Places*, ed. Upton and Vlach, 13; Newton, *Louisiana*, 173, 183–85.

23. Dell Upton, "Vernacular Architecture (Upland South)" in *Encyclopedia of Southern Culture*, ed. Wilson and Ferris, 115.

Tennessee but in the new frontier areas of south Georgia, Mississippi, Alabama, Louisiana, and Texas.[24]

As the original error of misreading the large number of surviving examples in mountain areas has been realized and as more and more early examples have been discovered, it has also become clear that the dog-trot did not originate in Tennessee or anywhere else in or west of the Appalachian Mountains. More likely the place of origin was the frontier Virginia piedmont, and the time of origin not the 1820s, but much before that date, during the mid- or early eighteenth century or maybe even earlier.[25]

If the time and place of the origin of dog-trots—the when and where—are beginning to be nailed down, what of the how and why? Some scholars have noted that the origin of dog-trot design may be related to the problem of enlarging a log house.[26] Those observations, although undeveloped, are very probably the key to answering the questions of how and why the dog-trot design, for adding to a log house is a real problem. In frame, brick, or stone construction, one can simply add a room wherever one wants; it can be nailed on or mortared on and the roof extended to cover it. But with log construction it is nothing like that easy. There is no simple and effective way to tie a new log wall into an existing log wall, no way easily to add to a log cabin, which was a problem commonly faced by frontier settlers. The only thing one could do was build another log cabin.[27] Yet it was not only difficult but senseless to build the second cabin adjacent to the gable of the existing cabin and extend the roof on it, because it would leave you with a wasteful, clumsy, rot-inviting, double-log-thick wall in the middle of the now two-room

24. Glassie, *Pattern in the Material Folk Culture*, 88–89; Hulan, "Middle Tennessee and the Dogtrot House," 37–46. Dog-trots, for example, were already being built in faraway Texas between 1815 and 1820; see Jordan, *Texas Log Buildings*, 120.

25. Jordan, *Texas Log Buildings*, 120; Jordan, *Old World Heritage*, 155.

26. Martin Wright, "Log Culture in Hill Louisiana" (Ph.D. dissertation, Louisiana State University, 1956), 34–35; Wilson, "Some Similarities," 14; Jordan and Kaups, "Folk Architecture in Cultural and Ecological Context," 63. See also Jordan, *Texas Log Buildings*, 113–48, which implicitly treats double-pen, central-chimney, dog-trot, triple-pen, four-pen, and two-story houses, as well as shed rooms, porches, and cellars, as solutions to the problem of enlarging a log cabin.

27. Technically, a single-room log cabin is called a "single-pen," a two-room log house is a "double-pen," etc. Indeed, before the spaces between the logs were chinked, floors put down, and a roof put on, the structure looked much like a pen for livestock.

house. Better to place the new pen apart from the old one and simply connect the two by bridging the intervening space with a floor and roofing it over, in effect creating a porch through the middle of the house, which was in fact the way dog-trot passageways were thought of, as porches rather than as halls. One could then add two frame shedrooms at the rear and a detached dining room and kitchen behind the main structure and have a six-room house, plenty of room by any standards of the time and place.

The same exactly was true if one set out in the beginning to build a large log house rather than a one-room cabin. The choices were limited. One could construct what is called a saddle-bag house by building one pen or cabin with a chimney at one end and then building another pen abutting the chimney on the opposite side. But that left one with two independent cabins joined by a chimney and an intervening four- or five-foot useless open space. The arrangement was altogether unsuitable for family use. Or one could build what is called a "double-pen house," simply a double-size log cabin, with a dividing log wall notched across the center, but that required quite long, thirty-foot or more, timbers for the front and rear walls, difficult to handle and in some areas, such as the mountains and Texas, difficult to find.[28] And when finished, one still had only a two-room house. Or it could be made two stories high to get four rooms, but that required an even more difficult engineering operation of pushing thirty-foot logs twenty or more feet into the air. Far simpler, far more sensible, to build two detached cabins or pens and join them with a dog-trot.

But how was such a solution to the problem of enlarging a log cabin arrived at? Did the frontier craftsmen in the early- or mid-eighteenth-century Virginia piedmont stumble on the solution as they were attempting to build or enlarge log houses? Or did they take a preexisting structural type of log building and simply convert it to use as a house? The latter is most likely exactly what they did. And the form they took was the traditional two-crib English barn. The floor plan of the small English barn is identical to that of a dog-trot house; and executed in logs, the elevation of

---

28. Some writers have noted that the size of log pen was limited by the weight of a timber (as much as two men could lift) and by the tapering of tree trunks (the length of a same-diameter section that could be cut from a trunk). Kniffen and Glassie, "Building with Wood," 51n29, or as rpr. in *Common Places*, ed. Upton and Vlach, 180; Johnston and Waterman, *Early Architecture of North Carolina*, 7. Other writers disagree; see Newton, *Louisiana*, 183.

a small English barn is identical to that of a dog-trot. In English barns the two cribs were used for storage of grain, and the roofed intervening area—the dog-trot in the later house—was used as a threshing floor.[29]

Many writers have noted the close similarity, the virtual identity, of such barns and dog-trot houses but have brushed aside the English barn as the prototype of the dog-trot house with two arguments. Some scholars have pointed out that because the South's colonial tidewater farmers threshed their grain crops in the field and stored their tobacco and corn crops in different-type packhouses and cribs, few English two-crib barns were built in the area.[30] True. But that does not mean local people did not know how to build such barns or were unfamiliar with the form. They were not. They, like each succeeding wave of British immigrants, were altogether familiar with the English barn. In the face of that fact, the argument loses most of its force.

The second and more recent argument against the two-crib barn as prototype is that such barns were not common in the coastal lowlands, exactly the area in which dog-trot houses were common. And conversely, the argument continues, double-crib barns were quite common in the upland mountain areas, exactly the area where dog-trots were not.[31] Again,

29. What are called "pens" in log houses are called "cribs" when referring to barns. Jordan, *Old World Heritage*, 30–36, 108; Henry Glassie, "The Double-Crib Barn in South-Central Pennsylvania"; Glassie, "Old Barns of Appalachia"; Glassie, "Barns Across Southern England: A Note on Transatlantic Comparison and Architectural Meaning," *Pioneer America*, VII (January 1975), 9–19; H. Wayne Price, "The Double-Crib Log Barns of Calhoun County," *Journal of the Illinois State Historical Society*, LXXIII (Summer, 1980), 140–60; Eric Arthur and Dudley Witney, *The Barn: A Vanishing Landmark in North America* (Toronto, 1972), 59–83; George E. Evans, *Ask the Fellows Who Cut the Hay* (London, 1956), 92–94; Eric Sloane, *An Age of Barns* (New York, 1967); George E. Evans, *The Farm and the Village* (London, 1969), 82–83; Mable E. Christie [M. E. Seebohm], *The Evolution of the English Farm* (London, 1927). After noting that dog-trots and two-crib barns are "genetically related," Jordan and Kaups, "Folk Architecture in Cultural and Ecological Context," 59, dismiss the barn as the possible prototype of the house as an "even less palatable prospect" than development from British building tradition, for a barn serving "as the model for a house" is, they declare, "an unlikely and perhaps unprecedented sequence."

30. Jordan, *Texas Log Buildings*, 166–67; Glassie, "Appalachian Log Cabin," 12; Glassie, "Old Barns of Appalachia," 30; Glassie, "Double-Crib Barn in South-Central Pennsylvania"; Price, "Double-Crib Log Barns of Calhoun County"; Upton, "Farm Buildings" in *Encyclopedia of Southern Culture*, ed. Wilson and Ferris, 65–67.

31. Glassie, *Pattern in the Material Folk Culture*, 101; Zelinsky, "Log House in Georgia," *Geographical Review*, XLIII (1953), 180–83; Donald Hustlar, *The Log Architecture of Ohio*

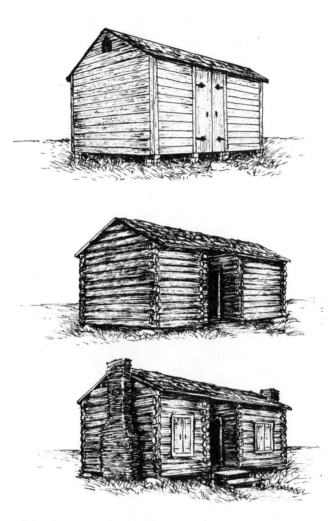

Evolution of the American dog-trot house from the English barn. Top: English
frame two-crib barn. Middle: American log two-crib barn. Bottom: American log
dog-trot house.

Drawings by Melissa Lindenmuth

true. But writers who have sought to use that observation as an argument against the English barn have missed the point, for the observation strengthens, not weakens, the probability of the barn as prototype. To wit: In the uplands, where double-cribs frequently occurred, who would have wanted to live in a house that looked like a barn? Even frontiersmen had that much fashion consciousness, not to mention the obvious discomfort of freezing hill-country winds blowing through open dog-trots. On the other hand, in the hot coastal plain, where double-crib barns were usually unknown—they were as useless for the cotton grown by later settlers as they had been for the tobacco and grain grown by earlier ones—few remembered, after a generation or two, that their comfortable, breezy dog-trot houses were actually lineal descendants of old English barns.

So in trying to find the origin of the dog-trot house, we find ourselves again back in the company of Virginia colonial carpenters, the same carpenters whose ancestors probably developed notched-log construction. But the route back to them in both instances is still largely one of conjecture, supported by a good deal of deduction and some bits of empirical evidence. The future, however, offers hope of considerably more solid evidence, particularly from two quarters. One, southern historians are increasingly getting interested in vernacular architecture, and their expertise in local records will be extremely critical in documenting and dating original owners and builders. And two, the Virginia Archaeological Survey, which represents the most thorough and comprehensive work being done anywhere in the country today in the field of historical archaeology, is virtually daily turning up new and valuable data.[32] There is every prob-

---

(Columbus, Ohio, 1977), 203, 242–43; Weslager, *Log Cabin in America*, 303; Douglas K. Meyer, "Diffusion of Upland South Folk Housing to the Shawnee Hills of Southern Illinois," *Pioneer America*, VII (July 1975), 59–62; David Sutherland, "Folk Housing in the Woodburn Quadrangle," *Pioneer America*, IV (July 1972), 22–23.

32. The Virginia Archaeological Survey is not an organized or systematic series of digs. Instead, it is a central clearing house for archaeological work in the state. Housed in the Division of Resource Information Services within the Department of Historic Resources, the survey grants state funds, on a matching basis, for digs and maintains over 29,000 archaeological site files. Especially important, the survey systematically collects field reports from all digs going on in the state and deposits the reports in its research library. This represents an extraordinary advance, for now all reports from all digs are available to scholars at one location. One of the problems with historical archaeology in the United States has been—and outside Virginia continues to be—that field reports of digs are hard to come by. They are not systematically filed in any one location, but only deposited in a hit or miss

ability that the field reports of the Virginia survey, together with the work of more and more historians, will shed some important new light on, and perhaps even answer some of the big questions about, the origins of log construction and of house types, particularly the dog-trot.

---

fashion with local libraries, agencies, or sponsoring authorities—which means that unless one happens to know a particular dig is going on and specifically requests copies of the reports, finding them is, all too often, a matter of sheer luck.

Bradley G. Bond

Herders, Farmers, and Markets on the Inner Frontier: The Mississippi Piney Woods, 1850–1860

Long before northern lumber barons moved their mills to the Deep South and began denuding virgin pine forests, the Carter family relocated from Bulloch County, Georgia, to the southeastern corner of Mississippi. Eighty years before John Kamper, Fenwick Peck, and the Gardiner brothers each purchased for a pittance section after section of pine forest, the Carter family "bought a little improvement in the piney woods." For three generations in the antebellum period, the Carters raised hogs, cattle, and corn; after 1820 they planted cotton, too.[1]

In the 1880s, when professional lumbermen began cutting centuries-old forests, they closed a portion of what Frank Owsley once referred to as the southern "inner frontier," a passed-over land inhabited by poor, self-consciously backward-looking folk. According to Owsley and piney-woods historians, successive waves of herdsmen and farmers occupied the subregion for more than one hundred years before the arrival of the timber barons. Settlers sought to escape the hubbub of market-oriented life in the Atlantic coast states and found a sparsely settled country in which they might eke out an existence by planting a few row crops and raising livestock, by hunting and fishing, by cutting timber and burning char-

1. Quoting Casandra Carter to Jane Everett, November 25, 1811, in Carter Family Letters, typescript photocopies in the possession of the author. The author wishes to thank Louis Clifford IV of Gautier, Mississippi, for making available his copies of the correspondence.

coal.[2] Or so contend historians of the early frontier and their acolytes, who depict the piney-woods plain people of the late antebellum period as cut from the same cloth as their eighteenth-century predecessors.

If the prevailing historical image of piney-woods people differs from William Faulkner's Anglo-Saxon frontiersman, who roared "with Protestant scripture and boiled whiskey, Bible and jug in one hand and like as not an Indian tomahawk in the other, brawling, turbulent, uxorious and polygamous," the difference appears in degree not kind. As surely as the tall man of Faulknerian mythology sought affirmation of his God-given right to political independence and of his Jefferson-inspired desire for economic autonomy, so too, supposedly, did piney-woods residents loathe governmental authority and the market. Unfortunately, historians too often fail to recognize what Faulkner understood: in the early nineteenth century (certainly by 1840), ordinary folk like the Carters formerly of Georgia—herders and farmers all—made the wild Anglo-Saxon and his anticommercial behavior obsolete.[3] For the Carters and thousands of folk like them, too poor to afford prime cotton lands, too ambitious and adventurous to remain back East, went to the piney woods of the southwestern frontier seeking not economic isolation or a mere subsistence, but access to markets of their own choosing. Compelled by a desire to make something of themselves, the Carters and other plain farmers began closing the "inner frontier" and creating its antithesis—a market-oriented society—long before rapacious lumber barons arrived.

In the summer of 1811, Matthew Carter, Sr., left Georgia bound for the frontier. His overland journey to the piney-woods section of Jackson

2. Frank L. Owsley, "The Pattern of Migration and Settlement on the Southern Frontier," *Journal of Southern History*, XI (May 1945), 155. See, too, Owsley, *Plain Folk of the Old South* (Baton Rouge, 1949), *passim*; Paul H. Buck, "Poor Whites of the Ante-Bellum South," *American Historical Review*, XXXI (October 1925), 54; and Grady McWhiney, *Cracker Culture: Celtic Ways in the Old South* (Tuscaloosa, 1988), *passim*. On plain people in the piney woods, see Nollie Hickman, *Mississippi Harvest: Lumbering in the Longleaf Pine Belt, 1840–1915*, 12; Herbert Weaver, *Mississippi Farmers, 1850–1860* (Nashville, 1945), 88; Ann Patton Malone, "Piney Woods Farmers of South Georgia, 1850–1900: Jeffersonian Yeomen in an Age of Expanding Commercialism," *Agricultural History*, LX (Fall, 1986), 52; and Mark V. Wetherington, *The New South Comes to Wiregrass Georgia, 1860–1910* (Knoxville, 1995), 6–26.

3. William Faulkner, *Essays, Speeches, and Public Letters*, ed. James B. Meriwether (New York, 1965), 14. On the rough-and-tumble ways of southern plain people, see McWhiney, *Cracker Culture*, 148–50.

County took five weeks and two days. Members of Carter's immediate and extended families removed with him, and they all arrived safely, as did their possessions. After scouting the northern part of Jackson County along the Chickasawhay River and locating acreage suitable to his needs, Carter wrote his Georgia kin. He wanted to assure them that the traveling party had made the move without incident and that the new place looked as promising as he had anticipated: "I am well pleased with the prospect of the country for I think it good, that is the cain land, water and range; and how the trade will be, is unknown. Now things can be got reasonable. Provisions is hi but we have lade in a supply of corn and 20 cows and c[alve]s." Casandra Carter, Matthew's wife, recognized too that the Mississippi piney woods offered abundant opportunities for livestock to fatten and humans to prosper, but in contrast to her husband, she evinced misgivings about her new home. Like other southern pioneer women whose husbands too often moved, she longed to see familiar faces. Five months after arriving in the piney woods, Casandra Carter told a friend of her disillusion: "As for being satisfied I can't relate. The men seems to be satisfied, as for the two girls they are often in tears for you all and wishes to be with you." In April 1812, ten months after relocating to the piney woods, Casandra's discontent surely increased when her husband died.[4]

Despite her dissatisfaction and the sudden death of Matthew, Sr., Casandra remained in the piney woods. Other members of the pioneering Carter family remained, too. Even Matthew Carter, Jr., decided to stay. When the Carters arrived in Jackson County, the younger Matthew Carter had left the family and spent several months fruitlessly searching for a tract of land in the Pearl River Valley, on the western edge of Mississippi's piney woods.[5] Surviving correspondence fails to explain his decision to return to his mother's side. Perhaps land prices in the more fertile Pearl River Valley exceeded his ability to pay, or perhaps the death of his father coupled with young Carter's reluctance to place yet another expanse of wilderness between himself and family members convinced him to call the banks of the Chickasawhay River home. Regardless of his reasons for remaining, Carter overcame his initial doubts about the eastern

---

4. Matthew Carter, Sr., to Griffin Mizell and Susanna, June 11, 1811, Casandra Carter to Jane Everett, November 25, 1811, both in Carter Family Letters.

5. Matthew Carter, Sr., to Griffin Mizell and Susanna, June 11, 1811, *ibid.*

piney woods and, like his father, came to believe that the area held great promise for his financial well-being.

Eleven months after his father died, Matthew, Jr., revealed his changed attitude when he chastised Griffin Mizell, his brother-in-law, for considering removing from Telfair to Ogeechee County, Georgia. Ogeechee, "an old worn out place," could not compare to south Mississippi, Carter said: "This is a fine fresh country, well watered and healthy, and the land produces very well. . . . It is only 40 miles from where I live to Mobile where I can buy shugar and coffee on better terms than ever I did in Savannah, and the schooners pass up and down the river and we can get any kind of necessaries from them, and they give a good price for our produce." Boasting even more, Carter opined that the piney woods offered ambitious men ample opportunities to prosper; in the future, he believed, those opportunities would multiply: "It is the opinion of the citizens of this country that it will be the best place of trade that is in America." As if good land and water, prosperity, and a vibrant market might not convince Mizell to abandon Georgia, Carter even volunteered to help his brother-in-law move.[6] Mizell, however, never heeded the advice of his kinsman and remained in Georgia.

Twelve years after first trying to convince Mizell to join him on the road to prosperity, Carter began to rue his own decision to remain in piney-woods Mississippi. Beginning in 1825, a six-year cycle of disasters ruined his crops and injured his livestock. River floods, depleted rangeland, drought, cotton rot, "blowing flies," and two "backward" springs wreaked their havoc and prompted Carter to contemplate moving.[7] But despite the misfortunes that afflicted his farm, he maintained his faith in the region. In the midst of an especially cold spring that occurred coterminously with a downturn in local market prices, Carter told Mizell that although times looked bleak in south Mississippi, he expected his Georgia relations suffered more than did he. "Money [is] scarce, produce of every kind low," Carter said, "but the convenience of a good market [at Mobile] enables us to get such necessaries as we need, on very good terms." Readily available credit and "the advantage of a good market" eased his suffering. In 1829, Carter drew encouragement from a construction boom

6. Matthew Carter, Jr., to Griffin Mizell, March 1, 1813, *ibid.*

7. Matthew Carter, Jr., to [Griffin Mizell], May 25, 1826, Matthew and Ann Carter to Griffin Mizell, November 4, 1827, Carter to Mizell, November 16, 1828, June 7, 1829, April 3, 1831, Carter to [Mizell], August 12, 1832, all *ibid.*

taking place at the mouth of the Pascagoula River. Already, he wrote Mizell, "the largest kinds of vessels" plied the river, and the movement of settlers and businesses to the swampy bottom augured development of a market town and personal, financial recovery. The following year, as if in testimony to his rekindled sense of hope, Matthew Carter built a new house.[8]

Within a decade Matthew Carter, Jr., died, but he passed to his son the legacy his father had left him: an affection for the piney woods and a commitment to market participation. In the late 1840s, William Barbour Carter thought of the piney woods as "our poor country." Yet to him the poverty of the place proved difficult to describe, for it was reflected not in the health of his household, the peace of the countryside, or the prosperity of the people. A decade later, in terms similar to those used by his father, William observed: "Our uplands are poor. We have good swamp lands but there is some ill-conveniences attending to it." Nevertheless, he proclaimed, "I think we have a pretty good country for poor people. I suppose our market to be about as good and convenient as any in the Union."[9]

Long before northern lumber barons opened the Mississippi piney woods to market forces that would radically transform the subregion, three generations of the Carter family assigned market participation a high priority in their lives. The image of the two Matthew Carters and William trumpeting the praises of the market and their ability to partake of its benefits, however, conflicts with the portrait of plain people (those with no slaves or fewer than six) offered by antebellum travelers to the region and by twentieth-century historians.

Most contemporaries believed piney-woods soils inhospitable to market production and piney-woods residents averse to the labor and risks that market production entailed. Such caricatures so prevailed that people who never passed through the region repeated them. In the early 1840s, Henry Benjamin Whipple of New York, later the Episcopal bishop of Minnesota, traveled through the coastal South, and although he avoided the piney woods, he discounted the subregion as alternately too sandy or too swampy to foster widespread cultivation. Eugene W. Hilgard likewise

8. Matthew and Ann Carter to Griffin Mizell, November 4, 1827, Carter to Mizell, June 7, 1829, September 26, 1830, all *ibid.*

9. William Barbour Carter to Matthew Mizell, October 19, 1848, Carter to Mizell, July 7, 1857, both *ibid.*

repeated, in his *Report on the Geology and Agriculture of the State of Missis-sippi*, popular perceptions of the piney woods: although the region pre-sented residents with stunning natural beauty and fertile river bottoms and hammocks, its sandy, coarse soil—soil that would "hardly pay for improvement on the large scale"—retarded market production. As for the people living in the piney woods, contemporary travelers character-ized them as farmers and herdsmen consciously seeking isolation. Timo-thy Flint referred to residents as "a peculiar race of petits Paysans," and W. H. Sparks remembered them as poor farmers who reveled in their iso-lation and whose children lived "as wild as the Indians they had sup-planted."[10] Exceptions to the portrait of common whites as peasants or noble savages exist. John Francis Hamtramck Claiborne, who as a news-paper reporter pursuing two gubernatorial candidates in the early 1840s visited the region and became its most vocal booster, believed the piney woods to be "literally a land of 'milk and honey.'" The region's backward-ness and poverty, stereotypes falsely fomented by hasty travelers, belied the fact that residents raised livestock and crops for the market.[11]

Marginalized by most antebellum contemporaries, the southern piney woods and the people who lived in the evergreen forests of the coastal plain have also been marginalized by historians. Just as travelers tended to avoid the region, choosing instead to cling to well-known byways, few historians have ventured into the piney woods' past. The same holds true, if to a lesser extent, for ordinary southern folk, although in recent years historians have undertaken rewarding studies of common people. Some scholars continue to portray common whites in much the same manner as did antebellum travelers: in the historical imagination, plain people too often appear as poor, self-sufficient souls who chose to live as they did to avoid the intrusive influence of forces that would enslave them, especially the market economy.[12] Such a depiction may correctly render the atti-

10. Quoting Eugene W. Hilgard, *Report on the Geology and Agriculture of the State of Mis-sissippi* (Jackson, Miss., 1860), quoting 357, but see, too, 349–50; Timothy Flint, *Recollec-tions of the Last Ten Years* (Boston, 1826), 317; W. H. Sparks, *The Memories of Fifty Years* (4th ed.; Philadelphia, 1882), 332. Henry Benjamin Whipple, *Bishop Whipple's Southern Diary, 1843–1844*, ed. Lester B. Shippee (Minneapolis, 1937), 190–91. See, too, the com-ments of Thomas Affleck on the poverty of piney-woods soils in U.S. Patent Office, *Report of the Commissioner of Patents for the Year 1849* (Washington, D.C., 1849), 155.

11. Quoting J. F. H. Claiborne, "A Trip Through the Piney Woods," Mississippi Histori-cal Society *Publications*, IX (1906), 516.

12. For two recent studies of plain people that offer competing interpretations, see Charles C. Bolton, *Poor Whites of the Antebellum South: Tenants and Laborers in Central*

tudes and behavior of Faulkner's wild Anglo-Saxon, but it inappropriately describes his heirs and assignees.

The contention that plain people disdained the market appears throughout southern historiography and has taken on the quality of orthodoxy. Formation of that orthodoxy originated with efforts to refute Douglas C. North's postulation that southern farmers depended on midwestern suppliers of meat and grain to make up foodstuff shortages caused by the southerners' emphasis on cotton cultivation. Initially, historians attempted to prove that southern farmers collectively produced sufficient foodstuffs to feed the region through local trade, but when primary sources failed to offer adequate evidence of an intraregional meat and grain market, scholars began examining individual farmers' ability to feed their households. By the early 1970s a number of economic historians proclaimed all classes of farmers such accomplished producers of meat and grain that they did not need to depend on their neighbors or midwestern suppliers to fulfill their foodstuff needs. According to North's critics, planters wisely used their labor to achieve self-sufficiency while producing cotton; small-scale farmers, on the other hand, concentrated on foodstuffs, not staple crops—a variety of production that Gavin Wright and Howard Kunreuther have labeled "safety-first." According to the safety-first model, farmers, acting on complementary ideological and economic impulses, devoted the bulk of their capital and labor to foodstuff production, and thus insulated themselves from market fluctuations. By making mostly foodstuffs, they ensured their families at least a minimal level of subsistence and guaranteed that they would neither accrue debts nor lose their farms while trying to make cotton.[13]

North Carolina and Northeast Mississippi (Durham, N.C., 1994), and Bill Cecil-Fronsman, *Common Whites: Class and Culture in Antebellum North Carolina* (Lexington, Ky., 1992). See also Steven Hahn, *The Roots of Southern Populism: Yeoman Farmers and the Transformation of the Georgia Upcountry, 1850–1890* (New York, 1983); and Mary Beth Pudup, "The Limits of Subsistence: Agriculture and Industry in Central Appalachia," *Agricultural History*, LXIV (Winter, 1990), 61–92, esp. 62, 84.

13. Douglas C. North, *The Economic Growth of the United States, 1790–1860* (1961; rpr. New York, 1966), 123–37; Albert Fishlow, "Antebellum Interregional Trade Reconsidered," 187–200, and Robert Fogel, "American Interregional Trade in the Nineteenth Century," 213–24, both in *New Views on American Economic Development: A Selective Anthology of Recent Work*, ed. Ralph L. Andreano (Cambridge, Mass., 1965); Samuel B. Hilliard, *Hog Meat and Hoecake: Food Supply in the Old South, 1840–1860* (Carbondale, Ill., 1972), *passim*; William K. Hutchinson and Samuel K. Williamson, "The Self-Sufficiency of the Antebellum South: Estimates of the Food Supply," *Journal of Economic History*, XXXI (Sep-

In recent years, southern historians, taking their cue from scholars who study the rural Northeast, have refined the depiction of plain people's agricultural production. David F. Weiman, Lacy K. Ford, and Paul D. Escott contend that in the late antebellum period, railroad construction in isolated subregions provided access to markets and prompted farmers, especially nonslaveholders, to discard their apprehensions about market participation and their safety-first habits of production. Despite these scholars' work, which challenges the universal application of the safety-first model, southern historians appear slow to reject the idea that small farmers, if they produced for the market at all, avoided the risks of their participation by achieving self-sufficiency. Unlike some scholars of the rural Northeast who reject outright the notion of "near-total independence" and who point to the absence of specialization and local interdependence for necessaries as evidence of small-scale farmers' participation in the market, southern historians cling to the idea of self-sufficiency.[14]

For two reasons, the Mississippi piney woods offers historians an exemplary region in which to test whether plain folk despised the market and

---

tember 1971), 591–612; Robert Gallman, "Self-Sufficiency in the Cotton Economy of the Antebellum South," *Agricultural History*, XLIX (January 1970), 22–23; Gavin Wright and Howard Kunreuther, "Cotton, Corn, and Risk in the Nineteenth Century," *Journal of Economic History*, XXXV (September 1975), 529–30.

14. Quoting Bettye Hobbs Pruitt, "Self-Sufficiency and the Agricultural Economy of Eighteenth-Century Massachusetts," *William and Mary Quarterly*, XLI (July 1984), 333. For a brief account of historiographic concerns in the field of rural northeastern development, see Christopher Clark, *The Roots of Rural Capitalism: Western Massachusetts, 1780–1860* (Ithaca, 1990), 9–14. Paul D. Escott's "Yeoman Independence and the Market: Social Status and Economic Development in Antebellum North Carolina," *North Carolina Historical Review*, LXVI (July 1989), 275–99, contains a summary of historiographic developments on the southern front. Several recent additions to the historiography of market development include: David F. Weiman, "Farmers and the Market in Antebellum America: A View from the Georgia Upcountry," *Journal of Economic History*, XLVII (September 1987), 639; and Lacy K. Ford, "Rednecks and Merchants: Economic Development and Social Tensions in the South Carolina Upcountry, 1865–1900," *Journal of American History*, LXXI (September 1984), 315–18, and Ford, "Yeoman Farmers in the South Carolina Upcountry: Changing Production Patterns in the Late Antebellum Era," *Agricultural History*, LX (Fall, 1986), 17–37. See also Martin Crawford, "Mountain Farmers and the Market Economy: Ashe County During the 1850s," *North Carolina Historical Review*, LXXI (October 1994), 430–50; Donald W. Buckwalter, "Effects of Early Nineteenth Century Transportation Disadvantage on the Agriculture of Eastern Tennessee," *Southeastern Geographer*, XXVII (May 1987), 18–37.

practiced safety-first production. First, according to many historians, plain people exhibited a predisposition for anticommercial behavior, and just such folk filled the piney woods. In the three interior counties selected for close examination in this study—Covington, Jones, and Perry—non-slaveholders and small slaveholders headed 73 percent of farming households in 1849 and 81 percent in 1859. Second, unlike plain folk in the Carolinas, who in the 1850s responded to the appearance of railroads by neglecting the dictates of safety-first production, thereby jeopardizing their self-sufficiency, antebellum farmers in the Mississippi piney woods never saw railroads traverse their subregion.

Because of the preponderance of ordinary people and the absence of an advanced transportation system, historians might expect to find in Covington, Jones, and Perry Counties limited market participation and widespread safety-first production. Yet documentary evidence indicates that piney-woods residents suffered no qualms about buying in the market and that they sold livestock—mostly cattle, but likely swine and sheep, too. They also depended on the market for supplies they could not themselves command. Furthermore, an examination of census records—the only plentiful source for the subregion—reveals that piney-woods people failed to produce sufficient grain to feed their households adequately. Although grain deficits did not result in human starvation or reliance on the market to purchase grain for livestock, farmers in the piney woods could not feed their stock sufficiently to ensure their survival or to secure high prices. Their action represented a form of risk taking that precluded their adoption of safety-first as an ideal. For the safety-first model demands not only that farmers feed their dependents adequately, but also that they be predisposed to avoid risks. Piney-woods farmers, however, did not think of agricultural production as merely a means of subsisting—a condition that, after all, had been available to them on the worn-out lands of their former homes in Georgia and the Carolinas. On the piney-woods frontier, ordinary white farmers like the Carters sought something better than they had known. To improve their material condition, they violated safety-first principles by endangering the welfare of their livestock, their chief commodity, while also making as much for their households as their limited resources allowed.[15]

15. For criticism of the safety-first model, see Robert McGuire and Robert Higgs, "Cotton, Corn, and Risks in the Nineteenth Century: Another View," *Explorations in Economic History*, XIV (April 1977), 171.

Disputing the orthodox view of rural white southerners as oriented toward safety-first mandates that historians examine whether farm households possessed the land, finished products (including clothes and tools), grain, meat, and drink necessary to subsist independent of the market or others. Since livestock, game, and water (by some accounts alcohol, too) abounded in the piney woods, the availability of the first three variables alone matters to the investigation of safety-first.[16] Based on data about 1,412 plain folk gathered from the manuscript returns of the 1850 and 1860 censuses, it can be safely asserted that small-scale farmers in Covington, Jones, and Perry Counties owned their farms but that home manufacturing and grain production likely fell short of meeting household needs.[17]

Tenancy and landlessness in the antebellum South have recently received scholarly attention. In their study of Georgia's 1860 manuscript census, historians Frederick Bode and Donald Ginter posit a variety of methods for calculating tenancy. They advocate counting as tenants individuals who identify themselves as farmers on the population schedule of the census but who do not appear on the agricultural schedule. Using their method, 31 tenants lived in Covington County in 1860; 76 lived in Jones; and 13 lived in Perry. Bode and Ginter argue as well that tenants likely appeared on the agricultural schedule, and they identify as renters farmers who reported owning no improved and unimproved acreage and who also reported no value for their real estate. Using their second method, nonslaveholding and small-slaveholding tenants in Covington and Jones Counties did not exceed 2 percent of all plain farmers in 1849, although Covington County's proportion of renters increased to 13.8 percent in 1859. Jones County tenants made up 1.2 percent of the county's population of small farmers in 1859. On the other hand, Perry County

16. On the use of alcohol, including homemade sweet potato beer, see Claiborne, "Trip Through the Piney Woods," 519, 522, 534.

17. The statistical analysis on which this essay is based originated with the construction of a database composed of all farm units listed in the Manuscript Census, Covington County, Jones County, and Perry County, Mississippi, Schedule IV (Agriculture), 1850 and 1860. Data about each farm unit was augmented with information obtained from the Manuscript Census, Mississippi, Schedule I (Free Inhabitants) and Schedule II (Slaves), 1850 and 1860. Altogether, data about 1,819 farm families was compiled, although the information about only 1,412 plain folk was used in the analysis. Hereinafter the databases will be referred to as *Piney Woods Farm Survey* (1850) and *Piney Woods Farm Survey* (1860).

census records reveal 85 tenants (53.5 percent) among small farmers in 1849 and 78 tenants (29 percent) in 1859. With the exception of small farmers in Perry County, plain people in south Mississippi typically controlled land, the single commodity on which rural self-sufficiency depended.[18]

The high rate of tenancy established for Perry County owed to the fact that the federal government located a land office at Augusta, the county seat. Temporary residents, who offered their labor for a share of the crop or who rented land outright while waiting to purchase farms elsewhere, inflated the percentage of tenants among the farming population. The persistence rate for plain folk in Perry County bolsters the assertion that the land office attracted a disproportionate population of transient farmers. In the last decade of the antebellum period, 28.9 percent of ordinary farmers in Perry County persisted, while in Jones and Covington Counties, counties with few tenants, the persistence rates were 45.9 percent and 42.6 percent, respectively.[19]

In another way, too, the availability of public lands accounts for the generally low tenancy rate. In the late antebellum period, public lands sold for prices that all but the most woebegone might afford. During the 1830s, when the Chickasaw and Choctaw land cessions opened to white settlers the northern two-thirds of Mississippi, farmers and speculators from the Atlantic seaboard flooded into the newly available territory. On the fertile Indian cession lands, cultivators intended to raise cotton and a variety of other row crops. By and large they ignored the vast and reportedly infertile public domain farther south. After the Panic of 1837 and the ensuing decade-long depression, which stymied public land sales, farmers turned their attention southward, as they realized that cheap and plentiful lands existed only in the piney woods. Between 1850 and 1860 the Augusta land office sold 176,887 acres at an average price of less than $1 an acre. During the period, land sales at Augusta accounted for 40 percent of all federal land sold in Mississippi, and purchasers sparked a population boom. Perry County saw its population increase 38 percent in the twenty-year period 1840 to 1860; Covington County's population grew by 62 percent; and Jones County's population shot up by 164 percent. In

18. Frederick A. Bode and Donald E. Ginter, *Farm Tenancy and the Census in Antebellum Georgia* (Athens, Ga., 1986), 23; *Piney Woods Farm Survey* (1850) and (1860). On tenancy in north Mississippi, see Bolton, *Poor Whites of the Antebellum South*, 85.

19. *Piney Woods Farm Survey* (1850) and (1860).

Perry and Jones, the bulk of the population change occurred between 1850 and 1860; in Covington, the population increased by approximately 30 percent in both decades. Considering the vast public domain of south Mississippi and the price for which public land sold, the established piney-woods tenancy rate should not surprise.[20]

Even though widespread farm ownership suggests a variety of near-universal self-sufficiency, farm-level data on household manufacturing indicate that a majority of plain folk produced too few finished goods to subsist. To achieve self-sufficiency in all things, farm families needed to make their own tools and clothing. Most, however, lacked the raw materials, equipment, and skill to do so. Historian Rolla Milton Tryon has calculated that Mississippians in 1849 and 1859 manufactured at home goods valued at $1.92 and $1.75 per capita, respectively. Production in the piney woods, Tryon shows, exceeded the statewide per capita value by a large margin, but his calculations fail to determine whether individual farmers achieved self-sufficiency in home manufacturing. Based both on Lewis Gray's assertion that slaves annually required between $5 and $15 per capita in manufactured goods and on the assumption that ordinary whites required clothing and tools similarly valued, the number of plain folk producing an insufficient supply of finished goods can be estimated. In 1849, 40 percent of piney-woods plain folk manufactured at home products valued at less than $5 per capita; in 1859, the percentage fell slightly, to 36 percent. Roughly two-fifths of farm families, then, produced at home an insufficient quantity of finished products to supply household needs. But that percentage perhaps understates the actual level of dependence. Calculating the percentage of farm families manufacturing goods valued at less than $10 per capita renders a truer portrait of individuals' failure to supply household demands for finished products. In 1849, 76 percent of piney-woods farm families made goods valued at less than $10 per capita, and in 1859, the percentage stood at 60 percent.[21] It may be

20. On the movement of people into the Choctaw and Chickasaw land cessions, see Bolton, *Poor Whites of the Antebellum South*, 72–74; Mary Elizabeth Young, *Redskins, Ruffleshirts, and Rednecks: Indian Allotments in Alabama and Mississippi, 1830–1860* (Norman, Okla., 1961), *passim*. Records of land sales at each federal office in Mississippi can be found in the annual U.S. Department of the Interior, *Report of the Secretary of Interior* for the years 1835–1860. On population change, see *Sixth Census, 1840: Compendium*, I, 56–70; *Seventh Census, 1850*, 440–47; and *Eighth Census, 1860: Population*, 254–70.

21. Rolla Milton Tryon, *Household Manufacturers in the United States, 1640–1860* (1917; rpr. New York, 1966), 305, 355–56; Lewis Cecil Gray, *History of Agriculture in the*

argued, then, that one-half to three-quarters of plain folk failed to meet household needs for manufactured goods.

To make up shortages, farmers turned to the market and their neighbors. While the piney woods remained throughout the antebellum period a subregion denied easy access to markets, roads and waterways provided connections to local and regional market towns. By the late antebellum period, every piney-woods county, as well as the counties surrounding the subregion, contained at least one market town, and a contemporary map indicates that roads connected the towns to one another and to more distant markets: Madisonville in Louisiana, Natchez, Mobile, Jackson, Paulding, Leakesville, Columbia, and Mississippi City. Entrepreneurs like Thomas Jefferson Ross, a farmer and miller who lived in Lawrence County near the Covington County border, used wagons to haul necessaries from Mount Carmel, Williamsburg, Monticello, and Hazelhurst. Ross sold to his neighbors the salt, leather goods, whiskey, tobacco, and farm implements that he purchased elsewhere. Farmers, generally during the spring but at other times as well, drove cattle, hogs, and turkeys over the roads leading to Mobile, Madisonville, and Gulf Coast towns.[22]

Rivers, too, provided access to markets. The Pearl River, which skirted the western edge of the piney woods, lay within one day's journey of Williamsburg (the Covington County seat), and Columbia, a regional market town, stood on the river's eastern bank farther to the south. During the 1830s steam packets began irregular operations on the Pearl River, providing at least part of the piney woods direct access to New Or-

---

Southern United States to 1860 (2 vols.; 1933; rpr. Gloucester, Mass., 1969), I, 544; *Piney Woods Farm Survey* (1850) and (1860).

22. On roads in the piney woods, see Thomas Cowperthwait and Company, "A New Map of Mississippi with Its Roads and Distances," 1852, in Mississippi Department of Archives and History, Jackson [hereinafter cited as MDAH]. On Ross's commercial activities, see Thomas Jefferson Ross, Account Books, in Cook Memorial Library, University of Southern Mississippi, Hattiesburg [hereinafter cited as USM]. On the movement of livestock to markets, see Joseph B. Lightsey Diary, December 16–26, 1851, in MDAH; John D. W. Guice, "Cattle Raisers of the Old Southwest: A Reinterpretation," *Western Historical Quarterly*, VIII (April 1977), 167–88; Claiborne, "Trip Through the Piney Woods," 521; Robert Baxter, "Cattle Raising in Early Mississippi: Reminiscences," *Mississippi Folklore Register*, X (Spring 1976), 1–23; Mrs. Arthur Turner, "Turkey Drives: South Mississippi, Greene County," *Mississippi Folklore Register*, III (Summer 1969), 31–32. For an account of difficulties trying to find supplies in the piney woods, see Miss Adeline Russ Diary, [?] 5, 1836, in Henry Weston Family Papers, MDAH. On the significance of Mobile to south Mississippi farmers, see Whipple, *Southern Diary*, ed. Shippee, 90.

leans and Jackson. Although Covington County residents likely benefited from their propinquity to the river, too many miles separated the Pearl from farmers in Jones and Perry Counties to permit their use of it. Yet farmers in the eastern piney woods did not lack waterways connecting them to markets. Matthew Carter, Jr., for instance, commented on the importance of sailing vessels that plied the Pascagoula River system and provided him access to markets, and the recent excavation of a partially submerged keelboat discovered on the banks of the Leaf River one mile north of old Augusta suggests that farmers too far upstream to see schooners in their neighborhoods might have found connections to distant markets via their shallow rivers.[23] Even though railroads did not penetrate the antebellum piney woods, residents nonetheless took advantage of roads and waterways to obtain access to markets, access they sorely needed in order to sell their surplus livestock and to purchase a variety of necessities.

Just as most nonslaveholding and small-slaveholding farmers in the piney woods turned to the market for finished goods, a majority likely produced insufficient grain to feed their households adequately. Literary evidence about grain production in the piney woods is scant and impressionistic; literary sources also tend to have been produced by planters. Duncan McKenzie, a Covington County planter, for instance, responded to the depression of the 1840s by eschewing cotton cultivation and making mostly corn, which he intended to sell to area farmers who continued to plant cotton. But the low price paid for cotton prevented his potential customers from acquiring cash to purchase McKenzie's crop. His scheme to emphasize corn cultivation while others concentrated on cotton ultimately failed, and McKenzie returned his attention to cotton. In 1857 another south Mississippi planter, R. A. Evans, sold nearly 7,000 bushels of oats in Jackson, but in the following year a grain shortage forced him to curtail the amount he fed his stock and to purchase grain locally.[24]

23. Matthew Carter, Jr., to Griffin Mizell, March 1, 1813, June 7, 1829, both in Carter Family Letters. The keelboat, estimated to have measured 52 feet by 14 feet, appears to have been a homemade vessel designed to haul goods to and from market. Barrel staves excavated nearby suggest that the vessel carried tar or molasses at the time it capsized. Based on construction techniques, the boat was probably built between 1830 and 1850. See Hattiesburg *American*, September 2, 1990.

24. Duncan McKenzie to Duncan McLaurin, December 28, 1845, in Duncan McLaurin Papers, Perkins Library, Duke University, Durham, North Carolina; R. A. Evans Journal, July 21, 1857, January 18, May 25, December 25, 1858, MDAH.

McKenzie's and Evans' habits of grain cultivation suggest that they looked upon grain production primarily as another avenue to the market, and secondarily as a method of supplying household needs. To McKenzie and Evans, occasional shortfalls mattered less than their ability to compensate for shortages through purchases made possible by the selling of marketable crops.

Other sources more plainly state that piney-woods farmers made insufficient grain. In February 1861, the Paulding *Eastern Clarion*, the only newspaper in the piney woods, advocated that its readers prepare for the coming Civil War by planting less cotton and more corn. By reorienting their operations to a subsistence mode of production, southern farmers and planters could feed themselves. One month before the firing on Fort Sumter, the *Eastern Clarion* declared that contrary to the pronouncements of the Springfield (Illinois) *Journal* efforts by central Mississippi counties to obtain grain from midwestern farmers reflected not the perils of secession, but an ordinary occurrence. "The cotton States have always relied upon the grain growing and provision raising States of the West for their supplies of those articles, and we have been their best customers," the *Eastern Clarion* announced. Mississippians chose to purchase grain, when had they wished, they could have fed themselves.[25] According to literary sources, piney-woods cultivators, especially planters, did not think or act like safety-first producers.

While literary sources fall short of definitively explicating production habits, data gathered from manuscript census records offer historians additional insight. Through the years, historians have exploited variations on a technique first used in the 1970s to convert raw census data into a form beneficial to understanding whether individual households produced sufficient grain to meet their needs. Simply stated, the technique involves calculating the difference between the amount of grain produced on each farm and the amount of grain needed by humans and livestock. Appropriating the methods of historians who have previously studied foodstuff production (particularly the assumptions and formulas employed by Raymond Battalio and John Kagel), I calculated the available supply of grain on each Covington, Jones, and Perry County farm operated by a plain farmer.[26] In doing so, I first deducted from grain crop totals a supply

25. Paulding *Eastern Clarion*, February 13, March 15, 1861.

26. Raymond C. Battalio and John Kagel, "The Structure of Antebellum Southern Agriculture: South Carolina, A Case Study," *Agricultural History*, XLIX (January 1970), 26–29. See, too, Gallman, "Self-Sufficiency in the Cotton Economy," 3–23; Roger Ran-

of seed for the next year and then converted all grain crops into corn equivalents. Enumerated wheat converted to the equivalent of corn at a rate of 1.3:1; potatoes at a rate of 4:1; oats at 2:1; peas and beans at 1.285:1; and rice at 1:1. Demand for grain was calculated by allocating to adult human consumers—those aged fifteen and over—16.25 bushels of grain per year; children received one-half that amount. Adult livestock was allocated the following amounts of grain: horses, 21.6 bushels; hogs, 5 bushels; milk cows and other cattle, 2.25 bushels; sheep, .5 bushels; and oxen and mules, 14.25 bushels. Immature livestock received half rations.[27]

Some historians, pointing to the observations of travelers and agricultural reformers, may object to the established feeding requirements. After all, contemporaries often commented on the niggardly treatment afforded piney-woods livestock and the use of vegetation and grains unenumerated by the census. In defense of the assumptions undergirding the formula, it should be noted that, individually, piney-woods farmers owned small numbers of the most voracious consumers of grain—horses, mules, and oxen. Furthermore, cattle and hogs, the livestock most common in the region, consumed relatively little grain. (Although swine are allocated 5 bushels, only 45 percent of the herd, the percentage assumed to have been slaughtered each year, received the ration demanded by the formula.)[28] Put another way, the largest consumers of grain as described by the feeding allocation comprised a low percentage of the grain consumers on plain folks' farms. Admittedly, however, the formula functions as a

---

som and Richard Sutch, *One Kind of Freedom: The Economic Consequences of Emancipation* (Cambridge, Eng., 1977), Appendix E; and J. William Harris, *Plain Folk and Gentry in a Slave Society: White Liberty and Black Slavery in Augusta's Hinterlands* (Middletown, Conn., 1985), 200–201.

27. Battalio and Kagel, "Structure of Antebellum Southern Agriculture," 26–29. The Seventh and Eighth Censuses neglected to count separately adult and immature livestock. I assumed that 94 percent of horses and mules listed in the agricultural census of 1850 were adults and that 90 percent of the remaining varieties of stock, except swine, were immature. The 1860 census counted only adult oxen, and I did not attempt to estimate the size or consumption requirements of young oxen.

28. On the feeding practices of small farmers, see McWhiney, *Cracker Culture*, 76. On the percentage of hogs fed, see Hilliard, *Hog Meat and Hoecake*, 104. The mean number of mules and oxen on common whites' piney-woods farms was 0 in both census years; the mean number of horses was 2, except in 1860 in Perry County, when it was 1. *Piney Woods Farm Survey* (1850) and (1860).

rough guide to understanding whether plain farmers made sufficient grain to feed their families adequately.

A summary of the data produced by the calculations outlined above appears in Tables 1 and 2. Briefly stated, the tables intimate that a majority of nonslaveholding and small-slaveholding farmers in Jones and Perry Counties produced an insufficient supply of grain, while Covington County farmers more ably fed their families. Of plain farmers in Jones and Perry Counties, roughly 60 percent in both census years produced inadequate supplies of grain; the percentage of deficit farmers in Covington County remained closer to 40 percent. Differences in the percentage of farmers producing insufficient grain in Jones and Perry Counties on the

TABLE 1

Plain Farmers Producing Inadequate Grain, 1849

County	Landholding Status (N)	Number Deficit	Percent Deficit
COVINGTON	Tenants (2)	1	50.0
	0–19 acres (32)	15	46.9
	20–49 acres (97)	48	49.5
	50–99 acres (25)	4	16.0
	100 or more (6)	3	50.0
County Total	All cohorts (162)	71	43.8
JONES	Tenants (3)	1	33.0
	0–19 acres (56)	37	66.1
	20–49 acres (99)	60	60.6
	50–99 acres (20)	12	60.0
	100 or more (3)	0	0.00
County Total	All cohorts (181)	110	60.8%
PERRY	Tenants (85)	64	75.3%
	0–19 acres (21)	14	66.7%
	20–49 acres (37)	17	45.9%
	50–99 acres (13)	4	30.8%
	100 or more (3)	2	66.7%
County Total	All cohorts (159)	101	63.5%

Source: Piney Woods Farm Survey (1850) and (1860).

TABLE 2

Plain Farmers Producing Inadequate Grain, 1859

County	Landholding Status (N)	Number Deficit	Percent Deficit
COVINGTON	Tenants (42)	22	52.4
	0–19 acres (42)	27	64.3
	20–49 acres (129)	47	36.4
	50–99 acres (69)	13	18.8
	100 or more (23)	6	26.1
County Total	All cohorts (305)	115	37.7
JONES	Tenants (4)	4	100.0
	0–19 acres (80)	58	72.5
	20–49 acres (170)	113	66.5
	50–99 acres (67)	37	55.2
	100 or more (15)	4	26.7
County Total	All cohorts (336)	216	64.3
PERRY	Tenants (78)	53	67.9
	0–19 acres (91)	51	56.0
	20–49 acres (57)	26	45.6
	50–99 acres (35)	17	48.6
	100 or more (8)	3	37.5
County Total	All cohorts (269)	152	55.8

Source: Piney Woods Farm Survey (1850) and (1860).

one hand and Covington County on the other owe to several forces. Covington County, although geographically a part of the piney woods, contained soils better suited to intensive cultivation than soils in the other counties. Covington also lay closer to major market towns—Jackson, Natchez, and New Orleans—and closer to steamboats on the Pearl River. Good soil and proximity to markets, in turn, likely attracted a different class of farmers to Covington County, a supposition borne out by the fact that of the three piney-woods counties, Covington had the highest concentration of slaveholders owning more than five slaves.[29]

29. In Covington County, owners of more than five slaves constituted 20 percent of all farmers listed on the agricultural census. They accounted for 16 percent of farmers in Perry

Besides the observation that Covington County farmers proved to be more-able grain producers than nearby plain folk, Tables 1 and 2 suggest two additional observations. First, they indicate, if imperfectly, that the operation of economies of scale determined grain cultivation on small farms; second, they demonstrate that plain folk generally, though not without exception, raised more grain in 1859 than in 1849.

Discounting classifications that include a small number of farmers, it appears that those in the smallest landholding cohorts more likely made inadequate grain than farmers in other landholding cohorts. Any number of forces, including some that elude quantification, may explain the observed economies of scale, but the size of insufficient farmers' livestock herds, when considered in relation to their diminutive landholdings and their supply of labor, adequately accounts for their failure to make sufficient grain. In other words, farmers producing inadequate grain possessed proportionately too few acres and commanded too few laborers to feed themselves and their sizable livestock herds properly. Compared with farmers identified as sufficient grain cultivators, those with deficits owned on average more cattle and hogs than did their capable grain-producing neighbors; they also commanded fewer laborers to work in their corn and potato patches.[30]

Farmers who, according to Tables 1 and 2, produced insufficient grain might have, of course, fed their livestock reduced rations and thereby compensated for their supposed shortages. To ensure against inflating grain consumption and exaggerating the number of insufficient producers, it is necessary to test farmers' volatility to changes in the formula. Assuming that the prescribed feeding allocations for humans and livestock overestimate by 20 percent the amount of food consumed, a number of changes in the rates of self-sufficiency appear. Under the amended formula for calculating grain consumption, the number of deficit farmers in Covington County decreases by more than 18 percent in 1849 and by 12.5 percent in 1859. The number of insufficient Jones County farmers

---

County in 1849 and 11 percent in 1859; in Jones County, they made up 5 percent of the population in both census years. *Piney Woods Farm Survey* (1850) and (1860).

30. For example, deficit farms in Covington County in 1849 included on average 19 cattle, 43 swine, and 1.67 laborers; self-sufficient farms had on average 16 cattle, 37 hogs, and 2.04 laborers. Likewise, deficit farms in Perry County in 1859 included on average 21 cattle, 33 hogs, and 1.5 laborers; self-sufficient farms had 11 cattle, 29 hogs, and 1.5 laborers. *Piney Woods Farm Survey* (1850) and (1860).

falls by almost 15 percent in 1849 and by 14 percent in 1859. In Perry
County, decreases in the number of deficit farms are more modest: in
1849, 4.4 percent fewer farmers are identified as insufficient, and in 1859,
9.7 percent fewer enter the deficit category. (See Table 3.) Even though
changes in the percentage of farmers producing too little grain are perhaps significant in Jones and Covington Counties, farmers identified as
inadequate producers under the amended formula represent those who sat
on the cusp of sufficiency.[31] By employing the most stringent economy
and allowing their herds to subsist on depleted rangeland, they might
have been able to stretch grain supplies. Even conservative use of grain
supplies, however, would not have helped most farmers in Jones and Perry
Counties; regardless of the formula used, approximately one-half of plain
folk in the two easternmost piney-woods counties made an inadequate
supply of grain for their dependents—humans and beasts.

The established level of insufficiency among piney-woods common
white farmers suggests that a significant number eschewed safety-first
production. Their action represented a variety of risk taking pursued for
the sake of market participation. Unlike farmers in other subregions who
wagered that the sale of staple crops would offset grain and meat shortages, those in the piney woods engaged in a doubly risky gamble. For by

TABLE 3

Amended Percentage of Plain Farmers Producing Inadequate Grain, 1849–1859

	County	Original Percentage Deficit	Amended Percentage Deficit
1849	COVINGTON	43.8	25.3
	JONES	60.8	45.9
	PERRY	63.5	59.1
1859	COVINGTON	37.7	25.2
	JONES	64.3	50.3
	PERRY	55.8	46.1

Source: Piney Woods Farm Survey (1850) and (1860)

31. *Piney Woods Farm Survey* (1850) and (1860).

falling short of grain, they endangered not only their families' health but also the welfare of the commodity that provided them access to the market: livestock. Whereas planters living in Mississippi subregions blessed with fertile soils emphasized cotton cultivation at the risk of self-sufficiency, piney-woods farmers, too poor to buy good land in substantial quantity, chose to specialize in stock raising. Cotton planters engaged in a circular pattern of thought about land, slaves, and cotton; they increased their cotton production in order to obtain more land and slaves. Plain folk in the piney woods perhaps embraced a similar manner of thinking. In order to participate profitably in the market, they raised cattle and hogs; to compensate for the price that their scrawny stock brought (less than one-half the average sum paid for stock raised elsewhere in the South), they owned large herds.[32] Herding represented, in short, the poor man's way to pecuniary progress. But the journey was a risky one, especially when attempted on broken rangeland and without sufficient tillable acreage for grain crops. Plain people, however, accepted the risks, in part because, unlike piney-woods residents in territorial Mississippi, they viewed herding as a temporary occupation. Herders who farmed intended, once their risky behavior paid off in cash, to purchase acreage and establish themselves as farmers—even cotton cultivators—who also herded.[33]

32. On the undernourishment of piney-woods livestock, see Kenneth Davidson Isreal, "A Geographical Analysis of the Cattle Industry in Southeastern Mississippi from Its Beginnings to 1860" (Ph.D. dissertation, University of Southern Mississippi, 1970), 36–38. Ebenezer Ford, a Marion County correspondent of the Patent Office, reported in 1850 that fortunate piney-woods herders sold their stock at $10 to $12 a head, and he anticipated that dependence on depleted range land would send the prices lower. See U.S. Patent Office, *Report of the Commissioner of Patents for the Year, 1850* (Washington, D.C., 1850), 260. In 1852, Ford reported selling in Mobile his better-cared-for cows at $20 and his steers at $40. See U.S. Patent Office, *Report of the Commissioner of Patents for the Year, 1852* (Washington, D.C., 1852), 642. Thomas Affleck of Hinds County reported that milk cows sold for $15 to $40 depending on age; see U.S. Patent Office, *Report of the Commissioner of Patents for the Year, 1849* (Washington, D.C., 1849), 160. Thomas Jefferson Ross of Lawrence County sold slaughtered beef for approximately $10, and he sold swine on the hoof for $1 a head or one cent per pound slaughtered; see Thomas Jefferson Ross Account Books in USM, esp. the entries for Clement Mobley, 1860; Jasper Sanders, 1859 and 1860; and James Weathersby, 1860.

33. For an alternative view of southern stock tenders, see Forrest McDonald and Grady McWhiney, "The Antebellum Southern Herdsman: A Reinterpretation," *Journal of Southern History*, XLI (May 1975), 147–66, esp. 153–58.

If south Mississippi herders in fact wagered on the livestock market to supply them the wherewithal to become farmers, historians might expect to find them divesting themselves of their herds in the 1850s, acquiring more acreage, cultivating more row crops, and becoming better able to feed their households adequately. Census records verify that a significant number of piney-woods farmers abandoned specialized livestock raising in the decade before the Civil War. The transition from herder to farmer, however, had begun earlier. Assuming that a 1:3 countywide ratio of people to cattle indicates the concentration of specialized stock-raising, geographer Kenneth Davidson Isreal has pointed out that Covington County ceased being a part of cattle country before the federal government took the 1850 census. Jones and Perry remained stock-raising counties in 1849, but by 1859 the ratio of cattle to inhabitants in Jones County had dropped, leaving among piney-woods counties only Perry with enough stock to be considered a part of cattle country. Four other measures of stock-raising activities in the subregion further suggest the dissipation of herding. First, between 1849 and 1859 the percentage of stock-raising specialists, those plain farmers possessing three or more cows per capita, declined by one-half. Second, over the same period, the number of plain farmers owning herds of at least 50 cows plummeted from 58 to 26. Large herds of swine, too, began disappearing: in 1849, 185 ordinary farmers ran swine herds of at least 50, whereas ten years later, 147 did. Besides the reduced number of herding specialists and the decreased presence of large herds, the raw number of cows and swine declined in two of the three counties. (See Table 4). Jones County alone saw its cattle and hog populations climb, but even there the increase did not keep pace with human population growth.[34]

34. *Piney Woods Farm Survey* (1850) and (1860); Isreal, "A Geographical Analysis of the Cattle Industry in Southeastern Mississippi," 110–11. See also Terry Jordan, *Trails to Texas: Southern Roots of Western Cattle Ranching* (Lincoln, Nebr., 1981), 46. Folk wisdom holds that sheepherding become widespread only after the Civil War, but as Table 4 indicates, the transition to sheepherding perhaps began before 1860. It should be noted, however, that large herds of sheep were not widely dispersed among plain folk, and in 1859 newcomers owned a disproportionate number of sheep. Piney-woods residents raised sheep for their wool, which they likely sold in Mobile and New Orleans, although they perhaps also sold it ten miles north of Biloxi at the trading village that would in the postbellum period come to be called Woolmarket. From the village, schooners laden with the produce of piney-woods farmers sailed down the Biloxi River into the Bay of Biloxi and on to New Orleans. On Woolmarket, see Miss Marjorie Stewart, "The W. C. Stewart Family History," 1971, in M. James Stevens Notebooks, USM; and Hattiesburg *American*, March 30, 1957.

TABLE 4

Piney-Woods Livestock, 1849–1859

	County	Cattle	Swine	Sheep
1850	COVINGTON	6,335	12,140	2,339
	JONES	5,059	9,035	1,203
	PERRY	12,193	12,345	1,655
1860	COVINGTON	6,083	11,323	4,569
		(−4%)	(−7%)	(95%)
	JONES	5,409	13,378	3,145
		(7%)	(48%)	(161%)
	PERRY	8,966	10,631	3,852
		(−27%)	(−14%)	(133%)

Source: Piney Woods Farm Survey (1850) and (1860).

Plain-folk farmers who persisted between the censuses of 1850 and 1860 offer an additional indication of the decline in stock tending as an occupation. Of 207 persisting farmers, 56 percent reported owning fewer cattle in 1859 than in 1849, and 68 percent owned fewer swine. Archibald Fairley and Robert Laird are two examples of plain people who began making the shift from herding to farming. In 1849, Fairley, a forty-nine-year-old herdsman, reported owning 102 cattle and 100 hogs. He also possessed four slaves, who apparently worked as stockhands, since he cultivated few row crops. Ten years later he had reduced the size of his livestock herds by more than one-half, and he raised more grain. Laird, in 1849 a fairly diversified Covington County farmer who kept sizable herds of stock, followed a similar path. Although he increased the size of his cattle herd from 18 to 20, he cut by 60 percent the number of hogs that he owned. Laird also became a slaveholder in the 1850s. His five slaves apparently spent a portion of their time cultivating cotton, of which he reported making 19 bales in 1859.[35]

As common farmers in the piney woods began divesting themselves of their herds, they purchased considerable acreage. In response to the abeyance of the depression of the 1840s, which opened the floodgates to piney-woods immigration, newcomers and established settlers, hoping to

35. *Piney Woods Farm Survey* (1850) and (1860).

preempt others with designs on land they prized, purchased acreage in the public domain. Longtime residents used the cash they accrued through selling livestock to augment their holdings; newcomers apparently arrived with cash to purchase land or found credit terms to their liking. The widespread desire for land accounted for an increase in the number of improved and unimproved acres owned. In Covington and Perry Counties, plain farmers owned 60 percent more improved acres in 1859 than they did in 1849, while in Jones County, the increase exceeded 120 percent. Holdings of unimproved acreage exploded even more dramatically; in Covington and Perry Counties the increase surpassed the 200 percent mark, and Jones County plain farmers owned over 900 percent more unimproved acres in 1859 than in 1849. (See Table 5). Persisting farmers like Murdock McGilberry of Jones County participated in the great land rush. When the census taker visited him in 1849, McGilberry reported owning 25 improved and 65 unimproved acres. A decade later his holdings had increased to 65 improved and 735 unimproved acres. To purchase approximately 650 acres over the period of ten years, McGilberry would have needed to raise a substantial amount of capital. Undoubtedly he obtained some of it by selling stock, and perhaps also by selling the one adult slave he owned in 1849.[36]

TABLE 5

Percentage Change in Holdings of Improved and Unimproved Acres, 1849–1859

	County	Improved Acres	Unimproved Acres
1850	COVINGTON	15,855	26,698
	JONES	6,568	8,986
	PERRY	5,886	28,033
1860	COVINGTON	25,740	102,129
		(62%)	(283%)
	JONES	14,641	93,179
		(123%)	(937%)
	PERRY	9,635	93,133
		(64%)	(232%)

Source: Piney Woods Farm Survey (1850) and (1860).

36. *Ibid.*

As piney-woods farmers began selling off their cattle and augmenting their landholdings, they planted more row crops, including cotton. Among persisting farmers, a majority (55 percent) increased their production of grain crops in the decade before the Civil War, while 115 (56 percent) baled more cotton (36 percent of persisters initially appeared on the 1860 census as cotton growers).[37] Perry County resident Isaac E. Carter represents an extraordinary example of a piney-woods farmer's transition to cotton cultivation. In 1849, Carter owned 170 acres and raised exclusively livestock and grain crops. On the eve of the Civil War, he reported controlling 700 acres, including 125 improved. Although he maintained in both census years a substantial herd of cattle, Carter entered the cotton-cultivating and slaveholding class of Mississippi in a revolutionary fashion. Whereas ten years earlier he had baled no cotton and owned no slaves, in 1859 he made 14 bales and owned 22 slaves. Although Carter's passage out of the plain-folk class seems an anomaly, other common whites shared his sudden interest in cotton cultivation. Jesse M. Bowden, a twenty-eight-year-old Georgia native living in Jones County made the transition from stock raiser to farmer in a more modest manner than did Carter. In the late 1840s Bowden kept 18 cows and 30 hogs on his 30-acre farm. He raised a little grain—too little, in fact, to feed his stock and family adequately. Within a decade, however, Bowden's circumstances changed significantly. Even though he owned only 35 improved acres, his unimproved holdings escalated from 0 to 485. In 1859, Bowden kept smaller herds of cattle and swine than he had ten years earlier; he harvested nearly six times more grain; and for the first time, he reported making cotton—3 bales.[38]

On the eve of the Civil War, the transformation of the piney woods from herding to farming frontier, albeit incomplete, had begun. Some persisters began concentrating on farming, not stock raising, and the shift proved generally salutary to their grain storehouses, although roughly one-half of persisters continued struggling to make for their households a sufficient supply of grain. Their protracted struggle reflects the fact that the shift from herding to farming did not dampen the willingness of pro-

37. Between 1849 and 1850, cotton production in the piney woods increased. In Covington County, bale production rose from 1,150 to 2,999; in Jones, the number of bales increased from 213 to 630; and in Perry County, farmers reported making 310 bales in 1859, an increase of only 2 bales over the 1849 total. *Ibid.*

38. *Ibid.*

ducers to engage in risk taking. Even though the risks they took might have no longer focused on livestock, they, like other cotton cultivators on the southwestern frontier, risked their household's well being on their ability to cover grain shortages by selling their staple crop and other agricultural products.[39] That they would engage in risky behavior seems hardly surprising, since many had throughout their residence in the piney woods gambled on their ability to sell undernourished livestock profitably, a gamble that paid off and permitted them to become cotton cultivators. Nonpersisting farmers (those appearing only on the 1850 census) and newcomers (those first appearing on the 1860 census) accounted for the overwhelming majority of grain-deficit farms; following the example of their persisting neighbors, they risked their ability to feed their households adequately in order to raise large herds of livestock.

Without documentary evidence, historians confront great difficulty attempting to understand the antebellum piney woods and the people who lived in the subregion, and the effort itself necessarily inspires speculation. Nonetheless, census records indicate that a majority of common white farmers in the piney woods owned land and did not need to turn to others for that commodity, which defined rural self-sufficiency; census data also demonstrate that most failed to produce a supply of finished products sufficient to subsist without relying on the market. The general failure of plain farmers to make adequate grain, although hardly certain, is suggestive. For if grain shortfalls actually occurred, the decision to emphasize livestock tending represented a form of risk taking that precluded farmers' pursuit of safety-first habits of production. Had small-scale farmers in the piney woods acted like safety-first producers, they would have either made more grain or raised fewer animals. Had they thought like safety-first producers, they likely could not have expanded the size of

39. Persisting farmers more ably made grain, whereas nonpersisting farmers struggled at the task, a phenomenon that should be anticipated, since by remaining in one county persisters intimated their satisfaction with the area and their ability to succeed there. Of persisting farmers living in Covington County in 1849, 62 percent produced grain surpluses; in 1859, 69 percent did so. In Jones County, 42 percent made enough grain for their families, and in 1859, 40 percent produced surpluses. In Perry County, 46 percent produced surpluses, and in 1859, 52 percent did. Furthermore, in Covington County, 45 percent of persisters achieved self-sufficiency in grain in both census years; and in Jones and Perry Counties, approximately 36 percent and 28 percent, respectively, made adequate grain in 1849 and 1859.

their landholdings in the 1850s as dramatically as census records indicate. For the safety-first model suggests stasis, except for the lucky few. And piney-woods people on the eve of the Civil War did not expose themselves to the rigors of frontier living for the sake of economic stagnation or for the sake of pursuing the lifestyle of William Faulkner's wild Anglo-Saxon Protestant. Piney-woods farmers, like the Carter clan, were often refugees from sterile regions of the Carolinas and Georgia and moved to the old southwestern frontier to secure a place for themselves in the market economy. They arrived understanding that regardless of their poverty and regardless of the absence of an advanced transportation system, the safety-first model would serve them poorly. Consequently they determined to make as much for their households as their limited resources would allow, but to do so without curtailing their ability to produce for the market and without fear of taking risks.

J. WILLIAM HARRIS

The Question of Peonage in the History of the New South

In October 1921, L. K. Salsbury, the head of the largest cotton plantation in the world, met with his top managers in the Delta town of Scott, Mississippi. The year 1921 had been a tough one for cotton planters; the high prices of the war years had broken abruptly in 1920 as a sharp recession hit the nation, and they had not recovered. The profits of the plantation, owned by the Delta & Pine Lands Company, had soared to more than half a million dollars in 1919; the next year they were replaced with a loss of more than a third of a million.[1]

Salsbury's concern in this meeting was above all with the African American sharecroppers who actually raised D&PL's cotton. The company, he told the managers, had reduced prices in the plantation stores

The first version of this essay, prepared while I held a generous fellowship at the National Humanities Center, was presented to audiences in the History Department of North Carolina State University and the Institute for Research in the Social Sciences at the University of North Carolina, Chapel Hill. I am especially grateful for comments and suggestions from W. Jeffry Bolster and Terry Kay Rockefeller.

1. "Annual Statement to Stockholders," Delta & Pine Lands Co. of Mississippi, January 31, 1921, in Annual Statements and Presidential Reports, Delta & Pine Lands Company Records, Special Collections, Mitchell Memorial Library, Mississippi State University, Starkville [hereinafter cited as DPL]. The wholesale price of cotton fell from 35 cents per pound in 1919 to 16 cents in 1920 and was 17 cents in 1921; U.S. Bureau of the Census, *Historical Statistics of the United States, Colonial Times to 1970* (Washington, D.C., 1976), 517.

until profits from that source had disappeared entirely; it had lowered charges for doctor bills; it had eliminated charges for services such as plowing. "We did this," he continued, "because we had on the books against the tenants all we felt that we had any possibility of getting and there was no use to put charges on them when we knew the most we could do could be to lose our money and run our tenants off." The managers, he went on to say, might even want to pay the tenants more for their cotton and seed than it was worth in order to "pull our tenants all out of the hole, make them pay their debts, and put them in position where they can clear a little money and where we know next year that they will all make money."[2]

Many readers, one suspects, may be prompted by Salsbury's words to recall the question on the back cover of the children's magazine: "What's wrong with this picture?" For Salsbury's admonitions and advice seem to take for granted a situation exactly the opposite of the one most of us who study and teach southern—or American—history generally think was the case. The story that many of us have told in our lectures probably goes something like this:

After the Civil War, impoverished former slaves resisted gang labor but came to depend on landlords and country merchants to sell them food and farming supplies on credit. Southern states gave this system legal force by allowing a merchant or landlord to take a lien on crops, which gave creditors the right to take the harvest to settle the sharecroppers' debts and to seek criminal prosecution of a sharecropper who could not pay in full. The landlords and merchants took advantage of the weak bargaining power of the ex-slaves by charging unusually high prices and interest rates. Once in debt, African American sharecroppers found it almost impossible to settle their accounts; the lucky ones broke even each year, while most fell deeper and deeper into debt. These indebted black farmers faced imprisonment and forced labor unless they toiled on the land according to the instructions of their creditors. Increasingly, merchants and landlords cooperated to maintain this lucrative system, and many landlords them-

---

2. Financial Records: Minutes: Managers' Meeting, October 21, 1921, in DPL. For very similar arguments from Salsbury, see *ibid.*, "We split accounts [that is, canceled half debts due] and paid money to practically every tenant on the place" because "for the last two years . . . the plantation had too many croppers fail to pay out; . . . most of the tenants have run away, so we are not carrying over so many old bad accounts—most of them have been charged over to profit and loss. I am sure it was a wise thing to split accounts with our tenants when settling with them this year."

selves became merchants. Thus, the ex-slaves became trapped in the vicious circle of debt peonage.

This view of the New South's rural economic history as dominated by crop liens and peonage has a long history. It was articulated more than a hundred years ago in an article by George Holmes entitled "Peons of the South," and echoed by many of his contemporaries.[3] The model that late-nineteenth-century writers had in mind when they bemoaned "peonage" was Mexico. As one historian of Latin America has summarized the situation in the Yucatán, for example, "labor conditions were harsh; workers were imported by force; debt was systematically used to provide a legal basis for coercion; and plantation owners, aided by local police or the army, were able to restrict workers' movement and tie them to the estates." On the hemp haciendas of this area, debts might pass from generation to generation, corporal punishment was frequent, and runaways were hunted down by the local police.[4] The southern-peonage model was summarized in the classic works of C. Vann Woodward, and it continues to appear as a standard assumption in the works of modern writers, whether they be prize-winning senior scholars, influential cliometricians, or the authors of cutting-edge dissertations. It is, one might say, the textbook version of New South agriculture. In fact, my foregoing summary of the standard view closely paraphrases an excellent recent multiauthored textbook survey of U.S. history.[5]

3. George K. Holmes, "Peons of the South," *Annals* of the American Academy of Political and Social Science, IV (1893), 265–74.

4. Arnold J. Bauer, "Rural Workers in Spanish America: Problems of Peonage and Oppression," *Hispanic American Historical Review*, LIX (1979), 36. See also Alan Knight, "Mexican Peonage: What Was It and Why Was It?" *Journal of Latin American Studies*, XVIII (1986), 41–74; and Gilbert M. Joseph, *Revolution from Without: Yucatán, Mexico, and the United States, 1880–1924* (Cambridge, Eng., 1982), 72–79.

5. The textbook is James Henretta *et al.*, *America's History* (Chicago, 1987); the original version appears on p. 502. For a similar example, see Mary Beth Norton *et al.*, *A People and a Nation* (Boston, 1994), 523. References to "peonage" in the New South are so ubiquitous that the point here hardly needs documentation, but a representative sampling includes Holmes, "Peons of the South"; C. Vann Woodward, *Origins of the New South, 1877–1913* (Baton Rouge, 1951), 181; Roger Ransom and Richard Sutch, "Debt Peonage in the Cotton South After the Civil War," *Journal of Economic History*, XXXII (1972), 641–69; Jonathan M. Wiener, "Class Structure and Economic Development in the American South, 1865–1955," *American Historical Review*, LXXXIV (1979), 970–82.

Why, then, was a Mississippi planter telling his managers in emphatic terms that they must keep their sharecroppers *out* of debt and let them clear some money at the end of the season as a way of keeping them for the next year?

We might guess, of course, that Delta & Pine Lands was atypical because of its huge size or because it was owned by absentee British investors. However, we can be sure that DP&L's great size did not make it immune to competition from neighboring plantations. On the contrary, Salsbury in this October meeting warned his managers to stay constantly alert to that competition. The tenants, he warned, would be "moving about more this year than ever before." Now was the time to lay plans for the next season. "Let's don't sit down and wait for the tenants to come in, let's reach out for them. . . . A good manager . . . has got to be looking after his labor until the first of next year and then begin over again without stopping."[6]

It is also pretty clear that Salsbury was acting on neither paternalistic nor philanthropic impulses. On the contrary, he criticized his managers for too often allowing their thinking to be controlled by the sentiment that said, "'Well, we have got to take care of the negroes'.—We must take care of our tenants, but on the other hand *we must take care of ourselves.* We are not philanthropists. . . . We must think of the stockholders who have their money invested and haven't realized anything in return."[7]

Perhaps it is not the plantation but the time that confounds our expectations about the relationship between debt and sharecropping. By 1921 the Great Migration of African Americans to northern cities was well under way; perhaps that made the 1920s quite different from the 1880s or the early years of the twentieth century with respect to peonage and forced labor. At the same time, it would be logical to assume that planters faced with increased black mobility would have a greater incentive than ever to tie down their workers by debt or other means.[8]

Let us review the reasons many of us have been convinced of the widespread existence of peonage in the New South. The evidence falls into

6. Financial Records: Minutes: Managers' Meeting, October 21, 1921, in DPL.

7. *Ibid.* (emphasis in original).

8. Thus Pete Daniel's standard monograph on peonage suggests that the 1920s actually may have seen an upsurge of peonage in the South; Daniel, *The Shadow of Slavery: Peonage in the South, 1901–1969* (Urbana, Ill., 1972), 132–48.

three broad categories. First, we know that debt itself was pervasive throughout the agricultural South; that millions of rural farmers were sustained through credit advanced by landlords and merchants; and that this credit was typically secured with liens on growing crops.[9] Second, we know that southern planters often expressed their desire or determination to limit, if not eliminate, labor mobility and fix black workers to their plantations, and that in response to those desires, southern states enacted a wide variety of laws designed to restrict mobility.[10] Third, we have the extensive analyses by historians and other scholars of peonage and forced labor in southern agriculture, most notably the research of Pete Daniel in the extensive records of federal prosecutions for peonage after 1900.[11]

Still, debt is not the same thing as debt bondage; laws are better evidence of intention than of results; and only a tiny proportion of southern planters were actually prosecuted for peonage. None of this evidence, in other words, shows that most poor southern tenants were typically or even often caught in genuine peonage.[12]

It is important to remember that debt pervaded every level of postbellum southern agriculture, not just the bottom level of sharecroppers. The planters'

9. On the general operations of the lien system, see Thomas D. Clark, "The Furnishing and Supply System in Southern Agriculture Since 1865," *Journal of Southern History,* XII (1946), 24–44; Woodward, *Origins of the New South,* 180–84; and Harold D. Woodman, *New South—New Law: The Legal Foundations of Credit and Labor Relations in the Postbellum Agricultural South* (Baton Rouge, 1995), 28–66.

10. These laws will be discussed in more detail below. See William Cohen, *At Freedom's Edge: Black Mobility and the Southern White Quest for Racial Control, 1861–1915* (Baton Rouge, 1991); Oscar Zeichner, "The Legal Status of the Agricultural Laborer in the South," *Political Science Quarterly,* LV (1940), 412–48; Jennifer Roback, "Southern Labor Law in the Jim Crow Era: Exploitative or Competitive?" *University of Chicago Law Review,* LI (1984), 1161–92; and Woodman, *New South—New Law,* 85–93. Ralph Shlomowitz, "Planter Combinations and Black Labour in the American South, 1865–1880," *Slavery and Abolition,* IX (1988), 72–84, provides extensive evidence that informal agreements among planters after the Civil War failed to limit mobility.

11. Daniel, *Shadow of Slavery;* John Dittmer, *Black Georgia in the Progressive Era, 1900–1920* (Urbana, Ill., 1977), 72–82; Neil R. McMillan, *Dark Journey: Black Mississippians in the Age of Jim Crow* (Urbana, Ill., 1990), 145–49. For a summary of the argument see Jay R. Mandle, *The Roots of Black Poverty: The Southern Plantation Economy After the Civil War* (Durham, N.C., 1977).

12. Daniel himself seems unsure about this; in one place he writes of peonage both as an "extreme manifestation" of the South's social system and as "virtually countless." Daniel, *Shadow of Slavery,* 23.

loss of financial wealth, including their use of slaves as collateral, in the Civil War, combined with the South's weak system of banking, made merchants the only possible source of credit for most farmers, as only merchants had credit to give.[13] Under the circumstances, it is hardly surprising that merchants lending to poor people demanded the only collateral many of them had, their growing crops. Even Matthew Hammond, one of the severest contemporary critics of the credit system, acknowledged that lien laws themselves could not be blamed for southern farmers' problems, because for many farmers there was no alternative way to get credit.[14] Hundreds of thousands of farmers could have literally starved without advances of supplies. When the South Carolina legislature abolished the crop lien in 1877, farmers clamored to have it restored, as without it they had no way to finance their operations.[15] In fact, without the credit system, it is hard to imagine how African Americans could have established any autonomy at all, which was precisely the complaint of writers like Charles Otken, who denounced the lien system not merely because it "enslaved thousands of good people," but also because it "derange[d] negro labor" by making black workers independent of their landlords.[16]

To be sure, this credit was expensive for sharecroppers and tenants— both directly, in the form of high interest rates, and indirectly, in the form of higher prices for credit sales.[17] As numerous scholars have pointed out,

13. Richard Holcombe Kilbourne, Jr., *Debt, Investment, Slaves: Credit Relations in East Feliciana Parish, Louisiana, 1825–1885* (Tuscaloosa, 1995); Harold Woodman, *King Cotton and His Retainers: Financing and Marketing the South's Cotton Crop, 1800–1925* (Lexington, Ky., 1968).

14. Hammond, *Cotton Industry*, 143.

15. Lacy K. Ford, "Rednecks and Merchants: Economic Development and Social Tensions in the South Carolina Upcountry, 1865–1900," *Journal of American History*, LXXI (1984), 294–318; Woodman, *New South—New Law*, 50. Georgia also eliminated merchant liens in 1874 but quickly restored them in 1875 before the new law could even take effect; Woodman, *New South—New Law*, 40–41.

16. Charles Otken, *The Ills of the South* (New York, 1894), 24, 36. In a pioneering study of African American farmers in North Carolina, Sharon Holt shows that many of these farmers used credit from local merchants or landlords to finance their slow and painstaking rise to landownership; Holt, "Making Freedom Pay: Freedpeople Working for Themselves, North Carolina, 1865–1900," *Journal of Southern History*, LX (1994), 229–62.

17. Roger Ransom and Richard Sutch, *One Kind of Freedom: The Economic Consequences of Emancipation* (Cambridge, Eng., 1977), 128–32, 237–43; Clark, "Furnishing and Supply System." The actual amount of effective interest is a matter of considerable dispute but could clearly go as high as 50 percent.

however, there is good reason to think that for most country and town merchants, monopolies were rare, competition fierce, and business failures frequent.[18] Supply stores typically clustered together in small towns and villages and had to compete with one another for customers, as a perusal of advertising in local papers shows.[19] They usually operated on narrow margins and frequently went broke. Richard Kilbourne recently estimated that at least 25 percent of store customers defaulted on their accounts in East Feliciana Parish, Louisiana, in the late 1870s, which suggests that a very high interest rate was inevitable for these operations.[20]

It is in any case debt bondage, not debt itself, that creates peonage. To show that American sharecroppers were peons, it is not enough to show that they were poor and indebted; it is also necessary to show that, like Mexican peons, they were tied by debt to their plantations.

A good deal of statistical evidence suggests quite the opposite, for it is clear that annual labor turnover on plantations in the South was simply enormous. For example, as Michael Wayne has shown, cotton plantations during late Reconstruction in the Natchez area faced very high annual turnover. For the immediate post-Reconstruction decade, the tax records of Georgia indicate that a large majority of nonlandowning black tenants and laborers changed employers at least every two years.[21] The U.S. Census in 1910 showed that well over half of the black sharecroppers in

18. Kilbourne, *Debt;* Gill Insong, "Furnishing Merchants and the Rural Credit Market of the American South: Alabama, 1870–1920" (Ph.D. dissertation, Yale University, 1990).

19. The *Georgia Gazetteer and Business Directory* (1881), for example, lists 27 stores in Hart County in 1881; 18 of these clustered in Hartwell, the county seat; three other hamlets had 5, 3, and 1 store, respectively. In the village of Linton, in Hancock County, there were 3 stores in 1881; a few miles away in Sparta were 10 more. Similar results obtain for other counties: in Greene, 23 stores in 6 locations, 5 with more than 1 store; in Taliaferro, 8 stores, all in Crawfordville; in Hancock, 33 stores in 8 locations. See Ford, "Rednecks and Merchants," for similar evidence for South Carolina.

20. Kilbourne, *Debt,* 8, 149.

21. Michael Wayne, *The Reshaping of Plantation Society: The Natchez District, 1860–1880* (Baton Rouge, 1983), 208–209; J. William Harris, "Marx, the Market, and the Freedmen: Land and Labor in Late Nineteenth Century Georgia," in *Looking South: Chapters in the Story of an American Region,* ed. Winfred B. Moore, Jr., and Joseph F. Tripps (Westport, Conn., 1989), 193; Steve Engerrand, "'Now Scratch or Die': The Genesis of Capitalist Agricultural Labor in Georgia, 1865–1880" (Ph.D. dissertation, University of Georgia, 1981), 175–92. Georgia's late-nineteenth-century tax records make it possible to trace landlord-tenant relationships on a year-to-year basis because black farmers and farmworkers who did not own their land are listed according to their employer or landlord.

Georgia and Mississippi had been on the same farm for one year or less. The turnover rates, in other words, are comparable to estimates of the annual turnover among industrial workers in the Northeast in the same period.[22] Such a high level of labor mobility is quite difficult to reconcile with the widespread existence of long-term peonage, based on debt or any other means.

The statistical evidence is corroborated vividly by the records left by farmers and planters who hired black labor in the late nineteenth and early twentieth centuries. Take, for example, the experience from 1878 to 1882 of the overseer on the Newstead Plantation in Washington County, Mississippi. At times he felt it perfectly appropriate to try to exercise the kind of authority over his workers that most white workers would not have tolerated. In 1881 he "rattled down several freedmen about their rascality"; the next year he "drove Bill Williams out of the quarter."[23] More often, though, his journal offers a running commentary on the fierce competition for labor and the problems of keeping it. In 1880 the overseer paid labor agents for six hands recruited from the Gulf Coast; the next year he was so short of hands at picking time that he had to hire wage labor, "a most expensive way of gathering a crop." His freedmen tenants, he complained, "won't work when they can hire [themselves out for wages on other plantations]." In January 1879, after settling up with several hands, he wrote, "I shall lose on the majority a small balance," and the next day he noted that "a good many of my hands are leaving," which he thought would cost him over $100 in advanced wages and supplies.[24] The next year the story was repeated: Jack Dunlap "goes owing me money . . . Henry Sanders informed me he intends to leave; I nursed him out of a bed of sickness." In the middle of the next summer, "Macks's wife quit . . . Negroes quit whenever they feel like it."[25] Nowhere in his jour-

22. "Stability of Farm Operators, or Term of Occupancy of Farms," *Thirteenth Census*, 1910. The rates were 56 percent of reporting farms in Mississippi and 58 percent of reporting farms in Georgia. See also Jacqueline Jones, *The Dispossessed: America's Underclasses from the Civil War to the Present* (New York, 1992), 104–26. For estimates of industrial turnover, see Daniel T. Rodgers, "Tradition, Modernity, and the American Industrial Worker: Reflections and Critique," *Journal of Interdisciplinary History*, VII (1977), 663.

23. Newstead Plantation Journal, November 30, 1881, July 11, 1882, in Southern Historical Collection, University of North Carolina, Chapel Hill [hereinafter cited as SHC].

24. *Ibid.*, January 24, 25, 1879.

25. *Ibid.*, January 14, 1880, February 4, December 29, 1881, July 11, 1882.

nal does he mention any method of keeping workers who were determined to leave, whether at midyear or after the harvest.

Worries about retaining labor surface frequently in the letters of
George Collins, who operated a plantation in Tunica County, Mississippi,
during this same period. In 1880, Collins wrote to his wife that "there is
the greatest commotion in the neighborhood more changes of managers
& consequently moves among the laborers themselves everybody trying
to secure the best class."[26] At the end of that year Collins planned to hire
a new manager from a neighboring plantation, who Collins hoped would
bring along new hands as well. "Now in this," he told his wife, "I don't
think I am infringing on my neighbours, as both Crews & the hands have
declared they will not stay where they are."[27] In 1882 he continued to
struggle to get and keep labor for the entire crop year. In April he lost two
tenants just after part of the crop had been planted, including one, named
Bedford, who left because the manager on the plantation "got after him
with a stick."[28] In June, Collins was "as busy as it is possible to be" and
complained that he was "so short of hands that I have to work a good deal
myself & unless I am there it seems nothing is done." The state of the
neighborhood crops was "obliging the planters to pay high day wages," yet
despite the money, "the weather is so hot that hands don't like such severe labor."[29] In the picking season that fall, "cotton pickers are scarce &
high & we have more than double what our own hands can pick, I hire
all I can get & shall send to M[emphis] tomorrow & try to get more. I
wish I had 100 for two or three weeks they would help me out wonder-
fully." The next week he was off to get cash to pay pickers, as "the crop is
opening so fast that it frightens me. . . . Prompt payment is the only way
to secure pickers."[30] Clearly these workers were not tied to the land like
Mexican peons.

A decade later the same themes dominate much of the diary kept by
Clive Metcalf, owner of a big Delta plantation. Sometimes Metcalf's "favored" hands left unexpectedly: "Aaron came to pay me the Bal[ance]
due me and he is going away. Well the more you do for a negro the less he

26. George Collins to Anne Collins, January 10, 1880, in Cameron Family Papers, SHC.
The plantation was owned by Collins' father-in-law, Paul Cameron of North Carolina.

27. Collins to Anne Collins, October 26, 1880, in Cameron Family Papers, SHC.

28. Collins to Anne Collins, April 28, 1882, in Cameron Family Papers, SHC.

29. Collins to Anne Collins, June 27, 1882, in Cameron Family Papers, SHC.

30. Collins to Anne Collins, November 3, 7, 1882, both in Cameron Family Papers, SHC.

will thank you." The end of every year meant a nervous time of settling up and recruiting hands for the next year: "I am worried to death from settling with Negros and getting them satisfied for X mast [Christmas]." And: "The negroes are very much dissatisfied evry where. They are leaving Brighton evry day. Why it is no body knows."[31] At times, to be sure, Metcalf benefited from other people's labor troubles. In 1890 a neighbor rented her place to local store owners and almost all her hands left because they were "vary [sic] much dissatisfied. A good many have applied to us for situations."[32]

It would be wrong to exaggerate the power of black workers, who after all had to make accommodations with *some* landholder if they expected to feed themselves and their families. Still, overstating the real power of planters distorts the story as well. As Metcalf put it, "What in the world will a man do with out labor in thes [sic] country? For one can not work the land with out the Negroes."[33] Metcalf, it must be remembered, was in a struggle not only with African American labor, but also with his neighbors, who were equally anxious to get workers. This is what made a planter like Metcalf think that he was at least as much dependent on his tenants as the other way around. As he noted with exasperation in his journal: "A man is a fool for renting his land. The doggone negroes want you to knock off your But. And give them every thing."[34]

In response to planters' desires to have more control over their labor, southern legislatures passed numerous laws designed to restrict black mobility or to limit black economic autonomy. Anti-enticement laws, for example, were intended to prevent one landlord from recruiting another's tenant. Professional labor recruiters were charged prohibitive license fees. Laws might authorize draconian punishment for the theft of a pig or, in an attempt to prevent thefts of cotton from the fields, outlaw the sale of unginned cotton after dark.

Perhaps potentially most important, African Americans could be charged with vagrancy if they were "idle" or with fraud if they allegedly violated the terms of their contracts by working for someone else. A study of Greene County, in piedmont Georgia, found that the county court there prosecuted some four dozen blacks in 1874 for either vagrancy

31. Clive Metcalf Diary, December 19, 21, 31, 1888, in SHC.

32. Metcalf Diary, January 1, 1890, in SHC.

33. *Ibid.*, January 3, 1890.

34. *Ibid.*, May 11, 1890.

or contract violations, sentencing many to the chain gang; similar laws were apparently used frequently by operators of Florida's turpentine camps.[35]

It should be noted that many of the state laws designed to restrict mobility did not, in any case, apply to end-of-year changes, but aimed only to relieve such planter headaches as losing a worker in midcrop. More important, many complaints by white southerners suggest that these laws were often less than effective in practice. In the 1890s, for example, the editor of Greene County's weekly newspaper called for something stronger than the current "utterly worthless and ineffective" contract law—something that might solve the "vexatious" labor problems that arose every year in chopping season. Even though sharecroppers by then had been living on landlord credit for months and were typically well into debt, the "first thing you know" when demand for labor is high is that "your laborer is hard at work in SOMEBODY ELSE'S COTTON PATCH," drawn away by higher wages.[36] Indeed, by the 1890s cases of vagrancy and contract violations had apparently almost disappeared from the county court.[37] As the editor's complaint makes clear, one problem was that the laws tried to regulate not only black workers, but also white employers. As another editor put it in 1881, "Our landowners need protection from each other in their struggle for labor."[38]

On occasion, when sudden, massive outmigration from local areas erupted, the law might be used with some effectiveness to restrict black mobility. Labor-agent licensing laws, for example, helped planters in the Georgia piedmont shut down a local "exodus," touched off by a labor agent from

35. Jonathan M. Bryant, *How Curious a Land: Conflict and Change in Greene County, Georgia, 1850–1885* (Chapel Hill, 1996), 157–58; Michael David Tegeder, "'The Onliest Way Out Is to Die Out': Debt Peonage and Southern Law Enforcement During the 1920s" (Paper delivered at the 1994 Annual Meeting of the Southern Historical Association, Louisville).

36. Greensboro (Ga.) *Herald-Journal*, November 9, 1888.

37. According to research by Edward L. Ayers, the *Herald-Journal* listed 129 cases for the county court in the 1890s and mentioned the verdict in 101 of these; 27 defendants were found not guilty, 63 were sentenced to the chain gang (the others apparently were found guilty but not sent to the chain gang). Ayers writes that 40 cases involved theft, 19 violence, and the rest "were scattered"; it is not clear whether breakdown of alleged crimes is based on all cases before the court or on the convictions. Edward L. Ayers, *Vengeance and Justice: Crime and Punishment in the 19th-Century American South* (New York, 1984), 324n7.

38. Oglethorpe (Ga.) *Echo*, February 13, 1881.

the Mississippi Delta, in 1899–1900.[39] But most migration was not the result of active professional recruitment; it arose out of the many individual decisions made by African Americans (and many whites) in their kitchens and churches, talking among themselves about the advisability of moving to places where pay might be higher or conditions better. African American laborers continued to pour into the relatively high-wage Delta from the southeastern states between 1870 and 1910, regardless of attempts at legal restrictions. Outside of the occasional spectacular case, it was difficult and expensive to enforce legal restrictions that bore on white employers as well as black workers. This was one reason laws tying workers to particular estates, farms, or plantations were routinely ignored.

Vagrancy statutes had the advantage for planters of affecting black workers without simultaneously restricting white employers. In the Georgia "exodus" of 1899–1900, at least one sheriff threatened to use the vagrancy laws to arrest potential emigrants.[40] But if the surviving court records I have examined are any indication, in many counties vagrancy statutes were rarely used. There was not a single case of vagrancy among the ninety-three criminal cases brought before a justice of the peace in Columbia County, Georgia, between 1897 and 1902.[41] Vagrancy prosecutions were rare in the County Court of Hancock County, Georgia, between 1896 and 1905. There were no vagrancy cases in 1896, and in the five cases for 1897, three of the defendants were acquitted. Again in 1898 no vagrancy cases came before the court. Only in early 1901 was there a spate of vagrancy prosecutions, with eight cases in the February and March terms. Perhaps these were related to the "exodus" of the year before. In any event, charges were dropped in five of the eight cases and the other three defendants were found not guilty. The next year the Hancock court again saw no vagrancy cases.[42] The same story emerges from state authorities'

39. William F. Holmes, "Labor Agents and the Georgia Exodus, 1899–1900," *South Atlantic Quarterly*, LXXIX (1980), 436–48.

40. *Ibid.*, 444.

41. The justice of the peace records for the 129th Militia District were microfilmed with those of the county ordinary: Columbia County Justice of the Peace Minutes, 1897–1902, Georgia Department of Archives and History [hereinafter cited as GDAH]. Columbia was a lower-piedmont cotton county, over 70 percent black in 1900.

42. Hancock County, County Court Minutes, 1896–1904, in GDAH. Like Columbia, Hancock was an old plantation county, almost three-fourths black in 1900. For similar findings for other Georgia counties, see Engerrand, "'Now Scratch or Die,'" 192–222.

records concerning prisoners held in county chain gangs. In February and March of 1901 the state received reports from eight camps in the eastern piedmont, a center of outmigration. Only 1 of the 187 piedmont prisoners had been convicted of vagrancy; the others had been found guilty of assault and battery, gambling, disorderly conduct, and other crimes.[43] Vagrancy laws were no more effective than anti-enticement or labor-agent laws in tying African Americans to the land.

Contract laws also appear to have given most white landlords little practical control over their laborers. Breaking a contract was on its face a civil rather than a criminal offense, and as Harold Woodman has pointed out, "Winning a civil suit against a propertyless tenant could be a pyrrhic victory."[44] Woodman further notes that "the courts made criminal suits difficult to sustain."[45] True, "criminal surety" laws offered the opportunity to secure labor by paying convicts' fines and requiring labor in recompense, but Georgia's supreme court threw out its criminal-surety statute in 1894.[46] Similarly, after the turn of the century, several states passed statutes intended to criminalize the violation of a contract by a farm tenant; the new laws made the very existence of a contract "presumptive evidence" of criminal fraud when tenants left plantations at midyear. But both the U.S. Supreme Court and some state courts found these laws invalid.[47]

Thus law in general and debt in particular were far less of a coercive force than historians have often portrayed them to be. In planters' records,

---

43. Monthly Reports of the Misdemeanor Chain Gangs, 1898–1901, in GDAH. The reports are for February 1901 from Burke, Elbert, Greene, Wilkes, and Oglethorpe in the piedmont, with the latter two reporting two camps each; and for March 1901 from Hancock in the piedmont. The Elbert and Burke reports did not list crimes of the convicts, but both counties do list crimes on earlier reports, and the pattern is the same. For example, in November of 1899 the Elbert and Burke camps together held fifty-six prisoners, none of whom had been convicted of vagrancy.

44. Woodman, *New South—New Law*, 41–42.

45. *Ibid.*

46. Cohen, *At Freedom's Edge*, 232; Engerrand, "'Now Scratch or Die,'" 136–37.

47. The Supreme Court invalidated an Alabama statute in *Bailey v. Alabama* in 1911; see Daniel, *Shadow of Slavery*, chap. 4. A Georgia law was passed in 1903 and thrown out by the state supreme court in 1911; the Mississippi law of 1900 that "barred a laborer who had broken a contract from entering into a second contract without the permission of the first employer" was struck down in 1913 by Mississippi's courts. See Cohen, *At Freedom's Edge*, 232.

debt plays a role that is both smaller and decidedly more ambiguous than it is in the writings of many historians. In 1880, for example, George Collins of Tunica County wrote that "the negroes are falling behind & there are several on the place from whom I can not collect their accounts & will have most probably to loose it, as they are of the trifling class that will never have anything & Nat [his manager] never ought to have kept them on the place nor have allowed them to run up the bills they have made."[48] High debts were a burdensome mistake, not a boon, to Collins, and they did not help to attach workers to his plantation.

Certainly the planter's or merchant's control over credit was a powerful resource in recruiting labor, as many workers literally could not have survived without "furnish" in the early months of the year, before wage work was widely available. It was the planter and merchant, too, who kept the books. But debt was just one of the many factors, ranging from the current price of cotton to a family's ownership of a mule, affecting the market for labor. As a contemporary analyst, Robert Brooks, noted of piedmont Georgia in 1911, "Negroes frequently get hopelessly in debt to their landlords. In order to extricate themselves they go to a neighboring planter and borrow enough to square up with the creditor, promising to become tenants to the lender and work out the new debt. So great is the competition for laborers that planters take on hands under such circumstances and are glad to get them."[49]

Examples of how planters and African American workers alike tried to work this situation to their advantage in the early years of the twentieth century can be seen in the papers of LeRoy Percy, one of the biggest planters in the Mississippi Delta. In 1905, Norman Hasty, one of his tenants, wanted to work for a different planter. Percy wrote the planter that Hasty had rented 43 acres the previous year, had bought a mule on credit, and now owed Percy a total of $409. Percy was willing to let Hasty settle the debt for $300 in cash or for a wagon and two mules. The cash, no doubt, would come from the new landlord. This was in May, in the full swing of planting season, not at the end of the year.[50] The next year John Williams wanted to move to Percy's place, but another planter had al-

48. George Collins to Anne Collins, December 9, 1880, in Cameron Family Papers.

49. Robert Preston Brooks, "A Local Study of the Race Problem," *Political Science Quarterly*, XXVI (1911), 214.

50. LeRoy Percy to A. S. Sinclair, May 31, 1905, in Percy Family Papers, Mississippi Department of Archives and History [hereinafter cited as MDAH].

ready advanced him moving expenses of almost $30; Percy promised to pay off this debt and also pay the cost of a wagon needed to move Williams to his new house on Percy property.[51] The next year, for another tenant who would come with a mule, Percy offered to pay off a debt of nearly $300.[52]

For Percy and these tenants, debts were, to be sure, liabilities in both the accounting and moral senses, but they were liabilities that could be bought, sold, and traded in the market. Tenants, especially black tenants, were most certainly poor, but they also worked in an economy in which competition for labor was often intense and in which collusion among landowners was anything but easy. As L. K. Salsbury of the Delta & Pine Lands Company put it, "If we had to contend and compete with men who were solvent and good business men—men who make money and prosper—it would not be so hard, but when we have got to compete with concerns that are grabbing the last straw—paying as much as $200.00 for a single family, we have got to be *quick on our feet* and *on our toes* every single minute. These are the kind of men who are setting the example in the Delta and they are the ones we have to follow and compete with for labor. It is not the man who is solvent . . . that sets the price on a family. It is the man who is 'broke' and making his last kick."[53]

It seems, therefore, that we must conclude, along with several recent historians, that peonage was a rather uncommon condition for African American tenants and workers, one that occurred in special circumstances—for example, in the relatively isolated turpentine camps, which attracted the attention of peonage investigators far more often than their importance in the South's economy would suggest.[54] In plantation areas,

51. LeRoy Percy to Herman Wilczinski, December 21, 1906, *ibid.*

52. LeRoy Percy to J. E. Branton, March 6, 1907, *ibid.* See also Percy to John L. Hebron, January 4, 1908, in which he writes that his rule is that "where a negro leaves without anything, I never expect anyone to take up his account, and have never asked for a payment of the account under these circumstances, and where a negro moves on my place without anything I don't pay his account." It should be noted, however, that Hebron apparently disagreed with Percy on this.

53. Financial Records: Minutes: Managers' Meeting, January 20, 1925, in DPL.

54. Daniel, *Shadow of Slavery*, 36–40; Tegeder, "'Onliest Way Out.'" Similarly, Alan Knight has argued that the newer, isolated timber camps and tobacco plantations of Mexico were areas in which coercive forms of labor control—including not only debt peonage, but also vagrancy and convict labor laws—most flourished; elsewhere "peonage" generally rested "upon non-coercive foundations." Knight, "Mexican Peonage," 68–69, 45.

however, as the author of a prize-winning study of labor mobility concluded, "black movement was occurring regardless of laws, court decisions, and even the threat of mob action."[55]

Still, even if it is true that debt peonage was exceptional, rather than typical, for southern farm tenants, it might be argued that the term itself can serve as a useful metaphor for the life of the tenant. Many, perhaps most, southern tenant farmers were poor, in debt, dependent, and had little chance of significant upward mobility. Is not *peon* a good word to summarize such a condition? And correspondingly, if we replace peonage with the idea that labor was mobilized primarily by markets, are we not whitewashing that poverty, dependence, and injustice?

Interestingly enough, a close look at the ways in which historians have used the term *peonage* shows that, in fact, they have more often meant it metaphorically than literally. Pete Daniel is one of the few writers who have carefully restricted its use to cases of forced labor based on debt.[56] Those contemporaries who first diagnosed "peonage" in the New South were mainly concerned with the relationship of farm owners—even large planters—to merchants. Their complaint was that indebtedness generally led to merchant insistence on "overproduction" of cotton, which in their eyes was bad for the South. The problems of the poorest black ten-

55. Cohen, *At Freedom's Edge*, 274; Woodman, *New South, New Law*, 92; Charles L. Flynn, Jr., *White Land, Black Labor: Caste and Class in Late-Nineteenth-Century Georgia* (Baton Rouge, 1983), 109–11. It is notable that some of these conclusions come in the work of authors whose previous research had emphasized coercion and immobility. Compare, for example, Cohen quoted here with Cohen, "Negro Involuntary Servitude in the South, 1865–1940: A Preliminary Analysis," *Journal of Southern History*, XLII (1978), 31–60; and Mandle, *Roots of Black Poverty*, with the same author's *Not Slave, Not Free: The African American Economic Experience* (Durham, N.C., 1992), esp. 23. Economic historians who have criticized the "peonage" argument include Gavin Wright, *Old South, New South: Revolutions in the Southern Economy Since the Civil War* (New York, 1986), 112–15; Price V. Fishback, "Debt Peonage in Postbellum Georgia," *Explorations in Economic History*, XXVI (1989), 219–36; and several of the essays in Gary M. Walton and James F. Sheperds, eds., *Market Institutions and Economic Progress in the New South, 1865–1900: Essays Stimulated by "One Kind of Freedom: The Economic Consequences of Emancipation"* (New York, 1981). Compare also Bauer, "Rural Workers in Spanish America," 62: "Most of the new research [on Mexico] is consistent in its rejection of debt as a controlling feature of labor."

56. However, Daniel in places suggests that "peonage" is but one name for "forced servitude," based on such heterogeneous foundations as contract law, violence, and illiteracy, rather than debt. Pete Daniel, "The Metamorphosis of Slavery, 1865–1900," *Journal of American History*, LXVI (1979), 88–99.

ants were not of much interest to these early writers; if anything, they complained that black labor was already too independent and that planters could best serve the South by supervising them more strictly. For Grady McWhiney and Forrest McDonald, "peonage" stands somewhat vaguely for tenant farming and poverty. Their concern is for the alleged loss of independence by white small farmers and herders in the nonplantation regions of the South. For economists Roger Ransom and Richard Sutch, "peonage" means mainly the ability of merchants to extract high interest payments and intensive cotton production from indebted African American farmers.[57] Thus, "peonage" has served as a kind of floating signifier, applied to the condition of whatever social group the analyst of the moment is most sympathetic toward—white landlords at one time, white small farmers at another, the poorest of African Americans at a third. This variability alone suggests that "peonage" has lost its power as a useful term of analysis.

But there is a more important reason for avoiding the use of "peonage" to characterize economic and social relations in the rural New South. The word itself inevitably summons up images of all-powerful planters ruling servile, dependent sharecroppers by coercion. In doing so, it fundamentally distorts the nature of those relationships, for it not only misrepresents the major sources of planter power, but it also understates both the extent and nature of African Americans' resistance to that power.

On one side of the equation was planter power, backed up by force, but based more importantly on two other foundations. White planters controlled, first, most of the economic resources in a market society, and second, most of the political and legal resources in a racist society. The combination of economic and political power was important, and allows us to see both the similarities and the differences between the condition of the South's rural black labor force and that of the contemporary northern industrial working class.

The similarities, which have been pointed out by historians such as Harold Woodman and Barbara Fields, lay in the fact that planters competed with one another in a largely free market for labor, and that the South's rural workers, lacking property themselves, depended on planters

57. Holmes, "Peons of the South"; Hammond, *Cotton Industry*; Forrest McDonald and Grady McWhiney, "The South from Self-Sufficiency to Peonage: An Interpretation," *American Historical Review*, LXXXV (1980), 1095–1118; Ransom and Sutch, *One Kind of Freedom*, 149–70.

for employment.[58] Like workers in the North, southern blacks lacked property, but also like workers in the North, they did have mobility, and their ability to move to new employers placed important limits on the power of planters to coerce them.

The differences lay in the fact that the rural south as a market society lacked some of the crucial components of what historian Thomas Haskell has called the capitalist "form of life." As Haskell writes, the capitalist marketplace may be "a scene of perpetual struggle," but "contrary to romantic folklore," it is "not a Hobbesian war of all against all. Many holds are barred. Success ordinarily requires not only pugnacity and shrewdness but also restraint." Among those restraints, Haskell argues, are the "'lessons' taught (and simultaneously presupposed) by the market," the first of which "taught people to keep their promises."[59] In the late-nineteenth-century rural South, we may say with admitted oversimplification, the failure of the legal system to enforce even a minimum equality before the law for African Americans meant that white landlords did not, as a rule, have to keep their promises.

This lack of legal restraint, rooted in white control of the political system, meant that African Americans found it far more difficult to organize themselves openly to resist landlord power. Attempts to organize unions were crushed with violence, and black voters had no chance to influence local or state authorities to back them in any confrontations with white economic power.[60]

But far more fundamental was the fact that tenants and laborers could not consistently enforce even the minimal rights they did possess under the law. As Hortense Powdermaker discovered when she arrived in Indianola, Mississippi, in the 1930s, African Americans lacked not just legal and political rights, but also economic rights. "The Middle Ages," she wrote, "had an established system of duties and responsibilities between lords and serfs. But the rules on which the sharecropping system was based

58. Woodman, *New South—New Law*, 104–108; Barbara Jean Fields, "The Advent of Capitalist Agriculture: The New South in a Bourgeois World," in *Essays on the Postbellum Southern Economy*, ed. Thavolia Glymph (College Station, Texas, 1985), 73–94.

59. Thomas L. Haskell, "Capitalism and the Origins of the Humanitarian Sensibility, Part 2," *American Historical Review*, XC (1985), 550–51.

60. For examples of violence used against unions and union organizers, see William H. Harris, *The Harder We Run: Black Workers Since the Civil War* (New York, 1982), 27–28, 33–35.

were broken more often than followed."[61] It would be easy to present almost endless examples of the failure of legal equality, but the consequences
for landlord-tenant relations in much of the southern countryside are summarized with crystal clarity in a 1938 exchange between two Mississippi
Delta planters, the author William Alexander Percy and his friend Oscar
Johnston, coincidentally the successor to L. K. Salsbury as manager of the
Delta & Pine Lands Company. "I have a hunch," Percy wrote to Johnston,
" . . . that you underestimate the amount of dishonesty practiced by landlords in this section in their settlements with their tenants. I am certain
that such dishonesty is wide-spread and disruptive of inter-racial relations,
disintegrating to the planters and conducive to making the tenant distrust
or even hate the white man." Percy went on to suggest that it might be for
the best, "much as I dislike government interference," if the federal government would regulate and monitor the terms of landlord-tenant contracts. The problem, he added, was not the contracts themselves, most of
which were "entirely defensible in theory," but the planters whose dishonesty made the contracts "indefensible in practice."[62]

Johnston accepted the premise, if not the conclusion, of Percy's argument. Although he thought government regulation would be useless, he
admitted that "dishonest practices are widespread, sometimes I fear that
such practices are the rule rather than the exception. Almost daily I have
indisputable evidences of this. This morning enroute from my house to
the office I had a pathetic tale told me by a negro who is moving with us
this year, and who comes literally almost naked, having been stripped of a
few work tools, a few goods and other belongings, under circumstances
which I have ever[y] reason to believe are indefensible." The problem,
which Percy and Johnston were at least willing to acknowledge between
themselves, was not "peonage," but a more insidious kind of injustice. As
Johnston put it, "I once heard a 'planter' say that the most difficult problem he had to solve in connection with his farming operations was to determine the difference between his money and his tenants' money. He

61. Quoted in James C. Cobb, *The Most Southern Place on Earth: The Mississippi Delta
and the Roots of Regional Identity* (New York, 1992), 155.

62. William Alexander Percy to Oscar Johnston, November 8, 1938, in Oscar Johnston
General Correspondence, DPL. Percy was the son of the LeRoy Percy earlier mentioned
and was the author of the minor classic *Lanterns on the Levee: Recollections of a Planter's Son*
(New York, 1941).

frequently found it impossible to make the distinction, and I fear usually erred in his own favor."[63] Black folklore put the case just as clearly in its own way, as in the story of the black man and the white man who simultaneously came across two boxes at a crossroads. The black man ran to the biggest one, which turned out to be filled with hoes and shovels. The white man claimed the smaller one, which contained the pencils and paper that whites have used ever after to control the men with the hoes.[64]

The central issue was not peonage, but that whites had it in their power to grant or to withhold the justice that should have been the indisputable right of every African American. Some white lawyers, judges, and jury members were honest men and upheld the integrity of their legal system with fair verdicts, if only to reassure themselves that they were, indeed, honest men.[65] Yet even in the best of cases, most blacks could expect little from the expensive and cumbersome courts when planters "erred in their own favor" in weighing the cotton and adding up the interest rates. Nastier planters could simply juggle the books, or even resort to violence, with scant probability of legal liability.

The occasional egregious cases of true agricultural peonage resulted not from the normal operation of the law, but from its perversion and corruption. One example occurred in Oglethorpe County, Georgia, which the U.S. district attorney in Atlanta considered the "the center and hotbed of this Peonage System" in the early twentieth century.[66] He believed the key violator in the county was James M. Smith, owner of the largest plantation in the state, who had "become a multi-millionaire by the employment of convict labor on his vast estate and by some strange process,

63. Johnston to Alexander, November 10, 1938, *ibid.*

64. Cobb, *Most Southern Place,* 155.

65. See instances cited in Woodman, *New South—New Law,* 82–85; Pete Daniel, "The Legal Basis of Agrarian Capitalism: The South Since 1933," in *Race and Class in the American South Since 1890,* ed. Melvyn Stokes and Rick Halpern (Oxford, Eng., 1994). See also below.

66. E. A. Angier, Atlanta, to Attorney General, July 30, 1903, in Pete Daniel, ed., *Peonage Files of the U.S. Department of Justice* (microfilm edition, Frederick, Md., 1988–), reel 1, frame 598. Oglethorpe's reputation for peonage was widespread. The editor of its own weekly paper in 1881 complained that planters were reducing blacks to "involuntary servitude" by threatening prosecution for minor offenses and paying bonds for the accused: Oglethorpe *Echo,* March 18, 1881. See also W. E. B. DuBois, *The Negro Landholder of Georgia,* U.S. Department of Labor Bulletin No. 35 (1901), 750.

converting free labor into convict labor." Others in the area, the district attorney maintained, were merely Smith's "cheap imitators."[67]

The key to Smith's "strange process" was his local political power. He had launched his political career during Reconstruction by serving as one of fifty "deputy sheriffs" mobilized to repress the black vote in Oglethorpe County in 1870. He had represented the county in the state house of representatives and senate, and by the 1890s "ruled" its politics. After giving up his elected offices he continued to be a member, and often the chairman, of the county Democratic Party's executive committee. He served frequently on the grand jury, "invariably" sitting as chairman when he did so. He was on the county commission that revised the jury lists. Smith donated or loaned money to individuals and to local churches and schools, was a director of the local bank, and bought controlling interest in the largest nearby daily newspaper. The reporter for the county weekly in Oglethorpe, according to Smith's biographer, served in effect as his publicity agent.[68]

With this combination of wealth and political influence, Smith built up a gigantic planting operation, in part by landing contracts to lease county and state convicts. These workers were in effect slaves, whose exploitation was authorized by the clause of the Thirteenth Amendment allowing forced labor as "punishment for crime." Workers like these could still be driven by overseers with whip in hand; a friendly reporter from a neighboring county noted one gang of sixty hands, many in chains, hoeing "faster than we have ever seen before."[69]

Smith's political influence was surely also crucial in his control of the numerous "free labor" hands and sharecroppers on his place. In one case that we can trace in the records of the U.S. Department of Justice, Smith purchased the contract of a man convicted in a neighboring county of illegally selling liquor. When this man's contracted time was up, in mid-July, he left Smith's plantation. Within days Smith's bookkeeper swore before a friendly justice of the peace that the man had been "gambling" and "carrying a concealed weapon," and a month later he had been ar-

67. E. A. Angier to Attorney General, December 3, 1903, in Daniel, ed., *Peonage Files*, reel 1, frame 657.

68. E. Merton Coulter, *James Monroe Smith, Georgia Planter, Before Death and After* (Athens, Ga., 1961), 93–100, 150–63. It should be noted that Coulter's is a highly admiring biography.

69. Greensboro (Ga.) *Herald-Journal*, September 14, 1894.

rested, convicted, and returned to Smith's fields.[70] Smith's operation mightily impressed a young Georgia visitor who would later remember it, rather fondly, as a model of a well-run plantation based on coerced labor; the visitor's name was Ulrich B. Phillips.[71]

Very few planters could wield the kind of political influence Smith did, but more could try simple violence to control their workers. Although my reading of the evidence leads me to believe that violence was not a customary part of the labor market—in part because it could easily lead to losing rather than keeping labor—there is no question that it was a potential part of it. To cite one example, planter J. N. Johnson of Mississippi wrote to LeRoy Percy's overseer in 1906 about a former tenant who had moved to Percy's property. "I have learned that you have a negro General Joyce on your land . . . Id like to know if there is any chance of my getting what he owes me—and if there is no chance to get it in money, I'd like to know if he is any where in your neighborhood, and I'll take it in the other currency that will be worth something to him." The threat of a beating is obvious. Percy refused to allow Johnson on his property, but we can scarcely doubt that Johnson had beaten tenants before this.[72] In Elbert County, Georgia, in May of 1901, Tom McClanahan, a white planter, went in search of one of his tenants, Robert Smith, who had left him to work on another plantation. When "the negro showed fight," McClanahan shot him.[73] A planter in the Mississippi Delta told the story of a tenant he had caught trying to sneak away. "Whipped him till he couldn't stand up," the planter said. "Thought that would hold him for a while. . . . He couldn't stand up when I got through with him."[74] Most planters could safely assume that they would never be prosecuted for such crimes.

As strong as it could become in abusive cases, the planters' power was far from absolute, and not only because it required a flouting of the law.

70. Mentha Morrison, "Col.," Lavonia, Ga., to "Mr. President," October 22, 1903, in *Peonage Files*, reel 1, frames 610–11; C. D. Camp to E. A. Angier, November 28, 1903, *ibid.*, frames 642–54.

71. Ulrich B. Phillips, "Plantations with Slave Labor and Free," *American Historical Review*, XXX (1925), 738–53. Phillips, of course, became his generation's leading historian of slavery in the United States, and he interpreted it as a rather benevolent institution.

72. J. N. Johnson to McPeak [Percy's overseer], April 27, 1906, LeRoy Percy to J. N. Johnson, May 25, 1906, both in Percy Family Papers, MDAH.

73. Elberton (Ga.) *Star*, May 2, 1901. Smith was apparently not killed.

74. Quoted in Cobb, *Most Southern Place*, 104–105.

African Americans did not passively accept their subordinate position. Lacking public power, they responded with what the anthropologist James Scott has aptly termed the "weapons of the weak"—"cautious resistance and calculated conformity" that manifested themselves in many ways and that formed the other side of the equation of power in the countryside.[75] This resistance is another important reason to reject "peonage," with its connotations of helplessness and servility, as a proper description of planter-tenant relations.

The resistance itself started with the same courts that usually denied justice to African Americans. Despite the received wisdom that blacks would never use the courts or lawyers, it is clear that many did. A federal investigation of James M. Smith's plantation was touched off by a letter from a convict's wife to none other than Theodore Roosevelt. Other cases began with complaints to a district attorney from black victims, their wives, or their parents.[76] Local courts might on occasion be sources of protection for black workers, especially if they could find white patrons or allies. In Greene County, Georgia, in 1893, for example, a "prominent" planter named Alec O'Neal was charged with buying unginned cotton after dark from Jim Armstrong, an African American farmer. After separate trials that "excited considerable interest," both O'Neal and Armstrong were acquitted.[77]

75. James Scott, *Weapons of the Weak: Everyday Forms of Peasant Resistance* (New Haven, 1992). For an analysis of urban African Americans that draws on Scott's work, see Robin D. G. Kelley, "'We Are Not What We Seem': Rethinking Black Working-Class Opposition in the Jim Crow South," *Journal of American History*, LXXX (1993), 75–112. A full accounting of such resistance would include a wider range of behavior than can be discussed here. As Scott says of the Malaysian village he worked in, "The struggle between rich and poor in Sedaka is not merely a struggle over work, property rights, grain, and cash. It is also a struggle over the appropriation of symbols, a struggle over how the past and present shall be understood and labeled, a struggle to identify causes and assess blame, a contentious effort to give partisan meaning to local history. The details of this struggle are not pretty, as they entail backbiting, gossip, character assassination, rude nicknames, gestures, and silences of contempt which, for the most part, are confined to the backstage of village life. In public life—that is to say, in power-laden settings—a carefully calculated conformity prevails for the most part" (p. xvii).

76. See n70 above and Daniel, ed., *Peonage Files, passim;* for another example, see Bryant, *How Curious a Land,* 158.

77. Greensboro (Ga.) *Herald-Journal,* April 28, 1893. The paper's report did not explicitly link the two trials, which occurred on the same day. Similarly, Columbia County's Superior Court in 1902 and 1903 saw a single prosecution for "enticing away a cropper" and

Most blacks, most of the time, however, could not count on courts to protect them from abuses of white power. Their resistance was necessarily more informal and hidden. Like slaves of earlier generations, sharecroppers who felt cheated or who stared out at a failing crop had their own ways of trying to even the odds a bit. The complaints of many whites that black sharecroppers were too "improvident" or "lazy" may not have been mere racism; why should a tenant convinced he had no chance of breaking even for the year put out extra effort or try to avoid high charges at the local store? Or why not sneak off to work in "somebody else's cotton patch" when demand and wages were high? By the early years of the twentieth century, James M. Smith himself was complaining bitterly about what he called "the new generation of Negroes . . . who had few of the graces and none of the dependability of their forebears." He claimed to see this decline not only in instances of gambling, drinking, and carrying concealed weapons, but also in stealing of tools and hogs and in nighttime thefts from the fields of corn and cotton. Worse still, according to Smith, he had lost $150,000 as a result of suspicious fires. His promises of rewards of $500 had uncovered no culprits.[78]

Even raw violence, although rarely checked by the courts, had its limitations. For one thing, violence might be counterproductive for the planter seeking labor. The Delta planter who had whipped his tenant discovered that "the next morning he was gone. Never got a trace of him. I'd sure like to know how he got off."[79] As LeRoy Percy told one of his own managers, "I just drop you a line to say that I know the report has been circulated among the negroes that you are rather rough with labor, and this is being used for the purpose of keeping hands from going to Tralake. I simply mention this so that you may be on your guard. A difficulty at

---

one for buying seed (*i.e.*, unginned) cotton; the defendant in the first case was not indicted; in the second, found not guilty. Columbia County Superior Court Minutes, 1897–1908, microfilm in GDAH. For the difficulty of using local courts to repress blacks in Reconstruction Mississippi, see Christopher Waldrep, "Substituting Law for the Lash: Emancipation and Legal Formalism in a Mississippi County Court," *Journal of American History*, LXXXII (1996), 1425–51.

78. Coulter, *James Monroe Smith*, 48–49. See also Albert C. Smith, "'Southern Violence' Reconsidered: Arson as Protest in Black-Belt Georgia, 1865–1910," *Journal of Southern History*, LI (1985), 527–64.

79. Cobb, *Most Southern Place*, 104–105; see also *ibid.*, 107, for the story of LeRoy Allen, a plantation manager who had difficulty getting labor when he was mistaken for a brutal employer with a reputation for "resorting to the lash."

this time with any of them would be fatal to filling the place up. . . . No matter what provocation is given, if you can do so decently, don't have trouble with them at present."[80]

Moreover, the threat of violence was never a one-way proposition, whatever the fearful price that might be paid by any black man or woman who attacked a white person. In piedmont Georgia's "exodus" of 1899–1900, one bailiff sent to serve a warrant on a tenant who had allegedly skipped out on his contract was shot to death.[81] When a Greenwood, Mississippi, merchant, Gus Aron, "upbraided" Dennis Martin by "lightly slapping the negro on the face" for making too much noise, Martin drew a pistol and shot him dead.[82] A visitor to the Delta from South Carolina wrote in 1905 that "every white man here virtually carries his life in his hands for it is a place where the long arm of the law does not reach. If a white man gets into trouble with a negro he has got to shoot and shoot quick or get shot. Everybody carries a gun however contrary to the laws of the state it may be and is always in a state of preparedness."[83]

Ultimately, the mobility of black labor itself was one of the most important limitations to landlord power. Clearly, dissatisfaction with landlords was a major source of high annual plantation turnover. As one Warren County, Mississippi, resident explained his "movin'," "I'se been cheated outen my rights, short weighted at de gin, short weighted at de store on de place and my account has been tampered wid. I can't read nor write but I made a mark every time I bought something but de man at de store on de place out marked me, my old 'oman and nine children worked and went naked all of de year. . . . I am lighting a shuck off of dis place."[84]

L. K. Salsbury, with whom I began this essay, recognized that "without labor, it is impossible [to] make a crop of cotton." He drew the conclusion that "a manager's job is a great deal like that of a politician. The politician who does not play politics the entire time and keep his fences up is never a success."[85] Salsbury here half recognized a basic reality about the

---

80. LeRoy Percy to J. B. Ray, December 26, 1906, in Percy Family Papers, MDAH. Percy added that once the overseer got the plantation running properly for the year, it would be safer for him to resent "provocation."

81. Holmes, "Labor Agents," 441.

82. New Orleans *Daily Picayune*, December 8, 1890.

83. Cobb, *Most Southern Place*, 126.

84. Quoted in Cobb, *Most Southern Place*, 106.

85. Financial Records: Minutes: Managers Meeting, October 21, 1921, in DPL.

Jim Crow South: after the final suppression of the black vote, the politics of race and class in the rural South did not disappear; it moved from the courthouses and ballot boxes to the fields and cabins of white-owned plantations. The mobility of African Americans was not only real, but perhaps the single most important weapon they had in their struggle. This struggle, often silent and hidden, is ultimately obscured when we mistakenly see African Americans in the New South as mere peons.[86]

86. Historians of rural labor in Mexico and Latin America have made a similar point. See Bauer, "Rural Workers in Spanish America," and Knight, "Mexican Peonage."

II

Social Groups and Attitudes

SALLY G. MCMILLEN

Southern Women and the Sunday-School Movement, 1865–1915

I believe eternity will reveal triumphs of earnest womanhood in the Sabbath School work which will astonish the universe," Baptist minister Lansing Burrows proclaimed in 1872. "I believe the Sabbath school work of some patient women . . . will cover them with a shining glory such as they nor we have ever dreamed of." In his series of sermons defining the role of Christian women, Burrows identified Sunday-school teaching as a means to give modern women an elevated position in the church. Although females could never occupy the pulpit, they still could play an important role in the church by patiently nurturing and educating youngsters and guiding them toward conversion and salvation. In the quiet of the Sunday classroom, women would excel. In fact, it seemed that God had offered a gift to Christian women with the creation of the Sunday school, for they could finally achieve their full potential. Southern women now had "a glorious opportunity" to play a significant role in the church.[1]

Burrows was but one of many evangelicals who celebrated female participation in the Sunday school, an institution that became an important arm of most southern denominations by the late nineteenth century. The

---

1. Reverend Lansing Burrows, "Priscilla," Sermon No. 160, August 1872, in Lansing Burrows Personal Papers, E. C. Dargan Research Library, Sunday School Board of the Southern Baptist Convention, Nashville [hereinafter cited as SSBSBC].

schools added a new dimension to women's duties; not only could mothers influence their children in the home, but they could teach youngsters in the Sunday classroom as well. These dual responsibilities, many observers claimed, gave women enormous power to uplift and save the next generation. In addition, female pupils who attended would become more pious and purposeful under such guidance, and as adults, become devoted mothers and active participants in church and Sunday school.

This essay will explore women's roles and gender concerns in the southern Sunday-school movement in seven of the South's largest denominations. Female involvement as Christian mothers and Sunday instructors created a paradox, as is often the case in women's experiences. Defined within a limited domestic circle and excluded from most leadership positions in the Sunday school and church, southern females nevertheless guaranteed the success of this Christian enterprise. In the Sabbath classroom, women displayed skill, energy, imagination, brains, and talent. Here they taught, wrote, competed, organized, managed, created, and even petitioned. As Sunday-school pupils, females attended in far greater numbers than did males. And although educated middle-class white women may have predominated, the variety of women involved in the southern Sunday-school movement was striking.[2]

Benevolent institutions and reform efforts are often associated with the middle class, but the southern Sunday school was different. It touched the lives of rich and poor alike, as evidenced by its importance in churches throughout the South. Sabbath classes were ubiquitous; they served all southerners, rich and poor, urban and rural, black and white, young and old. They could be found in cities, villages, and farm and mountain communities and accounted for much of the growth of most southern denominations. Their appeal to the South's plain folk is most apparent in the Southern Baptist and National Baptist Conventions,

---

2. The seven denominations discussed here include the National Baptist Convention, the Southern Baptist Convention, the Presbyterian Church of the U.S., the African Methodist Episcopal Church, the Colored Methodist Church, the African Methodist Episcopal Zion Church, and the Methodist Episcopal Church, South. Page Putnam Miller draws a similar conclusion in studying three women in the early national period who engaged in Sunday-school work, though her women occupied "leadership" roles. See Miller, "Women in the Vanguard of the Sunday School Movement," *Journal of Presbyterian History*, LVIII (Winter, 1980), 311–25. Throughout the research for this paper, one is reminded of how few denominational and church histories focus attention on women.

which evidenced major increases in new Sunday schools and church members. Black and white southern Methodists were not far behind. What is remarkable is the universal appeal of the Sunday school. Southerners did not identify it as an institution to serve only a select class of people. Rather, women from all walks of life participated. As Sunday-school teachers, many found a means to uplift the region's young and to serve God; as pupils, they relished their weekly engagement in Sunday-school activities.[3]

Sunday schools found a receptive audience in the post–Civil War South. That conflict's by-products—physical devastation, poverty, and social and economic upheaval—made the region's youngsters ripe for Christian uplift. Many southerners had long practiced their Protestant faith, but the Sunday school held special promise to evangelicals after the war. Southerners needed to believe in a better future. An enterprise that focused on educating and saving the young, the Sunday school was the place where youthful minds could absorb Christian and moral lessons and seek God. Whites hoped that all youngsters would join a church, learn to live by God's word, adopt middle-class values, and achieve salvation. Former slaves, with little more than their freedom and faith in 1865, faced poverty, debt, racism, and violence; the church played an important role in offering hope that their daily struggles would eventually reap rewards. By attending Sunday school, religious leaders argued, black youngsters could acquire respectability and good manners, become devout Christians, and embrace racial pride. By promising to nurture, educate, and save the region's next generation, the Sunday school promised a far brighter future for every southerner. Regeneration of the region and its people seemed assured if youngsters attended Sabbath classes.[4]

The Sunday school expanded rapidly during the latter part of the nineteenth century; this episode of church history is often called the "Sunday School Movement." The South proved an especially attractive area for northern and southern evangelicals to spread their Christian message and promise of uplift. Hundreds of northern missionaries, representing such

3. Because sources do not identify the background of those participating in the Sunday school, it is impossible not to lump rich and poor alike in drawing conclusions about this institution.

4. For an exploration on the importance of Victorian values, see Gertrude Himmelfarb, *The De-Moralization of Society: From Victorian Virtues to Modern Values* (New York, 1995), 4–27, 78.

organizations as the American Sunday School Union, the American Baptist Publication Society, and the American Bible Society, and such denominations as the African Methodist Episcopal Church and the Presbyterian Church of the United States, came South to promote and organize Sunday schools. Missionaries and colporteurs distributed and sold Bibles and instructional materials and founded hundreds of churches and Sunday schools. Many southerners welcomed these enterprises, eager to have their children enter God's realm. Classes were formed for the privileged and for the economically destitute. Pupils memorized Scripture and biblical truths, absorbed lessons on piety and proper behavior, and—among the poor, both black and white—often learned how to read and write.[5]

Southern denominations became interested in the institution and gradually dedicated more resources and personnel to founding Sunday schools in their own name. They established Sunday-school boards and, by the turn of the century, organized their own publishing firms to produce Sunday-school literature. In these Sunday classes, children could learn church doctrine and use the literature produced by their own denominational publishing house. With some 75 to 85 percent of all new church members coming from the Sunday school, evangelicals rightly identified it as the most successful means to attract potential converts and influence young minds. Volunteer teachers could school the young in denominational tenets, gain each child's lifelong loyalty, and ultimately strengthen and extend the power of the church through expanded membership and larger donations.

As Reverend Burrows had observed, the Sunday school was especially attractive to women. Whether he was responding to their active participation as pupils and instructors, engaging in hyperbole to attract more

5. For a history of the Sunday school in this country, see Henry Frederick Cope, *The Evolution of the Sunday School* (New York, 1911); Robert A. Crandall, *The Sunday School as Institutional Agency for Religious Instruction in American Protestantism, 1872–1922* (Terre Haute, Ind., 1977); Robert W. Lynn and Elliott Wright, *The Big Little School: Two Hundred Years of the Sunday School* (2d ed.; Birmingham, Ala., 1980); Lynn E. May, "The Sunday-School: A Two-Hundred-Year Heritage," *Baptist History and Heritage,* XV (1980), 3–11; Jack L. Seymour, *From Sunday School to Church School; Continuities in Protestant Church Education in the United States, 1860–1929* (Washington, D.C., 1982); and Anne M. Boylan, *Sunday School: The Formation of an American Institution, 1790–1880* (New Haven, 1988). For information on Sunday schools and their impact on teaching reading and writing, see James D. Anderson, *The Education of Blacks in the South, 1860–1935* (Chapel Hill, 1988).

volunteers, or just reminding women of their assigned role is not clear. Perhaps it was a bit of all three. But certainly Burrows accurately identified the Sunday school as an appealing place for southern females. All sources—including contemporary observers, class lists and reports, and statistics and surveys—indicate that by the turn of the century, females formed the majority of Sunday-school teachers and pupils and played a significant role in the institution's success. As Tennessee Baptists proclaimed, "Woman is our most successful power in the Sunday school work."[6]

Women's majority status in the Sunday school is understandable. Southern women filled the churches each Sunday morning and made up the majority of members in southern denominations. But there were other reasons for their visibility in Sunday schools. Teaching there seemed a natural extension of women's maternal, pious nature. For women accustomed to being confined to the home, the Sunday school offered a sphere in which to spread their influence and develop a sense of community. Writers of Sunday-school papers and advice literature repeatedly promoted women's patient and loving nature as perfectly suited to teach Sunday school. "As a rule," stated one Baptist, women were "more faithful as teachers—not so hard to manage as male teachers." Allegedly, a woman's gentle touch and loving heart were especially effective in winning children to Christ, since in the Sunday classroom, children learned to worship and adore God. Thus, according to church leaders, a female's tender and compassionate nature, rather than a man's superior mind, made her a more suitable Sunday-school instructor. Sunday-school tales often emphasized that the best Sunday school teacher was not the individual who knew more, but the one who loved more. In promoting heart over head, who could better convey this lesson than a female?[7]

Despite the fact that church leaders heralded women as better suited to teach in the Sunday school, men organized and ran the institution. In the first half century of the movement, southern women rarely achieved an official, paid position in the upper reaches of the denominational hier-

6. "Woman's Work," *Minutes of the 15th Annual Proceedings of the Tennessee Baptist Convention, 1889* (Nashville, 1889), 37.

7. "The Influence of Women in the Church," *Working Christian*, n.s., III (November 11, 1880), 2. On the concept of heart over head, see "Best Sunday School Teacher," *Children's Friend*, VIII (July 19, 1873), 56, and "A Thought for Teachers," *Earnest Worker*, I (November 17, 1870), 48.

archy. Sometimes women rose to become secretary of a Sunday-school union or editor of publications aimed at primary pupils; these were roles that apparently fitted their feminine nature. Invariably, though, men managed Sunday-school boards and publishing departments and served as colporteurs, superintendents, and missionaries. A few northern women like Joanna Moore worked as Sunday-school missionaries, spending years in the South, spreading God's word, ministering to families, and opening Sunday schools for destitute whites and blacks. For southern women, this path to Christian outreach was all but closed. When Mrs. Della Deupru, who had founded a successful Sunday school in her hometown of Bear Brooks, Mississippi, boldly wrote the secretary of the Southern Baptist Convention's Sunday School Board and asked to be appointed an official colporteur to black children in her region, her request was denied. Typically, churches and missionary organizations hired men to tramp through an assigned area, traveling thousands of miles annually to organize Sunday schools. The conventional thinking was that southern women were not suited for such demanding, exhausting tasks and that their benevolent work was best done on a local level.[8]

Notwithstanding their absence from leadership positions, southern women were active in organizing local Sunday schools. Black and white women reacted spontaneously to perceived needs and a desire to do good to ensure that all children gained exposure to God's word. Even as southern denominations in the late nineteenth century began to form bureaucratic structures to oversee their work and systematize Sunday-school organization, many southern women worked behind the scenes, without official sanction or a paycheck. Hundreds, perhaps thousands, of them acted on their own and founded Sunday schools, seeing no need for denominational sanction. They often paid little heed to the reams of advice books and outlines that insisted on a systematic approach to Sunday-school organization. As traditional caretakers imbued with deep concern for youngsters' piety and salvation, southern women responded naturally and took the matter in hand.[9]

8. Joanna P. Moore, *In Christ's Stead: Autobiographical Sketches* (Chicago, 1902), and Mrs. Della Deupru to James Marion Frost, *ca.* 1898, in Frost-Bell Correspondence, SSB-SBC. See also Evelyn Brooks Higginbotham, *Righteous Discontent: The Women's Movement in the Black Baptist Church, 1880–1920* (Cambridge, Mass., 1993), 97–102.

9. See Miller, "Women in the Vanguard," 316, 320. Higginbotham argues that African American women were the principal conveyors of culture. The women she studies in the

Women's efforts to organize Sunday schools were often rather informal and frequently were directed at the South's neediest youngsters. Women might invite poor children into their homes or gather them under a tree or arbor to read Bible stories and Scripture and instill moral lessons. Mrs. Jenkins of Caton's Grove, Tennessee, formed a Sunday school in her home for some forty impoverished youngsters; she taught the class and recruited her husband to serve as superintendent. Near Black Mountain, North Carolina, a woman gathered several dozen poor children into her home, supplied them with shoes and clothes, and formed a thriving Sunday-school class. A young woman opened a school in a region of Texas where no sermon had been preached for forty years; beginning with three pupils, her Sunday school soon attracted more than forty children. Not only did she successfully teach them Christian ideals, but "the keeper of a grog-shop (or doggery) in the vicinity of the Sunday school" had also "been induced to abandon his business and engage in farming," noted a pleased observer. Thirteen-year-old Esther Trevino of San Antonio formed a missionary Sunday school for Mexican children and set about raising money to purchase chairs for her classroom. At the Log Cabin community outside Atlanta, women organized a union Sunday school; residents insisted that all children become good Christians. As Mrs. O. B. Logan, one of the founders, noted, "I knew it would never do to raise our children without the influence of a Sunday school." Community residents obviously agreed; they raised money to support the school and in a few years erected a new building for it.[10]

Over time, women's efforts to establish Sunday schools became less random and more systematic, especially with the formation of women's home missionary societies and a desire to reach more of the region's destitute. The Methodist Episcopal Church, South, for example, formed a

National Baptist Convention promoted middle-class ideals, hoping to uplift the race and gain the respect of whites. See Higginbotham, *Righteous Discontent,* 185–94.

　10. Mrs. Jenkins reported by W. B. Graves, December 24, 1870, and the Black Mountain woman noted by G. S. Jones, June 19, 1869, both to American Sunday School Union [hereinafter cited as ASSU] secretary M. A. Wurts, in ASSU Correspondence, Presbyterian Historical Society, Philadelphia [hereinafter cited as PHS]; "Sunday School Intelligence," *Earnest Worker,* II (November 23, 1871), 61; Reverend E. Trevino, "In the San Marcos Field," *Missionary Survey,* IV (March 1914), 188; and "Log Cabin Community Sunday School: Memories of Twenty-five Years," 1937, in Special Collections Department, Robert W. Woodruff Library, Emory University, Atlanta [hereinafter cited as Emory].

Woman's Home Missionary Board in 1886, and its women took the ini-
tiative in establishing Sunday schools in both rural areas and inner cities.
Sometimes these classes were associated with a settlement house, such as
those in Birmingham and Dallas that welcomed the urban poor. A Sunday school started by Mrs. J. W. Wallis at Birmingham's settlement house
attracted local mill girls. Some twenty young women enrolled initially;
the number soon expanded to seventy, and Wallis had to rent a vacant
store to house her thriving class. Many women saw their work among
children of the poor as especially critical, for the assumption was that parents of such destitute families rarely conducted prayers or offered Christian education in the home. The Sunday school had to fill this perceived
void.[11]

Women took bold steps to ensure the success of their school or a class
they taught. Many pupils could not afford Sunday-school lesson books or
children's magazines, and struggling schools could not purchase books and
aids needed to teach basic lessons. It was important to address such concerns, even if that meant writing to a stranger or exposing one's own limited education. Southern women took up pen (or pencil) and sought
help, scarcely thinking twice before requesting assistance and free materials from a denominational Sunday-school board or publishing house.
Their pleas generally were effective. In fact, southern women seemed emboldened by the task; youthful Christian souls were too important to lose
at such a vulnerable stage. And although female letter writers often
adopted a supplicating tone to a male superior, their message was nonetheless persuasive.

For instance, requests for assistance inundated the desk of the secretary
of the Southern Baptist Sunday School Board. Hundreds of letters from
mothers and female Sunday-school teachers sought advice on Sunday-
school work and requested free Bibles, hymn books, magazines, and even
financial aid. Mrs. Deupru, whose Sunday school had twenty-four "eager"
students, wrote the board, requesting Bibles and Sunday-school literature.
Mrs. James Day of Durham, North Carolina, asked for a dozen Bibles for

11. Mrs. J. W. Wallis, "City Missions," and Estelle Haskin, "Dallas, Tex., Settlement
House," both in *18th Annual Report of the Woman's Home Missionary Society of the Methodist
Episcopal Church, South* (Nashville, 1904), 44. See also Frances Morton, "What Brought Us
Together: The Women's Home Missionary Movement in Atlanta, 1880–1920," (Kelley
Honors Thesis, 1993, in College Archives, E. H. Little Library, Davidson College, David-
son, North Carolina).

the mill girls she taught. Sarah McCann Elmore sought advice on how to conduct Children's Day, a special Sunday-school celebration that was un-familiar to her. A barely literate Mrs. Mattie Moran of Michigan City, Mississippi, wrote her "kind breathering, beging for a little help" for her "littel church only a hule of a house." She requested Bibles and a half dozen hymn books for church members and Sunday-school pupils. Miss Wallie Morgan adopted a successful approach used by several women. In requesting financial support for her Morgansville, Kentucky, Sunday-school library, Morgan mentioned that a rival organization, the American Baptist Publication Society, had already donated $10 to her enterprise, and she hoped that the board would emulate, if not surpass, this "noble example." From Bay Ridge, Florida, Mrs. E. J. Morris managed to slip into her letter the fact that her Baptist Sunday school was purchasing Methodist literature. Not surprisingly, these requests yielded positive re-sponses, as did most that came across the secretary's desk.[12]

Women also wrote to set things right or issue a complaint. Miss Annie Hays was furious when she discovered that black adolescents could not join two Baptist youth organizations, the Baracas and the Philatheas, nor could they purchase the organizations' membership pins. After rereading each organization's charter, Hays complained to a Baraca officer in North Carolina, charging that such behavior was un-Christian and indicated that "Jim Crowism" had now infiltrated the church. Ten-year-old Mar-garet Dudley Reynolds of Rendalia, Alabama, wrote Baptist Sunday School secretary James Frost to correct an error in his tract "Our Bible." From Madison, Florida, Mrs. Mary Crockett returned copies of *Child's Gem* to the Baptist Sunday School Board because the lessons inside were missing entire verses. Such sloppy editing "dismayed" Crockett and insulted her pupils, "bright boys with immortal souls," who could read.[13]

12. Mrs. Della Deupru to James Marion Frost, *ca.* 1898; Mrs. James Day to Frost, Sep-tember 21, 1897; Sarah McCann Elmore [Mrs. H. L. Elmore] to Frost, August 7, 1897; Mrs. Mattie S. Moran to the Baptist Sunday School Board, October 22, 1897; Miss Wallie M. Morgan to the Southern Baptist Publishing Board, September 16, 1897; and Mrs. E. J. Morris to Frost, June 13, 1898, all in Frost-Bell Correspondence, SSBSBC.

13. Annie Hayes to Robert Nirwana Simms, n.d., in Robert Nirwana Simms Collec-tion, Manuscript Collection, William R. Perkins Library, Duke University, Durham, North Carolina [hereinafter cited as DU]; Margaret Dudley Reynolds to Dr. Frost, September 18, 1898, and Mrs. Mary Crockett to the Southern Baptist Sunday School Board, February 7, 1898, both in Frost-Bell Correspondence, SSBSBC. Simms was vice-president of the na-tional Baracas and started the Baraca movement in North Carolina.

Even though they founded and supported Sunday schools, southern
women rarely had charge of an entire school. White females who became
supervisors were unusual enough to elicit special comment. Alice Hamilton, who attended a Sunday school in North Carolina's Blue Ridge Mountains, mentioned its female superintendent. A woman might occupy the
post temporarily in her husband's absence. The Reverend Levi Pigott, an
itinerant Methodist minister, allowed his wife to oversee his Sunday school
while he traveled the circuit. In other instances, the lack of a male volunteer led to the appointment of a female. Two women in Greensboro,
North Carolina, became Sunday-school superintendents when no men
could be found to fill the posts. In a few instances, church members preferred a female. As a representative of the Presbyterian Woman's Board of
Home Missions to the southern highlands, Frances Louisa Goodrich
found herself elected Sunday-school superintendent when mountain
residents could not agree on one of two male candidates. During the
debate over filling the post, a man in the audience nominated Goodrich,
explaining that as a "woman's suffrage man," he favored "having a lady."
Her election apparently saved the day; her acceptance speech received a
warm ovation, and she happily assumed her new duties.[14]

If southern white Sunday-school advisers discouraged women from aspiring to this managerial post, no one claimed that women lacked the
brains or talent to handle the job. Concerns focused instead on women's
perceived character and delicate nature. James Axtell, author of several
Methodist Sunday-school advice manuals, insisted that men made better
supervisors than women because of the "onerous character of the duties,
which is sometimes a severe tax on one's personal strength." Women
should not get caught in the fray of managing and supervising an entire
school. Another concern, largely unspoken, was that men were held in
greater esteem. As a relatively new institution seeking acceptance and a
legitimate place in the church, the Sunday school needed the authority

14. Alice McGuire Hamilton, *Blue Ridge Mountain Memories: The True Story of a Mountain Girl at the Turn of the Century* (Atlanta, 1977), 67; Levi Woodbury Pigott, *Scenes and
Incidents in the Life of a Home Missionary, With a Biographical Sketch of Fenner S. Pigott* (Norfolk, 1901), 28; Frances Louisa Goodrich Diary, November 4, 1892, in Frances Louisa
Goodrich Papers, DU. Goodrich was the founder of Allanstand School and Allanstand
Cottage Industries, and she had significant influence on the southern arts and crafts movement. One should remember that women rarely served as superintendents or principals of
public schools.

that males lent the enterprise. Also, men could deal with the minister on an equal plane. Finally, advisers noted that men could effectively discipline unruly students. Yet Axtell had to admit that when given the opportunity, women made excellent supervisors. "Observation goes to show that in the comparatively few instances in which women are working as superintendents, their success is of a higher order than that of the other sex," he confessed. He suggested a compromise: appoint females as assistant supervisors. One white woman who held such a position, Mrs. Lilly Morehead of Leaksville, North Carolina, organized and ran a successful Sunday school. She had two hundred pupils and kept the school open year round. Everyone credited her, rather than her male supervisor, with its success, "for she is doing nearly all the work."[15]

Race affected gender when it came to running a Sunday school. As district and conference reports, Sunday-school class lists, and comments in Sunday-school newspapers indicate, black women were more likely than white women to supervise a school. AME church doctrine tried to clarify the matter by suggesting that all its Sunday schools appoint two supervisors, one male and one female. The man would have ultimate authority, and the woman would oversee female pupils and teachers. Whatever the dictates, by the turn of the century black women seem to have been supervising a number of Sunday schools. Mary Ann Kirkman noted that her mother was superintendent of her AME Sunday school. Sunday-school workers in Covington, Georgia, elected Hattie Hutchinson as superintendent, and the members of the Tampa Sunday School District, most of whom were women, served under Mrs. M. B. Johnson as district supervisor. Virginia AME members routinely noted female supervisors. Mrs. Harriet Barrett of Richmond District was touted as "the best in the district," while Sister Bell of the Bedford Circuit received praise for running "one of the best schools in the district." Kate L. Smith was a one-woman show. She led the choir, was president of the Board of Deaconesses, and long served as Sunday-school superintendent. As one admirer noted, "No more zealous and faithful one can be found."[16]

15. James Wickleff Axtell, *The Organized Sunday School: A Working Manual for Officers* (Nashville, 1902), 64–65, 71; and R. H. Griffith, "Banner Sunday School of North Carolina," *Baptist State Sunday School Convention of North Carolina, 1874* (Raleigh, 1875), 11.

16. "Report on Sabbath-Schools," *15th Quadrennial General Conference of the African Methodist Episcopal Church* (N.p., 1872), 136; Mary Ann P. Kirkman, "Letter," in *Sunday School Monitor*, I (July 11, 1902), 3; Hattie Hutchinson, "Sunday School Organization,"

Though usually absent from leadership positions, in sheer numbers women dominated the southern Sunday-school movement as pupils and teachers. Observers were struck by the number of female pupils who filled the Sunday classroom. Class lists indicate that the majority of pupils and teachers were female. For instance, at the Greenwood, South Carolina, Presbyterian Church in 1892, sixteen of the twenty-one Sunday-school teachers were female. Female predominance also tended to increase with time. St. Paul's United Methodist Church of Goldsboro had an equal number of male and female teachers in 1868; only three years later, eight of its eleven teachers were women. In 1895, Goldsboro church leaders again confirmed that, with a few exceptions, its teachers were all female. During early childhood, gender participation seemed relatively equal, confirming a mother's influence over youngsters and the appeal of these classes to most little children. However, adolescent male dropouts were common, and classes for teenagers were often all female.[17]

Sunday-school teaching seemed a perfect task for women; most observers and advisers agreed with Lansing Burrows' thoughts and celebrated female participation. A teacher who could instill Christian lessons and teach children the world's most important book now claimed an elevated position and had "come to stand alongside the ministry of the gospel preacher," according to Methodist W. G. E. Cunnyngham. What power a woman now had to turn young hearts to God! Southern Presbyterians regarded Sabbath-school teaching as a woman's means to reach new heights, for "if by her sin entered into the world, by her also comes salvation." Baptists insisted on women's secondary, but glorified, position

---

Sunday School Monitor, II (January 23, 1903), 3; "District Reports, Richmond," *Journal of the Virginia Annual Conference of the African Methodist Episcopal Church* (Richmond, Va., 1899), 81; "District Reports, Bedford Circuit," *Journal of the Virginia Annual Conference of the African Methodist Episcopal Church* (Richmond, Va., 1914), 50; and Reverend Revel Alcorn Adams, *Cyclopedia of African Methodism in Mississippi* (Natchez, 1902), 186.

17. Lois Johnson Grier, ed., *First Presbyterian Church of Greenwood, South Carolina, 1883–1958* (privately printed, 1958), 68; "New Bern District," North Carolina Conference of the Methodist Episcopal Church, South, *Conference Records, 1893–1909*, DU. See also "The Gender of the Teacher," *North Carolina Sunday School Beacon*, II (June 1901), 2. Statistical surveys of Sunday-school teachers rarely differentiated them by gender. Determining the makeup of Sunday-school classes is also difficult because anyone who came to Sunday school was listed on the roll. The class lists I have seen with attendance marks show many boys on the roll, but most attending less frequently than the girls. The feminization of teaching was occurring in public schools as well.

in the Sunday school. M. G. H. Barnwell of South Carolina saw the Sunday school as a true blessing, "where woman can labor without infringing on the delicacy of her nature," and he exclaimed, "Thanks be to God for this delightful field of labor." A North Carolina minister, E. A. Yates, felt that the opportunity to teach Sunday school would keep a southern woman well satisfied with her sphere of influence and Christian duty. There would be no reason to move into the public fray as northern women were doing; she could "obtain her rights" and "correct her wrongs" within the boundaries of the Sunday-school classroom. Women did not need to demand equality, for "the religious training of the boys is the best palladium of woman's rights," he insisted. Anthony Bascom suggested nothing would do but to honor these women by erecting a memorial to female Sunday school teachers.[18]

Southern women eagerly answered the call for instructors. Sunday schools seemed perpetually short of teachers and initially welcomed almost any Christian volunteer; one did not need proved competency or a certain level of education, although the preference was that one could read. Age was scarcely a factor; young teenagers as well as grandmothers proved effective instructors. The institution attracted women from all walks of life whose dedication to God and knowledge of the Bible were more than adequate preparation for this work. Not until the turn of the century would denominations become increasingly concerned about quality and encourage teachers to attend special training courses and summer chautauquas to improve classroom performance.

Sunday-school teachers enjoyed a good deal of leeway in their approach to instruction. There were no absolute requirements or guidelines initially, although by the 1870s nearly all southern denominations endorsed the Uniform Lesson plan and encouraged Sunday schools to use it. Teaching styles were individualized. Some women drilled their pupils relentlessly and insisted that they memorize a set number of scriptural pas-

18. W. G. E. Cunnyngham, *The Sunday School: Its History and Management* (Nashville, 1902), 11; "Woman's Position as Teacher in the Church," *Presbyterian Standard,* XLIV (March 12, 1902), 13; M. G. H. Barnwell, "Woman's Work," *Working Christian,* VII (November 25, 1875), 2; Reverend E. A. Yates, "The Relation of Methodism to the Origin and Progress of the Sunday School Work," in Reverend L. S. Burkhead, *Centennial of Methodism in North Carolina, Containing the History and Addresses . . . Delivered at the North Carolina Annual Conference* (Raleigh, 1876), 216; and Anthony Bascom, *Fifty Years in the Ministry* (Macon, Ga., 1937), 74.

sages and the catechism each week. Roll call might include students' reciting a Bible verse they had memorized during the week. Teachers often rewarded outstanding pupils with ribbons, Bibles, a set of crockery, and in at least one instance, a silver bowl. Storytelling proved a popular method to instruct young children. Some women had to make do with very little. Elizabeth Hooker taught a Sunday school in the Appalachian Mountains with almost no classroom aids. Her pupils, some of whom were illiterate, sat on wooden benches, and she taught lessons orally by using simple words that she had printed on cards. Miss Mary Ogilve conducted an afternoon mission Sunday school in Richmond that attracted children of various nationalities. She found that the Uniform Lesson plan was too complex for these youngsters, and instead, she spent class time relating simple gospel stories. Some teachers added practical lessons, such as Miss Elizabeth Taylor's sewing class at a Methodist missionary Sunday school in Galveston, Texas. Role playing and a touch of the dramatic could impart important lessons to impressionable minds. Mrs. C. M. Carnahan always spoke in childlike language to her young pupils. She relished the theatrical approach. In one lesson on temperance, she mimicked a drunkard, reeling around the classroom to demonstrate the horrors of alcohol and insisting that her youngsters never step inside a saloon.[19]

The ideal teacher was someone like "Miss Fannie," in a north Georgia community, who had taught the same dozen "maidens" throughout their five years in her Sunday school. The girls apparently adored her. Fannie's nature was reserved and unassuming, and she devoted her life to pleasing her pupils. When mere youngsters, the girls came to her home to make dolls and have dinner or afternoon tea. Fannie always remembered birthdays by sending a card to each child; when on holiday, she sent each one a postcard and bought each a souvenir. Never one to rest on her laurels, Miss Fannie attended normal institutes to perfect her classroom performance.[20]

19. Elizabeth R. Hooker, *Religion in the Highlands: Native Churches and Missionary Enterprise in the Southern Appalachian Area* (New York, 1923), 87; "City Missions," *17th Annual Report of the Woman's Home Missionary Society of the Methodist Episcopal Church, South* (Nashville, 1903), 38; "City Missions," *20th Annual Report of the Woman's Home Missionary Society of the Methodist Episcopal Church, South* (Nashville, 1906), 116; and Mrs. C. M. Carnahan, "The Primary Teachers' Conference," *Minutes of the 28th Annual Session of the Kentucky Sunday School Union, 1893* (Louisville, 1893), 66–67.

20. "How One Teacher Holds Her Class," *North Georgia Conference Sunday-School Year Book, 1903–04* (Atlanta, 1904), 12–13.

Sunday-school teaching could be a demanding chore. If no male super-intendent was available when pupils misbehaved, the female teacher did the disciplining. Mary Ogilve, who managed a Dallas settlement house as well as its Sunday school, had little time to waste on unruly children. She quickly discharged those who failed to behave and focused her attention on the "teachable." Women might spend hours each week preparing for Sunday morning. This explains why advice manuals stated a preference for single or elderly women to teach Sunday school; when married, a mother's first duty was to serve home and family. Yet an exceptional mother might do both. One exemplary woman proved faithful both to her home and to her Sunday-school class. Although overwhelmed by household duties and burdened by poor health, she always found her place teaching on Sunday and labored for years to lead her pupils to God. Her glorious reward finally came, for, according to her husband, she saw her pupils "all go down into the liquid grave [of baptism] to 'arise in new-ness of life.'"[21]

The meticulous found it hard to be satisfied. The creation of the Uni-form Lesson plan in the 1870s was supposed to ease weekly class prepara-tion by presenting standard lesson outlines and a suggested topic for each week, but many teachers still spent hours preparing a lesson to make it fresh and appealing. Bessie Lacy of Charlotte, North Carolina, was espe-cially dedicated and felt frustrated that she had so little free time to pre-pare her weekly lesson. By the turn of the century, rising expectations about what the Sunday school should accomplish added new pressures. Denominations began to insist that supervisors and teachers keep accu-rate statistics and submit them to the denominational Sunday-school board. Sunday schools measured their success by classroom attendance, weekly donations, and most important, the number of pupils who con-verted and joined the church. Not all children complied with such goals, however exceptional the teacher might be. One woman in charge of a Sunday-school class was upset by her pupils' lack of progress. "To teach them seems to me a more hopeless task each year," she despaired. Some women continued their work with similar misgivings; they felt a deep commitment to serve God and uplift the South's destitute yet believed that their efforts did not match their goals.[22]

21. Haskin, "Dallas, Tex., Settlement House," 44; "Notice," *Kind Words,* XIV (June 22, 1875), 143.

22. Bessie Lacy to her brother Fred, April 18, 1888, in Drury Lacy Collection, Southern Historical Collection, Wilson Library, University of North Carolina at Chapel Hill [here-

Most women Sunday-school teachers found a meaningful role in the classroom, a place for self-expression where they could influence youngsters and lead them toward God. Despite the demands, women often commented on their deep love for teaching. Like Miss Fannie, some dedicated their lives to the task, finding it the most meaningful moment of their week. Women relished their impact on children and the opportunity to uplift the next generation. "The crowning feature of all our work has been the Sunday school," enthused Estelle Hawkins of the Woman's Home Missionary Society. "To look into the faces of 80 or 100 of these children each Sunday and to hear them sing, is indeed an inspiration to any heart." To others, this weekly responsibility provided welcome relief from farm and household chores and maternal duties. Teaching gave women an outlet beyond the confines of home and a chance to engage in purposeful, Christian work. Few rural women had the time or opportunity to participate in civic reform and club work or attend social gatherings, activities more typically associated with the urban and privileged. Sunday-school teaching, however, was a task undertaken and enjoyed by numerous women, rich or poor, black or white. Typically the church was the center of a southern woman's life outside her home.[23]

Female teachers devoted themselves to their Sunday-school classes. Miss Battie Shropshire of Rome, Georgia, and Mrs. Lottie Estes of Anderson, South Carolina, each taught Sunday school for more than fifty years. A Hartsville, South Carolina, woman taught Sunday school for more than sixty-five years and called the work the bright spot in her week. Miss Mabel Kennedy of St. Louis was one of many dedicated individuals who instructed two Sunday-school classes each week, one in the morning with eighty-five young women and another in the afternoon with fifty-two pupils. A North Carolina woman called her Sunday-school instruction "Heavenly work" and was thrilled when her daughter followed in her footsteps. Miss Annie Mutch could scarcely contain her delight. "How can I tell you of the girls in my Sunday school class. They are so dear to my heart!" she exclaimed. With trepidation, an elderly woman approached the weighty responsibility of helping youngsters achieve salva-

---

inafter cited as SHC]; Unidentified writer in a selection of letters in the *14th Annual Report of the Executive Committee of Colored Evangelization of the Presbyterian Church of the U.S., 1905* (Richmond, Va., 1905), 6.

23. Estelle Haskin, "City Missions," *19th Annual Report of the Woman's Home Missionary Society of the Methodist Episcopal Church, South* (Nashville, 1905), 12.

tion, fearing that her "nervous and excitable" constitution could not survive youthful energy and noise. She happily discovered that she loved teaching youngsters; the task had given her golden years real meaning.[24]

The number of teachers increased substantially as new Sunday schools sprang up throughout the South; so did the stream of advice and dictates concerning ideal behavior directed to teachers. It wasn't that the quality of teaching was declining; denominations were just becoming increasingly competitive over young souls and worried about the appeal of their Sunday classes. Quality was critical. Each church had to create the best Sunday school possible in order to attract new members into the fold— for it had long been observed that nearly all new church members came from Sabbath classes. Teachers were at the heart of this effort. Evangelicals insisted that standards be established, and writers and moralists were only too happy to produce volumes to guide behavior and improve instruction. Nothing was too insignificant when fashioning the ideal teacher. Punctuality was essential, for if children were to learn to live by the clock, adults must set a good example. Women were urged to dress modestly so that their pupils' eyes would never leave the Bible page to admire a new outfit. Teachers were to avoid parties on Saturday nights; to shun dancing, drinking, and tasteless language; and to appear alert and lively every Sunday morning, always "blameless before God."[25]

With the formation of Sunday-school publishing houses by the late nineteenth century, denominations began producing and selling their own literature for schools, pupils, and families. Not only would this ensure that children read sound literature and learned the correct interpretation of the Bible; it would also result in larger sales and profits for the

24. Georgia Hamlet, A *History of the First Baptist Church, Anderson, South Carolina, 1821–1979* (Anderson, S.C., 1979), 57; Malcolm Stuart Sweet, *Unto Everlasting Life; The History of the Hartsville Presbyterian Church, 1867–1952* (Hartsville, S.C., 1954), 121; Mabel Kennedy, "Mabel Kennedy, St. Louis Centenary Methodist Church," *22nd Annual Report of the Woman's Home Missionary Society of the Methodist Episcopal Church, South* (Nashville, 1908), 149; "City Missions," *23rd Annual Report of the Woman's Home Missionary Society of the Methodist Episcopal Church, South* (Nashville, 1909), 134; "To Her Grandson," *Baptist Courier*, March 19, 1885, p. 4; and "The Experience of an Elderly Lady as a Sunday School Teacher," *Earnest Worker*, III (February 27, 1873), 170.

25. Axtell, *Organized Sunday School*, 43; Israel P. Black, *Practical Primary Plans for Primary Teachers of the Sunday School* (New York, 1903), 77; and Samuel W. Cope, *The Great Evil and Its Remedy; or, Parental Responsibility in the Moral and Religious Training of Children* (Nashville, 1889), 89.

denominational publishing house. Female teachers and church members could play an effective role in marketing these publications. For instance, Baptist Sunday School Board secretary James Frost solicited Baptist women for his marketing scheme, urging them to become unofficial salespersons to increase the circulation of the board's publications. Churches also insisted that teachers use only literature published by their denominational firm.[26]

For female pupils, the Sunday classroom and its personnel, activities, and lessons offered a comforting and pleasing environment. These classes empowered young girls and gave them a rare opportunity to excel and gain confidence. With the majority of teachers being female, girls often found a role model, though some expressed equal pleasure with a male teacher. Julia Rankin of Guilford County, North Carolina, adored both her teacher and class. "I love to go because I love our teacher dearly," she wrote. Rankin relished the weekly Bible quizzes and the chance to question her teacher. AME member Sarah Wade of Tampa declared simply, "I love the Sunday school." She also loved her teacher's drilling pupils on the Bible. "I have answered any questions the teacher has asked," she bragged, and apparently her answers were never wrong. When her friends mocked her enthusiasm, she commented that their laughter "gives me courage."[27]

Years later, women often looked back on their Sunday-school days with fond memories, especially noting the influence of a superior teacher. Ermine McGaha loved her Sunday class. As an adult, she wrote to her former teacher: "When quite young, providence placed me in your Sabbath School Class. Your unwavering faith, so manifest in your zeal—and your correct understanding of the Scriptures, commanded my love and reverence. What would my life have been without such teachings?" Poems and hymns often celebrated a female instructor. As one stanza rhapsodized, "She came amidst her children, / Like sunshine 'mongst the flowers; / Cheering with love's soft radiance, / Those blessed Sabbath hours." Who could make a greater impression on a young girl than a Sunday-school class taught by a devoted and loving instructor?[28]

26. James Marion Frost, "The Sunday-School Board," *Religious Herald*, LXV (September 4, 1902), 7.

27. Julia Rankin to William Henry Wills, June 16, 1870, in Wills Collection, SHC; and Sarah Wade, "Letter," *Sunday School Monitor*, I (July 11, 1902), 3.

28. Ermine McGaha to James Harvey Joiner, n.d., in James Harvey Joiner Collection, SHC.

In the Sunday classroom, girls spoke freely and participated actively. Whether in single-sex or mixed classes, girls often outdid themselves. They were singled out for their superior work and exemplary behavior. They won prizes for memorizing the most Bible verses or catechism, for being punctual and responsible, and for never missing class. Participating in competitive Bible games and membership drives or memorizing the most verses appealed to young girls. Although many impoverished pupils lacked even a penny for the weekly collection basket, they eagerly engaged in activities to raise money for their Sunday school's benevolent work. A Sunday-school superintendent in Yalaha, Florida, reported on his pupils' enthusiasm in aiding the school's missionary fund. His female students gathered wild grasses and wove them into bonnets, which they then sold at a local market. Girls might make potholders, plant and raise corn, or gather eggs to sell. In one instance, seven girls spent their vacation raising money for their Sunday school's missionary project by working and doing good deeds. One girl gathered eggs for her grandmother; another earned $1 by not saying "gracious"; another read the Bible to a blind woman; one wiped the dishes for her mother; another fed the chickens; one promised not to scowl; and the last girl gathered and sold flowers. Girls took part in Sunday-school pageants and parades, an acceptable venue where women could publicly display their talents and character.[29]

Especially for impoverished youngsters living in overcrowded, dingy homes and toiling daily to aid family survival, an hour or two in the quiet of a Sunday-school room must have provided welcome moments of peace and Christian uplift. Winning a ribbon for memorizing a psalm, earning a blue ticket for promptness, competing in a Bible spelling bee, performing in a stirring theatrical production, or even receiving a Children's Day program decorated with flowers and crosses could have enormous meaning to these children, many of whom had little else to brighten their days. Two girls from the AME Sunday school at Wayman's Chapel in Wilmington, North Carolina, appeared in a Sunday school tableau and must have been pleased with the response to their performance. They "reflected

29. James E. Drake, "Florida Correspondence," *Sunday School Magazine*, VI (1876), 105; "A Missionary Vacation," *Earnest Worker*, XXIV (October 1893), 114. Anne Firor Scott notes that in a religious setting, "women could do things otherwise forbidden." Certainly this was true in the Sunday school. See Scott, *Natural Allies: Women's Associations in American History* (Urbana, Ill., 1992), 85.

great credit on themselves by the superior manner in which they rendered their parts," commented one admirer. To observers, the young women had displayed the race's "high state of culture." Imagine how delighted Annie Perley of Charlottesville, Virginia, must have been to see her name in a Sunday-school magazine, cited for attending 312 successive classes, or Mary Baring from East Tennessee, mentioned for recruiting 123 new pupils for her Sunday school.[30]

Sunday-school activities outside the classroom engaged the energy and management skills of women. Parades, pageants, and picnics were extremely popular Sunday-school activities; women were usually responsible for their organization and success. They created and sewed costumes for pageant performances and parades. They cleaned and decorated church sanctuaries and dining halls for holiday banquets. They made the fried chicken, lemon pies, biscuits, and lemonade for picnics. Women marched through village streets in Sunday-school parades and boasted about the magnificent demonstrations and enthusiastic participants. Sometimes women moved front and center by delivering speeches or actually leading the parades. Miss Naomi Young, like many others, was queen of a splendid Sunday-school parade in Nevada County, Arkansas, riding atop a carpeted platform on a throne covered in gold paper, surrounded by her royal court dressed in white. Women organized fairs to raise money to purchase furnishings, maps, organs, stereopticons, and library books. In one instance, AME women held an enormous bazaar and raised nearly $600 to aid their floundering publishing house.[31]

Women also played a significant role in writing Sunday-school literature, hymns, and poems. By the turn of the century, southern denominational publishing firms were churning out material for pupils, workers, and parents: Sunday-school magazines, lesson leaflets, hymnals, library volumes, and tracts filled with sentimental, uplifting lessons. Demand was high for new copy to fill the pages of these publications, and women con-

---

30. Cicero Daniel, "Wilmington, N.C., Item," *Christian Recorder*, XII (July 20, 1872), 7; G. M. J., "312 Successive Sabbaths," *Sunday School Magazine*, IV (1874), 69; "Sunday School Intelligence," *Earnest Worker*, II (November 30, 1871), 68.

31. Beulah Brummel Braden, *When Grandma Was a Little Girl* (Oak Ridge, Tenn., 1976), 76; Pigott, *Scenes and Incidents*, 91–94; and H. M. Turner, "Quadrennial Report of Manager H. M. Turner of the Publishing Department," *17th Quadrennial General Conference of the African Methodist Episcopal Church* (N.p., 1880), 113. This AME bazaar took place in Philadelphia but indicates women's dedication to a cause.

tributed a good deal of it. Naturally, most female authors were well educated and rarely represented the South's plain folk. They felt it their duty
to convey middle-class values and instill good behavior in all Sunday-
school pupils, rich or poor, black or white. Themes in their writings focused on cleanliness, honesty, generosity, punctuality, obedience, and humility—important lessons for all children to learn, especially the poor,
whom the writers often assumed had little exposure to such values in the
home.

Whether written by men or women, Sunday-school literature upheld
traditional ideas about gender, reinforcing male superiority and women's
submissiveness and domesticity. Stories in Sunday-school magazines described little girls helping their mothers by cooking, dusting, sewing, and
caring for younger siblings. Illustrations depicted girls in starched dresses
and frilly bonnets or hair ribbons, sitting quietly reading to a younger sib-
ling or holding a broom, ready to tackle a household chore. In a typical
tale, Susy Baird dreamed of becoming a woman exactly like her mother—
a missionary wife, president of her sewing circle, a Sunday-school teacher,
and head of the ladies' prayer meeting. Tales taught girls always to behave
in a ladylike manner. Invariably, a girl's worst habit was vanity; writers
urged females to dress simply and to focus on improving their character
rather than enjoying a new frock. Young girls rarely disobeyed their parents, or if they did, they suffered the consequences. All denominations
insisted upon women knowing their rightful place; white Baptists were
most insistent upon reinforcing this message.[32]

Females were society's moral force; they corrected the errant and supposedly engaged in exemplary behavior. In Sunday-school fiction, boys
inevitably disobeyed; girls often reminded them to behave. In one typical
story a young girl warned her older brother not to disobey their mother by
picking apples from a tree, because "God can see you." Like most children
in such stories, he was a quick learner and needed only one reminder to
avoid trouble. Through these stories children were to learn lessons in
benevolence, kindness, selflessness, and of course, the benefits of attending Sunday school. Frequently children in these tales appeared to be far
better Christians than adults; in fact, youngsters who went to Sunday

32. "A Mother's Example," *Kind Words*, II (May 22, 1873), 87. For an illustration of
three girls marching with brooms, see *Our Little People*, XXVI (May 1906), cover. For a discussion of middle-class values, see Higginbotham, *Righteous Discontent*, 14–15, and Himmelfarb, *De-Moralization of Society*, 4–8.

school were often the ones to redeem less worthy grownups by leading them to the church and to Christ.[33]

Yet Sunday-school lessons and stories also instilled in young girls the important but subtle lesson that as Christians they could be bold and assertive, a strength that came from believing in God and behaving properly. For instance, a little girl overheard a man swearing to God, and she insisted that he never use such bad language because God was her father. Another story described a little girl who attended Sunday school against her parents' wishes. They threatened to banish her from home if she persisted, but she would not forgo her weekly class. Finally, the parents secretly followed her to see what transpired in the classroom. One look convinced them of the importance of Sunday school, and they welcomed their daughter with open arms. But the child realized that she had an important lesson to teach them, and she refused to cross the threshold until her mother and father promised to attend church. Soon the entire family spent every Sunday morning worshiping God, thanks to the girl's devotion to Sunday school. In another story, Lucy Jones was voted the best child in her Sunday-school class because she was never tardy, always obeyed her teacher, was helpful and kind to other children, memorized and recited all her Bible verses, and "loves and obeys God." And it was a young Methodist girl on her deathbed who made her irreligious father promise that he would turn his life over to God. No sooner had little Sallie been buried than he rushed to the preacher to fulfill his final promise to his daughter. As long as the goal was Christian in nature, apparently women's assertiveness was acceptable.[34]

But an ideal female was also loving and self-sacrificing. One story that appeared in a missionary magazine for black children illustrates this point. A guest had just arrived at a hotel, and he noted that a young woman, Betty Gordon, was being feted with a grand celebration upon her departure. Curious about such popularity, he asked what had elicited this adoration. Was she especially brilliant? witty? rich? beautiful? famous? A negative response followed each inquiry. The hotel proprietor finally responded that she was being honored because she never thought of herself.

---

33. "God Sees You," *Kind Words*, II (January 15, 1873), 45. See also Bernard Wishy, *The Child of the Republic: The Dawn of Modern American Child Nurture* (Philadelphia, 1968), 85.

34. "A Gentle Reproof," *Child's Gem*, XIV (December 12, 1897), 3; "The Little Daughter," *Children's Friend*, XVIII (April 7, 1883), 27; and "A Little Preacher," *Good Tidings*, IX (November 19, 1887), 186.

"She simply forgot that there was such a person as Betty Gordon and with her warm heart and quiet sympathies threw herself into the lives of others." Such selflessness was an ideal for which all good Christian women should strive.[35]

These messages hit a responsive chord in many white youngsters. In the Sunday school, by lesson, story, prayer, and example, children learned that the meek shall inherit the earth. Southern females were ideal candidates for the meek, for they knew from their upbringing and childhood lessons that they could quietly civilize and influence the world and uplift others. Southern women did not expect to alter the world or use a shrill voice to engage in radical reform. Most never pondered such possibilities, and many agreed with southern men that northern women who engaged in demonstrations and public activities stepped well beyond their assigned role. In Sunday school, as teachers they taught, and as pupils they accepted, guidelines on how to live right and how to uplift others by dedicating themselves to God. Women were not forced to accept such lessons—although they had scant opportunity to learn others. Men reinforced this view of the proper female role; they preferred submissive women. Responding to northern women's involvement in temperance and suffrage in 1874, one male wrote: "The law of God forbids woman to speak in public, even in the quietude of the church. . . . We have seen the same impious pretense of religion used to oppress and degrade the manhood of the South and subordinate this fair portion of our land to the domination of an ignorant, degraded, and rapacious race—let us at least be spared the spectacle of seeing women of the South brought down to the level of this movement."[36] Most women would not have challenged his thoughts or sought to alter their subordinate position and domestic role. Sunday-school lessons and literature were appealing because they reinforced beliefs that most white women had absorbed for years. Black women, too, often embraced such middle-class values and lessons because they seemed to promise acceptance in a white world.[37]

35. "Self-Consciousness," *Good Tidings*, III (May 19, 1883), 78. This may seem to be a curious journal for northern Methodists to distribute to black Sunday schools, but white churches and missionary organizations did not concern themselves with making the material relevant to this audience.

36. "The Ladies Temperance Movement," *Earnest Worker*, IV (March 12, 1874), 188.

37. Jean E. Friedman, *The Enclosed Garden: Women and Community in the Evangelical South, 1830–1900* (Chapel Hill, 1985). Friedman focuses primarily on the antebellum

Even those southern women who had acquired a public voice celebrated females' limited sphere and quiet influence in church and home.
Annie Armstrong, corresponding secretary of the Woman's Missionary
Union of the Southern Baptist Convention, seemed a force to contend
with in public. Her correspondence suggests an opinionated, assertive
woman, at least on issues that affected her organization. She was a strong
advocate of the Sunday school as long as it supported Baptist missionary
endeavors. Notwithstanding her own position, she insisted that women
never assume men's roles or perform their work. "Our brethren are the
God-appointed leaders," she wrote. Mrs. Charlotte Hawkins Brown, principal of Palmer Memorial Institute in North Carolina, speaking on the
importance of educating black women, reiterated a familiar theme: "To
instruct a Woman is to instruct a man; to elevate a woman is to lift up a
man and to purify society." Overall, most southern women, black or
white, accepted their secondary role in church and society.[38]

One troubling thought that fostered a degree of panic was the possibility that northern ideas and reform activities might filter southward and
impact southern women. During the late nineteenth century, middle-
class northern women launched an effort to secure the vote, an idea that
generated little support in southern Sunday-school literature. Many men
regarded this movement with horror; so did some women. Such threats
from northern female activism made it all the more important to ensure
southern women's commitment to Sunday school, church, and home.
Baptist minister C. E. Askew commented in 1914 that Christian women
had no need to gain the right to vote because, by training their men to be
moral, wives could direct the vote as they saw fit. He urged women to become good teachers and Christians and not advocate female suffrage. A
woman did not need direct power, for "she is the head of the stream and it
will go as she directs, thus she should train the men right!" A writer for
the *Earnest Worker* was horrified by organized mobs of northern women.
He noted that the demand for women's rights had made an "ominous ad-

South, arguing that kin, community, and church kept southern women tied to their "enclosed garden." See also Higginbotham, *Righteous Discontent.*

38. Annie Armstrong to James Marion Frost, July 24, 1896, in Annie Armstrong Cor-
respondence, SSBSBC; Charlotte Hawkins Brown, "What the Educated Woman Stands
For," *Minutes of the 39th Annual Baptist State Sunday School Convention of North Carolina
(Negro)* (N.p., 1911), 10.

vance" since the Civil War, and female involvement in temperance work and suffrage would inevitably lead to women's degradation.[39]

Mothers' duties on the homefront were another important means to ensure the success of the Sunday school. It was usually mothers who insisted on their children's attendance and timely arrival at Sabbath classes. Advisers urged mothers to awaken their youngsters early and get them dressed and ready. Promptness was on everyone's mind, for the sixty to ninety minutes in class were too precious to waste. Mothers should insist that their offspring learn their weekly lessons and memorize the assigned Scripture and catechism. Also, they should support and praise the work of Sunday-school teachers.

A child's physical appearance was crucial; even the most impoverished youngsters should be scrubbed and tidy, dressed in their Sunday best. Beulah Braden of rural Texas recalled the ruffled white dress with pink bow and patent leather shoes that she wore to the Coal Creek Sunday School's Children's Day. Many youngsters, of course, could not afford a ruffled dress, much less a pair of shoes. When destitute children could not acquire a decent frock or shirt for Sunday school and church, women assumed responsibility for providing them with appropriate attire. This concern extended beyond a mother's own youngsters. Fannie Heck asked her friends to donate their cast-off clothing for her impoverished Sunday-school pupils in Raleigh. Richmond women formed the Baptist Sunday School Relief Society, which collected clothing to dispense to the city's poor children. As one member declared, "We will not rest until we see them able to go to Sunday school." This was a cautious group, however: before distributing any items, a committee member visited each family to ensure a legitimate need. Women in communities throughout the South formed sewing circles and stitched Sunday-school clothing for the poor.[40]

Far more important was the fact that the Sunday-school movement could not succeed without committed, competent mothers fulfilling their Christian responsibilities at home. Repeatedly, Sunday-school leaders and

39. "Notice," and "Women in the Church," both in *Baptist Courier*, July 23, 1885, pp. 2, 188, respectively.

40. Braden, *When Grandma Was a Little Girl*, 75; Fannie Heck Biography in Fannie Heck File, North Carolina Baptist History Archives, Z. Smith Reynolds Library, Wake Forest University, Winston-Salem, North Carolina; and Mrs. S. G. Hughes, "An Appeal to the Friends of Little Children," *Religious Herald*, March 8, 1866, p. 2.

advisers reminded mothers that their most important role was to nurture their children and raise them in a Christian environment. This message was critical, for family worship seemed to be on the decline; in Samuel Cope's assessment in 1889, it was "negligible." Mothers should take this duty seriously and regard their offspring as "empty vessels," ready to be filled with Christian teachings from the moment of birth. Henry Cope insisted that mothers secure the salvation of their children while they were young and receptive to new ideas. Just as important was every mother's duty to create a "joyous, cheerful home." Baptists insisted that mothers lead their children to a glorious future. "The brightest jewels in the mother's immortal crown will be her sainted children—children led to Jesus through her influence. . . . Let our women keep themselves unspotted from the world." Pressure on mothers to do right by their children was constant. As Samuel Cope noted, children followed by example and were, "as a rule, very much like their mothers, for good or evil." If mothers were to raise good Christians, they had to consciously monitor their own behavior and act in a loving, pious manner. Yet however great the pressure and duties, the maternal role was one to celebrate; all southern women "should be ambitious to excel" in their sacred responsibilities. Failure to fulfill home duties could be a child's undoing. Nearly all Sunday-school supporters felt that Christian education began with proper maternal nurturing in the home.[41]

Yet mothers could not do everything, and critics either admonished parents for their failings or insisted that they send their children to Sunday school to receive Christian nurturing that mothers failed to provide at home. Sometimes mothers were blamed for a faltering Sunday school. Dr. G. O. Bullock excused his own efforts, claiming that "we have poor material to work with because we do not have proper mothers in the home." The National Baptists' Reverend G. W. Perry insisted that the "many imperfections in mothers" caused children to commit petty crimes, and he suggested that mothers organize themselves and adopt a plan to save their children. Others saw Sunday school as the solution to inadequate home instruction. Nannie Burroughs, speaking before a gathering of the National Baptist Convention, insisted that mothers send their off-

41. Samuel Cope, *Great Evil,* 126; "The Training of Children," *Working Christian,* II (October 9, 1879), 4; Henry Frederick Cope, *Religious Education in the Family* (Chicago, 1915), 222; Samuel Cope, *Great Evil,* 59; Black, *Practical Primary Plans,* 46, 165. See also J. A. Lyons, *The Sunday School and Its Methods* (Nashville, 1883), 49–54.

spring to Sunday school, for on their own they could not possibly teach them everything they should know about the Bible. The Sunday-school teacher was, in Burroughs' eyes, a mother's agent. Other commentators felt that modern mothers were too involved in "ceaseless household cares" to be "constantly aglow" with spiritual thoughts and to provide a solid Christian education. Some mothers did not know how to convey Christian lessons to their offspring, were unfamiliar with the Bible, or could not read; their children should be in the hands of an experienced Sunday-school teacher.[42]

In what was regarded as a rapidly changing, fast-paced, and increasingly immoral world, mothers needed to pay even more attention to their children than they had in the past. Too many parents by the late nineteenth century apparently failed to guard their offspring against sinful temptations such as alcohol, gambling, billiards, and dime novels. Church leaders lamented the state of modern society and its impact on the nation's youth. The situation did not bode well. Lincoln Hulley, president of Stetson University, insisted that southern mothers become chief of what he called a "domestic university" and never lose sight of their children's activities. He feared that parents were doing little to teach their offspring about the Bible and to fear and love God.[43]

Church leaders and advisers were as likely to celebrate women's role in the home and praise their efforts as they were to criticize. Mothers were central to the success of the Sunday school and the piety of southern youngsters; many seemed to be serving their families well. Positive reinforcement could spur on the indifferent; too much criticism might cause women to give up altogether. Sunday-school literature offered countless odes to mothers and their influence on young souls. According to an account in the *Baptist Courier*, some 100 ministers out of 120 surveyed claimed that "from the cradle" it was their mother who had led them to Christ. A typical story urging children to love their mothers concluded, "You will never meet an eye as tender, a hand as gentle, or a heart as kind

42. Dr. G .O. Bullock comments in the *Minutes of the Proceedings of the 42nd Annual Baptist State Sunday School Convention of North Carolina (Negro)* (N.p., 1914), 11–12; Reverend G. W. Perry, "Address," *Minutes of the 27th Annual Wake Baptist Association (Negro)* (N.p., 1893), 11; Nannie Helen Burroughs, "Woman's Relation and Responsibility to the Sunday School," *National Baptist Union*, VII (August 25, 1906), 7; and Marianna C. Brown, *Sunday School Movements in America* (New York, 1901), 177.

43. Lincoln Hulley, "Religious Education in the Home," *Religious Education*, II (1905).

as hers." Some saw mothers as divinely appointed instructors of their children. Southerners looked with horror at northern reformers and women's activists and sighed with relief that their women sought only to serve family and church. "Thank God, our favored southern land is a land of homes and in these sacred castles the father and mother are chief rulers," rejoiced J. A. Lyons, who dedicated his Sunday-school manual "to my old-fashioned Mother, from whose lips I first rec'd the Gospel of Christ." Grown sons often blessed their mothers for steering them away from alcohol, gambling, and other sinful pleasures.[44]

As it was with women superintendents, race was a factor in women's participation in other Sunday-school offices. Black women played a more significant and public role in their Sunday schools than did white women, not only as officers, but in other positions as well. In black churches, a sizable percentage of delegates attending Sunday-school conferences and conventions were female. At the 1895 North Carolina Black Baptist State Convention, 63 men and 26 women were present; in 1896, 45 of the 119 delegates were female; and in 1914, 100 men and 75 women attended. A black woman usually held at least one position on each state Sunday-school committee. Black women wrote and delivered the majority—and sometimes all—of the essays and papers presented at conventions, in part because black females were likely to be better educated than black men. Sunday-school conferences often set aside a special time to hear their stirring essays, such as "These Are the Tides in the Affairs of Men" and "Now Is the Time to Strew Flowers in Life's Pathway." The women discussed temperance, good manners, adolescent male problems, Jim Crow laws, primary teaching, improved missionary programs at home, the Sunday-school library, and Sunday-school work in Africa. By contrast, some white denominations refused to welcome any female delegates. In 1885 two Arkansas women tried to gain seats at the Southern Baptist Convention in Augusta, an effort that produced an outraged response from male delegates and members for months thereafter.[45]

44. Reverend Fay Mills, "Motherhood," *Baptist Courier*, March 12, 1892, p. 2; "Little Ones, Do You Love Your Mothers?" *Kind Words*, II (June 25, 1873), 130; and Lyons, *The Sunday School*, dedication, frontispiece.

45. *Minutes of the 23rd Annual Baptist State Sunday School Convention of North Carolina (Negro)* (Raleigh, 1895), 19, and *Minutes of the 24th Annual Baptist State Sunday School Convention of North Carolina (Negro)* (Raleigh, 1896), 9. Higginbotham states that female delegates at the annual meeting of the American National Baptist Convention were few in

Black laymen and church leaders did not appear threatened by female participation; in fact, at least in their public pronouncements, men celebrated black female talent and brain power as a symbol of their race. After hearing several papers presented by female participants, one North Carolina Sunday-school delegate boasted, "This convention has caused us to feel that our young women are not at all behind in the great march of intellectual progress." Miss J. A. Dood delivered the welcome address at a Sunday school convention, and all agreed that her effort was "a credit to her." Miss Carrie Hill delivered the closing speech at a Little Rock AME Sunday school picnic; one man heralded her speech as that spoken "with a distinction and self-possession which was commendable." Other comments such as "brilliant," "interesting and spicy" and "bright and charming" described essays that women delivered at AMEZ Sunday-school conferences. One minister was so thrilled by the intellectual level of essays he heard that he offered to pay a portion of any young woman's tuition who wished to attend Shaw University in Raleigh. A decade later, this fund had reached $2,000 and supported twenty-seven women pursuing a college education.[46]

With women's growing involvement and participation in the Sunday school, a new problem became evident by the end of the century: Sunday schools were too attractive to women and were losing male pupils and teachers. This trend was not what Sunday-school leaders had anticipated. However, it was probably inevitable, considering that women made up a considerable majority of the membership in southern churches and Sunday schools. Church leaders and observers tried to walk a delicate balance

---

number. In 1892 only 32 of the 213 delegates were women. Higginbotham, *Righteous Discontent*, 259n59.

46. "Women's Essays," *Minutes of the 24th Annual Baptist State Sunday School Convention of North Carolina (Negro)* (Raleigh, 1896), 16; Reverend H. Blake, "The Sunday School Convention of the South Carolina Conference District," *Star of Zion*, XIV (September 25, 1890), 1. Other examples include, "News from the Churches," *Christian Recorder*, IX (June 24, 1871), 3; "Children's Day—Tuscaloosa, Alabama," *Star of Zion*, XIII (July 25, 1889), 1; and Reverend R. K. Kearns, "Children's Day at Cedar Grove Church," *Star of Zion*, XVI (August 11, 1892), 1. Pastor Dew was the individual who donated money to help pay young women's tuition to attend Shaw; see *Minutes of the 24th Annual Baptist State Sunday School Convention of North Carolina (Negro)*, 18. For an assessment of this "Girl's Educational Fund" two decades later, see the Presidential Address, "Our Sunday School Convention as an Evangelical and Educational Force," *Minutes of the 37th Annual Baptist State Sunday School Convention of North Carolina (Negro)* (N.p., 1909), 20.

by celebrating the dedication of female teachers and the presence of female pupils, while decrying the paucity of young men, many of whom were leaving Sunday school or never showing up in the first place. A typical article in the *Earnest Worker*, "Where Are the Boys?" bemoaned their absence, questioning where young men could be found. The usual response was in barrooms or billiard halls, on streetcorners, or fishing by the river. Such activities seemed to lead them down the road to ruin. As the article answered to its own question, "The devil knows."[47]

In short, the southern Sunday school was becoming feminized. Sunday-school leaders who had envisioned the glorious possibilities of their enterprise now worried over how few young men became teachers and the consequent shortage of role models for young boys. In some cases, the latter concern seemed moot, since so few male pupils attended anyway. The *North Carolina Baraca* newsletter despaired over the problem, for "75% of the boys leave the Sunday schools in the transition from boyhood to young manhood." The Sunday school was supposed to serve as a breeding ground for preachers and missionaries; presumably, fewer men would pursue these occupations if they never attended Sunday school. The Sabbath classroom was supposed to keep young men engaged in purposeful activity and off the street on a day when they did not have to work or attend school; instead, they seemed to be hanging out in seedy places rather than absorbing biblical truths. Apparently, many young men regarded Sunday school as an institution solely for females and young children. It was sissy. A young boy might find it difficult to resist parents who insisted that he attend, but adolescents asserted their independence and found other ways to spend their Sundays.[48]

---

47. "Where Are the Boys?" *Earnest Worker*, XXX (November 11, 1899), 301. Concern about young men was evident on many fronts. Other examples include "A Chance for Boys," *ibid.*, XLI (April 1910), 179; "The Man Problem," *ibid.*, XL (September 1909), 454; and Henry F. Cope, "The Man in the Sunday School," *Sunday School Magazine*, XXXIX (January 1909), 7. See also Ted Ownby, *Subduing Satan: Religion, Recreation, and Manhood in the Rural South, 1865–1920* (Chapel Hill, 1990), and Wishy, *Child of the Republic*, 131–35.

48. *North Carolina Baraca Newsletter*, I (March 1904), 1. See also "Where Are All the Young Men?" *Sunday School Magazine*, November 1882, p. 490; "Our Young Men," *ibid.*, May 1890, p. 3; "Wanted—Men Teachers," *ibid.*, February 1910, p. 98; S. Waters McGill, "How to Retain Our Hold upon the Boys?" *Proceedings of the 32nd Annual Meeting of the Kentucky Sunday School Union* (Louisville, 1897), 51; and Dr. Bryon H. De Ment, *The Baraca Class: A Power in the Church, How It Helps the Pastor* (Syracuse, n.d.), 7. De Ment

More Sunday-school essays and convention papers began to focus on the boy problem and demand a solution to entice males into Sunday school and church. Youth organizations, including the Baracas, Christian Endeavors, and Varick Christian Endeavors, sought to reach young men by offering religious activities that would appeal to more mature masculine needs. Sunday-school officers urged teachers to present lessons that discussed boys' bodies and to relate exciting stories that emphasized the masculine character of Jesus and other men in the Bible. Churches began to make a special effort to attract male teachers, urging them to share their worldly knowledge in the classroom. The *North Carolina Beacon* encouraged males to volunteer to teach. Many women taught Sunday school, but men who had ventured into the world could offer something special by bringing their valuable experiences and knowledge back to the classroom. Moreover, men who taught Sunday school would become better fathers, for they could then use their classroom skills on their own children at home. Evangelicals insisted that the institution become more masculine, offer special activities and classes for young men, and encourage more adult males to participate and teach in the Sunday school.[49]

Such were the trends and tensions regarding women and gender that emerged in the southern Sunday-school movement by 1915. Statistics show that the southern Sunday school had achieved real success by the early twentieth century, at least in terms of pupil enrollment and adult participation as officers and teachers, in large part because of the significant role played by women. Southern women from a variety of backgrounds and deeply imbued with concerns about children and community reached out to improve the world by Christianizing the next generation. Women from all walks of life directed and guided youngsters in lessons to live right and obey God's word. They did not expect to reap rewards on earth, other than the joy of witnessing children learn the Bible, convert, and achieve salvation. Organizing and teaching in a Sunday school brought enormous rewards; women a century ago found great satisfaction by influencing children in this manner. Black and white women focused not only on molding children's immediate Christian char-

---

was professor of Sunday School Pedagogy at the Southern Baptist Theological Seminary in Louisville.

49. "The Gender of the Teacher," *North Carolina Sunday School Beacon*, II (June 1901), 2; Emily Sasser, "The Necessity of Young Men Attending Sunday School," *Proceedings of the Baptist State Sunday School Convention (Negro) of North Carolina*, 1894 (Raleigh, 1895), 34.

acter, but also on looking ahead and endeavoring to create a brighter future.

Girls both rich and poor, black and white, attended Sunday school and absorbed these teachings. How Sunday school actually impacted the hundreds of thousands of females who enrolled and whether it fostered better behavior and more loving hearts is unknown. Certainly many women felt that Sunday school made a difference. For many, it opened up a new world. But we can never know what the South—or the nation—might have been like without the Sunday school and without women working through it and their homelife to improve the next generation. What is especially noteworthy is the attention, energy, and concern that southern women from all walks of life gave to children. In the quiet of home and in the Sabbath classroom, various Christian women sought to "raise up a child" to improve the world by focusing on the South's next generation.

GARY B. MILLS

Shades of Ambiguity:
Comparing Antebellum Free People of Color
in "Anglo" Alabama and "Latin" Louisiana

A twentieth-century cockbreeder who trains both fighters and handlers once compared his experiences in Louisiana and Alabama. In Louisiana, he said, nobody bothered chicken fighters because *nothing*'s illegal in Louisiana. But in Alabama, *everything*'s illegal—so folks just find ways around it all.[1] In a nutshell, this formally uneducated "good ol' boy" has perceived a point that scholars of race relations are just now accepting after a century of study: when the posturing of public figures creates too-restrictive legislation, the citizenry winks, nods, and looks away.

A case in point is the comparative roles of antebellum free people of color in "Latin" Louisiana and the "Anglo" South. This essay posits part of the existing literature, some of it my own, against my long-term grassroots study of southern nonwhites.[2] It focuses particularly upon the con-

---

1. Interview by the present writer, December 10, 1981; the informant requested anonymity, given the illegality of his occupation.

2. For Louisiana, major studies include H. E. Sterkx, *The Free Negro in Ante-Bellum Louisiana* (Rutherford, N.J., 1972); Virginia Rosa Dominguez, *White by Definition: Social Classification in Creole Louisiana* (New Brunswick, N.J., 1986); and Gwendolyn Midlo Hall, *Africans in Colonial Louisiana: The Development of an Afro-Creole Culture in the Eighteenth Century* (Baton Rouge, 1992). Major studies of other southern states include Ira Berlin, *Slaves Without Masters: The Free Negro in the Antebellum South* (New York, 1974); E. Franklin Frazier, *The Free Negro Family: A Study of Family Origins Before the Civil War* (Nashville, 1932); John Hope Franklin, *The Free Negro in North Carolina, 1790–1860* (Chapel Hill, 1943); James Hugo Johnston, *Race Relations in Virginia and Miscegenation in*

trasts and similarities between Louisiana and Alabama. In both states, the study has stretched across all economic strata, comparing minutely the experiences, achievements, and frustrations of free people of color at all levels, against each other and against the apparent norms of white society. The essay broadly summarizes my findings to date—suggesting, sometimes, unconventional perspectives from which to view the ambiguous lives of antebellum southerners who were neither white nor slave.

Resources and Methodology

Traditional scholarly wisdom holds that few records exist to document the personal lives of slaves; and that assumption has been extended to southern free people of color. Thus, most studies have taken the traditional tools of white history—laws, newspapers, and personal papers of literate whites—and have theorized from them a "free black experience."[3] How does this scholarly wisdom fare when tested against the common sense of the Alabama cockfighter—that "people are gonna do what they're gonna do; if it's illegal, they find a way around it"? Can historians actually docu-

---

the South, 1776–1860 (Amherst, 1970); and Marina Wikranamyake, A World in Shadow: The Free Black in Antebellum South Carolina (Columbia, 1973).

For a sampling of related works by the present writer, see Gary B. Mills, The Forgotten People: Cane River's Creoles of Color (Baton Rouge, 1976); Mills, "Piety and Prejudice: A Colored Catholic Community in the Antebellum South," in Catholics in the Old South: Essays on Church and Culture, ed. Randall M. Miller and Jon L. Wakelyn (Macon, Ga., 1983), 171–94; Mills, "Liberté, Fraternité, and Everything but Egalité: Cane River's Citoyens de Couleur," in To 1865: Essays on the Region and Its History, ed. B. H. Gilley (Ruston, La., 1984), 93–112, Vol. I of Gilley, ed., North Louisiana, 27 vols.; and Mills, "Miscegenation and the Free Negro in Antebellum 'Anglo' Alabama: A Reexamination of Southern Race Relations," Journal of American History, LXVIII (1981), 16–34; also Gary B. Mills and Elizabeth Shown Mills, "Missionaries Compromised: Early Evangelization of Slaves and Free People of Color in North Louisiana," in Cross, Crozier, and Crucible: A Volume Celebrating the Bicentennial of a Catholic Diocese in Louisiana, ed. Glenn R. Conrad (Lafayette, La., 1993), 30–47.

3. At the risk of unfairly singling out one study, Berlin's Slaves Without Masters offers a detailed bibliography of manuscript sources that represents a typical cross-section of materials. Some 80 percent of the cited matter is either predominantly white family papers in university and state archives or minutes of legislative bodies. The remaining records include three urban census returns, one tax roll, and a few archival holdings that bear "free Negro" or "manumission" labels. No citations appear to land, probate, marriage, military, pension, and similar grass-roots-level resources that are so critical to understanding the personal lives of the free Negro class.

ment the reality of private life that ignores public law? Can we do this for so marginal a class as nonwhites too poor to create public records and too illiterate to create private ones?

The Alabama project, begun in 1976, is a massive, systematic, and comprehensive test based on the type of grass-roots research that traditional historians have assiduously avoided—primarily because it is so time-consuming. To be specific:

- First, an attempt was made to identify every free person of color who lived in or passed through the American territory and state of Alabama prior to the Civil War. It began with a line-by-line reading of every extant population census return for every county in every year—a search that included not only the better-known federal enumerations, but also state and local ones.

- Upon this foundation, efforts have been made to reconstruct the life of each of those people, using the basic grass-roots resources that are commonly the domain of the genealogist. This reconstruction began with a page-by-page search of every surviving book in the courthouse attics, basements, and outbuildings—as well as record rooms—of each of the fifty counties that existed prior to the Civil War. The material ranges from obviously valuable free papers to deeds, mortgages, and tract-book entries; marriage licenses and returns; wills, estate inventories, guardianship appointments, and accounts; civil and criminal court dockets, minutes, record books, and loose-paper files; pauper and road maintenance records; and, occasionally, tax rolls (in most southern states, antebellum tax records have survived in significant numbers, but that is not the case for either Alabama or Louisiana). This search of localized public records turned up numerous people not found in those sporadic censuses. The current count is 5,702.

- Beyond the records just described, many others have been profitably combed: church minutes (Baptist, Catholic, and to a lesser extent, Methodist); lawsuits appealed to the state supreme court; and land-entry files, military records, pension applications, treasury payments, and wartime damage suits housed at the National Archives. Extending these are a wealth of lesser-known federal census returns that began in 1850—agricultural schedules for landowners and tenant farmers; manufacturing schedules for blacksmiths, cigarmakers, and other craftsmen; mortality schedules for those who died within twelve months prior to each enumeration; and slave schedules for those who were not only nonwhite but members of the "master" class as well.

Three objectives exist for this close personal scrutiny: First, to identify the place of origin of each man, woman, and child, so that migration and other social patterns could be defined. Second, to identify the parentage of each, so that miscegenation could be quantified and family relationships established. And third, to determine the lifestyle of each and the degree to which it conformed to the parameters set by law and "Anglo" social thought.[4]

The present study draws upon the data assembled for forty-eight of the fifty antebellum counties. The jurisdictions of Baldwin and Mobile, which had a minority Anglo population during the period, are excluded.[5] The comparisons drawn between the stereotypes of conservative Alabama and freewheeling Louisiana touch upon five areas in which common practice has conflicted with the law: concepts of freedom in southern social thought, the establishment of a legal framework, the treatment of nonwhites in the state's court system, the nonwhites' pursuit of livelihood, and miscegenation.

Concepts of Freedom in Southern Social Thought

Before evaluating "free Negroes," one must evaluate the term *free*. Apart from constitutional law, reality is that the degree of freedom any person enjoys in everyday life is commensurate with personal success. Wealth, fame, or exceptional ability breeds social status, which breeds privilege.

4. The term *Anglo* is used throughout this paper in a generic sense comparable to the more popular *WASP* (White, Anglo-Saxon Protestant). Both terms ignore the strong Celtic, German, and other influences that also shaped southern society east of the Mississippi River and north of the Gulf Coast.

5. Several years into the project, it was split into two studies because early Alabama was a state with two societies. The Mobile region (which includes adjacent Baldwin County) was heavily rooted in the French and Spanish colonial culture that shaped Louisiana. Outside of Mobile and Baldwin, Alabama was populated basically by Americans from states to the east and north. As the dimensions of the project grew, responsibility for the Mobile-Baldwin study was assumed by a doctoral student, who built extensively upon the preliminary work done by the present writer. See Christopher Andrew Nordmann, "Free Negroes of Mobile County, Alabama" (Ph.D. dissertation, University of Alabama, 1990).

For free people of color, status was normally acquired through financial success, but it could accrue from military service or other endeavors. Accomplishments earned community respect, which won privilege—a greater freedom to live and work and socialize as one pleased, regardless of what the law actually said.

The antebellum South extended privileges to people of color in some ways and restricted them in others. Any perusal of statutes will starkly spotlight the constraints. Yet a study of an individual's everyday life and the manner in which he or she operated within and *around* the law can reveal an entirely different level of freedom.

Looking beyond the law books into the private sphere of thousands of specific individuals—not just in Alabama but throughout the South— compels me to make two conclusions. First, Anglo Alabama was more or less typical of the lower and trans-Appalachian southern states, where the number of free people of color was comparatively small and few urban areas were of consequential size. Second, in most respects the patterns found in Anglo Alabama parallel those traditionally cited for Louisiana.

One statistic could serve as both an example and a launching point for the arguments that follow. *Strictly* applying the prevailing laws forces a conclusion that almost 50 percent of Anglo Alabama's free Negroes were either *illegally manumitted* or *illegally residing* within the state. They lived as free because society allowed them to exercise privileges beyond the law. Community recognition became a de facto right.

There are several explanations for this phenomenon, all of which require a basic understanding of several values important to southerners.

Apathy has strongly influenced the social climate. Southerners, white and black, have long lived by that now-ridiculed adage *don't ask, don't tell.* They accord others much freedom in their personal lives, so long as another's action does not threaten them, negatively affect them, or openly offend them. Thus, the majority of Alabama's free people of color lived without those free papers "pattyrollers" supposedly demanded along every roadside. If whites did not ask their nonwhite neighbors for legal proof of freedom, the illegality was not exposed. If no one was affected, no one was offended and no one cared.

Honor has been inseparable from the southern code of *personal* rights. Traditionally, a southerner of integrity believed that one could not question the actions of others without insult. Thus, if a master wanted his slave to enjoy the privileges of freedom, it was basically that master's business. As the radical fringe of southerners (some of whom were, in fact, of northern origins) pushed for stronger laws against manumission, this traditional code of honor was sorely tested. Ultimately, the South's lawmakers gave in to the pressure; but countless constituents still felt that the laws existed only to intimidate those who might otherwise abuse society. As long as a master or his freedman committed no public abuse, they had the right to live and work as they pleased. In the words of Harry Toulmin, a framer of Alabama's first constitution and compiler of its first legal digest, when he illegally set free his slave Toney in 1824: "I do not wish to petition our Alabama Assembly about his emancipation. . . . I scorn to petition for what I believe to be a right."[6]

A *sense of community* has called for protection of the individuals who are contributing parts of that community. Antebellum Alabama was mostly rural; and thinly scattered farm families needed each other, regardless of race. This mutuality stretched into the villages and towns as well. Urban areas were comparatively small, housing was integrated, and most urban free people of color in Alabama followed service-oriented trades that the community needed in order to function smoothly.

Paternalism, which is normally discussed in terms of master-slave relationships, has been inherent in most aspects of southern society. Southrons have respected the European tradition of landed, privileged classes exercising protective roles over families of lesser status.[7] Thus, the free nonwhites and the quasi-free, in the plantation South at least, had their "protectors." When they moved, they often did so in the party of prominent whites; or they went to areas in which influential citizens knew their origins and could assume a guardian's role. When laws were passed that restricted nonwhite activities, the well-placed mentors saw to it that the community made an exception for the worthy free people of color.

This patriarchal relationship between whites and free nonwhites reached its peak (or its nadir, depending upon one's philosophy) as the antebellum era waned. Hardliners introduced restrictive laws in reaction

6. Washington County, Ala., Record of Wills, 1820–99, p. 7. For other views on the theme of honor, see Bertram Wyatt-Brown, *Honor and Violence in the Old South* (New York, 1986).

7. A brief discussion of the South's roots in patriarchy and paternalism can be found in David Hackett Fischer, *Albion's Seed: Four British Folkways in America* (New York, 1989), 274–80.

to northern "interference," realizing that the free Negroes they drove northward would be considered a social problem by many northern antagonists once those individuals arrived on northern doorsteps. Yet in Alabama, as in many southern states, the expulsion efforts were thwarted by personal exceptions. Respectable "illegals" formalized the traditional paternalistic relationship by officially declaring their protector to be their legal guardian, and their communities were satisfied.

Kinship has been the web holding southern society in place and the fuel firing most of its activities.[8] As will be discussed in the segment on miscegenation, kinship crossed racial lines far more often and influenced race relations far more significantly than is commonly credited to Anglo America.

Reputation, in the Bible-belt South, has been a religious creed for both blacks and whites. Following the biblical mandate that a good name is worth more than riches, "good" southerners traditionally have felt obliged to earn the respect of not just peers but all social classes. For nonwhites, the need has been economic and political as well as personal. A reputation for honesty would promote their personal endeavors and protect them from unwarranted suspicion when crimes were committed. For people of color who had little else, a good name could be their most valuable patrimony.[9] "Decent" white citizens viewed the racial implications differently, recognizing that the "free Negro problem" was a profitable fuse for political demagogues and newspaper editors to ignite. Thus, when the *class* as a whole was publicly attacked, the *individual* free Negro of good reputation was defended in his community by the white citizenry that valued its own reputation.

Respect is, arguably, the most misunderstood motivator of southern society—being a caste-based system in which each level of society was ac-

8. This theme is touched upon by Fischer, *ibid.*, 220–22, and far more fully developed by Darett B. and Anita H. Rutman, *A Place in Time: Middlesex County, Virginia, 1650–1750* (2 vols.; New York, 1984).

9. Armstrong Williams, talk-show host, writer, and businessman, poignantly described the traditional value of reputation for southern African Americans in a 1996 Father's Day column: "When I was growing up in Marion, S.C., I would go into a store and try to get something on credit. When the clerk would ask me who my father was, my reply that I was the son of James Williams would earn instant respect. He would say, 'Get whatever you want; your daddy is a good man.' Even today when I'm back home, I receive the residual respect of the good name passed on as your patrimony." See "My Father Taught Me How to Be a Man," Tuscaloosa *News*, June 16, 1996. For one biblical reference, see Proverbs 22:1.

corded its own type of respect. Contrary to popular thought, these levels were chiseled by social factors that often surpassed race. As in other class-based milieus, the enjoyment of respect depended upon an individual's conformity to the class in which he or she was born. As long as free people of color contributed to the community and did not threaten the foundations of local society, they enjoyed respect within the level set by money, education, and (at least *public*) morality.

The present study has uncovered no convincing evidence that these fundamental engines of southern society worked differently in the Latin or Anglo South. Universally, southerners have tended to ignore laws that contradict local customs, family codes, and a community sense of justice. Thus, if a master wanted his slave to be free, that right was his or hers. The higher the master's position and respect in the community, the more right he or she enjoyed. To deny that right would be to question the master's honor, integrity, and judgment. At the same time, the community held masters responsible for the behavior of unshackled slaves. So long as masters exercised good judgment in choosing those to whom they granted privileges, the community commonly allowed them the liberty to exercise that judgment.

A myriad of other nuances, as well, affected the status and experience of free people of color in both Alabama and Louisiana, whether freeborn, manumitted, or quasi-free. The day laborer who "worked about" did not have the same esteem and protection as a skilled craftsman. A man or woman set loose by a master of dubious social status might find less privilege than the quasi-free attached to a community leader. If known to be the offspring of a prominent family, a freed person had increased status, and he or she was much less likely to be constrained by society and its laws.

The Establishment of a Legal Framework

Race-related legislation was cyclical in Anglo Alabama, as in Louisiana and elsewhere in the South. Commonly, those cycles were reactive rather than proactive. Some were knee-jerk responses to one or another highly publicized, inflammatory incident occurring elsewhere. Late in the antebellum era, racial restraints became defiant political measures passed by a populace that valued "minding one's own business" and resented northern pressure for the South to conform to northern dictates.

Throughout most of its antebellum history, Anglo Alabama passed laws to curb new manumissions. For half the era, its statutes barred incoming free Negroes at the state line. Evidence is abundant on those two points. Yet by identifying each free person of color involved, by dating individual manumissions or arrivals in the state, and by tracking each person through to the end of the antebellum era, another reality is laid bare: the laws were widely ignored.[10] The reason is not surprising. Southerners are tolerant to a fault with individuals they know and get along with. The unknown is a different matter; and the idea of *masses* of unknown, uncontrolled blacks was an antebellum bogeyman that radicals planted and nourished. Laws restricting free nonwhite population growth eased the fears of all by keeping *unknown, uncontrollable* free Negroes out of the state. But case-by-case nonenforcement of those laws protected the black friends and gave society the right to choose whom it would accept.

The system was discriminatory, yes. But it had a solid precedent in Anglo America—ironically in *northern* Anglo America. Roots of the attitude are seen in the "warning out" practice of early New England. There, the body politic of each town considered itself responsible for the welfare of only those individuals who had been officially "admitted" to that town. Strangers who showed signs of dallying or visitors who stayed too long were "warned out." Gaining legal admission to the town required newcomers to prove good citizenship. The official "warning out" put them on notice that they were there only with community forbearance.[11]

So was it with many of Alabama's manumitted slaves and freeborn nonwhites coming into the state. They knew their residence was not legal; but so long as they lived within the parameters of society and maintained themselves and their dependents, they were allowed to remain and to entertain the hope of permanent status. Most southern whites were

10. Eugene Genovese foretold this in a 1972 essay in which he noted: "Wherever we look, we find communities ignoring a variety of restrictions placed upon manumission and the rights of Free Negroes," although adequate data had not been assimilated at that point to see the breadth and depth to which these laws were popularly nullified throughout the South. See Genovese, "The Slave States of North America," in *Neither Slave nor Free: The Freedmen of African Descent in the Slave Societies of the New World*, ed. David W. Cohen and Jack P. Greene (Baltimore, 1972), 258.

11. Ann S. Lainhart, "Records of the Poor in Pre-Twentieth-Century New England," *National Genealogical Society Quarterly*, LXXXI (1993), 262. New England's warnings out, of course, were rooted in Old England's traditional "poor laws."

comfortable with the ambiguity. They wanted a legal framework that lent a sense of security and satisfied the feeling that "something oughta be done"—so long as the law did not infringe upon their individual right to "do whatever I damn well please."

The principle is apparent in Alabama's reaction to the Nat Turner rebellion of 1831. Raising the specter of free blacks inciting rebellions closer to home, a few white radicals in the black-belt county of Dallas (county seat: Selma) followed the lead of counterparts in other states from Louisiana to the Tidewater and proposed the removal of free Negroes from the state. They were immediately assailed by the black-belt press, which swore the proposal would be opposed by "every friend of this unfortunate class of beings, and lover of domestic security." [12] Amid the ensuing ideological battle, the legislature compromised with an 1832 act that, on the one hand, gave local communities the right to rule on manumission requests within their own jurisdictions but, on the other, attempted to limit growth of the free Negro class. Its language barred new arrivals from other states and decreed that newly manumitted slaves were to move from the state within twelve months, never to return. [13]

The first restriction of the law was met with almost utter disregard. Free Negroes continued to come into the state, making no attempt to hide their illegal status. To the contrary, they gave public evidence, in official forums, that could have been used to force their expulsion, had there been a local inclination to do so. For example:

- Peter Brandford brought his free paper to the courthouse of the piedmont county of Jefferson for recording in 1838, attesting that he was freed in Wilkes County, Georgia, in 1836. [14]
- Lavina Bert, alias Bowens, had a copy of her free paper made in Hertford, North Carolina, before leaving that state in 1834, and she presented it the next spring to the county clerk of Madison County, in Alabama's Tennessee Valley, for official recording. [15]

12. Tuscaloosa *State Intelligencer*, December 10, 1831. The anti-free-Negro reaction in Louisiana actually began in 1830, fueled by an inflammatory incident in that state; see Sterkx, *Free Negro in Ante-Bellum Louisiana*, 98–101.

13. John G. Aikin, *A Digest of the Laws of the State of Alabama . . . in Force at the Close of the Session of the General Assembly, in January, 1833* (Philadelphia, 1833), 545.

14. Jefferson County, Ala., Deed Book 6, p. 317.

15. Madison County, Ala., Deed Book P, 297.

- Amelia Ann Johnson filed her proof of freedom in the black-belt county of Marengo in 1835, saying that she and her child had just arrived in the state, following her enslaved husband, George Kincaid, from Prince Edward County, Virginia.[16]

Francis "Frank" Wickfall of South Carolina provides an even clearer example of the disregard that community leaders showed for the expulsion laws. When Wickfall, in 1846, presented his free paper to officials in Tuscaloosa (which until recently had been the state capital) for recording, he reported that he was a free Negro who had served out an apprenticeship in South Carolina and had moved to Tuscaloosa in company with a white tradesman. His wife, Agnes, was not mentioned and filed no papers of her own. Throughout the 1850s, as radicals turned up the heat on free Negroes, Wickfall continued to operate his tannery in Tuscaloosa and adjacent Fayette County. Wickfall's only concession, late in the antebellum period, was to choose white associates to serve as his "guardians," officially. Neither wealthy nor well connected, Wickfall was still honest and hardworking. Area citizens knew him to be a solid, contributing member of society and had no qualms about winking at a law that would offend an inoffensive member of their community.[17]

Other free Negroes who entered Alabama came from as far away as New York and Philadelphia—individuals whose northern roots, theoretically, would have made them a threat to the southern slave system. Yet neither court records nor newspapers yield any account of action taken against them. The conclusion of Louisiana's major study of free Negro rights—that "efforts to keep free Negroes out of Louisiana were a failure either because of laxity in the administration of the law or a humane attitude on the part of government officials"—could be equally applied to Anglo Alabama.[18] In this regard, both the Alabama and Louisiana findings contrast markedly with one widely accepted opinion—namely, "Border counties in almost every southern state sported a disproportionately

16. Marengo County, Ala., Deed Book C, 368.

17. Tuscaloosa County, Ala., Deed Book 4, p. 157; Orphan's Court Book 6 [1857], pp. 194, 299, 481, and Book 7 [1860], pp. 391, 409; Commissioner's Court Minutes [1861], pp. 39–40; 1850 U.S. census, population schedule, Fayette County, Ala., p. 35, dwelling 485, microfilm M432, roll 5, National Archives [hereinafter cited as NA]; 1860 U.S. census, pop. sch., Tuscaloosa County, Ala., p. 732, dwell. 1105, microfilm M653, roll 25, NA.

18. Sterkx, *Free Negro in Ante-Bellum Louisiana*, 95.

large free Negro population. Free Negroes found these borderlines a stra-
tegic boon in their endless battle with the law. When one state threatened them, they simply slipped across the state line and waited for the
furor to pass."[19] Specifically in Alabama, the free Negro settlement pattern reflects significant density in the major urban areas and the productive river valleys; it was not tied to the state's borders.

The federal census of 1850 clearly documents the extent to which the
law was disregarded. Beginning in that year, census marshals were directed to record the name, racial status, age, and birthplace (as well as
other pertinent data) of *every* free person in their districts.[20] From their
returns, a list can be compiled of known free Negroes in Alabama who
were born outside the state after the passage of the 1832 law and who
were, thus, in the state "illegally." In the case of adults, in-migration often
can be dated within two years or so by checking birth-state data for each
child in the household. For those living in households with no other free
nonwhites, the time of migration often can be established by studying
this detail for the white family with whom they lived. Under the law, of
course, children born of illegal parents were illegal as well.

Federal law also required that the original copy of each county's census
be deposited with the clerk of the county court, open to the public for examination.[21] If, as commonly held, free Negroes instinctively avoided
public records and public officials for fear they would be expelled, then
the public display of census data proving them to be illegals was a serious
threat.[22] Yet the analyzed 1850–1860 data for Alabama reveal a different
scenario and a different mindset. To summarize:

- In 1850, over 20 percent of all free nonwhites in Anglo Alabama
  (n = 217 individuals, 64 families) gave the census marshal data
  that proved they had entered the state after February 1, 1832 —
  officially recording their illegal status.

19. Berlin, *Slaves Without Masters*, 173.

20. Bureau of the Census, *Twenty Censuses: Population and Housing Questions, 1790–
1980* (Washington, D.C., 1979), 14–17.

21. George Minot, ed., *The Statutes at Large and Treaties of the United States of America
from December 1, 1845, to March 3, 1851* (Boston, 1851), 31st Cong., 1st Sess., Vol. IX,
430. Also, Margo J. Anderson, *The American Census: A Social History* (New Haven, 1988),
13–14.

22. For example, see Berlin, *Slaves Without Masters*, 328.

- Two-thirds of these individuals were still in the state in 1860, when census takers next made their rounds.

- Of the one-third not enumerated in 1860, most can be accounted for by death or by natural attrition due to migration patterns of the era.

The second restriction of the 1832 law—that manumitted slaves should leave the state and not return, under penalty of being sold back into slavery—was observed more in name than in spirit. Numerous wills gave lip service to the law. In execution, it often was blatantly disregarded. Between the 1832 law and the close of the era, Alabama's free nonwhite population nearly doubled. Numerous individual cases explain why. Consider this one: In 1837, Richard Blunt, a newly freed mulatto of Montgomery County, bought the freedom of his daughter Penelope "Penny" Blount (later Wilson) of Montgomery. He then visited the county courthouse with two white friends; together they filed a power of attorney by which he authorized them to take her to New England for manumission. Presumably, she did leave. Clearly, she returned. When the first every-name census was compiled in 1850, Penny was registered right there in Montgomery, the state capital, where the census marshals reported that all her children were born in Alabama—in 1835, 1840, 1841, 1844, 1845, and 1848, respectively.[23]

Even more blatant is the case of Dallas County's two Charity Smiths—both surviving "widows" of the same man. Tom Smith, who was locally manumitted in 1828, died intestate in early 1850, leaving a free wife of advanced years and a younger slave wife, whose children were still in bondage. The administrator of his estate petitioned for the second family's freedom. A special act was passed by the legislature in January 1852, requiring the administrator to post a $2,000 bond guaranteeing that the family would leave the state within two years.[24] (The general law of the state required a move within six months.)[25]

23. Montgomery County, Ala., Conveyances, o.s. Books P, 3–4, and X, 654; 1850 U.S. census, pop. sch., Montgomery County, Ala., p. 133, dwell. 996, microfilm M 432, roll 12, NA.

24. Dallas County, Ala., Probate File 96 (Tom Smith); *Malinda and Sarah [Smith]* v. *Gardner*, 24 Ala. 719. See also Dallas County Record of Wills, A, pp. 13–14, for the 1826 manumission of Tom himself.

25. John J. Ormand, Arthur P. Bagby, and George Goldthwaite, *The Code of Alabama* (Montgomery, 1852), 391.

Did the newly freed Smiths leave? No. The son Miles moved to Mobile immediately after his father's death, where he lived as free for two years before his legislative manumission. The daughter Rebecca married and moved to the neighboring black-belt county of Perry, where she and her husband went before the court in 1856 to select a "guardian." Still showing no qualms over the illegality of her continued existence in the state, her attorney petitioned the Dallas court in 1858 for settlement of her father's estate; and he plainly stated Perry as her place of residence. Pending before the Dallas court, at the same time, was a petition of the older Charity in which she claimed old age, poverty, ill health, and immense worry over "her daughter," who was still in slavery. Her plea to emancipate the child was duly advertised in the local newspaper, and the manumission was granted. No one raised the question of how Charity, who had been manumitted in 1828, could have a preteen, enslaved "daughter." Nor did any locals insist that the adolescent Priscilla be removed from Alabama within six months, as the law required. Except for old Charity and two sons of the younger Charity whose deaths are documented during the 1850s, all members of the family were recorded by the 1860 census marshals as free residents of Dallas and Perry Counties.[26]

From instances such as these, it could be argued that Alabama's nonentry and expulsion laws were less a punishment than a *tool* to be used as needed. When they were not needed, public energies or funds were not wasted on their enforcement—a pattern that typifies southern thought. The central authority may pass laws for the good of the whole; but the execution of those laws, and the decision whether and when to execute any specific law, was properly a matter of self-determination at the local level.

The quasi-free—slaves living on their own, working on their own, and sometimes paying a percentage of their income to their master—also enjoyed more legal rights than law dictated. It is probably impossible to estimate the number or ascertain the exact status of these slave elites, who made considerable economic and social strides while still formally enchained. Legal records are relatively meager because these people were

26. Dallas County, Ala., Probate File 96; Probate Minutes K, pp. 45, 128; *Malinda and Sarah v. Gardner*, 24 Ala. 719. Also Perry County, Ala., Probate Minutes H, 1856, p. 590; 1860 U.S. census, pop. sch., Dallas Co., Ala., p. 818, dwell. 398, microfilm M653, roll 8, NA; 1860 U.S. census, pop. sch., Perry County, Ala., p. 722, dwell. 631, microfilm M653, roll 20, NA.

not a legal entity, although they might be recorded by census takers who found them living independently and assumed them to be free. Yet a revealing number of cases exist in which enterprising slaves filed documents to buy or lease property. Occasionally they asked the court's assistance in collecting a debt for money loaned to others.

Civil War damage claims are especially rich in detail on their activities. In the case of Cain Leach of Lauderdale County in the Tennessee Valley, for example, witnesses described Leach as "practically a free man," being "entirely at liberty to choose his own work and his own company," and "a free man, having his own time." Another witness explained, "The man [whom Leach] belonged to was a very lenient man and very good to his slaves. . . . [Leach] was a very energetic man, and very saving." With a willing master, an ambitious slave such as this one could live as free, work on his own, buy and sell, and do whatever else it took to acquire property.[27] Leach, however, was not counted as free on the federal censuses.

Joseph Commons of nearby Madison County, by his own statement, was quasi-free—although the census marshals in his case gave him the benefit of the doubt. Commons, who appears in sundry public records between 1838 and 1870, buying, selling, and suing, testified before the Southern Claims Commission in 1872 that he "was a free person of color, having purchased before the Rebellion my freedom, [although I] had never been legally made free by an act of the State Legislature." His wife Lucy said, "He was a free man, and had been since the Florida War." Joseph owned nine horses, cattle, a stable, a house and lot in Huntsville, and a farm three miles from town. He did laundry, dyed clothes, and traded for a living. If questioned as he went about his antebellum business, this quasi-free could have presented a pass issued him by an Alabama Supreme Court justice who wrote that the laws restricted outright manumission but that all "humane and generous people" of Alabama should allow Joe Commons to live free without molestation.[28] All did.

27. *Cain Leach* v. *U.S.*, Record Group 56, Records of the Southern Claims Commission, commission no. 4531, office no. 46, report 3, 1873, NA.

28. *Joseph Commons* v. *U.S.*, Southern Claims Commission, comm. no. 401, ofc. no. 29, rpt. 2, 1872, NA. For Commons' free paper, see Madison County Deed Record Q, p. 581. His subsequent activities can be tracked through such records as Madison County Deed Record R, 1838–1840, pp. 493–94; Marriage Book 4 [1843], 31; and Chancery Record N [1845], 261–64; also 1850 U.S. census, pop. sch., Madison County, Ala., Huntsville, p. 11, dwell. 96, microfilm M432, roll 9, NA.

Treatment of Free Negroes in the Court System

Most studies of southern race relations assume from the statutes that Louisiana's free nonwhites enjoyed far more rights before the court than did those of the Anglo states, including the right to testify in all civil suits. Sterkx, for example, opines that "free Negroes of Louisiana . . . enjoyed a better legal position than *any* of their counterparts in other states of the South."[29] Genovese modifies that statement slightly, noting that Delaware law also permitted free Negroes to testify against whites.[30] Other studies have posed the South's free nonwhites—in both Louisiana and the Anglo states—as a social problem, a population prone to various forms of vice.[31] The Anglo Alabama project does not uphold this image.

Strictly speaking, free nonwhites in Alabama had the right to a jury trial, although not to a jury of their peers. Legislation enacted three years after statehood decreed that trials of free Negroes were to be generally "conducted in the same manner and under the same rules" as the trials of free whites, although black testimony might be given less weight than white testimony in certain cases.[32] By 1833 the courts were appointing attorneys at public expense when free Negroes could not afford their own.[33] Then as now, no one could argue rationally that the quality of representation was the same for the pauper as for the rich man. Nor could it be contended that this safeguarding of free Negro rights was born of liberalism, because there were social restrictions passed simultaneously. However, it does reflect a societal willingness to protect whatever rights its laws did grant.

In reality, there occurred very few criminal cases involving this anomalous class. Extant court records of Anglo Alabama's forty-eight counties have yielded only thirteen such cases for a population of nearly three

---

29. Sterkx, *Free Negro in Ante-Bellum Louisiana*, 171, emphasis added.

30. Genovese, "Slave States of North America," 262.

31. For a sampling of this view, see William B. Hesseltine and David L. Smiley, *The South in American History* (2d ed.; Englewood Cliffs, N.J., 1960), 196–97; Derek Noel Kerr, "Petty Felony, Slave Defiance, and Frontier Villainy: Crime and Criminal Justice in Spanish Louisiana, 1770–1803" (Ph.D. dissertation, Tulane University, 1983), 190, 265; John H. Russell, *The Free Negro in Virginia, 1619–1865* (Baltimore, 1913), 160; Franklin, *Free Negro in North Carolina*, 88–89, 101; and Berlin, *Slaves Without Masters*, 186.

32. Harry Toulmin, A *Digest of the Laws of the State of Alabama . . . in Force at the End of the General Assembly in January, 1823* (Cahawba, Ala., 1823), 204.

33. Aiken, *Digest of the Laws of the State of Alabama . . . 1833*, 125.

thousand free Negroes.[34] Charges ranged from gaming (a frequent offense for whites as well) to failure to perform community service on the roads, to malicious mischief in a revenge killing of another man's hogs, to trading with slaves, to keeping a house of ill fame, to what was surely the ultimate offense: rape of a white woman. Of these thirteen cases, ten ended in convictions; but one of the convictions was overturned at the appeals-court level—as was the sentence imposed in the rape trial. For the remaining three cases, the extant records report no outcome; but the accused in each case is later found, as free, in other records.[35] The only clear conclusion to be drawn from so few cases is that free nonwhites in Alabama were not a lawless class.

The rape case particularly speaks to public attitude and court protection. John Thurman was tried and convicted at the local level, under an indictment that labeled him a "mulatto." Contemporary Alabama law decreed a death sentence for any "free Negro or mulatto" committing rape "upon the body of a white female." However, the state's law also defined a

34. These thirteen are *State v. John Thurman*, 18 Ala. 276; *State v. M'Donald*, 4 Porter 449; *State v. Jeptha*, Dallas County Circuit Court Record, 1853–54, [vol.] No. 2, p. 218; *State v. Isaac Jacobs*, Saint Clair County Circuit Court Minutes, 1842–47, [illegible page number]; *State v. Henry Frost*, Lowndes County Final Record, 1848–49, pp. 9–10; *State v. Green King*, Perry County Circuit Court State Trial Docket, 1856–60, [unpaginated, see Fall Term, 1859, case no. 1920]; *State v. Edney and Adeline Jacobs*, Madison County Minute Book [Chancery], 1831–34, p. 42; *State v. Richmond Terrell*, Madison County Minutes, Circuit Court, 1844–46, pp. 303–42; *State v. Charles Jumper*, Madison County Circuit Court Minutes, 1852–53, p. 364; *State v. William Patterson*, Madison County Circuit Court Minutes, 1852, p. 398; *Mayor and Alderman v. Polly Martin*, Madison County Circuit Court Book 34, 1836–37, pp. 42–43; *State v. James Williams*, Clarke County General Records of Suits, County Court, 1824–[1833], pp. 397–99; and *State v. Jonathan Meiggs*, Clarke County Circuit Court Record, 1829–30, p. 56. The cited Clarke and Perry records have been deposited at the Alabama Department of Archives and History, Montgomery [hereinafter cited as ADAH]; the others remain in the local courthouses. Additionally two free Negroes have been found enumerated in the state penitentiary and two others in the county jails, for whom no criminal proceedings have been found in extant records; see 1850 U.S. census, pop. sch., Coosa County, Ala., pp. 5B-6, dwell. 80 (state penitentiary, for John Marshall and James Weaver), microfilm M432, roll 4, NA; 1850 U.S. census, pop. sch., Fayette County, Ala., p. 102, dwell. 653 (county jail, for Phealas Shiflma), M432, roll 5, NA; 1860 U.S. census, pop. sch., Coosa County, Ala., p. 116, dwell. 833 (state penitentiary, showing no free Negroes), microfilm M653, roll 7, NA; and 1860 U.S. census, pop. sch., Morgan County, Ala., p. 11 (317), dwell. 62 (county jail, for George Fines), microfilm M653, roll 19, NA.

35. Specifically: Richmond Terrell, Polly Martin, and William Patterson.

mulatto very narrowly as "the offspring of a negress by a white man or of a white woman by a negro." Thus, Thurman's attorney appealed his conviction to the state supreme court, arguing that he was a quadroon (three-fourths white) and should not be subjected to the more punitive law for mulattoes and Negroes. The proceedings identify Thurman as the offspring of a white mother and a mulatto father. They say he was well known in his community as a free man of color and describe him as "having kinky hair and yellow skin." Alabama's supreme court fretted over a larger issue: if a law created for mulattoes were to be applied to quadroons, where would the extension stop? Would it be necessary, the jurists asked, "to pursue the line of descendants, as long as there is a drop of negro blood remaining?" Caring naught for such folly, the court decreed that Thurman "was not a mulatto within the meaning of the statute." Overturning his death penalty, the justices ordered that he be resentenced as a white man.[36]

The other conviction overturned at the state's highest level treats another sensitive subject: the oft-repeated fear that free blacks were in league with abolitionists to incite slave revolts. Only one such accusation has been found in Alabama, and it coincided with the reaction in the early 1830s to Virginia's Nat Turner revolt. The nonwhite male charged with this offense was convicted on the local level. However, at the time he made his "inflammatory" remarks, he was on a three-day binge and was well known in his community to talk loosely when drunk. The fact that a local white was motivated to pursue the defense of this impoverished, alcoholic free Negro all the way to the state supreme court makes its own testimony as to the kind of social protection that Alabama's nonwhites could enjoy.[37]

The sentences meted out by Alabama courts to the eight free people of color whose convictions went unchallenged were neither more nor less stringent than those given whites for similar crimes. Severe punishment was decreed only once—and its severity may well explain the rareness of the crime. Convicted of robbery, James Williams was ordered to repay his victim, suffer thirty-nine lashes, spend one hour each day for two days in the town pillory—with one ear nailed thereto each day, after which the ear would be cut off—and be branded in the hand with the letter *T.* A

36. *State v. Thurman,* 18 Ala. 276.
37. *State v. M'Donald,* 4 Porter 449.

white man of the same county who committed the same crime was given a similar sentence.[38] Within a couple of years, the state penitentiary opened and incarceration replaced branding and the pillory for whites and nonwhites alike.[39]

In both Alabama and Louisiana, the more radical elements of the 1850s called for the reenslavement of free Negroes for various causes. Both groups proposed it for free people of color convicted of crime, and both legislatures rejected it. As a sop to satisfy their "something oughta be done" constituents, both passed optimistic legislation in 1859 "permitting" free Negroes to voluntarily return themselves to slavery.[40] Alabama also reduced from a year to six months the grace period before a newly manumitted slave was supposed to leave the state or face reenslavement (1852) and, two years later, adopted Georgia's longstanding precedent of "permitting" free Negroes to formalize their relationship with a white protector by choosing him as "guardian."[41] (In keeping with prevailing discrimination against women, no females of antebellum Louisiana were similarly chosen to be a legal representative.) The second provision became, in reality, an illegal but socially acceptable substitute for the first—as previously implied by the examples of Rebecca Smith and Francis Wickfall.

The largest percentage (59 percent, $n = 79$) of legal actions in Alabama involving free nonwhites were debt cases, a situation not dissimilar to society as a whole. The free Negro image emerging from these cases is not one of dishonesty or financial instability. Less than 1 percent of the total free nonwhite population was involved in the surviving litigation. Of these cases, 5 percent were blacks' suits against other blacks. Roughly 60 percent represented whites suing blacks. In the remaining 35 percent, the plaintiffs were free Negroes and the defendants were white.

38. *State v. Williams*, Clarke County, Ala. Also *State v. Collins*, Clarke County Circuit Court Minutes G, 1837–39, p. 25, ADAH. Although the local trial minutes decree the two exposures in the stock, they do not mention the nailing and amputation of the ears. The specifics of the pillory activities are provided in the prevailing statute; see Aikin, *Digest of the Laws . . . 1833*, 113.

39. C. C. Clay, *A Digest of the Laws of the State of Alabama . . . in Force at the Close of the Session of the General Assembly, in February, 1843* (Tuscaloosa, 1843), chap. 15.

40. Sterkx, *Free Negro in Ante-Bellum Louisiana*, 196–98; *Acts of the Seventh Biennial Session of the General Assembly of Alabama . . . 1859* (Montgomery, 1860), 63.

41. Ormand et al., *Code of Alabama . . . 1852*, 391; *Acts of the Fourth Biennial Session of the General Assembly . . . Commencing on the Second Monday in November 1853* (Montgomery, 1854), 49.

This last figure belies another stereotype. Under the Alabama law that was enacted in 1832 and followed for the rest of the antebellum period, black testimony could be prohibited in cases involving more than $20.[42] Yet free nonwhites not only testified *but sued whites* in cases far in excess of the legal limit: 56 percent of the debt cases involved $100 or more, and 26 percent involved $1,000 or more—a circumstance that places the Alabama free Negro, in a de facto sense at least, on an equal footing with the legal rights reported for Louisiana.[43] Not only was free nonwhite testimony accepted by the courts, but the verdict was returned in the free Negro's favor in over half of the cases. When all types of civil action between free blacks and whites are analyzed, verdicts were returned in favor of nonwhites in 66 percent of all cases and in 77 percent of cases in which blacks sued whites.

The Free Negro's Pursuit of Livelihood

Existing literature on southerners of this caste paints a bleak and one-dimensional picture of their economic activities: Free Negroes, as a class, were impoverished, although spectacular exceptions could be cited, particularly in Louisiana. Free Negro ranks were financially burdened by the aged and infirm whose unconscionable masters supposedly dumped them upon society.[44] Although some free nonwhites did own slaves, they are generally assumed to have been benevolent souls buying freedom for friends and loved ones.[45] In practice, individual cases of all of the above can be documented in Alabama, as they can for all antebellum states, North or South; but reality is far more complex than the stereotype suggests.

With regard to wealth—or a lack thereof—extensive figures have not yet been developed from the accumulated Alabama data. In the sample counties in which statistics have been tabulated, average nonwhite wealth remains noticeably below the average for white property holding, although

42. Aikin, *Digest of the Laws of the State of Alabama . . . 1833*, 294.

43. On this point, specifically see Sterkx, *Free Negro in Ante-Bellum Louisiana*, 171, although Sterkx provides only anecdotal data rather than statewide statistics.

44. Typical discussions of this viewpoint are presented by Berlin, who synthesized numerous previous works. See, for example, *Slaves Without Masters*, 152. Supporting anecdotes are for the upper South states of Maryland and Virginia.

45. Typical here is Genovese's discussion in "Slave States of North America," 266.

minimal difference exists in the mean and median figures. Comparative statistics published for Latin Louisiana sometimes reflect the opposite situation—an example being the Franco-African, slaveowning families of Isle Brevelle in Natchitoches Parish. There, average nonwhite wealth actually exceeded average white wealth in certain periods.[46]

The elite free Negroes of Anglo Alabama were the tradesmen, a few of whom achieved quite comfortable economic status. They lent money to whites. They built nice homes. They invested in real estate. They privately educated their children.[47] But they were not the norm. More typical were those one might label *lower-middle class:* steady job holders of marginal or limited education, living frugally in a modest house, with a horse or two that could be equated to a modern used car or pickup truck. Single mothers and uneducated males who worked for minimum wage, weather permitting, seldom escaped poverty. On rare occasion there was the charity case, on public dole. All of this could be said for contemporary white society as well, but one notable difference existed: free Negro males in Anglo Alabama never cracked the glass ceiling that enterprising white males *could* crack—and the one that some exceptional free Creoles *de couleur* in Louisiana, such as the Metoyers of Natchitoches and the Donatos of Opelousas, did crack.[48]

It is exceedingly hard to find evidence of masters in Alabama manumitting old and decrepit slaves without means of support.[49] The examples often cited for large urban areas of older states were incongruent with the social milieu of rural and small-town Alabama. One of the state's most strictly enforced laws of manumission, dating from 1805, was a require-

46. An explicit comparative table is found in Mills, *Forgotten People,* 110. Elizabeth Shown Mills has extended that analysis to include a less elite free nonwhite community in the same parish, finding a modest but far less impressive economy; see "(de) Mézières-Trichel-Grappe: A Study of a Tri-caste Lineage in the Old South," *Genealogist,* VI (1985), 4–84, esp. 14.

47. Among the numerous examples are Solomon Perteet and James Abbott of Tuscaloosa, John Rapier of Lauderdale County, and John Robinson of Madison County.

48. For the Metoyers, see Mills, *Forgotten People;* for the Donatos, see Carl A. Brasseaux, Keith P. Fontenot, and Claude F. Oubre, *Creoles of Color in the Bayou Country* (Jackson, Miss., 1994).

49. For abstracts of all manumissions found in Anglo Alabama's county-level records (but not in legislative records), see Gary B. Mills, "Free African Americans in Pre–Civil War 'Anglo' Alabama: Slave Manumissions Gleaned from County-Court Records," *National Genealogical Society Quarterly,* LXXXIII (1995), 127–42, 199–214.

ment that the master post bond to ensure that the freed slave would not become a public charge.[50] Although all county governments had some welfare mechanisms in place, none tolerated the shifting of a financial burden from an able individual to the community as a whole.

Typical of those who did free the aged and infirm is the following sampling representing diverse cultural and economic elements of the state: Francis Ashurst, Montgomery County, willed in 1831 that Abra(ha)m and Priscy should be set free and that his executor, R. J. W. Crockett, should support them from estate funds.[51] Ruth Otterson of Greene County willed in 1843 that "Joseph & Chancy, old Negroes made free by the last will of Samuel Otterson deceased be taken care of by my said executors . . . out of any money or means in the hands of my executors and that they be allowed to choose their own place of residence."[52] John Watson of Coosa County willed in 1851 that the old couple January and Nelly were to live as free; that they be allowed to remain "for the rest of their life" on the forty acres he set aside for them; and that if they should be unable to support themselves, his executor should do so out of his estate.[53] Only one manumission has been found of an elderly or infirm slave without an attached provision for support: Gallanus Winn of Madison County, in his 1839 will, rewarded "the kind attendance of [his] old Negro woman Hanna," by giving her freedom—but specified no property, cash, or pension.[54]

The most controversial question—to what extent free Negroes bought slaves as an investment versus an act of love and charity—is one for which quantifiable figures do not yet exist. Wishful thinking aside, Alabama's free nonwhites did both, as did their counterparts in Louisiana. Young Delia Logwood of Lawrence County, in the Tennessee Valley, bought her husband and kept him in slavery even though both she and he had the kinship and political support of whites prominent enough to have obtained his manumission.[55] Wade Potter, a free black of coastal Es-

50. Toulmin, *Digest of the Laws of the State of Alabama, . . . 1823,* 632.

51. Montgomery County, Ala., Will Book 2, pp. 161–62.

52. Greene County, Ala., Probate File 969.

53. Coosa County, Ala., Will and Orphan's Records 2, pp. 42–43.

54. Madison County, Ala., Probate Record Book A, p. 30.

55. *Delia Logwood v. U.S.,* Southern Claims Commission, comm. no. 21129, rpt. 6, 1876.

cambia County, bought a concubine who later became his wife—one whom associates testified appeared to be white.[56] The previously mentioned Tom Smith of Dallas died owning a slave wife and three children by her, but he also owned ten other slaves whom his family made no effort to manumit. Solomon Perteet of Tuscaloosa bought his wife and her child and had them freed by an act of the legislature; then he bought and freed a friend and that friend's grandson, who labored to pay him back. But there is no record of his purchasing a slave as a capital investment.[57] In contrast, his enterprising townswoman Martitia Payne bought a number of slaves—including one runaway from the county jail—without freeing any of them.[58]

From an economic standpoint, the presumption that slaves owned by free Negroes were "undoubtedly family members" is an economic injustice. Whether a blood relationship existed or not, the slave represented hard-earned capital. A thousand dollars was a thousand dollars, whether spent on a spouse, an unrelated servant, or a tract of land. Work, thrift, and acumen were all required for a free Negro to accumulate such sums; the purchase represented a major financial investment and an increased labor force, as it did for anyone else.

From an ideological standpoint, modern ideals of "black brotherhood" and repulsion at the thought of Negroes owning Negroes is also unrealistic. All races, all people, and all nations have had members who profited at the expense of others with the same skin color. Alabama's free people of color were humans, with human cravings and ambitions. Just as there were white Alabamians who argued that slavery was acceptable because the Bible condones it, there were free black Alabamians—devout Christians—who undoubtedly felt the same. In the same manner that the white Alabamian was likely to say "Sure, this law is needed; just don't apply it to me," there clearly were free black counterparts who said "All men should be free; but as long as slavery exists, I might as well get a piece of the action." To deny them the right to feel thusly is to deny them *a* right.

56. *Wade L. Potter v. U.S.*, Southern Claims Commission, comm. no. 637, ofc. no. 113, rpt. 9, 1879.

57. Tuscaloosa Co. Deed Record Books G, 480–81; J, 211–12; and Q, 312.

58. Tuscaloosa Co. Deed Record Books H, 560; Q, 82; and T, 231, 233, 241.

Miscegenation

Of all the ways that the Anglo South has been held up as superior to Latin Louisiana, none has caused more tongues to wag than miscegenation. Thereon is built the moral stage upon which Anglo America has repeatedly upbraided Louisiana—without fair cause. As statistics slowly displace cultural bias and subjective assumptions, historians are discovering that sexual attraction transcends race everywhere.

It takes only a few census statistics to slay either culture's self-righteousness. Comparing the percentage of mulattoes with the total free colored population in 1860, one finds mulattoes representing 90 percent of free nonwhites in Louisiana and 78 percent in Anglo Alabama—a statistic neither should have felt smug about. Louisiana's slight edge can be accounted for by the fact that Louisiana's free-Negro society was the older one—seeing more generations in which the offspring of each original act of miscegenation could multiply itself. Comparing the percentage of mulattoes with the total slave population reveals that 10 percent of Louisiana's slaves had mixed racial origins, while the same could be said of 8 percent of those in Alabama.[59] Again, the difference is negligible, especially considering that Alabama had no truly large urban center such as New Orleans to foster libertine attitudes and erode social controls. On the other hand, Louisiana's fabled quadroon balls and the oft-cited but yet-unquantified scandals in which white New Orleanians presented slave children for baptism and acknowledged paternity are all hard to find in Anglo Alabama.

What one does find in Alabama is another situation that upsets conventional thought about miscegenation in the Anglo South. Interracial marriages were performed legally in Alabama until 1852. The marriage code passed that year did not nullify interracial marriages, once they were performed; and Alabamians who surreptitiously formed interracial unions after the 1852 law were not prosecutable.[60] By comparison, Louisiana's *Code Noir* of 1724 forbade black-white marriages, and parts of the Anglo South dallied long after Louisiana in passing similar laws.[61] In this one re-

---

59. Joseph C. G. Kennedy, *Population of the United States in 1860 . . . Eighth Census* (Washington, D.C., 1864), xiii.

60. Ormand *et al.*, *Code of Alabama . . . 1852*, pp. 376–77.

61. *Code Noir ou loi municipal servant de règlement* (New Orleans, 1778); Genovese, "Slave States of North America," 262.

gard, the old cockfighter did err in his comparison of Louisiana and Alabama. One perceived social "vice" *was* illegal in antebellum Louisiana—miscegenation—so Louisianians simply found their way around it. By contrast, Alabama contemporaries tolerated interracial marriages, while cluck-clucking over the relationships that produced miscegenation in Louisiana. Moral one-upmanship is an age-old game.

Conclusion

A comparison of the Alabama study with historical interpretations of other southern states finds little of the exceptional prejudice that supposedly characterized the Anglo South in comparison with Louisiana. My preliminary grass-roots research in other states suggests that the Alabama pattern holds true in the lower and trans-Appalachian South from which Alabama's population came, especially for rural and small-town regions.[62] (Maryland and Virginia, which contained more massive numbers of free Negroes in the antebellum era, are notable exceptions.)[63]

However, none of this denies the fact that free people of color—in Alabama, Louisiana, or any other slave regime—were severely constrained by the ambiguity of their estate in life. They could never know just how serious public opposition against their class might become. They could never know when the political blasts of fire-eaters might be specifically aimed at them. They could never know when fate might deprive them of their protectors or whether they would be able to find compatible replacements. Always they had to guard their tongues, exercising constant diligence in playing the Sambo role. Some succeeded splendidly within these constraints. Most got along.

Free people of color in Latin Louisiana clearly had a head start on economic growth along the Gulf. Alabama was abandoned early as the capi-

62. Published writings of some other researchers reflect similar conclusions about race relations and free-Negro absorption into the general white populace. See, for example, the interdisciplinary work of the government historian and genealogist, Virginia Easley DeMarce, "'Verry Slitly Mixt': Tri-racial Isolate Families of the Upper South—A Genealogical Study," *National Genealogical Society Quarterly*, LXXX (1992), 5–35; and DeMarce, "Looking at Legends—Lumbee and Melungeon: Applied Genealogy and the Origins of Tri-racial Isolate Settlements," *National Genealogical Society Quarterly*, LXXXI (1993), 24–45.

63. The more radical prejudice of nineteenth-century Maryland and Virginia, states that had considerably more free people of color than other southern areas, is a point well made by Berlin's *Slaves Without Masters*.

tal of the Louisiana colony because New Orleans was more strategically positioned. Nearly a century of population development occurred thereafter in Louisiana before any significant settlement existed in Alabama north of Mobile and Baldwin. Real growth in Alabama did not happen until after the War of 1812; and the half-century that remained of the antebellum era could not produce a sufficient number of generations or adequate population density to create the kind of separate social class that evolved for free people of color in Louisiana.

Thus, numerically and economically, the status of Louisiana's free people of color was indeed superior to that found in Anglo Alabama. But a comparison of the *private* and *legal* lives of free Negroes in the two societies yields overriding similarities. Among the elite colored tradesmen of Huntsville and Montgomery and the wealthy colored nabobs of New Orleans and Isle Brevelle, there were the same drives to succeed, similar interracial friendships, and parallel patterns of interracial sex. For all classes, in both societies, there was virtually the same legal and social insecurity. Both knew theirs was an uncertain world, and the "privileges" of second-class citizenship were similarly bittersweet.

GRADY MCWHINEY

Crackers and Cavaliers: Shared Courage

Confederate military leaders, like most historic figures, varied as much in manners and characteristics as they did in appearance and brains. Some were polished, worldly, and sophisticated; others seemed scarcely more than violent rustics—bold, impulsive, and dashing. A number could be described as simple country gentlemen who displayed remarkable bravery in battle. So gallant were a few that contemporaries called them "Cavaliers" even if their family background, social standing, and conduct sometimes fell below Cavalier standards.

Not many genuine Cavaliers inhabited the Old South or the Confederate States of America, but by 1861 the Cavalier ideal had become fixed in southern popular culture. After antebellum writers romanticized plantation life, abolitionists helped distort the Cavalier image by picturing the Old South as a three-tiered society composed of arrogant, aristocratic planters, "mean poor" whites, and cruelly treated black slaves.

Many southerners believed that after the English Civil War one of the contesting factions, the Roundheads, had colonized the North and another, the Cavaliers, had settled in the American South.[1] According to this view, Yankees descended from those Puritan Roundheads and southerners from the more aristocratic Cavaliers.

---

1. Clement Eaton, *The Growth of Southern Civilization* (New York, 1961), 150; William R. Taylor, *Cavalier and Yankee: The Old South and American National Character* (New York, 1961), 15.

That such beliefs rested more on myth than on reality dissuaded few believers; the Cavalier cult depicted southerners not as they were but as the depicter portrayed them. Just before the Civil War, southerner Daniel R. Hundley wrote in considerable exaggeration: "The Southern Gentleman is usually possessed of an equally faultless physical development. His average height is about six feet, yet he is rarely gawky in his movements, or in the least clumsily put together; and his entire physique conveys . . . an impression of firmness united to flexibility." According to yet another contemporary: "The Southern aristocrat trained his sons in a code of behavior which was self-consciously chivalric. The items in this code were noblesse oblige, a sense of personal and family honor, and above all, a due and proper regard for the beauty and virtue of white women."[2]

But disagreement existed on what constituted Cavalier characteristics. In Virginia fiction, Cavaliers were "expected at all times to be graceful and dignified, as well as courteous and thoughtful. They sought to attain qualities of fortitude, temperance, prudence, justice, . . . and courtesy." Scholars acknowledge that plantation conditions fostered outdoor living, which in turn encouraged familiarity with horses and guns and thus stimulated interest in the profession of arms. Slavery required patrols and militia units to cope with threats of servile insurrection, and the lack of commercial and industrial opportunities in the Old South's agrarian economy helped turn many young southerners toward military careers. All these activities promoted the Cavalier image, as did such trappings of chivalry as attention to manners, stately ladies, lavish hospitality, heraldry and ancestry, romantic oratory and place-naming, dueling, military affairs, and the use of horses in hunting, tournaments, and racing. The horse and horsemanship were inextricably linked to the chivalric ideal, and the cult of manners became so intertwined with concepts of personal honor and integrity that all appeared part of a single theme. Because the planter class regarded a business career with disdain, their sons rarely considered occupations other than law, politics, plantation management, or the military.[3]

A nineteenth-century biographer defined George Washington as a Cavalier not just because he was brave and inspired confidence, but be-

2. Daniel R. Hundley, *Social Relations in Our Southern States* (1860; rpr. Baton Rouge, 1979), 28–29; Willard Thorp, ed., *A Southern Reader* (New York, 1955), 243.

3. Ritchie Devon Watson, Jr., *The Cavalier in Virginia Fiction* (Baton Rouge, 1985), 4; Rollin G. Osterweis, *Romanticism and Nationalism in the Old South* (New Haven, 1949), 87, 91, 96, 98.

cause he displayed self-control and regularity of character as well as tenderness and compassion rather than ambition. Washington possessed two additional Cavalier traits of significance: "he lived on his horse and idolized his mother and his wife."[4]

Just after the Civil War, John A. Wise revealed the impact of Sir Walter Scott's fiction in shaping not only his own but the views of many other southerners. He listed as desirable for Virginia Military Institute cadets the following Cavalier traits: "courtesy, self-respect, deference to superiors, contempt for effeminacy or cowardice, a dauntless courage, a joyous simple outlook, a healthy love of life, tempered by the romantic code of [Sir Walter Scott's] Fitz-James. Such, my comrades," insisted Wise, "is the ideal Cadet, as you and I love to picture him."[5]

Not every Cavalier, of course, met these standards. In 1860 one of the Old South's most popular magazines admitted that "Cavaliers had many human failings; they were indeed earthy; they fought, they drank, they swore, they loved." A Yankee writing after the Civil War asserted that "the central trait of the 'chivalrous Southron' is an intense respect for virility. If you will fight, if you are strong and skillful enough to kill your antagonist, if you can govern or influence the common herd, if you can ride a dangerous horse over a rough country, if you are a good shot or an expert swordsman, if you stand by your own opinions unflinchingly, if you do your level best on whisky, if you are a devil of a fellow with women, if, in short, you show vigorous masculine attributes, he will grant you his respect."[6]

The real Cavalier, not the character of fiction or idealization, but the flesh and blood man, may not have been so different from another stereotyped southerner, the Cracker, with whom Cavaliers shared a cause and a culture. At the time of the Civil War the overwhelming majority of white residents of the Confederacy—most planters, farmers, and plain folk; indeed, everyone except a few aristocrats, some townsfolk and professionals, and a sprinkling of foreigners and unacculturated Yankees—were part of Cracker culture, whether they acknowledged it or not. Some Crackers were rich, others poor, and still others neither; but they all more or less

4. James K. Paulding, *Life of Washington* (New York, 1835), quoted in Taylor, *Cavalier and Yankee*, 250.

5. Wise quoted in Osterweis, *Romanticism and Nationalism*, 92.

6. *DeBow's Review*, XXVIII (January 1860), 7–16; John W. DeForest, "Chivalrous and Semi-Chivalrous Southrons," *Harpers Monthly*, January 1869, pp. 196–97, quoted in Thorp, ed., *A Southern Reader*, 270–71.

acted alike and shared the same values. And that is the point: the word *Cracker* did not signify an economic condition; rather, it defined a culture.

Scotch-Irish settlers, "in whose dialect a *cracker* was a person who talked boastingly," brought the term to the South, where during the colonial period it became associated mainly with Scottish, Scotch-Irish, Irish, or Welsh herdsmen of Celtic origins. "The Cracker was typically a Scotch-Irishman," noted a scholar. In 1766 a colonial official informed the earl of Dartmouth: "I should explain to your Lordship what is meant by Crackers, a name they have got from being great boasters; they are a lawless set of rascalls on the frontiers of Virginia, Maryland, the Carolinas, and Georgia, who often change their place of abode." A German visiting the Carolina backcountry found longhorn cattle, swine, and slovenly people whom he identified as "Crackers." A Spanish official reported in 1790 the "influx [into Florida] of rootless people called *Crackers*." He described them as rude and nomadic, excellent hunters but indifferent farmers who planted only a few patches of corn, and as people who kept "themselves beyond the reach of all civilized law."[7]

Cracker became part of the American vocabulary, but almost always it has been used disparagingly to describe the mudsills of the South. Contemporaries and scholars alike usually equated Crackers with poor whites. Few writers chose, as did historian Lewis C. Gray, to distinguish between the two: "The distinctive characteristics of the poor whites were recognized in the various special appellations by which they were contemptuously known in different parts of the South, such as, 'piney-woods people,' 'dirt-eaters,' 'clay-eaters,' 'tallow-faced gentry,' 'sand-hillers,' and 'crackers.' The term *crackers*, however, was sometimes applied also to mountaineers and other small farmers." Gray also acknowledged that many of the Old South's herdsmen were called Crackers. To most travel-

---

7. Delma E. Presley, "The Crackers of Georgia," *Georgia Historical Quarterly*, LX (1976), 102–16; Gary S. Dunbar, "Colonial Carolina Cowpens," *Agricultural History*, XXXV (1961), 130; Joe A. Akerman, Jr., *Florida Cowman: A History of Florida Cattle Raising* (Kissimmee, Fla., 1976), 59; Terry G. Jordan, *Trails to Texas: Southern Roots of Western Cattle Ranching* (Lincoln, Nebr., 1981), 34; Johann David Schopf, *Travels in the Confederation [1783–1784]* . . . , trans. and ed. Alfred J. Morrison (new ed.; 2 vols.; New York, 1968), II, 222–23; James A. Lewis, "Cracker—Spanish Florida Style," *Florida Historical Quarterly*, LXIII (1984), 188, 191; see also Leroy V. Eid, "The Scotch-Irish: A View Accepted Too Readily," *Eire-Ireland*, XXI (1986), 82–105.

ers in the antebellum South and the Confederacy, especially those from England and the North, a Cracker was any southerner whose ways differed significantly from their own, and many visitors to the South delighted in laughing and sneering at the rustic ways of the Crackers.[8]

It is understandable why visitors usually failed to distinguish between Crackers and poor whites, who shared the same culture: all poor whites were Crackers even though not all Crackers were poor whites. Frederick Law Olmsted, an observant Yankee who visited the South in the 1850s, noted that some Crackers "owned a good many negroes, and were by no means so poor as their appearance indicated." Crackers all shared the common heritage of being southerners. "We do not remember ever to have seen [poor whites] in the New-England States," remarked southerner Daniel Hundley in 1860. "They are . . . found in Ohio, Pennsylvania, Indiana, and all States of the [Old] North-west, though in . . . these last they came originally from the South." The characteristics of poor whites drawn up by Hundley, which match a list compiled much later by Lewis C. Gray, credit them with being courageous, lazy, lustful, quarrelsome, violent, ignorant, superstitious, drunkards, gamblers, and livestock thieves. Both observers agreed that poor whites were unconcerned with money. "Dollars and dimes," Hundley claimed, "they never bother their brains any great deal about." The list compiled by Hundley and Gray, allowing for exaggeration, is a fair but an incomplete outline of Cracker traits.[9]

The easiest way to understand Cracker characteristics, and indeed to understand Cracker culture, may be to contrast some of the major differ-

---

8. Lewis C. Gray, *History of Agriculture in the Southern United States to 1860* (2 vols.; Washington, D.C., 1933), I, 484, 149; Henry Benjamin Whipple, *Bishop Whipple's Southern Diary, 1843–1844*, ed. Lester B. Shippee (Minneapolis, 1937), 257; Rosalie Roos, *Travels in America, 1851–1855*, ed. Carl L. Anderson (Carbondale, Ill., 1982), 97–98.

9. Frederick Law Olmsted, *The Cotton Kingdom: A Traveller's Observations on Cotton and Slavery in the American States*, ed. Arthur M. Schlesinger (new ed., New York, 1953), 206; Hundley, *Social Relations*, 257, 262, 265, 266, 268, 269, 272, 276, 282; Gray, *History of Agriculture*, I, 484. John Hebron Moore concluded that "the culture of cotton farmers and cotton planters of the Old Southwest were virtually identical (except for the so-called river planters of the Natchez region), and that both groups emerged from the backcountry of South Carolina and Georgia about 1800." Moore also observed that the Mississippi River planters, or "the great agriculturists," as he called them, followed a more cosmopolitan lifestyle as well as a totally different "system of farming." See his *Emergence of the Cotton Kingdom in the Old Southwest: Mississippi, 1770–1860* (Baton Rouge, 1988).

ences between antebellum southerners and northerners. A wide range of
observers generally described southerners as more hospitable, generous,
frank, courteous, spontaneous, lazy, lawless, militaristic, wasteful, imprac-
tical, and reckless than northerners, who were in turn more reserved,
shrewd, disciplined, enterprising, acquisitive, careful, frugal, ambitious,
pacific, and practical than southerners. The Old South was a leisure-
oriented society that fostered idleness and gaiety, where people favored
the spoken word over the written and enjoyed their sensual pleasures.
Family ties reportedly were stronger in the South than in the North;
southerners, whose values were more agrarian than those of northerners,
wasted more time and consumed more tobacco and liquor and were less
concerned with the useful and the material. Yankees, on the other hand,
were cleaner, neater, more puritanical, less mercurial, better educated,
more orderly and progressive, worked harder, and kept the Sabbath better
than southerners.[10]

These characterizations, which attempt to distinguish Rebs from
Yanks, also suggest similarities between Cavaliers and Crackers. No individual southerner—Cracker, Cavalier, or whatever—possessed all of the
peculiarities described, but Cavaliers and Crackers shared with most
other white southerners such ideals as hospitality, frankness, generosity,
and courtesy; they sanctioned a leisure-oriented, agrarian society with
strong family ties, where people favored the spoken word over the written
and enjoyed their sensual pleasures, delighting in music, dancing, gambling, hunting, fishing, horse racing, talking, telling stories, eating, drinking, smoking, chewing tobacco or dipping snuff; they shared a strong
sense of personal and family honor, and tended to be rash, violent, and
brave.

Some Confederate military leaders possessed traits that failed to enhance their careers. A striking example: General George B. Crittenden,
eldest son of Senator John J. Crittenden of Kentucky. The younger Crittenden had demonstrated courage in 1842 by joining Colonel William
Fisher's disastrous Texan filibustering expedition into Mexico. Captured
and compelled by the Mexicans to draw beans from a jar to decide which
of the adventurers would be executed, Crittenden picked a white bean,
which meant he would be spared; he gave it to a friend and then was

10. Grady McWhiney, *Cracker Culture: Celtic Ways in the Old South* (Tuscaloosa,
1988), 268.

lucky enough to select another white bean. Brevetted for heroic conduct during the Mexican War, he joined the Confederacy against his father's advice. After the Confederate disaster at Mill Springs early in 1862, where he was accused of being "in a beastly state of intoxication" during the battle, Crittenden received command of a corps in General Albert Sidney Johnston's army, but on April 1, 1862, General William J. Hardee found him drunk and his command in a "wretched state of discipline." Arrested on the spot, censured by a court-martial, and pronounced unfit for command by General Braxton Bragg, Crittenden resigned his commission in October 1862.[11]

There were plenty of drunks in the Confederacy, and far too many of them held high military command. Generals Roswell Ripley and Nathan G. Evans were two of the army's "most notorious drunkards." General Henry Hopkins Sibley was another; after his failure to take New Mexico for the Confederacy, his uncontrolled drinking cost him his command. General Benjamin Franklin Cheatham, commanding a division in the Army of Tennessee, attacked lackadaisically at Murfreesboro, sending "his brigades . . . into action individually rather than simultaneously—and he was drunk." Officers found ardent secessionist John Dunovant too inebriated to attack and "lying drunk by the roadside" instead of leading his regiment forward during the Secessionville campaign. Arrested and imprisoned, he was later released and promoted to brigadier general. Dunovant died in 1864 leading his brigade in a headlong charge; his biographer noted that "Dunovant commanded troops in heavy fighting only four days of the entire war, three of them defeats. It is difficult reconciling [high praise for him] . . . with the reality of Dunovant lying drunk on the . . . Road and lying dead after a foolhardy frontal foray. Brave the brigadier unquestionably was, but his bravery was the rashness of irresponsibility."[12]

Hardly anything appears more extreme than contrasting the reckless Dunovant and the dutiful Robert E. Lee, the epitome of all Cavalier virtues.

---

11. Lawrence L. Hewitt, "George Bibb Crittenden," in *The Confederate General*, ed. William C. Davis (6 vols.; N.p., 1991), II, 42–43; Ezra J. Warner, *Generals in Gray: Lives of the Confederate Commanders* (Baton Rouge, 1959), 65–66.

12. Warner, *Generals in Gray*, 276–77, 83–84; Jeffry D. Wert, "Nathan George Evans," in *Confederate General*, ed. Davis, II, 107–108; Arthur W. Bergeron, Jr., "Henry Hopkins Sibley," *ibid.*, V, 153–54; Edwin C. Bearss, "Benjamin Franklin Cheatham," *ibid.*, I, 174–81; Richard J. Sommers, "John Dunovant," *ibid.*, II, 86–87.

Son of Revolutionary War hero "Light Horse Harry" Lee and "one of the finest women the State of Virginia ever produced," Robert Edward Lee established his military reputation during the Mexican War. For twenty months he served on General Winfield Scott's staff and worked in close proximity with the army's commander. Scott reported that Lee "greatly distinguished himself" during the siege of Vera Cruz. At Cerro Gordo, Scott based his victorious strategy on the reconnaissance made by Lee, who again received Scott's praise, along with promotion to the brevet rank of major for his gallant and meritorious conduct. Lee further distinguished himself on the march to Mexico City by twice crossing difficult terrain on a dangerous reconnaissance that Scott called "the greatest feat of physical and moral courage [ever] performed by any individual." Lee received two additional brevet promotions for heroic conduct in Mexico. Jefferson Davis recalled that Lee "came from Mexico crowned with honors, covered by brevets, and recognized . . . as one of the ablest of his country's soldiers." A fellow officer observed that General Scott had an "almost idolatrous fancy for Lee, whose military genius he estimated far above that of any other officer of the army." In an official letter Scott referred to Lee as "the very best soldier that I ever saw in the field."[13]

Almost everyone who knew Lee held him in high regard. A family friend once spoke of young Robert's "amiable disposition, & his correct and gentlemanly habits." One of his early teachers said that Lee "was a most exemplary student in every respect. He was never behind time at his studies; never failed in a single recitation; was perfectly observant of the rules and regulations of the Institution; was gentlemanly, unobtrusive, and respectful in all his deportment to teachers and fellow-students. His specialty was *finishing up*. He imparted a finish and a neatness, as he proceeded, to everything he undertook."[14]

General Joseph E. Johnston, who was a classmate of Lee's at West Point, claimed that "no other youth or man so united the qualities that win warm friendship and command high respect. For he was full of sym-

13. Douglas S. Freeman, *R. E. Lee: A Biography* (4 vols.; New York, 1934–35), I, 108; Emory M. Thomas, *Robert E. Lee: A Biography* (New York, 1995), 131–33, 136; J. William Jones, "The Friendship Between Lee and Scott," *Southern Historical Society Papers,* XI (1883), 623; Colonel Archer Anderson, "Robert Edward Lee," *Southern Historical Society Papers,* XVII (1889), 118–19.

14. Ralston B. Lattimore, ed., *The Story of Robert E. Lee: As Told in His Own Words and Those of His Contemporaries* (Philadelphia, 1964), 4–5.

pathy and kindness, genial and fond of gay conversation, and even of fun, that made him the most agreeable of companions, while his correctness of demeanor and language and attention to all duties, personal and official, and a dignity as much a part of himself as the elegance of his person, gave him a superiority that every one acknowledged. He was the only one of all the men I have known who could laugh at the faults and follies of his friends in such a manner as to make them ashamed without touching their affection for him, and to confirm their respect and sense of his superiority."[15]

Audacity, the military characteristic that most influenced Lee's generalship, was not exclusively a Cavalier trait. Crackers often were as bold as Cavaliers. Whether Lee's audacity, which sometimes bordered on recklessness, was simply part of his heritage or something he learned from Scott is less important than understanding that long before the conflict of the 1860s, Robert E. Lee was committed to aggressive warfare. From the outset of the Confederacy's struggle for independence, Lee suggested offensives to President Davis and urged other generals to be bold and aggressive. "What genius! What audacity in Lee!" exclaimed War Clerk John B. Jones during the Seven Days Campaign.[16]

A member of Lee's staff told General E. P. Alexander that "if there is one man in either army, Confederate or Federal, head and shoulders above every other in audacity, it is Gen. Lee! His name might be Audacity. He will take more desperate chances and take them quicker than any other general in this country, North or South."[17] And "General Lee, . . . not excepting [Stonewall] Jackson, was the most aggressive man in his army," concluded General Henry Heth. "No one ever went to General Lee and suggested an aggressive movement who was not listened to attentively."[18]

President Davis observed that after the war some critics charged Lee "with 'want of dash.' I wish to say," Davis announced, "that I never knew Lee [to] decline to attempt anything that man may dare."[19] The president's wife agreed. "General Lee was not given to indecision," she remem-

---

15. A. L. Long, *Memoirs of Robert E. Lee* (New York, 1886), 71.

16. John B. Jones, *A Rebel War Clerk's Diary*, ed. Earl Schenck Miers (Baton Rouge, 1993), 86.

17. E. P. Alexander, *Military Memoirs of a Confederate* (New York, 1907), 110–11.

18. Henry Heth, *The Memoirs of Henry Heth*, ed. James L. Morrison, Jr. (Westport, Conn., 1974), 214–15.

19. *Southern Historical Society Papers*, XVII (1889), 191–92.

bered, "and they have mistaken his character who supposed caution was his vice. He was prone to attack."

Other generals may have been as aggressive as Lee, but his boldness, revered by both Cavaliers and Crackers, established a model that southerners appreciated and honored. Audacity not only characterized Confederate heroes; it united even such diverse southerners as James Johnston Pettigrew and Nathan Bedford Forrest.

Pettigrew, who was killed in action during the retreat from Gettysburg, personified the Cavalier ideal and practiced the highest standards of southern chivalry. "One of the finest scholars ever to attend the University of North Carolina," he graduated first in the class of 1847. After dabbling in such intellectually satisfying pursuits as writing, college teaching, law, politics, and travel, he turned to the study of warfare. What he lacked in formal training, he learned from reading and observation. He served as both a private and a colonel; for a time, modesty forced this slender Cavalier to refuse President Davis' attempt to promote him from colonel to general. At the Battle of Seven Pines, Pettigrew fell with a neck wound that appeared to be fatal, yet before the action ended he suffered another wound, a bayonet slash in the leg, and capture. Following his exchange, he led both a brigade and a division through the carnage at Gettysburg. On the march to Pennsylvania, he remarked that "life was only to be desired for what could be accomplished in it and death only to be dreaded for what had been done amiss. For himself, Pettigrew said, he was ready to die at any time, at that very moment, if he could do so with honor and usefulness. He meant it." Bold and aggressive, he courted combat. "We whipped the Yankees," he stated, "every time we could get at them." At Gettysburg, as his men cheered and his division prepared to charge, he rode up and down the battle line, a perfect target for sharpshooters. Later, while he was rallying troops, his horse was shot from under him, and canister shattered his right hand, but Pettigrew was among the last to leave the field. "None had more deeply at heart . . . the cause for which he shed his blood," wrote a friend. "He gave himself up to it wholly, with all his fine energies, extraordinary talents, and the courage of a heart literally ignorant of fear. I have never met with one who fitted more entirely my 'beau ideal' of the patriot, the soldier, the man of genius, and the accomplished gentleman."[20]

20. Clyde N. Wilson, *Carolina Cavalier: The Life and Mind of James Johnston Pettigrew* (Athens, Ga., 1990), 190, 185, 192, 205.

General Forrest, perhaps the ideal Cracker, and surely a violent and an aggressive one, seemed to have little in common with General Pettigrew except courage. Son of a backcountry Scotch-Irish blacksmith, Forrest had raised livestock, sold slaves, and killed his uncle's murderer before turning his talents to slaughtering Yankees.[21] But when called upon to defend the Confederacy, Johnston Pettigrew and Bedford Forrest, despite their differences, reacted with equal bravery.

So did many other southerners. Courage may not have been universal throughout the Old South, but a remarkable number of Confederate military leaders displayed a willingness to die in battle. More than half of all Confederate generals—235 of 425—managed to get themselves killed or wounded in combat. "I have to stay in the forefront to make these men fight," confessed General James Dearing. "I'll get myself killed." In the last days of the war, this "reckless, handsome boy" did just that—he died in combat.[22]

He was not alone. General Samuel Garland, Jr., a graduate of the Virginia Military Institute and a descendant of President James Madison, suffered several wounds before receiving a fatal one at South Mountain. Garland was "the most fearless man I ever knew," insisted General D. H. Hill, and General Lee called him a "brave and accomplished officer." General States Rights Gist, a wealthy South Carolinian, whom General Beauregard regarded as "able and brave," died at Franklin leading a charge on foot after his horse had been killed. General Tom Green, a native Virginian, spent most of his life in Texas, where he participated in the battle of San Jacinto and in nine Indian and Mexican campaigns. He served in the War with Mexico and fought during the Civil War in the invasion of New Mexico, the liberation of Galveston, and in Louisiana. Described as "upright, modest, and with the simplicity of a child," Green "rejoiced in combat," noted his commanding officer, General Richard Taylor. "His men adored him, and would follow wherever he led; but they did not fear him, for, though he scolded at them in action, he was too kind-hearted to punish breaches of discipline. In truth, he had no conception of the value of discipline in war, believing that all must be actuated by . . . devotion to duty."

21. Edwin C. Bearss, "Nathan Bedford Forrest," in *Confederate General*, ed. Davis, II, 139–44.

22. These figures are based on data taken from Warner, *Generals in Gray*, and Mark Mayo Boatner III, *The Civil War Dictionary* (New York, 1959); see also Robert K. Krick, "James Dearing," in *Confederate General*, ed. Davis, II, 54–59.

General Green died leading his men "in his accustomed fearless way" while attacking a Union gunboat.[23]

Not every brave man died the first time he was shot. Twenty-one of the seventy-seven Confederate generals who were killed or mortally wounded in battle had been shot at least once before they received their fatal injuries. Some had been hit two or more times. William D. Pender survived three wounds before a shell shattered his leg and killed him at Gettysburg. Stephen D. Ramseur recovered from wounds received at Malvern Hill, Chancellorsville, and Spotsylvania, only to die at Cedar Creek. A remarkable number of Confederate generals received multiple wounds yet survived the war: thirty-one were wounded twice, eighteen three times, and a dozen were hit four or more times. Generals Clement A. Evans, William ("Extra Billy") Smith, and William H. Young were wounded five times. Young was hit in the shoulder and had two horses shot from under him at Murfreesboro; he was hit in the leg at Jackson and in the chest at Allatoona, where another horse was shot from under him and he was captured. Generals John R. Cooke, William R. Terry, and Thomas F. Toon were wounded seven times, but the record seems to have been set by William Ruffin Cox, who joined the 2d North Carolina Infantry as a major in 1861 and fought through the war with the Army of Northern Virginia. He was wounded eleven times.[24]

A mere listing of courageous Confederates would take days. Even brief sketches of selected bravery omit more heroes than they include. General Junius Daniel, West Point graduate and Louisiana planter, returned to his native North Carolina at the war's outset to command a regiment. Promoted to brigade command, he died leading his men at Spotsylvania. General Richard Brooke Garnett, a Virginia gentleman, whose horse had kicked him a few days earlier and made it impossible for him to walk, rode into battle at Gettysburg, where his brigade constituted the center of Pickett's massive assault. Garnett may have been the only Confederate in the charge to stay mounted throughout. As the assaulting column neared the crest of Cemetery Hill, he and his horse disappeared in the smoke and

23. Jeffry D. Wert, "Samuel Garland, Jr.," in *Confederate General*, ed. Davis, II, 164–67; Arthur W. Bergeron, Jr., "States Rights Gist," *ibid.*, 194–97; Anne Bailey, "Thomas Green," *ibid.*, III, 32–33; Richard Taylor, *Destruction and Reconstruction: Personal Experiences of the Late War*, ed. Charles P. Roland (Waltham, Mass., 1968), 176.

24. These figures are based on data found in Warner, *Generals in Gray*.

confusion. No one ever saw him again; "only his bloodied horse running to the rear."[25]

Heroes became commonplace: consider three Confederate generals named Gordon. First captured near Cumberland Gap in 1862, George Washington Gordon of Tennessee, after being exchanged, suffered a serious wound "while gallantly leading his regiment" at Murfreesboro. Promoted to general, he led his men in the deepest penetration of the Union center during the Battle of Franklin, where he was again wounded and captured. General James B. Gordon of North Carolina received Jeb Stuart's praise for disregarding wounds and continuing "by his brave example and marked ability to control the field" until he fell mortally wounded. And General John B. Gordon of Georgia, who rose to prominence in the Army of Northern Virginia, first demonstrated his courage and leadership at Sharpsburg, where five bullets struck him. "Not to promote him," an officer wrote, "would have been a scandal."[26]

During action in east Tennessee, General Archibald Gracie, Jr., after taking a rifle bullet in his arm, had the wound dressed and then went back into combat, where he received a more serious wound; he lived until 1864, when an exploding shell killed him in the Petersburg trenches.[27]

A deadly assault at Atlanta—only one of many—cost General Daniel C. Govan's Arkansas brigade half of its thousand men, but they captured eight artillery pieces, numerous wagons loaded with ammunition, and 700 Yankees, many of them members of the 16th Iowa. After the war Govan attended a reunion of the 16th Iowa and returned the regiment's captured colors.[28]

General Hiram B. Granbury, a Mississippian who migrated to Texas in the early 1850s, led his Texans at New Hope Church in "a dashing charge on the enemy, driving them from the field." At Franklin, leading yet another charge, he died within a few yards of the Federal breastworks.[29]

At Shiloh a bullet hit General Henry W. Allen, commander of the 4th Louisiana Infantry, in the mouth and tore away part of his cheek. Despite

25. William C. Davis, "Junius Daniel," 44–46, and "Richard Brooke Garnett," 168–69, both in *Confederate General,* ed. Davis, II.

26. Lawrence L. Hewitt, "George Washington Gordon," *ibid.,* III, 3–4; Jeffry D. Wert, "James Byron Gordon," *ibid.,* III, 6–7; Peter S. Carmichael, "John Brown Gordon," *ibid.,* III, 8–12.

27. William C. Davis, "Archibald Gracie, Jr.," *ibid.,* III, 21–22.

28. Edwin C. Bearss, "Daniel Chevilette Govan," *ibid.,* III, 17–19.

29. Lawrence L. Hewitt, "Hiram Bronson Granbury," *ibid.,* III, 24–25.

his wound, he continued to lead his regiment, recalled an officer, "like a whirlwind into the thick of the battle." Later, while directing an attack on an enemy battery at Baton Rouge, Allen rode to within fifty feet of the guns before being hit by canister. The blast killed his horse and permanently crippled Allen, who walked on crutches for the rest of his life. Elected governor of Louisiana in 1863, he resigned from the army and devoted himself to performing the miracle of securing supplies and industries for his state. An Allen biographer proclaimed him "spectacular," and Douglas S. Freeman called Allen "the single great administrator produced by the Confederacy."[30]

Many generals could say that they were lucky to survive the war. South Carolina Cavalier Wade Hampton, whom Jeb Stuart called "a brave and distinguished officer," had hunted bears with a butcher knife before the Civil War. A soldier described General Hampton leading a charge as "a veritable god of war." General Bryan Grimes of North Carolina had seven horses killed under him during the war, yet he received only one wound.[31]

Two generals named Gregg were not so lucky. Alabamian John Gregg, described as "personally without fear," had migrated to Texas before the war, sustained a severe wound at Chickamauga, led the furious charge of the Texas Brigade in the Wilderness, but survived until he directed an assault on the Charles City Road south of Richmond. Maxcy Gregg was equally courageous. He led his brigade of South Carolinians with such dash at Gaines's Mill that a contemporary called him "the sublimest spectacle I ever saw." At Second Manassas, Gregg strode among his men waving an ancestral sword and shouting, "Let us die here, my men, let us die here." Many did, contributing significantly to winning the victory. Gregg received a painful wound at Sharpsburg and a mortal one at Fredericksburg, where he managed to drag himself to his feet, wave his hat, and cheer on the Confederate counterattack. As his men charged the Federals, Gregg died holding on to a sapling.[32]

General William R. "Dirty Shirt" Scurry, who was born in Tennessee but grew to manhood in Texas, became a hero at Glorieta Pass during the

30. Arthur W. Bergeron, Jr., "Henry Watkins Allen," *ibid.*, I, 14–15.

31. Jeffry D. Wert, "Wade Hampton," *ibid.*, III, 50–53; Gary W. Gallagher, "Bryan Grimes," *ibid.*, III, 46–47.

32. William C. Davis, "John Gregg," *ibid.*, III, 36–39; Robert K. Krick, "Maxcy Gregg," *ibid.*, III, 41–43.

New Mexico campaign and demonstrated his courage on several other occasions until he was mortally wounded at Jenkins' Ferry. Refusing to be taken to the rear, where surgeons might have saved his life, he bled to death on the battlefield.[33]

Just as valiant were two generals named Adams. Daniel W. Adams of Louisiana, who had killed a newspaper editor in a duel before the Civil War, received three wounds fighting for the Confederacy. "It is difficult for me to decide which the most to admire, his courage in the field or his un-paralleled cheerfulness under suffering," wrote General D. H. Hill. At Shiloh, while directing a charge, Adams received a wound in the head that cost him his right eye; he received his second wound leading an as-sault at Murfreesboro, and his third at Chickamauga, where he was cap-tured. General John Adams of Tennessee, son of an Irish immigrant father, had received a brevet promotion for gallantry during the Mexican War. Wounded in the arm early in the battle of Franklin, Tennessee, Adams re-fused to leave the field, where his shattered brigade lost 450 men. Instead he rode up to the Federal breastworks and tried to leap his horse over them. A hail of bullets met the general and his horse, which fell on the mortally wounded Adams, who remained conscious for a time and bravely told a Yank: "It is the fate of a soldier to die for his country."[34]

Many southerners certainly bled and died for their country during the 1860s. The typical Confederate military leader either died in battle or suffered one or more wounds during the war; whether predominately Cracker or Cavalier, he needed courage because his men demanded it and because he demanded it of himself. Individual honor, of course, required bravery, but so did family, clan, and community. Unwilling to face their peers in disgrace, most Confederates despised cowards and dreaded dis-honor more than death. A foreign visitor recorded Colonel George Gren-fell's explanation "that the only way in which an officer could acquire influence over the Confederate soldier was by his personal conduct under fire. They hold a man in great esteem who in action sets them an example of contempt for danger; but they think nothing of an officer who is not in

---

33. Lawrence L. Hewitt, "William Read Scurry," *ibid.*, V, 133–35. See also Donald S. Frazier, *Blood and Treasure: Confederate Empire in the Southwest* (College Station, Tex., 1995).

34. Arthur W. Bergeron, Jr., "Daniel Weisiger Adams," in *Confederate General*, ed. Davis, I, 2–3; Terry Jones, "John Adams," *ibid.*, 4–5.

the habit of *leading* them. In fact such a man could not possibly retain his position. Colonel Grenfell's expression was, 'every atom of authority has to be purchased by a drop of your blood.'"[35] In other words, Confederate military leaders—whether Cavaliers or Crackers—preferred death in battle to the white feather of cowardice.

35. Arthur J. L. Fremantle, *The Fremantle Diary* . . . , ed. Walter Lord (Boston, 1954), 127.

III

Plain-Folk Democracy and Its Limits

LACY K. FORD

Popular Ideology of the Old South's Plain Folk:
The Limits of Egalitarianism in a Slaveholding Society

The monumental corpus of Eugene Genovese's highly controversial work casts a formidable shadow over the recent historiography of the Old South. For at least a quarter century precious little scholarly work on the pre–Civil War South has failed to engage Genovese's powerful yet much-disputed arguments for a distinctive antebellum southern society fundamentally at odds with the emerging capitalist world order. In the Old South, Genovese maintains, the master-slave relationship produced a social order defined by paternalism and planter hegemony rather than wage labor and bourgeois social relations. The peculiar dialectic of paternalism, with its resistance to accommodation and accommodation to resistance, constructed a social order in which slaveholders and their bondsmen found themselves locked in a perverse but unremitting mutual dependence.[1]

---

1. For a perceptive recent assessment of Genovese's influence on the historiography of the Old South, see David Brion Davis, "Southern Comfort," *New York Review of Books*, October 5, 1995, pp. 43–46. To follow the broad outlines of Genovese's thought and its evolution over time, see the following works by Eugene D. Genovese: *The Political Economy of Slavery* (New York, 1965); *The World the Slaveholders Made: Two Essays in Interpretation* (New York, 1969); *Roll, Jordan, Roll: The World the Slaves Made* (New York, 1974); (with Elizabeth Fox-Genovese), *Fruits of Merchant Capital: Slavery and Bourgeois Property in the Rise and Expansion of Capitalism* (New York, 1983); and *The Slaveholders' Dilemma: Freedom and Progress in Southern Conservative Thought, 1820–1860* (Columbia, S.C., 1992).

Strikingly, given historians' constructive propensity to quarrel with one another, no rival interpretive paradigm has emerged to challenge Genovese's insistence that the dialectic of paternalism defined the master-slave relationship in the Old South.[2] However, Genovese's intermittent efforts to argue that social relations between planters and white plain folk were mediated through the same ideology of paternalism have excited considerably more disagreement among historians.[3] Although assessing these animated historiographical contretemps between Genovese and his critics is no easy task, arguably the balance of recent scholarship disputes Genovese's theory of paternalism and planter hegemony in favor of the concept of *Herrenvolk* egalitarianism, a model that portrays white society in the Old South as marked by a high degree of egalitarian sentiment and personal or household independence among members of the dominant race, but willing to accept the absolute subjugation of black slaves. Suggested by the work of George Fredrickson and fleshed out in considerable detail by a variety of historians, the *Herrenvolk* democracy model asserts the hegem-

2. Recent assessments of the historiography of antebellum southern slavery that reveal the protean influence of Genovese's work include Peter Kolchin, *American Slavery, 1619–1877* (New York, 1993), esp. 93–168; Peter J. Parish, *Slavery: History and the Historians* (New York, 1989), esp. 26–96; and Charles B. Dew, "The Slavery Experience," in *Interpreting Southern History: Historiographical Essays in Honor of Sanford W. Higginbotham*, ed. John B. Boles and Evelyn Thomas Nolen (Baton Rouge, 1987), 120–61.

3. For a brief introduction to Genovese's view of white plain folk, see his "Yeoman Farmers in a Slaveholders' Democracy," *Agricultural History*, XLIX (1975), 331–42. Drew Gilpin Faust, "The Peculiar South Revisited: White Society, Culture, and Politics in the Antebellum Period, 1800–1860," in *Interpreting Southern History*, ed. Boles and Nolen, 78–119, offers a judicious evaluation of Genovese's influence and the arguments of his leading critics. See also Kolchin, *American Slavery*, 169–99, and Parish, *Slavery*, 124–48. Probably the most sweeping one-volume refutation of Genovese is James Oakes, *The Ruling Race: A History of American Slaveholders* (New York, 1982). Subsequently, however, Oakes's *Slavery and Freedom: An Interpretation of the Old South* (New York, 1990) offered a more favorable evaluation of Genovese's contributions. Since 1980, two historians have offered sweeping interpretations of antebellum southern distinctiveness that focus on cultural uniqueness rather than a singular regional political economy based on slavery. Bertram Wyatt-Brown, *Southern Honor: Ethics and Behavior in the Old South* (New York, 1982), emphasizes the persistence of a traditional code of honor in the region, while Grady McWhiney, *Cracker Culture: Celtic Ways in the Old South* (Tuscaloosa, 1988), locates southern singularity in the ethnic folkways of a Scotch-Irish culture that preferred leisure to work and encouraged a touchy, if informal, sense of personal honor even among commoners.

ony of an egalitarian ideology that emphasized the equality of all whites in the public sphere despite the glaring inequalities separating planters from common whites in terms of material well-being.[4]

Historians' current understanding of the common whites of the Old South also owes much to the pioneering work of Steve Hahn, whose award-winning *Roots of Southern Populism*, published in 1983, reinvigorated the study of plain folk. Hahn emphasized not simply the numerical preponderance of yeoman farmers in southern society, but also the ability of yeomen in white-belt areas to define a community-oriented political economy that defied the market ethos advanced by urban merchants and their black-belt planter allies. Southern yeomen, particularly hill-country yeomen on the geographic margins of the market economy, thrived as a class of independent producers who concentrated on subsistence production and community self-sufficiency that insulated them from the booms and busts of the encroaching capitalist economy. In Hahn's view, the southern yeomanry not only cherished this independence, but also clearly perceived that it was sustained by community cooperation as well as by individual or household autonomy.[5]

---

4. George M. Fredrickson, *The Black Image in the White Mind: The Debate on Afro-American Character and Destiny* (New York, 1971), esp. 61–68. See also Kenneth Vickery, "Herrenvolk Democracy and Egalitarianism in South Africa and the United States South," *Comparative Studies in Society and History*, XVI (1974), 309–28. Lacy K. Ford, Jr., *Origins of Southern Radicalism: The South Carolina Upcountry, 1800–1860* (New York, 1988), is one recent study informed by the *Herrenvolk* egalitarian model. Michael Wayne, "An Old South Morality Play: Reconsidering the Social Underpinnings of the Proslavery Ideology, " *Journal of American History*, LXXVII (1990), 838–63, cites a variety of works influenced by *Herrenvolk* egalitarianism and offers an insightful critique of them.

5. Steven Hahn, *The Roots of Southern Populism: Yeoman Farmers and the Transformation of the Georgia Upcountry, 1850–1890* (New York, 1983), esp. 1–133. Prior to the publication of Hahn's innovative study, the plain folk of the Old South had attracted surprisingly little attention from scholars since the work of the so-called Owsley school over thirty years earlier. Owsley and his students argued that a "middling sort" of landholding farmers constituted the majority of whites in the Old South and defined that society as one that scorned both aristocratic pretensions and grinding poverty. For an introduction, see Frank L. Owsley and Harriet C. Owsley, "The Economic Basis of Society in the Late Antebellum South," *Journal of Southern History*, VI (1940), 24–45, and Frank L. Owsley, *Plain Folk of the Old South* (Baton Rouge, 1949). In a much-cited article, Fabian Linden criticized the Owsleys' preliminary findings, pointing out that land and other resources were very unevenly distributed in the antebellum South and that a significant minority of white

In the years since it appeared, Hahn's book has proven enormously influential. The voluminous recent scholarship on the white plain folk of the Old South largely supports Hahn's case for the independence of the southern yeomanries and his argument that yeoman production and consumption patterns centered around household and community self-sufficiency. To be sure, studies by J. William Harris, Lacy Ford, Harry Watson, David Weiman, Donald Winters, Paul Escott, and others have presented impressive evidence that the yeoman farmers of the southern interior embraced the opportunities offered by market involvement more eagerly than Hahn realized. Apparently no small number of yeomen saw increased market production as a chance to enhance, rather than risk, their independence. Nevertheless, the bulk of this recent scholarship confirms Hahn's central contention that, regardless of their degree of market orientation, the yeomen of the Old South desperately feared the loss of their independence, equating dependence with degradation and virtual enslavement. Like petty producers elsewhere, they resisted "proletarianization" with as much vigor as they could muster.[6]

In the 1990s the renaissance of yeomen studies has entered its second generation as a number of monographs have appeared addressing ques-

---

households owned no property at all; see Linden, "Economic Democracy in the Slave South: An Appraisal of Some Recent Views," *Journal of Negro History,* XXXI (1946), 140–89.

6. For a sampling of the literature on the yeomanry that appeared in response to Hahn, see J. William Harris, *Plain Folk and Gentry in a Slave Society: White Liberty and Black Slavery in Augusta's Hinterlands* (Middleton, Conn., 1985); Lacy K. Ford, "Rednecks and Merchants: Economic Development and Social Tensions in the South Carolina Upcountry, 1865–1900," *Journal of American History,* LXXI (1984), 294–318, and "Yeoman Farmers in the South Carolina Upcountry: Changing Production Patterns in the Late Antebellum Period," *Agricultural History,* LX (1986), 17–37; Harry L. Watson, "Conflict and Collaboration: Yeomen, Slaveholders, and Politics in the Antebellum South," *Social History,* X (1985), 273–98; David F. Weiman, "Farmers and the Market in Antebellum America: A View from the Georgia Upcountry," *Journal of Economic History,* XLVI (1987), 627–47; Donald L. Winters, "'Plain Folk' of the Old South Reexamined: Economic Democracy in Tennessee," *Journal of Southern History,* LIII (1987), 565–86; and Paul D. Escott, "Yeoman Independence and the Market: Social Status and Economic Development in Antebellum North Carolina," *North Carolina Historical Review,* LXVI (July 1989), 275–99. For a thorough survey of the post-Owsley literature on the plain folk that appeared before much of the fascinating recent work, see Randolph B. Campbell, "Planters and Plain Folk: The Social Structure of the Antebellum South," in *Interpreting Southern History,* ed. Boles and Nolen, 48–77.

tions raised but not answered by the pathbreaking studies of the previous decade. Tracy McKenzie's multifaceted comparative study of yeoman communities in each of Tennessee's three grand divisions explored the question of upward social mobility for the plain folk, finding that wealth was unevenly distributed in the hills and valleys of east Tennessee as well as in the rich west Tennessee cotton lands, but that the overall material well-being and the prospects for upward social mobility among yeomen were actually better in staple-growing areas than in hermetic hill-country economies.[7] More recently, Bradley Bond's study of the political economy of nineteenth-century Mississippi contends that historians have incorrectly characterized the production patterns of many southern yeomen. His analysis of Mississippi piney-woods yeomen in the late antebellum period suggests that rather than following a "safety-first" strategy of ensuring self-sufficiency before allocating land and other resources to market crops, they instead pursued an "accumulation-first" strategy in which they produced as much as possible for the market while allocating to foodstuffs the minimum resources that they thought necessary to produce a subsistence. Bond concludes that this market-friendly approach kept many yeomen perilously close to shortfalls in subsistence production as they sought to enhance their cash incomes and property holdings.[8]

Two other recent studies of the plain folk have rightly noted conceptual limitations of earlier works. Charles Bolton's study of poor whites in central North Carolina and northern Mississippi chided scholars for too often neglecting to make careful distinctions among the various gradations of white plain folk. Tenant farmers, agricultural day laborers, and industrial operatives, Bolton emphasized, usually owned no real property and thus had economic interests that diverged significantly from those of yeoman freeholders.[9] Moreover, by looking at the interior of yeoman households, Stephanie McCurry's study of common whites in the plantation-

7. Robert Tracy McKenzie, *One South or Many? Plantation Belt and Upcountry in Civil War-Era Tennessee* (Cambridge, Mass., 1994).

8. Bradley G. Bond, *Political Culture in the Nineteenth Century South: Mississippi, 1830–1900* (Baton Rouge, 1995), esp. 43–80, and Bond, "Habits of Foodstuffs and Market Production: A Look at Mississippi," *Journal of Mississippi History*, XLVI (1994), 1–20.

9. Charles C. Bolton, *Poor Whites of the Antebellum South: Tenants and Laborers in Central North Carolina and Northeast Mississippi* (Durham, N.C., 1994), 42–112. A similar point is made by Bill Cecil-Fronsman, *Common Whites: Class and Culture in Antebellum North Carolina* (Lexington, Ky., 1992).

dominated South Carolina lowcountry has broadened our attention from
its long-standing focus on the political economy of yeoman communities
to encompass the family and cultural values of the plain folk and thus shed
new light on the social conservatism of the black belt. McCurry's work reveals that the "masters of small worlds" who headed self-reliant households prized both their independence from direct planter control and their
patriarchal authority over dependent women and children in their own
households. Whatever common cause ordinary southern whites made with
elite slaveholders, McCurry contends, arose at least in part from their
shared embrace of the patriarchal ideal.[10]

In addition to this rich body of recent work on the antebellum southern yeomanry, historians have acquired a dramatically improved understanding of the plain folk of the Old South from the concurrent flourish
of scholarship examining the political culture and the ideology of the
Jacksonian South. This recent southern political historiography is voluminous and rich in state-to-state and locale-to-locale variations, but its
interpretive thrust can be readily summarized. It contends that the political culture of the Old South was strongly democratic for white males and
characterized by high levels of voter participation and, outside of Calhoun's South Carolina, by a competitive two-party system that encouraged voter loyalty.[11]

Yet despite the abundant recent scholarship on the common whites
and the politics of the Old South, little of this work has focused directly
on the political ideas of the plain folk. In all likelihood, the primary reason for this relative neglect is that the primary sources available to historians render the task of reconstructing the political thought of the common whites, as opposed to their production patterns, daunting. In an
effort to circumvent this problem, but admitting from the start that my
flanking approach involves relying heavily on the professions of elected

10. Stephanie McCurry, *Masters of Small Worlds: Yeoman Households, Gender Relations,
and the Political Culture of the Antebellum South Carolina Low Country* (New York, 1995).

11. For a sampling of this literature, see William J. Cooper, Jr., *Liberty and Slavery:
Southern Politics to 1860* (New York, 1983); J. Mills Thornton III, *Politics and Power in a
Slave Society: Alabama, 1800–1860* (Baton Rouge, 1978); Harry L. Watson, *Jacksonian Politics and Community Conflict: The Emergence of the Second American Party System in Cumberland County, North Carolina* (Baton Rouge, 1981); Ford, *Origins of Southern Radicalism,*
97–214; Daniel Dupre, "Barbecue and Pledges: Electioneering and the Rise of Democratic
Politics in Antebellum Alabama," *Journal of Southern History,* LX (1994), 479–512.

spokesmen for the plain folk, rather than on evidence gathered directly from the voices or pens of common whites, this essay will examine the ideology presented by champions of the plain folk at political moments when ideas should have been most salient—in the state constitutional reform movements of the Jacksonian era.

Across the South, the Jacksonian movement for constitutional reform advocated injecting ever-larger doses of political democracy, as that term was understood by antebellum white southerners, into state constitutions. But perhaps more important, analysis of the campaigns for state constitutional conventions and the proceedings of the conventions themselves reveals a consistent pattern of support for egalitarian reforms from yeoman-dominated white-belt areas and conservative support for the constitutional status quo from planter strongholds in the various portions of the tidewater and the black belt.[12] This pattern suggests that an examination of the egalitarian ideas of the constitutional reformers of the 1830s might offer valuable insights into the prevailing political ideas of plain folk. Thus, in an attempt to uncover the popular political thought of the Old South's plain folk, this essay will evaluate the ideas presented by egalitarian reformers, and to a lesser extent the conservative critique of those ideas, in the three full-blown constitutional conventions held in the South during the years of Andrew Jackson's presidency: the Virginia convention of 1829–1830, the Mississippi convention of 1832, and the Tennessee convention of 1834.

Doubtless the most contentious of the three, the Virginia Constitutional Convention of 1829–1830 represented the culmination of a political crisis that had roiled the Old Dominion for nearly two decades. Egalitarians from western Virginia, an area composed of the Valley and the trans-Allegheny portions of the state, demanded thoroughgoing reform of

12. The standard literature on the constitutional reform movement in the Jacksonian South is Fletcher M. Green, *Constitutional Development in the South Atlantic States, 1776–1860: A Study in the Evolution of Democracy* (Chapel Hill, 1930), and "Democracy in the Old South," *Journal of Southern History*, XII (1946), 2–23; Charles S. Sydnor, *The Development of Southern Sectionalism, 1819–1848* (Baton Rouge, 1948), 275–93; and Chilton Williamson, *American Suffrage from Property to Democracy, 1760–1860* (Princeton, 1960), esp. 138–57, 223–41. For an incisive recent commentary on state constitutional revision in the Old South, see Don E. Fehrenbacher, *Constitutions and Constitutionalism in the Slaveholding South* (Athens, Ga., 1989), 1–32. All of the state constitutions analyzed in this essay can be found in Francis N. Thorpe, comp., *The Federal and State Constitutions, Colonial Charters, and Other Organic Laws . . .* (7 vols.; Washington, D.C., 1909).

the state's 1776 constitution, which they considered "aristocratic" because it granted effective control of state government to tidewater and piedmont counties with heavy concentrations of slaves.[13]

The reform position, expressed chiefly by western delegates and their few scattered piedmont and urban allies, reflected a broader, *Herrenvolk* egalitarian commitment to the rough political equality of all white men (who could present at least a nominal claim to "independence") and an equally firm commitment to white majority rule as controlling principles of republicanism. At the convention, egalitarians fought for a variety of democratic reforms, foremost among them the liberalization of the suffrage and an end to the so-called county unit system of legislative apportionment. The long-controversial county unit system granted equal representation in the House of Delegates to every county in the commonwealth regardless of its white or free population, and thus favored the long-settled plantation areas east of the Blue Ridge. Moreover, Virginia's restrictive suffrage law, reaffirmed in the 1776 constitution, stipulated that voters must own a freehold or its equivalent in town property in order to vote.[14]

Although egalitarians ultimately evinced a willingness to compromise on details of an apportionment plan, these reformers advocated the so-called white basis as the only truly republican form of representation. Any apportionment formula that did not recognize "one white man, one vote" as its guiding principle, egalitarians claimed, risked relinquishing the sovereignty of the popular majority to the tyranny of a propertied minority.[15] Valley egalitarian and future Democratic governor James McDowell insisted that any legislative apportionment scheme that "results in vesting equal powers in unequal masses of men is repugnant to our

13. Alison Goodyear Freehling, *Drift Toward Dissolution: The Virginia Slavery Debate of 1831–1832* (Baton Rouge, 1982), 11–81, places the Virginia convention in context and offers the best succinct account of its proceedings. See also Robert P. Sutton, *Revolution to Secession: Constitution Making in the Old Dominion* (Charlottesville, Va., 1989), 52–102.

14. For a good brief introduction of these issues, see Freehling, *Drift Toward Dissolution*, 36–48, and Merrill D. Peterson, *Democracy, Liberty, and Property: The State Constitutional Conventions of the 1820s* (Indianapolis, 1966), 271–85.

15. William W. Freehling, *The Road to Disunion: Secessionists at Bay, 1776–1854* (New York, 1990), esp. 162–77, provides a particularly perceptive analysis of the Virginia convention as a microcosm of the larger political struggle between white-belt egalitarians and black-belt conservatives in the Old South. To a large extent, I have adopted his terminology for this essay.

ideas." Only apportionment by the white basis, McDowell maintained, could ensure the "perfect equality of our citizens."[16]

On the convention floor, Shenandoah Valley delegate and reformer John R. Cooke asserted that the American Revolution founded the republic "on the sovereignty of the people and the equality of men." True republican doctrine required that "all members of a community" who were "free agents by situation" were "equally entitled to the exercise of political power." Cooke emphatically maintained that the Virginia Declaration of Rights unequivocally proclaimed the *"principles of the sovereignty of the people, the equality of men, and the right of the majority"* as the heart of Virginia's founding political creed. But, Cooke continued, Virginia's 1776 constitution had "violated" this creed by "investing small masses of people in small counties, and large masses of people in large counties, with equal power in government."[17]

Another Valley egalitarian, Alfred Powell, argued that the convention could make "no excuse" for infusing "oligarchic, aristocratic" principles into the formula for representation. Representation based even in part on property, Powell charged, implied that "power is not derived from the people and vested in them" but "that a portion of political power belongs to and is vested in, *property.*" A "republican form of Government," Powell maintained, not only refrained from "giving to wealth political power" but rather sought "to prevent wealth from drawing to itself too great a portion of political power."[18]

Yet perhaps the most trenchant critique of the county unit system came from trans-Allegheny delegate Philip Doddridge. The erudite but sometimes uncouth Doddridge, described by one easterner as "busy as a bee, and dirty as a hog," emphatically maintained that the "majority of free white persons" had the "right . . . to govern the state." Moreover, Doddridge candidly contended, the "rule of the majority would be safe

16. Draft of Speech by James McDowell, April 20, 1829, in James McDowell Papers, Southern Historical Collection, University of North Carolina at Chapel Hill [hereinafter cited as SHC].

17. *Proceedings and Debates of the Virginia State Convention of 1829–1830* (2 vols., Richmond, Va., 1830), I, 54–62. An unabridged reprint edition of these volumes was published by DeCapo Press in 1971. See also entry of November 8, 1829, John R. Cooke Diary, in Virginia Historical Society, Richmond [hereinafter cited as VHS].

18. *Proceedings and Debates of the Virginia State Convention of 1829–1830,* I, 103–108.

now" were it not "for the possession of slaves in great masses, by the minority, residing mostly in a particular part of the State." The arguments made against the rule of the white majority, Doddridge claimed, implied that "however small their numbers," the "owners of slave property must possess all the powers of government" in order to "secure that property from the rapacity of an overgrown majority of white men." Such an oligarchic principle of government, Doddridge maintained, led to the "perpetual slavery" of the free white majority. As "long as you hold political dominion over me," Doddridge told eastern delegates, "I am a slave."[19]

Conservatives not only opposed the white basis of reapportionment, instead favoring bases that included property as well as population in the formula, but they also accused the egalitarians of grossly misunderstanding the Old Dominion's republican heritage. Conservatives claimed that at the heart of the Virginia founders' conception of self-government lay deep concerns for the protection of property and minority rights. According to conservative Culpeper planter and appeals court judge John W. Green, republicanism assumed only "that all power resides in the people," and not that "the possession of all power of government by the people gave to each member of the body politic equal weight in its government." Nor did a republican frame of government assume that "the majority shall rule by absolute power." Numerical majorities, Green contended, were "likely to decide rightly" if and only if "the majority have an *interest* in doing what is right."[20]

Green's conservative formulation of the republican creed seemingly resuscitated the old antifederalist proposition, long contradicted by James Madison, that self-government protected the rights of minorities only in small, homogenous societies in which "all have one common interest."[21] But Green's statement also opened the door for an innovative argument

19. For the characterization of Doddridge, see Hugh Blair Grigsby to John N. Tazewell, October 6, 1829, in Tazewell Family Papers, Virginia State Library, Richmond [hereinafter cited as VSL]; for Doddridge's remarks, see *Proceedings and Debates of the Virginia State Convention of 1829–1830*, I, 79–89.

20. For a perceptive brief analysis of conservative thought as it emerged at the convention, see Dickson R. Bruce, *The Rhetoric of Conservatism: The Virginia Convention of 1829–1830 and the Conservative Tradition in the South* (San Marino, Calif., 1982); *Proceedings and Debates of the Virginia State Convention of 1829–1830*, I, 62–64.

21. Jack N. Rakove, *James Madison and the Creation of the American Republic* (Glenview, Ill., 1990), 44–52; *Proceedings and Debates of the Virginia State Convention of 1829–1830*, I, 63.

explaining the need for the protection of minority interests from potential depredations at the hands of hostile popular majorities. In an eloquent speech that reflected the influence of his friend John C. Calhoun, Eastern Shore conservative Abel Upshur conceded that majority rule was an essential part of republican government, but he stressed that there "are two kinds of majority," a "majority in *interest*, as well as a majority in number." Upshur acknowledged that "as a general proposition," in "free Governments" power "ought to be given to the majority," but he maintained that the question of "what elements that majority shall be composed," whether of persons or interests or some combination of the two, was left open. The separate interests of society, Upshur contended, should each be represented in any majority, and since different interests arose "from property alone," then both "persons and property" deserved consideration. In Virginia—where, Upshur argued, slaveholders might be exposed to ruinous taxation if they lost control of the legislature—property was "entitled to protection."[22]

If Upshur succinctly summarized the emerging idea that all of society's clashing interests deserved representation in government, other conservatives elaborated on the concept. Littleton Waller Tazewell, a prominent Norfolk lawyer, maintained that even in a republic "the protection of interests" should be "the object of government." Representation, he continued, "should not be awarded in proportion to noses." Instead, Tazewell believed that "three grand interests"—agriculture, commerce, and manufacturing—existed in American society and "each ought to be represented." Tazewell denied that "the principles of all Republican Government required that representation should be apportioned according to numbers alone, and should be founded on white population only."[23] Tidewater conservative Benjamin Watkins Leigh agreed, recommending the adoption of a legislative apportionment plan that gave "as nearly equal a representation of the great interests of the state" as possible.[24]

No other issue at the convention proved as difficult to resolve as the question of representation. A plethora of compromise proposals failed. Finally, after subtle negotiations for votes of a mere handful of swing dele-

22. *Proceedings and Debates of the Virginia State Convention of 1829–1830*, I, 65–79.

23. *Ibid.*, 326–35; Hugh Blair Grigsby Diary, October 23, November 1, 1829, in VHS.

24. Benjamin Watkins Leigh to John Y. Mason, August 21, 1828, in Mason Family Papers, VHS; Grigsby Diary, November 3, 1829; *Proceedings and Debates of the Virginia State Convention of 1829–1830*, I, 151–73.

gates, the convention narrowly approved a plan apportioning both houses of the Virginia legislature on the basis of the 1820 white population. To the bitter disappointment of determined western reformers, this plan penalized the faster growing regions west of the Blue Ridge and left the tidewater and piedmont in effective control of the state government.[25]

Liberalization of the suffrage enjoyed broader support among convention delegates than did democratic representation, largely because many nonfreeholders in the east as well as the west resented their disfranchisement. Again egalitarian reformers invoked the rhetoric of white male equality to support their cause. Reformer James McDowell reasoned that the right of suffrage should stand "on a liberal basis comprehending all who possess sufficient independence to exercise so important a privilege." McDowell concluded that "every man keeping household in his own right" possessed such independence. He proposed extending voting rights to "every man of discreet age . . . who is not discredited as a pauper or infamous offender."[26]

Influenced by a memorial from nonfreeholders in Richmond, Lucas Thompson, a piedmont reformer, decried the freehold requirement as "invidious and anti-republican" and identified the extension of the suffrage as "the great cause of *non-freehold* emancipation." Vowing to "judge the professor of republicanism by his practice," Thompson continued his comparison of disfranchisement with enslavement. A "man who has no voice in the government . . . [and] holds his rights by the sufferance of him who has," he observed, "is already half a slave."[27] With his usual flair, the outspoken egalitarian Doddridge characterized the government of a minority over a majority an "aristocracy and oligarchy" and warned that if freeholders ever became a minority in Virginia, as it appeared they soon might, then a freeholders' republic was nothing more than an aristocracy.[28]

Reflecting later on the convention proceedings, James Madison, the architect of the American republican edifice, reiterated Doddridge's con-

25. Freehling, *Drift Toward Dissolution*, 78–81; Sutton, *Revolution to Secession*, 103–21.

26. Draft of Speech on Convention, April 20, 1829, and a fragment of a speech on "Elective Franchise," *ca.* 1829, in James McDowell Papers, SHC.

27. The Non-freeholders' Memorial was introduced early in the convention by United States Chief Justice John Marshall. See *Proceedings and Debates of the Virginia State Convention of 1829–1830*, I, 25–31, for the memorial and 410–419 for Thompson's remarks.

28. *Ibid.*, 419–28.

cern. Madison argued that the right of suffrage ought to extend at least far enough to include "a majority of the people" because a "Government resting on minority is an Aristocracy not a republic."[29] Moderate reformer Charles Morgan, a westerner, offered a straightforward racial justification for white manhood suffrage when he noted that Alabama, South Carolina, and most other slaveholding states had already "deemed it of utmost importance to make all free white men as free and independent as Government could make them" in order to promote the social harmony essential to public safety in a slave society. "Is it not now wise," Morgan admonished his fellow delegates, "to call together at least every free white human being, and unite them in common interest and government?"[30]

Conservatives, however, defended the freehold as the proper basis for suffrage in a republic. One western delegate skeptical of democratic suffrage, the Valley's Archibald Stuart, predicted that in "a few years we must see that for one landholder there will be many who have none. The rights of those who own the country will be invaded by those who hold no part of it." Experience having "taught us how even freeholders in a State of Independence may be influenced to commit foolish acts," said Stuart, "what then have we to expect if the idle, the vicious [and] worthless are to have agency in carrying on our government?"[31] Conservative Benjamin W. Leigh warned that extending the suffrage "to men who cannot be expected to give an independent vote" opened the door to the rise of faction, caucus, and party.[32] Philip N. Nicholas, a wealthy Richmond banker and scion of an old Virginia planting family, disputed as "ludicrous" the charge that Virginia was governed by an "aristocracy of freeholders." Nicholas noted that the yeoman freeholders of Virginia possessed an "independence of character" that poor whites who owned no real property lacked. The "great advantage of the freehold system," Nicholas contended, was that it "keeps Government in the hands of the mid-

29. James Madison to James K. Paulding, January 7, 1832, in William C. Rives Papers, Library of Congress, Washington, D.C. See also Drew R. McCoy, *The Last of the Fathers: James Madison and the Republican Legacy* (Cambridge, Mass., 1989), 217–52.

30. *Proceedings and Debates of the Virginia State Convention of 1829–1830*, I, 377–83.

31. Archibald Stuart to [?], *ca.* 1829, in Stuart Family Papers, VHS.

32. *Proceedings and Debates of the Virginia State Convention of 1829–1830*, I, 406–409. For a thorough explanation of Leigh's long-standing objections to an extended suffrage, see Benjamin Watkins Leigh to Peachy R. Gilmer, August 17, 1825, in William Leigh Letters, VSL.

dling classes, so far from being aristocratic, it is a safeguard against aristocracy." As "long as political power is placed as it now is in Virginia, in
the hands of the middling classes, who, though not rich, are yet sufficiently so to secure their independence, you have nothing to fear from
wealth," Nicholas concluded, but if you "extend the right of suffrage to
every man dependent as well as every man independent, you immediately
open the floodgates of corruption."[33] Leigh also felt compelled to deny
imputations of "aristocracy" issued by reformers. Leigh dismissed charges
that Virginia was ruled by an "aristocracy of wealth" as "downright
slang."[34]

Eventually the Virginia convention compromised the suffrage question, extending the suffrage to all taxpayers and established household
heads but stopping decidedly short of the white manhood basis egalitarian
reformers wanted. When the Virginia convention submitted the constitution to voters, the liberalized suffrage clause and the popular election of
the governor helped ensure ratification of a document whose representation provisions left egalitarians extremely dissatisfied. Virginians who
lived west of the Blue Ridge voted overwhelmingly against the new constitution, but a strong favorable vote from the east, and especially the
populous piedmont, ratified the controversial document.[35]

Picking up a theme from frustrated Virginia reformers, egalitarians at Mississippi's constitutional convention of 1832 focused on a war against "aristocracy." The state's original constitution, adopted when Mississippi
gained statehood in 1817, reflected the strong influence of the Natchez
region's planter and mercantile elite. While hardly as undemocratic as
Virginia's Constitution of 1776 or other seaboard constitutions of the
Revolutionary era, the Mississippi Constitution of 1817 was decidedly
"less liberal than most constitutions of the new states." It included
significant property requirements for officeholding, limited the suffrage to
white taxpayers and members of militia companies, and apportioned the
senate on the basis of white taxpayers. Moreover, the state's judiciary was
elected for life by the legislature, and part of that judiciary, the county
courts, administered local government.[36]

33. *Proceedings and Debates of the Virginia State Convention of 1829–1830*, I, 362–68.
34. *Ibid.*, 402–404.
35. Sutton, *Revolution to Secession*, 103–107; Freehling, *Drift Toward Dissolution*, 77–81.
36. Edwin A. Miles, *Jacksonian Democracy in Mississippi* (Chapel Hill, 1960), 33–43;
Winbourne Magruder Drake, "The Framing of Mississippi's First Constitution," *Journal of*

Although these conservative provisions suited the Natchez area elite, egalitarian reform sentiment flourished among whites in rapidly growing areas of northern and eastern Mississippi. Keenly aware of the egalitarian sentiments of the new white majority and their increasing political strength in areas remote from Natchez, one knowledgeable observer predicted that Mississippi would draft "a constitution much more democratic than any other in the United States. Not republican—but downright democratic." The same observer, skeptical Natchez-area conservative Stephen Duncan, classified the three factions represented at the convention as "whole hogs," "half-hogs," and "aristocrats" according to how much democracy, particularly with regard to the judiciary, delegates favored writing into the new constitution.[37] Leading conservatives at the convention admitted that "the complexion of the members is decidedly in favor of what they call Reform" and conceded that they could hope only to force "some modifications which will make the pill less bitter and more palatable."[38]

Once debate began, egalitarian reformers asserted that "the most liberal Democratic Republican principles" should guide the convention's course. Just as in Virginia, egalitarians found fodder for their reform in the original Mississippi Declaration of Rights. Patterned after its Virginia counterpart, Mississippi's declaration proclaimed that "all freemen, when they form the social compact, are equal in rights; and that no man or set of men are entitled to exclusive . . . privileges." Reformers claimed that an extension of voting rights would appeal to the state's "hardy yeomanry" and quickly pushed for the elimination of any "unnecessary restriction on the franchise." Egalitarians also claimed that "unequal representation" was "oppressive, unjust and contrary to the true meaning of our Republican institutions," and urged the apportionment of both houses of the legislature on the white basis.[39]

Mississippi History, XXIX (1967), 301–27, and "The Mississippi Constitutional Convention of 1832," *Journal of Southern History*, XXIII (1957), 354–70; John Hebron Moore, "Local and State Governments of Antebellum Mississippi," *Journal of Mississippi History*, XLIV (1982), 104–35.

37. Stephen Duncan to Levin Wailes, September 14, 1832, in Benjamin L. C. Wailes Papers, Mississippi Department of Archives and History, Jackson [hereinafter cited as MDAH].

38. John Quitman to Eliza Quitman, September 16, October 2, 1832, in Quitman Family Papers, SHC.

39. *Journal of the Convention of the State of Mississippi* (Jackson, 1832), 18–23, 45–48.

Perhaps recognizing their need to conserve intellectual capital for other issues, the so-called aristocrats offered little opposition to the democratic suffrage and representation proposals. In fact, conservative leader John Quitman, a northern-born, self-made Natchez nabob, praised "universal suffrage" as "inseparably connected with our republican institutions." Quitman also offered support for a democratic basis of representation. "Men should be represented," he maintained, "not property or territory."[40] Against such tepid conservative opposition, Mississippi reformers moved quickly to secure the elimination of both the state's limited tax-paying requirement for voting and its property requirements for office-holding. The convention also apportioned both houses of the legislature on the basis of white population.[41]

But the major fight at the Mississippi convention involved not suffrage or representation, but two controversial constitutional provisions concerning the judicial branch: the life tenure of appointed judges and the county court system of local government. In particular, the local government provision, which granted county judges (appointed by the legislature for life) executive, lawmaking, and judicial power over county matters, aroused widespread popular hostility. Free of any meaningful popular check on their actions, members of this powerful, tenured state and local judiciary assumed the appearance of a privileged aristocracy to many Mississippi egalitarians.[42] Democratic reformers, the so-called whole hogs, led by Vicksburg newspaper editor and future United States senator Henry Foote, demanded the popular election of all state and county judges as testimony to "the competency of the people to govern themselves." At the convention, egalitarians called "the principle of rotation in office" essential "to prevent those who are invested with authority from becoming oppressors." Reformers also argued that too much "independence in judges renders them irresponsible to the people and is contrary to the genius of Republicanism."[43]

40. John A. Quitman, "To the Electors of Adams County," July 1832, in J. F. H. Claiborne, *Life and Correspondence of John A. Quitman* (2 vols., New York, 1860), I, 116–26.

41. Drake, "Mississippi Constitutional Convention of 1832," 361–63; *Journal of the Convention of the State of Mississippi,* 18–52, 185–220; Vicksburg *Advocate and Register,* September 27, 1832.

42. Moore, "Local and State Governments of Antebellum Mississippi," 105–108; Harry Cage to John Quitman, May 1, 1832, in J. F. H. Claiborne Papers, MDAH.

43. Vicksburg *Mississippian,* January 9, 1832; *Journal of the Convention of the State of Mississippi,* 19; George Winchester to John Quitman, September 24, 1832, in J. F. H. Clai-

A determined Quitman lead the fight against egalitarianism. Popular election of judges, Quitman warned, "would . . . strike a fatal blow at the independence of the judiciary." Quitman maintained that constitutional checks were designed "for the benefit of the minority," to "protect them against the action of the majority." If "the judicial department is to be completely under the influence and control of the mere majority," Quitman continued, "that majority might as well govern without any restrictions." Predicting that an elected judiciary would be "too much influenced by sudden popular excitement," Quitman reminded reformers that an "independent" judiciary was not necessarily an "irresponsible" one.[44] Fellow conservative George Winchester echoed Quitman's concerns, maintaining that "tenure of office for good behavior" guaranteed judges "the independence they needed to insure impartiality."[45]

Ultimately, however, the "whole hog" approach prevailed in Mississippi, and the state's new constitution turned the selection of all judges over to the people. It also restructured local government, abolishing the despised county court system in favor of popularly elected county boards of police with extensive governmental responsibilities.[46]

Two years after the Mississippi reforms, Tennessee held a convention to revise the state constitution. Voters approved the call for a convention decisively in 1833, motivated in large part by a desire, similar to the one that had animated Mississippi reformers, to reform an arrogant and inefficient judiciary.[47] Newspaper editors from eastern Tennessee charged that a "spirit of aristocracy" flourished among state and local judges, and even

borne Papers, MDAH. Although Winchester was a conservative, his letter to Quitman not only states his own position but also articulates clearly the views of reformers he has talked to in his travels around Mississippi.

44. Quitman, "To the Electors of Adams County," in Claiborne, *Life and Correspondence of Quitman*, I, 116–23.

45. George Winchester to John Quitman, September 24, 1832, in J. F. H. Claiborne Collection, MDAH.

46. Moore, "Local and State Governments of Antebellum Mississippi," 107–16; Drake, "Mississippi Constitutional Convention of 1832," 363–65; Thorpe, *Federal and State Constitutions*, IV, 2055–57.

47. Paul H. Bergeron, *Antebellum Politics in Tennessee* (Lexington, Ky., 1982), 38–40; Jonathan Moore Atkins, "'A Combat For Liberty': Politics and Parties in Jackson's Tennessee, 1832–1851" (Ph.D. dissertation, University of Michigan, 1991), 7–11; Robert Cassell, "Newton Cannon and the Constitutional Convention of 1834," *Tennessee Historical Quarterly*, XXV (1956), 224–42.

Tennesseans skeptical of a constitutional convention acknowledged that the "defective nature" of the state's judiciary spurred the reform movement.[48]

On the whole, democratic reforms prevailed easily in Andrew Jackson's home state in 1834, largely because at the time Tennessee lacked a black-belt region comparable to those that sustained determined conservative opposition to egalitarian reform in Virginia and at least raised the specter of opposition to democratization in Mississippi. With a minimum of controversy, the Tennessee convention eliminated the existing connection between freeholds and voting rights and rejected proposals advocating a taxpaying requirement for voting in favor of white manhood suffrage. The convention also eliminated all property requirements for officeholding, and democratized representation in the state legislature by apportioning it on the basis of eligible voters (white males) instead of "taxable inhabitants" (a classification that included slaves) as the 1796 constitution had.[49]

Even judicial reform triumphed easily in Tennessee, albeit in a shape that would have been referred to as "half-hog" in Mississippi. The new constitution abolished the unpopular county courts in favor of elected justices of the peace. It made other county offices, such as sheriff and tax collector, elective as well. Through this reform the convention removed the legislative functions of local government from county court judges and placed them in the hands of officials directly accountable to the voters. At the same time, however, the new Tennessee constitution permitted the legislature to retain the power of choosing circuit and appeals court judges, thus giving the judiciary the measure of independence from voters desired by conservatives and cautious reformers.[50]

But if the Tennessee convention handled the issues of suffrage, representation, and judicial reform with a minimum of controversy, at least compared with other southern states, it found itself enmeshed in sensitive internal disagreements over slavery and the status of free blacks in the

48. Knoxville *Register,* November 27, 1833; William B. Campbell to David Campbell, August 8, 1833, in Campbell Family Papers, Perkins Library Special Collections, Duke University, Durham, North Carolina.

49. *Journal of the Convention of the State of Tennessee* (Nashville, 1834); Cassell, "Newton Cannon," 233–42.

50. Bergeron, *Antebellum Politics in Tennessee,* 38–39; Thorpe, *Federal and State Constitutions,* VI, 3426–44.

state. Memorials offered by antislavery societies from various locales around the state, but mostly from eastern Tennessee (where less that 10 percent of the population were slaves), opened the debate. These memorials challenged the morality of slavery, proclaimed its inconsistency with the ideals of the Declaration of Independence, and argued its apparent contradiction of the basic principles of republicanism.[51]

Rather than permit a lively public debate over the antislavery memorials, the convention appointed a special committee, chaired by John Mc-Kinney, an eastern Tennessee delegate, to consider them. The committee's report defended the convention's decision to "refuse to enter upon a lengthy discussion of the perplexing question." Convinced of the "utter impracticability" of all emancipation and expatriation plans, the committee concluded that such a debate would end in "the destruction of that harmony among members . . . so necessary . . . for the great work the people of Tennessee sent the convention here to perform." The committee conceded the "rectitude of the intentions" of the memorialists and acknowledged that proving slavery "a great evil" was "an easy task," but it added that "to tell how that evil can be removed is the question that the wisest heads and most benevolent hearts have not been able to answer."[52]

The special committee defended slavery as consistent with both biblical teachings and the principles of republican government. But neither Christianity nor republicanism explained the persistence of slavery in Tennessee. The committee's guarded proslavery argument rested not on a defense of slavery in the abstract, but instead on a racial justification of slavery as it existed in Jacksonian Tennessee. Where the slave and master were of the "same race and wore the same complexion," the committee declared, slavery had "long ago been extinguished." Moreover, following their emancipation, former slaves of the same race as their former masters successfully "mingled with the mass of the community." But, according to the committee, "the African slave stands in a different attitude—he bears upon his forehead a mark of separation which distinguishes him from the white man—as much after he is a free man as while he was a slave." Describing free blacks as a people "despised and trampled by the rest of the community," and arguing that their condition was "the most

51. For an overview of these issues, see Chase C. Mooney, "The Question of Slavery and the Free Negro in the Tennessee Constitutional Convention of 1834," *Journal of Southern History*, XII (1956), 487–509.

52. *Journal of the Convention of the State of Tennessee*, 87–93.

forlorn and wretched that can be imagined," the committee doubted that freeing slaves to become denizens of a biracial society dominated by whites represented a viable solution to the problem of slavery. Forever stigmatized by the identifying mark of race, the committee insisted, even the nominally free black "is a real slave." [53]

Branding the report "a kind of apology" for slavery, a minority of delegates, mostly from eastern Tennessee, dissented. The antislavery minority claimed that the special committee's report rested on premises "subversive of the true principles of republicanism." Skin color, they remonstrated, was not "a good reason for denying" blacks "the common rights of man." This dissident minority also chastised the committee for refusing to consider any of the specific emancipation and colonization proposals included in the memorials. [54]

Out of the limited exchange over slavery at the convention emerged a dramatic redefinition of the political status of free blacks in Tennessee, a move that revealed much about the racial assumptions of antebellum plain folk and the limits of egalitarianism in the Old South. As outlined above, critics of the antislavery movement used the plight of free blacks, who were generally poor and often endured social ostracism at the hands of both races, as a powerful argument against emancipation without colonization. Thus the report strengthened growing sentiment in favor of excluding free blacks from the suffrage. Tennessee's original 1796 constitution, which granted suffrage to "freemen" who met minimal freehold or residency requirements, permitted free blacks who were freeholders or longtime residents of a particular county to vote. But the idea of free blacks voting drew sharp criticism at the 1834 convention. [55] Egalitarian reformers complained about the contradictions involved in slaveholding society giving voting rights to black men who were otherwise considered "outside the social compact," while some delegates resisted the extension of the suffrage to all white males. Contending that white Tennesseans "reprobate and abhor" black voting, western delegate G. W. L. Marr believed the "political fabrics of Tennessee denied citizenship to all people of color, slave or free." Hence that the "supposed claim" of free blacks "to

53. *Ibid.*

54. *Ibid.*, 101–105.

55. Nashville *Republican and State Gazette,* July 1, 5, 15, 1834; Mooney, "Question of Slavery and the Free Negro," 503–506.

exercise the great right of free suffrage" should be "prohibited."[56] Non-slaveholder Terry Cahal agreed, arguing that continuing to allow free blacks to vote would result in the "degradation and injury" of whites by transforming Tennessee into "the asylum for free negroes and the harbour for runaway slaves."[57]

Following this brief but passionate discussion of the dangers of including free blacks as political citizens, the convention redefined suffrage in Tennessee. With one stroke of the pen, delegates inserted the word "white" into the constitutional requirement for voting. All free blacks, including freeholders, were disfranchised. To further define blacks out of the body politic, the convention excluded them from militia service and excused them from paying the poll tax required of whites.[58]

In the final analysis, Tennessee had reaffirmed its devotion to white man's democracy not only by expanding the political entitlement of the white plain folk but also by drawing the line of racial exclusion tighter and tighter around the region's free black population, defining egalitarianism in explicitly racial terms. As previously acceptable distinctions among whites collapsed under the pressure of the white egalitarian ideology, the racial justification of slavery and the exclusion of free blacks, including free blacks with property, character, and local reputation, from public life reinforced the popular perception that liberty was the exclusive right of whites.

Based on the preceding analysis of these three conventions, I conclude that the plain folk embraced four egalitarian principles as the core of their Jacksonian political creed. First, the plain folk emphasized the notion of equality of all citizens. Equality meant that all white men enjoyed equal political rights, privileges, and influence, and that no man or group of men should enjoy special privileges or influence due to wealth, family connections, or corrupt influence of any kind. Second, the plain folk embraced the idea of majority rule. By simple semantic definition, a republic existed where the sovereign people were governed by their own consent. Over time, however, the plain folk increasingly insisted that the will of

56. Marr's comments can be found in the *Journal of the Convention of the State of Tennessee*, 107.

57. Nashville *Republican and State Gazette*, July 10, 1834.

58. *Journal of the Convention of the State of Tennessee*, 209–14.

the people could be expressed only by the majority. Third, the plain folk were animated by hostility toward any public policy or private institution which they perceived as tending toward "aristocracy." In the American context, few were concerned with a formal hereditary aristocracy, a titled nobility of the European stripe, but rather with de facto aristocracies of various kinds, such as aristocracies of wealth, privilege, familial connections, and political or governmental preferment. Fourth, the plain folk were driven by their passion for exclusion. Indeed, the boundaries of political democracy in the antebellum South were as important because of whom they left out as whom they included. More often than not, the plain folk of the Old South were as interested in sharpening the racial and gender boundaries of popular republicanism as they were in effectively obliterating public recognition of class distinctions among whites.

The plain folk frequently invoked their Jeffersonian heritage in defense of their ideas, and indeed, it is easy to assume that their commitment to popular sovereignty, white equality, and majority rule, and their disdain for special privilege reflected a continuing allegiance to the republican faith of the founders. But the republican ideology of the founders was always an ambiguous construction, and it grew more rather than less problematic as it strained to accommodate challenges to its coherence generated by the market revolution.[59] In fact, the constitutional reform debate in the Jacksonian South revealed the growing bifurcation of an already-complex republican political tradition. Egalitarians cherished the republican heritage because of the legitimacy it gave popular sovereignty, the equality of white men, and the power of majorities. Conservatives embraced republicanism largely because of the way it checked and diffused democracy and because of the privileges it allowed property. The American republican experiment strained to balance, or hold in creative tension, as Madison hoped but doubted that it could, these potentially contradictory tendencies.[60]

59. Marc W. Kruman, "The Second American Party System and the Transformation of Revolutionary Republicanism," *Journal of the Early Republic*, XII (1992), 509–37. On the gender dimension of plain folk ideology in the Old South, see Stephanie McCurry, "The Two Faces of Republicanism: Gender and Proslavery Politics in Antebellum South Carolina," *Journal of American History*, LXX (1992), 1245–64.

60. Edmund S. Morgan, *Inventing the People: The Rise of Popular Sovereignty in England and America* (New York, 1988), 237–306; Robert A. Burt, *The Constitution in Conflict* (Cambridge, Mass., 1992), 34–76.

But as much as egalitarians and conservatives both proclaimed themselves the true heirs of the founders' republicanism, each camp had also transformed that ideology in important ways. Moving away from the founders' ideal of disinterested statesmanship, conservatives in the Age of Jackson openly avowed the need for protection of property, not because property was a guarantor of independence, but because property was a special interest that deserved protection. Abandoning the founders' concern for a "balanced" government, egalitarians in the Age of Jackson believed popular government meant not only government by consent of the governed, but also that the only true calculus of consent lay in the will of the majority. Moreover, whereas the founders had defined personal independence largely in economic terms, as the freedom from material dependence that allowed citizens to effectively shun the appeals of both the scheming demagogue and the ruthless capitalist, egalitarians of the Jacksonian era increasingly defined independence in terms of race. Citizenship became a racial entitlement. Virginia conservative William Colquhoun chided egalitarians on this point during the early 1850s. The idea that "the mere animal man because he happens to wear a white skin" can vote and govern resembled the "false reforms of the red republicans and socialists," Colquhoun opined, more than it did the ideas of the founders.[61]

From this Jacksonian transformation of republicanism emerged the first faint outlines of a new ideological competition that remained salient well into the twentieth century. Conservatism shunned the posture of "disinterestedness" to seek protection for the special interests of wealth, property, and capital, and advanced its claims on the government accordingly. Egalitarians sounded erstwhile populist notes about the economic independence of working households while vigorously defending racially exclusive definitions of citizenship. And beneath the passionate rhetoric, the Jeffersonian political economy of independent producers, which sustained all strains of early republican ideology, disintegrated in the vortex of a capitalist revolution that neither conservatives nor egalitarians could fully comprehend.

61. William S. Colquhoun to John Y. Mason, May 10, 1851, in Mason Family Papers, VHS.

Samuel C. Hyde, Jr.

Backcountry Justice in the Piney-Woods South

On a cold, cloudy Christmas Eve night in Franklin County, Mississippi, two horsemen chatted amiably as they entered a gully surrounded by a thick growth of immature pines. Suddenly, from a carefully prearranged spot, several shotgun blasts rang out, knocking the larger rider from his horse. His companion, though wounded, escaped amidst a hail of pistol shots. Acting with the inspiration of cold, vengeful hate, the assassins emerged from their place of concealment, fired a second load of buckshot into their victim's head, emptied a pistol into his heart, and battered his face with their gun butts. Whether the dead man realized before his death that he had been attacked within a stone's throw of the spot where he claimed the life of another the previous spring remained unclear; that the murderers considered their actions justified is certain.[1]

With the close of Reconstruction, large areas of the South returned to a semblance of the stability they had known in the antebellum period. But in other regions, unrestrained violence remained a fundamental component of everyday life. Lynchings, regulator movements, personal difficulties, and efforts to enforce restrictions on the production of moonshine all served to sustain the centrality of violence in southern culture. Far from a period of peace and prosperity, in many regions of the South the late nineteenth and early twentieth centuries witnessed exceptional levels of violence.

1. *Franklin Advocate* (Meadville, Miss.), January 2, 1908.

Much of the violence involved the systematic suppression of blacks or strident defenses of personal honor, both of which frequently enjoyed popular acceptance, indicating a degree of social homogeneity among the white population. By contrast, in some relatively isolated areas of the piney-woods and mountain South, scores of fierce feuds erupted, demonstrating the presence of sharp divisions within white society. Many of these feuds originated in the struggle for economic and political primacy that characterized much of the post-Reconstruction South; others resulted from the emergence of certain intrinsic attributes of life found in specific regions of the South and suddenly unfettered by the events of war and Reconstruction. Although slavery had certainly conditioned southerners to brutality, the concentration of violence in regions peripheral to the slave system and the exceptional levels of white-on-white violence in these same areas demonstrated the presence of other contributing causes. In many cases, the chaotic conditions dramatically illustrated a strong distaste for governance among many southerners and the necessity of powerful authority figures to maintain stability in the backcountry. Most significant, the turbulent conditions in the post-Reconstruction South provide important lessons in democracy, its limits, and the interrelationship between public virtue and stability.[2]

To many rural southerners, rather than a set of legal statutes, justice remained a pattern of societal norms allowing for respect of property rights, individual honor, and a maximum of personal independence. Any violation of this pattern amounted to a breach of justice requiring a specific response from the injured party. Upon learning that a youthful neighbor had approached his wife in an overly friendly manner, Robert Leard of Tangipahoa, Louisiana, promptly tracked the young man down and killed him. Under the piney-woods code of justice, anything less would have in-

---

2. For examples of southern violence, see Bertram Wyatt-Brown, *Southern Honor: Ethics and Behavior in the Old South* (New York, 1982); Richard M. Brown, *Strain of Violence: Historical Studies of American Violence and Vigilantism* (New York, 1975); Stephen Cresswell, *Mormons and Cowboys, Moonshiners and Klansmen: Federal Law Enforcement in the South and West, 1870–1893* (Tuscaloosa, 1991); Robert Ingalls, *Urban Vigilantes in the New South: Tampa 1882–1936* (Knoxville, 1988); Wilbur Miller, *Revenuers and Moonshiners: Enforcing Federal Liquor Law in the Mountain South, 1865–1900* (Chapel Hill, 1991); William Montel, *Killings: Folk Justice in the Upper South* (Lexington, Ky., 1986); Charles Mutzenberg, *Kentucky's Famous Feuds and Tragedies* (New York, 1917); Christopher Waldrep, *Nightriders: Defending Community in the Black Patch, 1890–1915* (Durham, N.C., 1993); and Altina Waller, *Feud: Hatfields, McCoys, and Social Change in Appalachia, 1860–1900* (Chapel Hill, 1988).

vited shame and ridicule upon the Leard family. Likewise, a bloody Mississippi feud resulted from the failure of one family to restrain its chickens from entering a neighbor's garden. In each case, as in countless others, judicial statutes and legally constituted authority remained perfectly irrelevant. Instead, a backcountry code of justice defined the proper response that best demonstrated individual honor and the power of independent conviction. An Alabama agrarian circular summarized the force of this creed, advising rural farmers that "if you wish to be loyal to every instinct of true manhood, if you want to maintain every principle of self respect and the respect of others, carry out your convictions." In many regions of the South, backcountry justice allowed for agreeable interpersonal relations independent of the demands of the established legal system. But it also frequently produced chaotic circumstances subject to the will of an individual interpreter, and most ominously, such situations were often resolved violently. Much as in many of our urban centers today, in large areas of the rural South, violent resolution of disputes remained the norm, not the unusual. Without strong leadership to restrain its excesses, the backcountry ideal would render stability exceptionally elusive in large areas of the late-nineteenth-century rural South.[3]

Many of the same areas that endured severely turbulent conditions in the late nineteenth century had earlier enjoyed relative stability. The antebellum harmony that many regions maintained rested on the firm direction provided by the planter elite, the consistent policy of racial suppression the slave system afforded, and the negligible emergence of economic development disruptive to the prevailing societal norm. The postwar collapse of planter power carried far-reaching implications in many regions. But the well-documented political significance of the curtailment of planter authority frequently overshadows the societal ramifications of the disintegration of strong leadership. In certain areas of the piney-woods South, the sudden removal of firm direction unleashed latent tendencies, such as fierce individualism and contempt for authority, that ultimately rendered society ungovernable.[4]

3. New Orleans *Weekly Picayune*, October 2, 1895; *Franklin Advocate* (Meadville, Miss.), July 30, 1914; "Address to the Alliance Members of the Second Congressional District," 1891, in Thomas Jefferson Carlisle Papers, Alabama State Archives, Montgomery [hereinafter cited as ASA].

4. For a description of planter dominance in the piney-woods South, see Samuel C. Hyde, Jr., *Pistols and Politics: The Dilemma of Democracy in Louisiana's Florida Parishes, 1810–1899* (Baton Rouge, 1996).

Abundant research has focused on the violent tendencies of southerners. Fewer studies have concentrated on the common elements of southern violence, particularly white-on-white violence, and especially the means by which organized lawlessness was suppressed and stability restored. The slaveholding elite had established a deferential social and political system that shaped the character of the antebellum South.[5] In many regions of the South, planter leadership provided the basis for social and political stability. Planter interests dominated statewide politics in virtually all the southern states. The planters' power also extended to local control of large areas of the rural South. The ruling elite's commitment to white supremacy allowed for limited, if controlled, opportunity for the common folk in an environment where restraints on economic competition furthered social stability. But the foundation for planter power remained a brutal system of human bondage. To the planters and many other whites, all other social and political concerns proved secondary to the maintenance of slavery. The planters' determination to preserve the practice that guaranteed their power created a dilemma for the mass of southern commoners: they either aspired to enter the ranks of the slaveholding elite, accepted a system often antagonistic to their own economic and political livelihood, or agitated for democratic reform. The plain folks' response to planter dominance proved central to the maintenance or absence of social stability in many regions of the South.

Planter leadership therefore presented an interesting contradiction for many southerners. Despite the evils of the antebellum South, the slaveholding elite created a system that generally promoted peace among the common folk. The presence of slavery highlighted the need to safeguard personal independence carefully, and demanded a measure of white unity. Moreover, by identifying a series of enemies common to white southerners—successively, abolitionists, Federal troops, and carpetbaggers—the planters sustained their power in many regions of the South through Reconstruction and, in the process, inhibited discord among the plain folk who recognized the need to rally in the face of a common threat. Some of

5. Some historians dispute the idea of planter dominance. Among the most notable examples are Frank L. Owsley, *Plain Folk of the Old South* (Baton Rouge, 1949), and Grady McWhiney, *Cracker Culture: Celtic Ways in the Old South* (Tuscaloosa, 1988). For some additional examples of southern violence, see Edward L. Ayers, *Vengeance and Justice: Crime and Punishment in the 19th-Century American South* (New York, 1984), and George Rable, *But There Was No Peace: The Role of Violence in the Politics of Reconstruction* (Athens, Ga., 1984).

the most intense post-Reconstruction violence occurred in regions conditioned to the strong leadership the planters had previously provided.

Although planter leadership furnished the basis for stability, planter political dominance frequently suppressed the ambitions of the common folk, created the fear of unseen enemies threatening southern liberty, and allowed for an education in violence through war and Reconstruction. As a result, at the close of Reconstruction many regions witnessed a rejection of the authority of the old elite. Many residents of these same areas proved reluctant to accept the leadership of a newly emerging elite whose business orientation exemplified the challenge of the New South, yet who lacked the deferential power and the common enemies the planters had employed to maintain their dominant position. By contrast, many regions that experienced continuing planter dominance in the same period enjoyed a restoration of stability, demonstrating the importance of strong leadership for containing the violent inclinations of many rural southerners.[6]

An excellent example of the relationship between strong leadership and stability can be found in Louisiana. And within Louisiana one region, the Florida parishes, provides an even clearer statement on the implications of this relationship. The eight parishes in the "toe" of Louisiana, between the Pearl and Mississippi Rivers, shared the statewide dichotomy between wealthy plantation country and poorer piney woods. The Felicianas and East Baton Rouge were among the wealthiest and most politically powerful parishes in the state; the eastern piney-woods parishes were far less developed. Yet the region endured a peculiar pattern of development. A long past of territorial ambiguity, which included periods of French, British, and Spanish overlordship, climaxed with an insurrection and the short-lived Republic of West Florida. For decades prior to incorporation with the rest of the state in 1812, the region served as a haven for Tories, army deserters, and desperadoes who exploited the prevailing instability and absence of American control. Disputed land claims, resulting from the conflicting grants of the various governing powers, aggravated the turbulent conditions. The general insecurity prompted

6. For examples of planter continuity, see William J. Cooper, Jr., *The Conservative Regime: South Carolina, 1877–1890* (Baton Rouge, 1991); Paul D. Escott, *Many Excellent People: Power and Privilege in North Carolina* (Chapel Hill, 1985); and Jonathan M. Wiener, *Social Origins of the New South: Alabama, 1860–1885* (Baton Rouge, 1978). See Hyde, *Pistols and Politics*, 202–203, 235–36, on a region that witnessed both a restoration of stability under planter leadership and a descent into chaos where planter authority collapsed.

an exasperated William C. C. Claiborne, the first American governor, to complain that "civil authority has become weak and lax in West Florida in which the influence of the laws is scarcely felt."[7]

Stability finally arrived with the successful introduction of a cotton-based economy and the determined leadership of Feliciana planters. During the late 1820s and 1830s, the cotton economy spread from the plantation parishes into the piney woods, bringing with it slaves, prosperity, and increasing planter control. Despite their willingness to follow the lead of their powerful neighbors, the piney-woods folk of eastern Louisiana shared the fierce attachment to independence and honor common to rural dwellers across the South. They lived their lives as proud, independent farmers shunning an urban, industrial existence and the complexities that often accompanied it. Yet the turbulent conditions that characterized the region demonstrated that the piney-woods existence in eastern Louisiana also involved a perverted perception of individual rights. From the colonial period into the early twentieth century, events in the Florida parishes demonstrated the unequivocal necessity of determined leadership to control the latent excesses of the population and maintain stability.[8]

Throughout the antebellum period, planters from the Mississippi River parishes dominated politics and the economy of the piney-woods region of eastern Louisiana.[9] To encourage white unity, planter politicians dramatically emphasized the presence of enemies common to regional whites, ranging from Spanish authorities to an assertive federal government. In

7. Dunbar Rowland, ed., *Official Letter Book of Governor William C. C. Claiborne* (6 vols.; Jackson, Miss., 1917), VI, 161–62; Hyde, *Pistols and Politics*, 21–45.

8. For a description of the arrival of the cotton economy, see John Hebron Moore, *The Emergence of the Cotton Kingdom in the Old Southwest* (Baton Rouge, 1988).

9. For examples of the planters' expanding economic control due to privatization of the means of market access, see *Journal of the Senate of the State of Louisiana*, 3d Legis., 1st Sess., February 1, 7, 1850; *Journal of the House of Representatives of the State of Louisiana*, 10th Legis., 2d Sess., January 13, February 9, 1832, and 3d Legis., 1st Sess., January 1, 1850. For examples of planter control of state and local government, see *Journal of the Senate of the State of Louisiana*, 1st Legis., 1st Sess., 1853, and 3d Legis., 1st Sess., 1850; *Journal of the House of Representatives of the State of Louisiana*, 4th Legis., 1st Sess., 1852, and 3d Legis., 1st Sess., 1854. See also East Baton Rouge, East Feliciana, West Feliciana, and St. Tammany police jury minutes, all in WPA Louisiana Parish Police Jury Minutes Collection, Louisiana and Lower Mississippi Valley Collections, Hill Memorial Library, Louisiana State University, Baton Rouge [hereinafter cited as LLMVC]; Notarial Records of Parris Childress, 1843–1851, in St. Tammany Parish Clerk of Court Archives, Covington, Louisiana; St. Helena Parish Records Collection, LLMVC; Manuscript Census, Louisiana, Schedule 1, Free Population, 1850 (microfilm).

particular, racist rhetoric and relentless press coverage portraying the planters as the bulwark against abolitionism furthered the planter appeal in a region heavily populated by small slaveholders.[10]

The planters' successful manipulation of events to achieve white unity exacerbated an unexpected tendency among eastern Louisiana's common folk. Political rhetoric centering on the threat to white southerners' independence posed by distant abolitionists stimulated an obsessive concern for individual liberty among the piney-woods dwellers. Concomitantly, the war in the Florida parishes degenerated into a guerrilla conflict. Atrocities committed by some undisciplined Union soldiers revived the traditional regional distaste for authority and provoked an energetic citizen response. In the absence of regular Confederate forces, bushwhacking emerged as a popular and effective means to strike back at the Federals. Shotgun blasts into the back of an enemy produced terror and proved exceptionally difficult to control. More important, bushwhacking manifested no sense of honor, which agreeable interpersonal relations in large areas of the South continued to require. As a result, for some, the events of the war served as a blueprint for the extralegal resolution of postwar grievances. The combination of contempt for authority, an emerging obsessive concern for individual liberty, and resolution of grievances by violence independent of the honor-bound restraints of the past proved an ominous mixture in eastern Louisiana.[11]

During Reconstruction the planter elite heightened the explosive potential of this dangerous combination by identifying another enemy com-

10. In 1850 the percentage of heads of households owning slaves in the piney-woods region of the Florida parishes ranged from a high of 66 percent in St. Helena to a low of 28 percent in Livingston. Figures for the remaining parishes in eastern Louisiana are: East Feliciana 76 percent, West Feliciana 55 percent, East Baton Rouge 29 percent, Washington 50 percent, and St. Tammany 37 percent. Manuscript Census, Louisiana, Schedule 3, Slave Population, 1850 (microfilm). Figures based on a 3 percent sample survey of heads of households in each parish.

11. Eugene Hunter to Stella, June 16, 1865, in Hunter-Taylor Family Papers, LLMVC; "Reminiscences of a Union Raid," in Josephine Pugh Papers, LLMVC; Patrick Geary, ed., *Celine: Remembering Louisiana, 1850–1871* (Athens, Ga., 1987), 111–21, 142, 144–48, 155. J. Burruss McGehee to James McGehee, February 5, 1904, Eve Brower to James S. McGehee, February 22, 1904, in James Stewart McGehee Papers, LLMVC. Amite City (La.) *Daily Wanderer*, December 8, 1864; *The War of the Rebellion: Official Records of the Union and Confederate Armies* (130 vol.; Washington, D.C., 1880–1901), Ser. I, Vol. XLI, Pt. 1, pp. 277–78; John Burruss to Edward, February 18, 1864, in John C. Burruss Papers, LLMVC; Howell Carter, *A Cavalryman's Reminiscences of the Civil War* (New Orleans, 1925), 113–14.

mon to southern whites, carpetbagger government, and encouraging its violent overthrow. As during the secession crisis, the natural tendencies and aspirations of the plain folk simmered while, at the behest of the antebellum elite, the common enemy was violently subdued. The close of Reconstruction concluded the interlude of fear and dependence on planter overlordship in the piney woods, initiating a revitalization of the demands for greater democracy.[12]

The stability that returned to many areas of the post-Reconstruction South did not return to the Bayou State. In Louisiana, years of chaotic conditions climaxed with the dramatic collapse of the Republican government. In most of the delta and sugar parishes, the planters' vast patronage allowed them to reassert their dominance easily, but in the piney-woods region of eastern Louisiana, local residents resisted the return of the prewar status quo. Voters in several of the piney-woods parishes demonstrated their newfound assertiveness by repudiating the old elite in the initial post-Reconstruction elections.[13]

The decline of planter authority in the piney woods created a political power vacuum and the opportunity for new leadership. But the men who filled this void lacked both the stature of the old elite and the unifying issues that the planters had so effectively manipulated in support of their dominance. The factionalization of politics and the rapid economic transformation occurring in certain areas, particularly along the line of the New Orleans–Jackson Railroad, rendered stability increasingly elusive. Indeed, societal equilibrium proved exceedingly difficult to secure in a region where, in the absence of a common threat, many refused to be governed. Furthermore, the fledgling political leaders faced the resentment of many of the old elite, who not only offered little assistance, but even withdrew their active support from a legal system in crisis. As a result, those who assumed positions of authority at this critical juncture possessed little experience and no regional tradition of leadership, facts well known to the public at large.[14]

---

12. New Orleans *Republican*, April 5, 1873; Amite City (La.) *Independent*, September 5, 1874; Amite City (La.) *Democrat*, September 4, November 20, December 11, 1875; *Tangipahoa Democrat* (Amite City, La.), September 26, 1874; *House Journal*, 1st Legis., 1st Sess., January 1876, 94–99.

13. Amite City (La.) *Independent*, December 6, 1879.

14. Map of the Line of the New Orleans–Jackson Railroad, *ca.* 1870, in Illinois Central Railroad Collection, Newberry Library, Chicago; *Report of the Manufactures of the United States at the Tenth Census, 1880* (Washington, D.C., 1883).

In the absence of an effective legal system, factions engaged in bitter competition to fill the prevailing political void. None of the groups commanded the level of political and economic patronage previously enjoyed by members of the antebellum elite. And one of the most powerful factions, dubbed the "Courthouse faction" by the New Orleans press, failed to provide consistent leadership regarding racial issues, a concern that had always commanded the intense interest of the planters.[15]

Despite the increasing factionalization of regional society and politics, racial concerns ultimately remained at the center of the southern psyche. Although the common folk proved willing to forsake the guidance of the antebellum elite, they continued to demand of their leaders an unqualified commitment to white supremacy. But during the last years of Reconstruction, some whites advocated racial cooperation as a tool to overcome the Republican government. As early as the fall of 1874 the impassioned debate surrounding this issue had created a rift in the once-solid ranks of Florida-parish Democrats. Increasing numbers of influential white Democrats preferred to grant blacks the suffrage that they in turn would control. In return for political support, blacks would be granted limited opportunities for advancement. Some of the most important supporters of the Courthouse faction opened their doors to black labor. For these "cooperationists," black employment provided a cheap and easily exploited source of workers. Even though all the emerging factions exploited blacks in one way or another, the Courthouse faction's reliance on black labor and votes seemed to compromise its commitment to white supremacy, a situation that proved intolerable to many whites.[16]

15. Tom Ellis to Steve Ellis, December 4, 1879, Steve to Tom, November 15, 1887, September 4, 1894, S. M. Robertson to Steve, August 11, 25, 1893, July 24, 1896, T. M. Akers to Steve, August 8, 1894, T. Babington to Steve, September 19, 1894, S. W. Settoon to Steve, September 9, 1895, Milton Strickland to Tom, February 15, 1896, all in Ellis Family Papers, LLMVC. Charles Lea to Hardy Richardson, March 20, 1879, in Hardy Richardson Papers, LLMVC; New Orleans *Daily Picayune*, April 4, July 4, 5, 1897; New Orleans *Times Democrat*, September 14, 1890, July 11, 1897; Amite City (La.) *Florida Parishes*, July 14, August 12, 1891.

16. Charles Kennon to Tom Ellis, November 11, 1870, October 6, 1874, Tom Ellis to Steve, April 1, 1884, all in Ellis Family Papers, LLMVC. Resolutions adopted by White League meeting at Bayou Barbary, Livingston Parish, September 5, 1874, in Mary Alley Scrapbooks, LLMVC. Amite City (La.) *Florida Parishes*, August 26, September 16, 1891; New Orleans *Weekly Picayune*, February 24, March 2, April 9, 1896, and *Daily Picayune*, February 22, July 4, 1897, January 10, 1898; Charles E. Lea to Uncle Hardy, March 20,

Opponents of cooperation, criminal elements, and others in conflict with the Courthouse faction coalesced into a tenuous alliance committed to its destruction. The press frequently referred to this group as "Branch Men," a name derived from the numerous branches or streams in the northeastern Tangipahoa Parish stronghold of some of the group's more notorious lawless elements. The Branch Men included some opportunistic families contemptuous of the power of the Courthouse faction. More ominously, they included the leaders of some of the more violent "white-cap groups" that terrorized the region. Usually inspired by economic competition, whitecaps menaced large areas of the rural South with their nocturnal adventures. In the piney woods of the Florida parishes, whitecap groups boldly raided mills and towns brutally intimidating their opponents. Although the whitecaps often served as self-appointed moral policemen, blacks remained the primary target of whitecap violence. Posting armed pickets on roads leading to targeted sites, whitecap leaders in the Florida parishes openly professed their determination to prevent blacks from working in local sawmills and brickyards.[17] The efforts of the Courthouse faction to contain the violence and protect its black laborers brought it into a fateful confrontation with the Branch Men.

Even more significant, the Courthouse faction, like the other political cliques that filled the power vacuum created by the decline of the old elite, lacked the deferential support the planters had always enjoyed, a situation dramatically amplified by their association with black laborers. As a result, local residents increasingly took the law into their own hands, provoking a series of bitter family feuds. The primary feud pitted supporters of the Courthouse faction against the most violent elements from among the Branch Men.

1879, in Hardy Richardson Papers, LLMVC. Testimony of Samuel H. Houston, in "Testimony Taken by the Select Committee on the Recent Election in Louisiana," *United States House of Representatives Report*, 44th Cong., 2d Sess., 1877, 263; testimony of J. W. Armstead, 297–99, Robert Wickliffe, 548–49, and John Kennard, 592, in "Testimony Taken by the Select Committee on Alleged Frauds in the Presidential Election of 1876," *United States House of Representatives Report*, 45th Cong., 3d Sess., 1879.

17. New Orleans *Times Democrat*, July 11, 1897; Amite City (La.) *Florida Parishes*, January 14, February 4, 11, 1891; New Orleans *Daily Picayune*, February 22, December 11, 1897; New Orleans *Item*, April 15, 1922. Kentwood (La.) *Commercial*, June 11, 1895; Sister to J. J. Stokes, February 6, 1893, in Joel A. Stokes Papers, LLMVC; Magnolia (Miss.) *Gazette*, November 9, 1882.

With the legal system in disarray and no individuals or factions capable of providing resolute leadership, feuding served as the principal means of societal regulation. Multiple unrelated family feuds developed across the piney-woods region of the Florida parishes. Little evidence exists to suggest that any of the feuding parties sought the intervention of the legal establishment; in essence, government remained aloof and irrelevant to the struggles. In an interview with the *Daily Picayune*, Tangipahoa Parish deputy sheriff Millard Edwards noted that those not involved in the feuding remained terrified of the participants and therefore would not support the peace officers.[18]

Although the unwillingness of some individuals to address the chaotic conditions can certainly be attributed to cowardice, this in itself does not account for the reaction of the majority. The tacit tolerance of lawlessness by the mass of the population signified instead the dominance of a corrupted perception of individual rights that served as the defining ideal of backcountry justice. In the Florida parishes, as in other regions of the South, violent resolution of perceived injustices had become not merely an accepted, but an expected, response among much of the population. The prevailing irrelevance of apathetic legal authority promoted a kill-or-be-killed attitude among many common folk involved in otherwise trivial disagreements. According to the New Orleans *Daily Picayune*, the prevailing chaos in the piney woods resulted from the presence of a plethora of peculiar people "who are exceedingly jealous of what they deem their rights, and it was mainly through their misconception of what those rights really were that the troubles originated."[19]

The oratory of the antebellum elite furthered this dangerous outlook. By employing only those aspects of the Jeffersonian tradition conducive to their social and political agenda, local power brokers promoted among many people an intense but distorted republican legacy that violently rejected government and other sources of restraint on individual liberty. The refusal of the mass of the population to address the lawlessness reinforced the impression that individual liberty was most effectively mani-

18. New Orleans *Daily Picayune*, October 22, 1894, March 27, July 4, November 22, December 15–16, 1897, and *Weekly Picayune*, August 2, 1894, June 27, 1895; Kentwood (La.) *Commercial*, December 4, 1897; *St. Helena Echo* (Greensburg, La.), July 9, 1892. Baton Rouge *Daily Advocate*, December 28, 1896, and rpr. in New Orleans *Daily Picayune*, December 21, 1897; New Orleans *Times Democrat*, December 23, 25, 1897.

19. New Orleans *Daily Picayune*, April 12, 1899.

fested through the barrel of a gun. In the spring of 1899, Louisiana adjutant general Allen Jumel noted that the feud-related violence had spiraled out of control because the victims "could not secure juries with the moral courage to bring in verdicts against the parties charged with crimes." As he scanned a mass meeting in support of one of the most violent group's right to eliminate those who threatened their liberty, Jumel added that "this was the fault of the people not the courts." Just as their political rhetoric had encouraged this dangerous tradition, only the firm direction provided by the planter elite had prevented its fruition from the antebellum period through Reconstruction.[20]

The dramatic escalation of violence corresponded chronologically and geographically with the retreat of planter dominance in eastern Louisiana. Complete regional official criminal statistics for the period are available only for the years 1877 and 1907. But existing records indicate that in the thirty-year period following the close of Reconstruction, the number of murders in the piney-woods parishes increased dramatically while the population less than doubled (see Table 1). The smallest change

TABLE 1

Homicides in Eastern Louisiana 1877 and 1907

Parish	Population	Homicides (1877)	Population	Homicides (1907)
East Baton Rouge	19,966	3	34,580	10
East Feliciana	15,132	6	20,055	7
West Feliciana	12,809	n/a	13,449	6
Livingston	5,258	0	10,627	11
St. Helena	7,504	0	9,172	6
St. Tammany	6,887	4	18,917	6
Tangipahoa	9,638	3	29,160	46
Washington	5,190	1	18,886	9

Homicide sources: 1877, "Report of the Attorney General," La. Legis. Docs (New Orleans, 1878), 44–47; 1907, "Report of the Attorney General" (New Orleans, 1908), 82–95.
Population sources: Tenth Census of the United States, 1880: Population; Twelfth Census of the United States, 1900: Population.

20. *Ibid.*, April 12, 14, 1899.

occurred in St. Tammany, where four reported murders in 1877 increased to six in 1907. Tangipahoa reported the most significant change, the number of murders there increasing from three to forty-six in the same period. Attempted murder and assault showed similar increases over the recorded level in 1877. Significantly, the plantation parishes of East Baton Rouge, East Feliciana, and West Feliciana did not experience similar increases. Violent crimes in each of the plantation parishes either decreased in number or remained about the same even though these parishes experienced population growth similar to that of the other four Florida parishes. Despite severely chaotic conditions during Reconstruction, the return of the antebellum elite to most positions of authority in the plantation parishes allowed for the restoration of stability.[21]

Although exceptional levels of violence prevailed in the piney woods of eastern Louisiana, the region did not constitute an anomaly. Similar patterns of violence prevailed in neighboring states. During the late nineteenth and early twentieth centuries, the southwestern counties of Mississippi, which had also enjoyed relative stability under the direction of a powerful slaveholding elite during the antebellum period, likewise experienced exceptional levels of organized lawlessness. Whitecaps, determined to regulate black labor practices, but also inspired by a strong sense of outrage against the growing economic power of local Jewish merchants, waged a campaign of terror designed to intimidate their opponents. The nightriders brazenly destroyed fences, burned barns, and committed murder. As in Louisiana, their activities provoked several blood feuds. Local residents acknowledged that the whitecaps operated in the belief that the "county courts could make no headway against them."[22]

21. "Report of the Attorney General," *Louisiana Legislative Documents*, 1878 (Baton Rouge, 1906), 1–40; "Report of the Attorney General to the General Assembly," *Louisiana Documents*, 1906–1908, Vol. I (New Orleans, 1908), 3–51; *Twelfth Census, 1900: Population*, 22–23; Sixteenth Judicial District Court Minute Books, multiple entries books 4–6, Tangipahoa Parish Clerk of Court Archives, Amite, Louisiana. Unfortunately, Justice Department records for the most chaotic period, 1892–1900, are incomplete. In some cases the district attorney failed to file a report; most significant, during the crucial years 1896–1898 he reported that all indictments and records in criminal cases were missing. See "Report of the Attorney General to the General Assembly of Louisiana, 1896–1898" (New Orleans, 1898), 51. Although the rates of murder in East Baton Rouge Parish did increase, this rise corresponded with the substantial population growth in that relatively urbanized parish.

22. Liberty (Miss.) *Southern Herald*, November 11, 1892, January 6, 1893; *Franklin Advocate* (Meadville, Miss.), September 28, 1899; Meridian *News*, May 6, 1893; Birmingham

Abundant evidence demonstrates the Mississippi malefactors' complete contempt for the law. In one Simpson County episode, a group of desperadoes locked a party of would-be arresting deputies in a barn and warned them to leave or be killed; the deputies readily complied. A more spectacular example of the prevailing disregard for the law occurred in Lincoln County. In the spring of 1893 a group of whitecaps seventy-five to eighty strong boldly entered the county seat at Brookhaven, surrounded the courthouse, and demanded the release of several of their members incarcerated there. Bloodshed was avoided when a group of prominent citizens led by the county judge persuaded the outlaws to depart in peace.[23]

Alabama nightriders also operated in flagrant disregard of the law. Their wanton acts of violence included the murder of innocent persons merely to demonstrate their brutal capabilities. In at least one Elmore County case, they displayed the remains of their victim along a public road as a warning to their opponents. Whitecaps in Cherokee and Cleburne Counties targeted those who informed federal marshals of the location of illegal moonshine distilleries. Multiple crimes frequently occurred during the Alabama assaults. A notorious Cleburne County episode involved arson, attempted murder, attempted rape, kidnapping, assault, and battery. As always, the terrorists operated in the knowledge that a significant proportion of local residents considered their actions justified. Supporters of Cherokee County whitecaps publicly proclaimed the group the true upholders of regional justice. The whitecaps' seeming absence of concern for the implications of their actions may have resulted from the questionable character of the local courts. In the last decades of the nineteenth century, a series of state officials urged the reform of the jury system to allow for selection by lot rather than individual appointment by a potentially crooked sheriff. The despair resulting from the dubious nature of the legal system led one Alabama piney-woods widow to complain that "it seems like there is no law here now."[24]

Age Herald, July 30, 1893; "Amite County Outlaw Days," 18–44, in WPA County History Collections, Mississippi Department of Archives and History, Jackson [hereinafter cited as MDAH].

23. *Meridian News*, May 6, 1893; *Franklin Advocate* (Meadville, Miss.), May 28, 1903; Birmingham *Age Herald*, July 30, 1893; New Orleans *Daily Picayune*, December 10, 1892; "Lincoln County Outlaw Days," 2–3, in WPA County History Collections, MDAH.

24. *Biennial Report of Attorney General William C. Fitts* (Montgomery, 1896), 17; *Biennial Report of Attorney General Henry C. Thompkins* (Montgomery, 1884), 9–10; *Biennial*

Numerous episodes of collective violence in Arkansas assumed a more exclusively racial focus. Nightriders in Pope and Conway Counties warned all blacks to depart the region, than launched armed assaults against the homes of those who remained. The effort to drive black workers from the area differed from events in southwestern Mississippi, where much of the trouble centered on the competition for black labor between local farmers and Jewish merchants accused of securing debt-ridden farms and operating them with black tenants. Yet as in the other states, the collective violence seemed to complement and reinforce individual acts of violent defiance to government. At the height of the Arkansas whitecap activities, in a well-publicized Izard County incident, several alleged "timber depredators" ambushed a small posse seeking to arrest them and killed a federal marshal in the process. Whitecaps in Pickens County, Georgia, swore to perjure themselves in court if necessary to sustain their nocturnal attacks on suspected revenue informers. When revenue agents arrested two of their members, an armed band boldly entered the county seat at Jasper and released them from jail. The Atlanta *Constitution* noted that "no resistance was given to the mob." Several particularly brutal Carroll County, Georgia, attacks allegedly resulted from a long simmering family feud.[25]

The similarities among the violent actions in each state highlight a corresponding pattern of antebellum development. The regions that endured some of the worst lawlessness were inhabited by people who remained of little consequence to antebellum power brokers. Although some of the affected regions of Alabama, Arkansas, and Georgia differed from eastern Louisiana and southwestern Mississippi in that they had not

Report of Attorney General T. N. McClellan (Montgomery, 1887), 9; *Biennial Report of Attorney General William L. Martin* (Montgomery, 1894), 12–20. Birmingham *Age Herald*, March 7, 15, June 21, 22, 24, 1893; Atlanta *Constitution*, March 18, 1893; Lusindia Tommas [sic] to Governor [sic] Jones, January 11, 1896, C. F. Curtis to Governor Oates, June 20, 1895, E. J. Mancill to Oates, March 23, 1896, William Young to Oates, April 6, 1896, all in Governor W. C. Oates Correspondence, ASA.

25. Governor James B. Berry to A. J. Witt, January 15, 1883, in Governor J. B. Berry Correspondence, Governor Daniel Jones to Samuel Caradine, March 1, 1897, both in Governor Daniel W. Jones Correspondence, Arkansas History Commission–State Archives, Little Rock [hereinafter cited as AHC]; *Randolph Herald* (Pocahontas, Ark.), April 6, 1893; New Orleans *Daily Picayune*, January 30, 1893; Little Rock *Arkansas Gazette*, February 24, 25, 1885; Atlanta *Constitution*, March 6, 9, 1890, February 12, March 24, 25, 27, 1893.

been subject to direct local control by a powerful planter elite, all shared the reality of possessing minimal political clout in a state dominated by planter interests. In essence, a tradition of relative political powerlessness applied to the inhabitants of most affected regions, creating conditions conducive to extralegal activities. Perhaps most significant, each of the states included in this study had, of course, experienced the ordeal of Reconstruction. Throughout the turbulent Reconstruction years many regional leaders had encouraged violence, depicting brutality as an honorable means to secure political control from an unjust oppressor. The Ku Klux Klan and other extralegal organizations proved splendidly successful in rejecting legal authority and achieving goals through terror. The prevailing contempt for federal authority that emerged during the Civil War intensified during Reconstruction and proved easily transferable to revenue agents and other representatives of authority during the late nineteenth century. In short, decades of qualified political influence furthered the appeal of backcountry justice as the only legitimate, popularly recognized source of social regulation. And in combination with stereotypical racial attitudes, amid the economic and political turbulence of the late nineteenth century, it created perfect conditions for instability.

Still another issue remained of fundamental importance in shaping perceptions of governance in each of these regions: the appeal of agrarian reformers. In many areas, the Populist Party's campaign to improve the economic fortunes of farmers struggling to survive in a system that often catered to the interests of big business reinforced contempt for government. Some Alabama Populists openly challenged the right of elected officials to govern them. Much of their rhetoric centered on the belief that the state Democratic Party employed questionable political maneuvers to frustrate the will of the majority and sustain the position of regional merchants. Yet the Populists also exposed blatant corruption within the legal system. According to one irate Calhoun County, Alabama, Populist, the common man "has been swindled by organized government in this county."[26]

26. J. M. Winfrey to Governor W. C. Oates, March 25, 1896, E. J. Mancill to Oates, March 23, 1896, Johnson Kiker to Oates, July 13, 1895, J. S. Snoddy to Oates, July 10, 1895, Sam Adams to Oates, October 21, 1896, all in Oates Correspondence, ASA; "Address to the Alliance Members of the Second Congressional District," 1891, in Thomas Jefferson Carlisle Papers, ASA; Calhoun County Farmers Mutual Association Records, 1896–1899, 97–152, ASA.

Disillusionment with government also appeared among agrarians in Arkansas and Louisiana. A leading Arkansas power broker complained that corruption and government mismanagement had created "widespread public disgust," noting that established politicians were "losing the battle to control the public mind" as they had once controlled it. A widely publicized circular titled "To the Granges of Arkansas" bluntly stated that "there is no protection for the farmer in the existing system." In some regions of Louisiana, the Populist Party functioned as the political arm of several whitecap groups.[27]

Despite the similarities among events in each state, an important difference developed concerning the suppression of the violence. The intensity of the popular commitment to backcountry justice demanded an organized response from respected local residents supported by determined state authority. Men of influence sought to convince residents, and especially juries, that true justice was not served by individual action; they also possessed the clout to secure the intervention of state authority. State government provided local police with the muscle to subdue the outlaws.

Perhaps one of the most dramatic illustrations of the fragile nature of democracy and the necessity of a coordinated response to restore stability in many regions of the backcountry South occurred in Sevier County, Tennessee. Situated between the largest urban center in east Tennessee, Knoxville, and the Great Smoky Mountains, Sevier County embodied the regional distinctiveness that separated the area from much of the remainder of the South. A virtual absence of blacks, and the overwhelmingly Unionist and pro-Republican sentiment characterizing the population during the Civil War and Reconstruction, permitted the emergence of a culture in many ways separate from that of the black-belt South. The post-Reconstruction instability that characterized the region, however, demonstrated that the dilemma of backcountry justice transcended standard racial and political patterns.

A tradition of resolving grievances independent of legally constituted authority encouraged the emergence of whitecap bands in the late 1880s and early 1890s. Less inspired by the demands for white supremacy that

27. T. F. Sorrells to Governor Churchill, May 12, 1881, in Luther C. Gulley Collection, AHC; Circular, "To the Granges of Arkansas," in Clark Grange No. 232, Pope County Arkansas Items, AHC; Kentwood (La.) *Commercial*, February 15, 1896; *St. Helena Echo* (Greensburg, La.), June 18, 1892; New Orleans *Daily Picayune*, December 23, 1896, February 22, December 11, 1897.

characterized nightriders in other regions of the South, the Sevier County whitecaps operated primarily as self-appointed enforcers of morality. Prostitutes, adulterers, and promiscuous women served as the principal victims of their nocturnal adventures. But as with other regulator bands, their extralegal activities encouraged escalating lawlessness. Whitecaps increasingly engaged in acts of robbery, assault, and even murder, confident of their immunity from prosecution. By the spring of 1897 nearly one hundred people had been attacked by the Sevier County whitecaps, and at least twelve had been murdered.[28]

A citizens' effort to control nightriders operating under the direction of a paramilitary group known as the "Blue bills" failed when the bloody cost of warfare between vigilante groups became apparent. Instead, the solution to the whitecaps' criminal activities emerged in the form of an alliance between leading citizens, local authority figures, and state government. The election of Sheriff Millard Fillmore Maples in a close and bitterly contested race heralded the onset of a more assertive local system of justice. Maples, who ran on a platform promising to contain organized lawlessness, soon realized that the problem was not arresting, but convicting, the outlaws. Stability in Sevier County frequently foundered on decisions by juries composed of men who shared the whitecaps' commitment to backcountry justice. Even more perplexing, several regional justices of the peace and the circuit judge were accused of dismissing numerous cases out of sympathy for the fugitives. Outrageous acts, such as the murder of a young couple by nightriders acting at the behest of a landlord determined to evict the victims, provoked public outrage. Influential citizens petitioned Governor Bob Taylor to support a measure to attach Sevier County to the Knox County circuit court, thereby circumventing the courts accused of sympathizing with the whitecaps. Governor Taylor offered his enthusiastic backing and a $500 reward for the arrest of the murderers.[29]

28. List of persons murdered and severely injured by whitecaps in Sevier County, manuscript in J. C. Houk Papers, Calvin McClung Historical Collection, Knox County Public Library System, Knoxville, Tennessee. For a detailed description of these events, see Thomas H. Davis, *The Whitecaps: A History of the Organization in Sevier County* (Knoxville, 1899).

29. D. A. Wayland to John C. Houk, March 20, 1897, M. F. Maples to Houk, March 22, 1897, D. W. Payne to Houk, March 23, 1897, G. E. Sharp to William Parton, April 1, 1897, all in J. C. Houk Papers, McClung Collection; William J. Cummings, "Community,

Despite some continuing support for the nightriders, the Tennessee legislature followed the governor's lead, approving a White Cap Bill that prohibited extralegal conspiracies to injure persons or property and barred participants of such acts from sitting on juries. In the same session the legislature approved the bill attaching Sevier County to the Knox circuit court, effectively transforming conditions in Sevier. Deprived of their protection from prosecution, as well as much of their popular support, whitecaps and other organized lawless groups rapidly declined. Where the independent efforts of citizens and local authority figures had failed, when combined—and supported by state authority—they proved overwhelmingly effective in restoring stability.[30]

Excepting eastern Louisiana, stability reemerged in each affected area when a combination of leading citizens, local peace officers, and state officials coordinated their efforts to suppress lawlessness. Whereas in Alabama, Arkansas, Georgia, Mississippi, and even other regions of Louisiana, governors acted aggressively to restore order, only a sustained statewide demand for the restoration of legal authority in the Florida parishes moved a reluctant Governor Murphy J. Foster to take action. Foster's discretion may have resulted from the fact that the Florida parishes lacked a clearly definable group of citizen leaders. In a very apparent way, eastern Louisiana differed from other areas in that the legal system was subject to, rather than separate from, the violence. Not only were the representatives of the legal system completely cowed by the violence, but feudists and nightriders so permeated the system itself that it proved ineffective, functioning as merely another partisan tool of the feudists. Unlike other regions, where a local judge or civic-minded group of influential citizens worked in cooperation with state officials to quell the violence, eastern Louisiana had no single person or group that commanded the necessary respect from a large enough segment of the population to enforce legal authority. As always, governance depended on the will of the governed. Studies by Tracy Campbell, William F. Holmes, Christopher Waldrep, Altina Waller, and others further demonstrate the

---

Violence, and the Nature of Change: Whitecapping in Sevier County, Tennessee, During the 1890s" (M.A. thesis, University of Tennessee, 1988), 63–65, 73–79.

30. Sevierville (Tenn.) *Star*, May 7, August 4, 1897; S. A. Sims to John C. Houk, March 18, 1897, M. F. Maples to Houk, March 22, 1897, B. D. Brabson to Jesse Rogers, March 31, 1897, J. Baird French to Houk, April 8, 1897, all in Houk Papers, McClung Collection.

interrelationship between a local elite, state authority, and stability in the late-nineteenth-century South.[31]

In eastern Louisiana, no such combination of forces emerged, and as a result, the region consistently sustained some of the highest rural murder rates in the nation through the outbreak of World War I. And throughout, only a few of the most violent individuals ever came to trial and none was ever convicted of murder. Although the territory continues to maintain inordinately high rates of violence today, by the early 1920s the emergence of a more modern, assertive legal system, along with increasing societal awareness of the economic implications of regional chaos, combined to restrain the most violent excesses.[32]

The violence that convulsed the late-nineteenth-century South served as a manifestation of the clash between the antiquated value system common to much of the backcountry and the demands of a more modern world. Local legal systems were frequently rendered impotent by peace officers or juries in sympathy with the backcountry code of justice, or out of fear of those who adhered to its violent ways. Accordingly, the transition from traditional to modern proved less painful in regions that enjoyed strong, enlightened leadership. The turbulence in eastern Louisiana demonstrated that planter power served an important role. The legacy of regional instability coupled with Jacksonian political rhetoric caused many among the

31. *Meridian News*, May 6, 1893; "Outlaw Days," 41, in WPA Amite County, Mississippi, Collection, MDAH; New Orleans *Daily Picayune*, November 3–4, 1892, January 4, December 21, 1897; Atlanta *Constitution*, March 24, 27, 1893; Franklinton (La.) *New Era*, December 17, 1898; Governor James B. Berry to A. J. Witt, January 15, 1883, in Governor James B. Berry Correspondence, Governor Daniel Jones to Samuel Caradine, March 1, 1897, in Governor Daniel W. Jones Correspondence, AHC; J. C. Collins to Governor W. C. Oates, June 22, 1896, Governor J. M. Stone [Miss.] to Governor Oates, December 7, 1895, C. W. Ferguson to Governor Oates, March 24, 1896, all in Oates Correspondence, ASA; Tracy Campbell, *The Politics of Despair: Power and Resistance in the Tobacco Wars* (Lexington, Ky., 1993); William F. Holmes, "Whitecapping: Agrarian Violence in Mississippi, 1902–1906," *Journal of Southern History*, XXXV (1969), 165–85; Waldrep, *Nightriders*; Waller, *Feud*.

32. New Orleans *Daily Picayune*, January 4, December 21, 1897, April 4–8, 12–14, 1899; Franklinton (La.) *New Era*, April 8, 1899; William B. Bankston and David H. Allen, "Rural Social Areas and Patterns of Homicide: An Analysis of Lethal Violence in Louisiana," *Rural Sociology*, XLV (1987), 223–37.

plain folk to resist regulation of their private affairs to the point of rejecting governance. Only the respect commanded by the planter elite as the
champion of southern whites offered a basis for stability.

Most significant, from the antebellum period through the close of Reconstruction planter leaders emphasized a commitment to white supremacy
that virtually guaranteed the allegiance of common whites, a commitment their successors as power brokers in eastern Louisiana failed fully to
appreciate. That planter dominance allowed for an orderly society is true,
but the planters' manipulation of the common folk repeatedly repressed
their aspirations, thus contributing to the emergence of a warped impression of individual rights. Moreover, the planters' political agenda reinforced an obsessive concern with personal liberty, raised the specter of
unseen enemies threatening that liberty, and produced a learning ground
for the effectiveness of violence in the form of war and Reconstruction.
By creating a popular obsession centered on the menace posed by common enemies, and by encouraging violent resistance to those enemies,
the ruling elite provoked the emergence of a dangerous tradition that
only the presence of powerful, respected leaders backed by state authority
could contain.

Those regions that endured similarly chaotic conditions yet enjoyed
either continuity of leadership from the antebellum period or witnessed
the emergence of a strong new generation of leaders saw the backcountry
code of justice fade away. Abundant racial violence continued, as it does
today, but in most regions that boasted forceful leadership, white-on-
white violence markedly declined. In much of the backcountry South,
the legal system itself produced no fear of retribution, and it worked only
where forceful leaders who commanded the respect of the public and the
clout to secure the intervention of state government were available to
support it. Essentially, confronted with fierce backcountry individualism
that included a propensity to violence, the late-nineteenth-century turbulence demonstrated that in some regions of the rural South democracy
worked best under oligarchic supervision. The events of war and Reconstruction, combined with popular resentment of governmental interference, produced a culture of violence that overwhelmed the system of justice and demanded an aggressive, coordinated response to restore stability.
Under such conditions the solution to the violence ultimately remained
not the incarceration of certain individuals, but the reconditioning of the
value system of the people to overcome the legacy of the antebellum

South and its turbulent collapse in order to confront the demands of modernity. Only leaders conscious of the values of the people and commanding their respect could direct the restoration of stability. As a result, the oft-overlooked dilemma in many regions of the late-nineteenth-century rural South remained overcoming the physical and ideological implications of antebellum planter power while maintaining order and prosperity. Unfortunately for the residents of some places, such as eastern Louisiana, events in their region epitomized the consequences of an inability to resolve that dilemma.

MICHAEL L. KURTZ

New South Demagoguery

One of the most renowned students of southern politics observed that the southern demagogue "is a national institution. His numbers are few but his fame is broad. He has become the whipping boy for all his section's errors and ills—and for many of the nation's. His antics have colored the popular view of a region of the United States."[1]

Made in 1949, this observation by V. O. Key, Jr., reflected the substantial local and national publicity, much of it highly critical, given to such flamboyant and colorful southern political leaders as Theodore G. Bilbo of Mississippi, Earl K. Long of Louisiana, James E. "Kissing Jim" Folsom of Alabama, and Eugene Talmadge of Georgia. In the contemporary South of half a century later, it is difficult to imagine a new "Cotton Ed" Smith or "Alfalfa Bill" Murray rising to power through ostentatious appeals to the poverty, ignorance, and bigotry of the region's rural masses. The modern South has a population far more heterogeneous and cosmopolitan than in the past, an economy structured on industry and technology, and a regional identity crumbling under the assault of jet planes, interstate highways, and telecommunications. With blacks possessing, for the first time in their regional history, real political power and influence, and a citizenry far more educated than before, the South no longer resembles, if indeed it ever did, that idyllic paradise so marvelously depicted by the

---

1. V. O. Key, Jr., *Southern Politics in State and Nation* (New York, 1949), 106.

Nashville agrarians six and a half decades ago. In the South of high rises, galleries, Disney World, and Cape Canaveral, the demagogue appears headed the way of such defunct characters in southern history as the slave, the sharecropper, and the overseer.[2]

But if the demagogue has all but disappeared as an integral part of southern politics, his legacy remains, modernized with the slick trappings of contemporary political campaigns: computerized polling data; issues discussed according to their "sound-bite" responses among "focus groups"; high-powered and high-paid consultants; professional fund-raising; and ten-to-thirty-second television commercials. Beneath those trappings, one finds the same phenomenon—politicians trying to win votes. Superficially, the two most prominent southern politicians of today, Bill Clinton and Newt Gingrich, appear to have little in common with Jeff Davis of Arkansas—the "Wild Ass of the Ozarks"—or with W. Lee "Pass the Biscuits, Pappy" O'Daniel of Texas, whose hysterical evocations of the "Lost Cause" and fiddle-and-banjo-thumping, foot-stomping campaigns mesmerized their audiences. Both Clinton, a Rhodes scholar, and Gingrich, a history Ph.D., have appeared on MTV and have publicly advocated the employment of cyberspace to communicate with their constituents.[3] Yet both have the same goal as their picturesque regional predecessors, winning elections, and they attempt to attain that goal by appealing to the passions and prejudices of the populace.[4]

From the last decade of the nineteenth century through the first half of the twentieth, the demagogue assumed center stage as one of the leading actors in the great drama of American politics. The dozens of southern politicians to whom the term has been applied all possessed distinctive, unique qualities of personality, character, rhetoric, and even of dress, qualities that set them apart from the ordinary breed of southern politicians and branded them with the mark of the demagogue. Those who wit-

2. See "The South Today," *Time*, September 27, 1976, pp. 28–99; see also "Forum," *ibid.*, 4–6.

3. For examples of Clinton's and Gingrich's affinity for cyberspace, see the Clinton home page on the World Wide Web at http://www.whitehouse.gov; and a Web site devoted to Gingrich at http://www.clark.net:80/pub/jeffd/mc_newt.html.

4. See excerpts from selected Clinton speeches on the World Wide Web at http://www.cg96.org/main/mac [the Clinton-Gore reelection home page]; also see the complete text of Gingrich's "Contract With America" on the World Wide Web at http://www.clark.net:80/pub/jeffd/contract.html [one link on a conservative home page].

nessed the demagogues in action thrilled at the sight of James K. Vardaman, Mississippi's "Great White Chief," as he entered a small town in the early 1900s with his long hair flowing down his back, his feet firmly planted in a bed of hay in an ox-drawn cart. Many Georgians still fondly recall Eugene Talmadge peering intently through his spectacles, his fingers nervously flicking his trademark "red galluses," as he lashed out with vitriolic attacks on Eleanor Roosevelt, Negroes, and Jews.

The list of such shenanigans could be extended almost endlessly, for all the demagogues employed them as campaign gimmicks. That such buffoonery represented transparent, blatant devices to prey on the ignorance and bigotry of the lower classes has led many writers to dismiss the demagogues as insincere charlatans, unscrupulous in their methods, caring nothing for the genuine needs of the people, and desirous only of winning their votes.[5] The national press and the most respected organs of southern journalism echoed this derogatory depiction. In a similar fashion, the South's aristocratic elite viewed the demagogues through identical lenses, often contributing to the journalistic denunciations and adding to them its own contempt and disdain, almost as if the demagogues, through their crudeness and vulgarity, sullied that genteel image of southern culture and manners the ruling hierarchy had tried so assiduously to cultivate. Such portrayals served to perpetuate a stereotyped image that the demagogues still carry.[6]

What those who scorned and denounced the demagogues failed to realize was that these men consciously and deliberately sought to shock elite sensibilities, not merely to rock the established boat of moonbeams, magnolias, and mint juleps, but to unleash a popular movement designed to overthrow the entrenched political order. Most of the demagogues in fact were highly educated and, in private conversation and social demeanor, quite articulate and erudite. Many came from middle- or upper-class families and could conduct themselves in a manner worthy of Ashley Wilkes at his most charming. Many shared the staunchly conservative social and economic views of the classes they attacked. But whereas their

5. See Ellis G. Arnall, *The Shore Dimly Seen* (Philadelphia, 1946), 40; Wallace Stegner, "Pattern for Demagogues," *Pacific Spectator*, XIV (1948), 389–411; and Katherine D. Lumpkin, *The South in Progress* (New York, 1940), 207–208.

6. For an example of the aristocratic portrayal of the demagogue, see the hostile depiction of Theodore G. Bilbo in William Alexander Percy, *Lanterns on the Levee: Recollections of a Planter's Son* (New York, 1941), 143–51.

opponents refused to descend to the level of the poor masses, the demagogues descended to it willingly, for they appreciated and understood the
deep yearning for recognition that these people had harbored for so long.
The demagogues also knew how to galvanize that yearning into political
action by communicating with the rural people in language they understood. To the plain folk of the South, the demagogue represented far more
than just another politician seeking their votes. He symbolized a real opportunity to compensate for generations of privation and ignorance, a
chance to "get even," to poke that pitchfork into President Cleveland's
ribs. The demagogue thus embodied the fears and frustrations of the plain
folk and provided a conduit for vocalizing those feelings and translating
them into political action.[7]

The southern demagogues had definite social and political goals, and
the fact that many of them realized most of those goals helped to transform the nature of twentieth-century southern politics. Far from being
mere rabble-rousers, the demagogues promoted surprisingly modern social
and political reforms. Such men as Tom Watson and Theodore Bilbo, at
least early in their careers, advocated certain far-reaching programs that
resembled some of the planks of the Populist and Progressive Party platforms. To be sure, some demagogues, like Cole Blease and Tom Heflin,
stood for programs indistinguishable from those of their conservative opponents. Others, like Bilbo, especially later in his career, descended so
deeply into the muck of racial bigotry that their liberal voting records
went virtually ignored. If nothing else, the demagogues tapped the aspirations of the plain folk of the South and called attention to their needs.[8]

The word *demagogue* derives from an ancient Greek term meaning
"leader of the people." The Greeks simply combined two words, *dēmos*
and *agōgos*, the former the root word for "people," the latter a derivation
of the root word for "leader." This originally neutral term quickly assumed
a derogatory connotation, and Athenian political rulers began to employ

---

7. See T. Harry Williams, *Romance and Realism in Southern Politics* (Athens, Ga.,
1961), 63, and Michael L. Kurtz, "The Demagogue Since 1890: A Southern Political
Stereotype" (M.A. thesis, University of Tennessee, 1963), 19, 24, 26, 29–30, 44.

8. T. Harry Williams, "The Gentleman from Louisiana: Demagogue or Democrat?"
Journal of Southern History, XXVI (1960), 3–21; Reinhard H. Luthin, "Flowering of the
Southern Demagogue," *American Scholar*, XX (1951), 185–95; Michael L. Kurtz, "The
Demagogue: A Southern Political Stereotype" (Paper delivered at the annual meeting of
the Southern Historical Association, Atlanta, 1976).

it to characterize their opponents, whom they regarded as unscrupulous and dishonest politicians stirring up mob emotions to gain power.[9] In *Orestes*, Euripedes called the demagogue "a man of loose tongue, intemperate, trusting to tumult, leading the populace to mischief with empty words."[10] In Book V of his *Politics*, Aristotle declared that "revolutions in democracies are generally caused by the intemperance of demagogues."[11]

For many centuries, *demagogue* fell into disuse, but in the sixteenth and seventeenth centuries, Thomas Hobbes, John Dryden, and Jonathan Swift revived it in its original, neutral meaning. Hobbes wrote: "In a Democracy, look how many Demagogues (that is) how many powerful orators there are with the people." Dryden referred to "the warriors and senators, and demagogues," and Swift called Demosthenes and Cicero "leaders (or, as the Greeks called it, a demagogue)." By 1850, the *Oxford English Dictionary* informs us, the word had branched into seven different forms: *demagogic, demagogism, demagoguish, demagogue* (as a noun), *demagogue* (as a verb), *demagogy,* and *demagoguery.*[12] In its American usage, *demagogue* became common in the late eighteenth and early nineteenth centuries, when Jeffersonians and Hamiltonians hurled the word at each other as a term of political derision.

In 1828, in his landmark *American Dictionary of the English Language,* Noah Webster reverted to the original meaning of *demagogue* as a "leader of the people."[13] However, his contemporary James Fenimore Cooper, in *The American Democrat,* published in the same year, provided a definition that remains the commonly accepted one today. According to Cooper, the demagogue "is usually sly, a detractor of others, a professor of humility and disinterestedness, a great stickler for equality as respects all above him, a man who acts in corners, and avoids open and manly expositions of his course, calls blackguards gentlemen and gentlemen folks, appeals to passions and prejudices rather than to reason, and is in all respects, a man of intrigue and deception, of sly cunning and management, instead of

9. Reinhard H. Luthin, *American Demagogues: Twentieth Century* (Boston, 1954), 3.

10. Richard H. Rovere, *Senator Joe McCarthy* (New York, 1959), 45.

11. Aristotle, *Politics*, Book V, quoted in Lycos search engine, World Wide Web, under "demagogue" search, referring to URL http://the-tech.mit.edu/Classics/Aristotle/politics .fivev.html. February 21, 1996.

12. *Oxford English Dictionary* (London, 1933), III, 172.

13. *An American Dictionary of the English Language* (New York, 1828), I, 159.

manifesting the frank, fearless qualities of the democracy he so prodigally professes."[14] This definition is quite similar to that given by the most respected authority on twentieth-century demagoguery, Reinhard Luthin. As Luthin wrote: "What is a demagogue? He is a politician skilled in oratory, flattery, and invective; evasive in discussing vital issues; promising everything to everybody; appealing to the passions rather than the reason of the public; and arousing racial, religious, and class prejudices—a man whose lust for power without recourse to principle leads him to seek to become a master of the masses."[15]

On countless occasions, writers and politicians have employed *demagogue* to denounce political candidates and incumbents with whom they disagreed. In 1868, Edward Bellamy assailed the "demagoguery and corruption of our public men."[16] In 1886, *Harper's Weekly* called Benjamin Butler a "dangerous demagogue . . . the symbol of disreputable politics."[17] In 1911, Theodore Roosevelt bemoaned the difficulty of winning the Republican nomination over William Howard Taft: "It becomes extremely difficult to beat a loud-mouthed demagogue."[18] In his 1965 account of the New York City mayoral race of that year, William F. Buckley, Jr., asserted that "Adam Clayton Powell, Jr., is a demagogue." In 1985, New York governor Mario Cuomo called conservative Republican Pat Buchanan's views "transparent demagoguery."[19] The term, in its pejorative connotation, continues in widespread use today and has even entered the world of cyberspace. My own World Wide Web search, conducted on the "Lycos" search engine, uncovered forty references to "demagogues" in Internet documents, and the AltaVista search engine revealed more than nine hundred. A brief sampling will illustrate the universal employment of the word to attack one's opponents. One home page attacked the "self-

14. James Fenimore Cooper, *The American Democrat* (1828; rpr. New York, 1956), 96. See also Robert E. Snyder, "The Concept of Demagoguery: Huey Long and His Literary Critics," *Louisiana Studies,* XV (1976), 61–83.

15. Luthin, *American Demagogues,* 3.

16. Edward Bellamy, *Looking Backward* (1868; rpr. Cambridge, Mass., 1967), 84.

17. Quoted in Hans Sperber and Travis Trittschuh, *American Political Terms: An Historical Dictionary* (Detroit, 1962), 116.

18. Quoted *ibid.,* 117.

19. William F. Buckley, Jr., *The Unmaking of a Mayor* (pbk.; New York, 1965), 21; "The Glib Gladiators," *Newsweek,* July 1, 1985, p. 43.

righteous religious demagogues." Another criticized the "arrogant demagogues in Congress."[20]

Numerous writers have attempted to delineate the unique characteristics of southern demagogues. Again, Reinhard Luthin made the most
comprehensive effort: "Promising everything to everybody, proclaiming
love for the 'common man,' preaching from the Bible, praising Founding
Fathers and Confederate heroes, protesting against 'nigger-lovin' Yankees
and Republicans, and purveying jokes, anecdotes, and histrionics, and
hillbilly music. . . . Hardy perennials of Dixie politics, they took to the
hustings in each Democratic campaign season. They attracted publicity
by their picturesque personalities, distinctive dress, unorthodox electioneering, pointless programs, and 'hot air' harangues."[21]

Reference works generally agree on the contemporary definition of the
term. The *American Political Dictionary* defines a demagogue as an "unscrupulous politician who seeks to win and hold office through emotional
appeals to mass prejudices and passions. Half-truths, outright lies, and
various means of card-stacking may be used in attempts to dupe the voters."[22] The *Random House Dictionary of the English Language* (1967) calls a
demagogue "an orator or political leader who gains power and popularity
by arousing the emotions, passions, and prejudices of the people." The
American Heritage Dictionary of the English Language (1969) defines a
demagogue as a "leader who obtains power by means of impassioned appeals to the emotions and prejudices of the public."

Numerous writers, usually referring to southern demagogues, have
added to these definitions. Some saw the mark of the demagogue as the
promise to establish a vague utopia, including panaceas for all social and
economic maladies. Others viewed him as an insincere charlatan whose
only motive for seeking public office lay in personal profit. Still others fo-

20. Lycos search engine, World Wide Web, February 21, 1996, under "demagogue"
search, referring to URL http://www.ua.com/cgi-bin/sfx/http://www.cc.org/cc/edu/reed
.html.; *ibid.*, referring to URL http://www.mecca.org/BME/STUDENTS/mdallara.html.
The AltaVista search engine, World Wide Web, July 1, 1996, under "demagogue" search,
revealed 918 references. One called Pat Buchanan a "Populist demagogue" [http://www
.vated.com/Buch2.html]; another stated that "Louis Farrakhan is a demagogue" [http://
www.spectacle.org/196/mmmarch.html]; yet another referred to the "rotund radio demagogue Rush Limbaugh" [http://www.ypn.com/vote/a865.html].

21. Luthin, "Flowering of the Southern Demagogue," 185.

22. William Safire, *Safire's Political Dictionary: The New Language of Politics* (New York,
1978), 163.

cused on campaign techniques and attached the label of demagogue to those politicians who engaged in irrational and inflammatory stump appeals. Some writers have delineated the conditions necessary to the rise of the demagogue. First, he seeks personal profit and advancement. Second, he is educated, but "not too much." Third, he carefully selects as his friends those whom the people support and as his enemies those whom the people oppose.[23]

Ellis G. Arnall, a governor of Georgia and a bitter opponent of Eugene Talmadge's, classified demagogues into three categories: the impostor; the power-hungry; and the sincere reformer whose disillusionment with political reality inspires him to resort to demagogic methods. In all three categories, Arnall contended, certain traits appear that mark the individual as a demagogue: (1) vague, ambiguous promises; (2) the use of armed thugs and bodyguards; (3) the frequent employment of scapegoats in campaign rhetoric; (4) an abiding fear of the educated, especially of college students and faculty; (5) showmanship. Historian Wilma Dykeman added three traits to Arnall's list: (1) "a way with words"; (2) "raising hell"; and (3) the use of "folksy nicknames." In a 1955 study of dictators and demagogues, G. M. Gilbert declared that a demagogue is "a person who seeks notoriety and power by exploiting the fears and desires of the people, offering scapegoats and dogmatic panaceas in an unscrupulous attempt to hold himself forth as the champion of their values, needs, and institutions. His behavior is guided more by its potential effect in beguiling public opinion than by any scrupulous regard for the truth, for basic social values, or for the integrity of the individual in his person, property, livelihood, or reputation."[24]

When examined carefully, these efforts at providing a meaningful definition of demagogue fail to establish a set of concrete criteria by which the term may be measured. These writers load their definitions with

23. Daniel M. Robison, "From Tillman to Long: Some Striking Leaders of the Rural South," *Journal of Southern History*, III (1937), 296–97; William T. Polk, *Southern Accent: From Uncle Remus to Oak Ridge* (New York, 1953), 192–93; Gerald W. Johnson, "Live Demagogues or Dead Gentlemen?" *Virginia Quarterly Review*, XII (1936), 3; Frederick E. Venn, "The Demagogue: A Textbook for Politicians," Pt. 1, *Independent*, April 26, 1924, pp. 219–20, and Pt. 2, May 10, 1924, pp. 256–58.

24. Arnall, *Shore Dimly Seen*, 40–41; Wilma Dykeman, "The Southern Demagogue," *Virginia Quarterly Review*, XXXIII (1957), 560–61; G. M. Gilbert, "Dictators and Demagogues," *Journal of Social Issues*, XI, 3 (1955), 51–52.

moral and ethical judgments that fall beyond the professional capabilities
of the historian to assess. For example, they often raise the issue of sincerity, ascribing to the demagogue such attributes as insincerity, unscrupu-
lousness, and dishonesty. Such terminology may appear meaningful in a
dictionary or in a book, but when applied to specific individuals, it loses
all meaning. All of the men commonly called "southern demagogues"
aroused feelings and emotions intensified by the spectacular character of
their campaign oratory and tactics. More often than not, the accusations
of insincerity originated in political counterattacks by their opponents,
rather than in objective inquiries into the genuineness of their intentions.
A further problem with these definitions is their lack of understanding of
the realities of American politics. As Allan P. Sindler observed: "An un-
biased application of these popularized standards of demagogy, then,
would lead to the conclusion that demagogy is an inherent part of all political appeals and a tactic of most politicians."[25]

Aware of the deficiencies in the common definitions of demagoguery,
several scholars have attempted to offer an alternative meaning of the
term. In a monograph on southern demagoguery, political scientist Allan
L. Larson argues that the question of sincerity cannot be evaluated by the
political scientist. Therefore, the key element in the new criteria for
demagoguery is the absence of such subjective terms as *insincere* and *unscrupulous*. Larson believes that a workable definition of a demagogue is "a
political leader or public figure which [sic] operates through appeals to the
passions." In Larson's analysis, when a politician engages in attempts to
persuade the public through rational discourse, "we may have politics of
the highest order." But those politicians who "pander to passion, prejudice,
bigotry, and ignorance, rather than reason, fall into another category, that
of demagogue." These demagogues arise during times of severe social and
economic distress, when people "look for a leader who will deliver them
from their problems."[26] By offering appealing but irrational solutions to
those problems, the demagogues win the voters' confidence and thereby
destroy their more principled and rational opponents in elections.

Larson's effort to restructure the parameters of demagoguery also fails
to supply concrete criteria by which the term can be measured. Through-

25. Allan P. Sindler, *Huey Long's Louisiana: State Politics, 1920–1952* (Baltimore,
1956), 111.

26. Allan Louis Larson, "Southern Demagogues: A Study in Charismatic Leadership"
(Ph.D. dissertation, University of Chicago, 1964), 76, 79, 85.

out American history, office seekers have employed essentially irrational appeals to win votes. Lyndon Johnson's campaign tactics in the presidential election of 1964 provide an outstanding example. So sharply delineated were the differences on the issues between Johnson and his Republican opponent, Senator Barry Goldwater, that they invited a campaign of rational discourse. Instead, Johnson opted for a campaign devoid of reasoned discussion. Flatly rejecting Goldwater's repeated pleas for a series of televised debates on the issues, Johnson took his case to the people by using campaign gimmicks every bit as flamboyant as those of many southern demagogues. In his study of the 1964 campaign, Theodore H. White observed that on the stump Johnson assumed a variety of personalities: "Fair-Shares Johnson"; "Preacher Johnson"; "Old Doc Johnson"; "Sheriff Johnson"; "Lonely Acres Johnson"; and "Uncle Lyndon." At the Oklahoma State Fair, "Fair-Shares Johnson" rode a horse, waved his Stetson hat, and after letting forth a whoop, declared that he had come to "talk to happy people." To an audience at the Mormon Tabernacle in Salt Lake City, "Preacher Johnson" stated that if everyone would "just go back to the Good Book and practice some of the teachings of the Lord . . . we won't be unhappy very long." "Lonely Acres Johnson" sobered a crowd with tales of the "awesome burden" of the presidency.[27] Johnson's campaign team preyed on popular fears about Goldwater's views on nuclear war by televising a classic commercial depicting a young girl in a field of daisies with a mushroom cloud replacing the child as a somber voice counted backward from ten to zero.[28]

Concurring with the contention that appeals to the emotions do not provide a useful criterion for an understanding of demagoguery, Allan Sindler offers a "broader category of demagoguery as distinguished from statesmanship," a category that embraces the quality of leadership. Sindler maintains that a true statesman will recognize a particular political, social, or economic issue, or "complaint," and will "intellectualize the complaint to a higher level of awareness" than the public is capable of reaching by itself, and he will recommend a "revision of the social, economic, or political framework as the necessary solution." In contrast to this statesmanly approach, the demagogue "personifies the complaint, intensifies

27. Theodore H. White, *The Making of the President: 1964* (New York, 1965), 359–60.
28. The famous commercial may be downloaded from the World Wide Web in a Quick Time version (for Macintosh) from http://www.pathfinder.com, using the All Politics link.

the original irrational elements or merely relieves tension by expressing feeling. By so doing, he seduces his followers into an emotional attachment to his person which effectively blocks any group awareness of either the real sources of their discontent or the real areas of solution."[29]

When applied to the real political world, as distinguished from the theorizing of the political scientist, Sindler's differentiation between statesman and demagogue lacks validity. Few American political leaders manage, if indeed they try at all, to educate voters about difficult problems and complicated, unpopular solutions to them. On the contrary, fearing voter retaliation, their inclination is to avoid serious discussion of pressing problems. Consequently, virtually all politicians run for office on campaign platforms dressed in evasiveness and decorated with generalization. In the 1996 presidential election, both the incumbent, Democrat Bill Clinton, and the challenger, Republican Bob Dole, utterly avoided serious, rational discussion of the imminent bankruptcy of the vast Social Security and Medicare entitlement programs, and of the harsh measures needed to avert it.[30]

Another critic of the common usage of *demagogue* was the historian T. Harry Williams, who observed that we have accepted the ancient Greek definition of a demagogue as a rabble-rouser. But, Williams stated, "implicit in Greek thinking about the subject was the assumption that in politics the masterful leader manipulated the mindless mass with the mere turbulence of his rhetoric." Williams argued that this Greek conception of demagoguery has little bearing on the American political scene, yet writers assume that men like Huey Long rose to power solely on their oratorical ability to attract attention. Because such usage ignores political reality, Williams called on students of southern politics to "dispense with the word demagogue in dealing with men like Long and employ instead a term suggested by Eric Hoffer, mass leader."[31] Williams believed that the southern demagogues met Hoffer's criteria for a mass leader, a man who does not

---

29. Sindler, *Huey Long's Louisiana*, 111.

30. For a candid discussion of Social Security and Medicare, see the material on 1996 Reform Party candidate Richard Lamm in Nancy Gibbs, "It's My Party and I'll Run If I Want To," *Time*, July 22, 1996, pp. 28–31. By way of contrast, see the Clinton and Dole positions on the two issues in their position papers for the 1996 presidential campaign, available from the Democratic and Republican National Committees.

31. Williams, "Gentleman from Louisiana," 17–19, 20–21.

hesitate to harness the frustrations of the masses into a crusade for genuine social and economic reform. The mass leader possesses several distinguishing characteristics. First, he sets a popular movement in motion by articulating the fears, resentments, and complaints of the masses, accomplishing this through a charismatic personality reinforced by an iron will strengthened by an unshakable faith in himself and in the cause he promotes. Second, he has enormous reserves of physical energy, enabling him to dedicate his total resources to the cause. Third, he instills fear in the populace, who simultaneously treat him with reverence and awe.[32]

Williams' substitution of *mass leader* for *demagogue* fails to resolve the fundamental problem of definition because it simply replaces one arbitrary label with another. Furthermore, Williams distorted Eric Hoffer's original concept of the mass leader. Hoffer used the term to denote such men as Adolf Hitler, Joseph Stalin, Benito Mussolini, Mohandas Gandhi, and Franklin Roosevelt, men whose influence clearly extended far beyond the boundaries of their native lands. Williams' contention that Huey Long belonged in the same category would find little support among scholars. It is also difficult to conjecture how such demagogues of very provincial scope as "Pitchfork Ben" Tillman, "Ma" and "Pa" Ferguson, and "Cotton Ed" Smith could seriously be classified as mass leaders on the same scale as Hitler, Stalin, and Roosevelt.[33]

The inability of scholars to arrive at a consensus on the meaning of *demagogue* has led some writers to recommend abolishing the word altogether. In his biography of Tom Watson, historian C. Vann Woodward argued that "the term 'Southern demagogue' should be recognized for what it is, a political epithet," correctly pointing out that "it does not contribute anything to our understanding of the men to whom it is applied." In discussing Huey Long, journalist Hamilton Basso remarked that the assertion that "Huey Long was a demagogue tells us nothing." In their history of the New South, historians Thomas Clark and Albert Kirwan made a pertinent observation about the word: "Southern political history, confusing at best, is hopelessly confounded by too free usage of the term demagogue. It would be better to forget the term altogether and to clas-

32. T. Harry Williams, *Huey Long* (New York, 1969), 411–19.

33. For a discussion of some of the issues raised in this analysis of the term *demagogue*, see Raymond Ostby Arsenault, "The Wild Ass of the Ozarks: Jeff Davis and the Social Bases of Southern Demagoguery" (Ph.D. dissertation, Brandeis University, 1979), 5–19.

sify politicians, if indeed they must be classified, as reformers or non-reformers, as progressives or conservatives. For although these terms are sweeping and subjective too, they do avoid evaluation of motives, a thing often not possible, and permit judgments based on the politicians' accomplishments rather than on their supposed beliefs."[34]

The validity of these arguments is persuasive. Over the past two decades, this author has collected several hundred examples of the usage of *demagogue*, and the collection reveals that the term is employed almost exclusively to reflect the political prejudices of the individuals using it.[35] Despite the lack of an acceptable definition, the word is so deeply embedded in southern historiography that even calls for its abolition by such distinguished scholars as Woodward and Clark have gone unheeded. It is therefore of value to discuss those characteristics of personal and political demeanor that have labeled certain southern politicians as demagogues. Because the political careers of the demagogues spanned a very long period, this study will concentrate in a general manner on those demagogues who flourished from the last two decades of the nineteenth century through the first three decades of the twentieth.

During those five decades, a host of men called "demagogues" rose to political power by championing the causes of the plain folk of the South: Robert "Fiddlin' Bob" Taylor of Tennessee; Benjamin Ryan "Pitchfork Ben" Tillman, Coleman Livingston "Coley" Blease, and Elliston D. "Cotton Ed" Smith of South Carolina; Jefferson "Jeff" Davis of Arkansas; James Stephen Hogg and James and Miriam "Ma and Pa" Ferguson of Texas; Thomas "Tom" Heflin of Alabama; James K. "The Great White Chief" Vardaman and Theodore G. Bilbo of Mississippi; and Thomas D. "Tom" Watson of Georgia. These men capitalized on the political discontent of the turbulent years of Populism and Progressivism and geared their campaign promises to the white lower classes, the plain folk, of their states.

34. C. Vann Woodward, *Tom Watson: Agrarian Rebel* (New York, 1938), preface; Hamilton Basso, "Huey Long and His Background," *Harper's Magazine*, May 1935, p. 668; Thomas D. Clark and Albert D. Kirwan, *The South Since Appomattox: A Century of Regional Change* (New York, 1967), 129.

35. For two examples of recent references to demagoguery, see Roger Rosenblatt, "The Demagogue in the Crowd," *Time*, October 21, 1985, p. 102, in which Rosenblatt calls Nation of Islam leader Louis Farrakhan a demagogue; and Joe Klein, "Powell's Race Problem," *Newsweek*, June 24, 1996, p. 39, in which Klein castigates both Colin Powell and Bill Clinton for their demagoguery.

In his study of Jeff Davis of Arkansas, Raymond O. Arsenault argued that early-twentieth-century demagogues, of whom Davis was only one of many, represented a radical agrarian insurgency that challenged the entrenched ruling class of New South planters and industrialists by developing a political movement based on a highly complex and innately social and cultural conflict between classes in the region. Arsenault further argued that these demagogues provided their constituents with much sound and fury, but little substantial improvement in their lives. Referring to Davis, but alluding to all of Davis' contemporary demagogues, Arsenault stated that "as an agrarian radical, he personalized the problems of downtrodden farmers; yet for the most part he practiced a politics of catharsis and symbolic action which probably inhibited radical change. He was an innovative politician who knew how to acquire and hold power, yet his administration produced more politics than government, more rhetoric than reform."[36]

In reality, the southern demagogues of the late nineteenth and early twentieth centuries could point to records of substantial accomplishment in the realms of social and economic reform. Between 1890 and 1894 in South Carolina, for example, Tillman persuaded the legislature to enact a host of measures that clearly reflected his affinity with Populist and Progressive reform: the establishment of Clemson and Winthrop Colleges; a more equitable distribution of state taxes; reapportionment of the legislature; the primary system for nominating candidates for statewide office; stricter state regulation of railroads; the reduction of weekly working hours for textile workers; and the adoption of a new state constitution containing a stringent antilynching provision and incorporating political and legal rights for women.[37] In Texas, Governor Hogg strongly advocated many of the political reforms of the Populists and Progressives, including secret ballots, the direct election of United States senators, and party primaries. Arsenault's review of Jeff Davis' meager record of reform in Arkansas simply cannot be projected to all of his contemporaries, as Tillman's and Hogg's records demonstrate.

Each of the so-called southern demagogues had a unique personality, rose to power for different reasons, and achieved a distinctive political record. They drew the bulk of their support from the poor-white and

36. Arsenault, "Wild Ass of the Ozarks," 496.

37. Francis Butler Simkins, *Pitchfork Ben Tillman: South Carolinian* (Baton Rouge, 1944), 155–70; Ernest M. Lander, Jr., *A History of South Carolina, 1865–1960* (Chapel Hill, 1960), 35–37.

small-farmer class, but also, as recent research has indicated, from the growing body of southerners employed in textile mills, working in the lumber industry, and holding a variety of occupations in small towns. These "plain folk" of the New South, either illiterate or having little formal education, regarded the demagogues as political leaders who could voice their grievances and who seemed to care for their genuine needs. Still feeling the effects of Reconstruction and living during a period of monumental economic change, the plain folk wanted schools, roads, medical care, and other necessities—programs the Bourbons and Redeemers utterly neglected. Like Huey P. Long, Sr., a modestly well-off farmer and land owner in Winn Parish, Louisiana, they found themselves confronted by forces that they scarcely understood—railroads, lumber barons, industrialists—and often proved amenable to Populist and even, in isolated cases like the elder Long's, to Socialist, appeals.[38]

Some demagogues, however, did not share these generally enlightened views. In a recent article, Bryant Simon discussed the reasons for the early-twentieth-century political phenomenon in South Carolina known as "Bleasism," named after the state's governor and senator, Coleman Livingston "Cole" or "Coley" Blease. Simon maintains that Blease constructed a large following of white male millworkers who became intensely devoted to him largely because he was the first politician to voice their grievances at a time when these people felt neglected by his opponents. Blease vehemently opposed virtually all programs that would have benefited the millworkers: child labor legislation, compulsory school attendance, minimum working hours, etc. Yet he retained their fierce loyalty because he made them feel as if he was one of them. Simon quoted an Aiken mill laborer: "Even though Coley don't ever do a durn thing for us poor fellows, he does at least promise us somethin', and that's more than any of the others do."[39] Blease, however, proved an exception to the

---

38. See Herbert Gambrell, "James Stephen Hogg: Statesman or Demagogue?" *Southwest Review*, XIII (1928), 338–66; Francis Butler Simkins, *The Tillman Movement in South Carolina* (Durham, N.C., 1928), 58–72; Dewey W. Grantham, *Southern Progressivism: The Reconciliation of Progress and Tradition* (Knoxville, 1983), 56–57. In Texas, James Stephen Hogg actively sought the votes of small farmers, both black and white, by espousing programs popular with the plain folk; see Alwyn Barr, *Reconstruction to Reform: Texas Politics, 1876–1906* (Austin, 1971), 117–39, 157, 240–45.

39. Bryant Simon, "The Appeal of Cole Blease of South Carolina: Race, Class, and Sex in the New South," *Journal of Southern History*, LXII (1996), 85–86.

general rule that the demagogues did indeed advocate social, political, and economic reforms every bit as far-reaching as did some of their more sedate urban Progressive counterparts such as Hoke Smith in Georgia and John M. Parker in Louisiana.[40]

The assumption that the demagogues gained political control solely through their picturesque personalities and unorthodox electioneering methods overlooks more fundamental reasons for their success. A more judicious assessment of their remarkable record of political accomplishment must take into consideration the fact that they possessed the imaginative appeal necessary to stir the political consciousness of the plain folk and to transform that consciousness into a potent political force. Insofar as they championed the causes of the plain folk, the demagogues represented, in however crude a manner, durable embodiments of the spirit and desires of a large majority of these people, making these political mavericks the vanguard of democracy in the New South. By "stroking the ego of democracy," as T. Harry Williams said, the demagogues assaulted a political power structure based on elitism and aristocratic control, highlighted by a disdainful neglect of the legitimate needs of the common people. Therefore those who judged the demagogues by their campaign tactics and public demeanor displayed a singularly myopic view of southern politics and society. A more balanced and objective means of evaluation lies in an analysis of their records while in office and in the social and economic conditions which produced them.

The main reason for the rise of the demagogue to prominence in the late-nineteenth- and early-twentieth-century South lay in the deep-rooted dissatisfaction of the plain folk with the historical tradition of neglect pursued by the conservative elite that had dominated regional politics for several decades. At the end of Reconstruction, this elite, often called Redeemers or Bourbons, either ignored or rejected all efforts at lifting from the plain folk the burdens of poverty, ignorance, and deprivation. Universally poor, semiliterate, and isolated from the mainstream of society, the plain folk made natural targets for demagogic appeals. Promising to lead these people out of their misery, the demagogues opened for them a vision of a new and better world. Like the revivalist exhorting the

40. See Dewey W. Grantham, *Hoke Smith and the Politics of the New South* (Baton Rouge, 1959), and Matthew Schott, "John M. Parker of Louisiana and the Varieties of American Progressivism" (Ph.D. dissertation, Vanderbilt University, 1969).

faithful to salvation, these popular spokesmen promised to purge the lives
of the downtrodden of the misery to which they were accustomed. By injecting the element of hope into a life devoid of any real opportunity for
material success, they made the frustrations of a soil-scratching, back-
wrenching existence more tolerable. The demagogues gave the plain folk
a sense of importance, a feeling that they belonged within, rather than
without, the political spectrum. The plain folk, many of them tenant
farmers and sharecroppers, others oppressed millworkers and lumberjacks,
admired the stately mansions and envied the wealth and status of the
elite but knew that they themselves lacked any real opportunity to obtain
those things. The demagogues voiced these frustrations and resentments
in language and mannerisms the plain folk understood. Through their
lively harangues, which mainly pitted the rich against the poor, they personified the class struggle between the dirt farmer and the planter. They
gave the residents of Tobacco Road a vision of Tara, and however distorted and unrealistic that vision may have been, the demagogues supplied a valuable and necessary catharsis to the latent and potentially explosive class divisions of New South society.

Each of the demagogues exhibited his own unique qualities of campaign style, political philosophy, and personal dedication to the goal of
genuine social and economic reform, but all shared certain characteristics
of political behavior. In general those characteristics embodied the development of methods of electioneering so radically different from the traditional that they called attention to certain recurrent and predominant
themes in the oratory of southern demagogues. Indeed, the employment
of these themes was what inspired political opponents to dismiss these
popular leaders as "demagogues."

The first of these themes, the exploitation of race as a political issue,
enabled many of the demagogues to win the backing of the white plain
folk. Mississippi's Vardaman and Bilbo, for example, engaged in racial bigotry of the most vicious kind because it proved a perennial vote-getter.
Dressed in flowing white robes, Vardaman appealed to rural whites to
back him, their "Great White Chief," in his battle against the "nigger
lovers." In 1903, commenting on President Theodore Roosevelt's controversial decision to invite blacks to the White House, Vardaman declared:
"Let Teddy take 'coons' to the White House. I should not care if the walls
of the ancient edifice should become so saturated with the effluvia from
the rancid carcasses that a Chinch bug would have to crawl upon the

dome to avoid asphyxiation."[41] Bilbo overcame a personal scandal—he was fired as a teacher in a girls' school because of "familiarity with his students"—by engaging in race-baiting of the most hateful nature. Winning the governorship in 1915, Bilbo could point with pride to a formidable list of reform measures: equalization of tax assessments, doubling the enrollment at the University of Mississippi, erecting charity hospitals, building roads, increasing aid to education, and enacting a stringent antilynching law. Later, as a United States senator, Bilbo would have a very solid pro–New Deal voting record. Yet his racism proved so intense that he is remembered more for his attacks on African Americans than for his accomplishments.[42]

One of the most prominent demagogues of the era, Tom Watson of Georgia, began his career as a reformer and as a moderate on the race issue. A graduate of Mercer College, Watson established a reputation as a powerful lawyer in rural Georgia in the 1880s. In the 1890s he joined the Populist Party and became its best-known southern member, running as its vice-presidential candidate in 1896 and its presidential candidate in 1904 and 1908. During this early phase of his career, Watson openly urged blacks to join with poor whites in the Populist crusade, thus making himself a target for racial demagoguery from his opponents. In 1905 he began publishing the muckraking *Tom Watson's Magazine*, which included articles by such established men of letters as Theodore Dreiser, Maxim Gorky, and Edgar Lee Masters. In 1906, Watson actively campaigned for the Progressive reformer Hoke Smith in Smith's successful gubernatorial campaign. In 1908, however, Watson underwent a radical

41. William M. Strickland, "James Kimble Vardaman: Manipulation Through Myths in Mississippi," in *The Oratory of Southern Demagogues*, ed. Cal M. Logue and Howard Dorgan (Baton Rouge, 1981), 75–76. See also Harris Dickson, "The Vardaman Idea," *Saturday Evening Post*, April 27, 1907, pp. 3–5, 61.

42. See Reinhard M. Luthin, "Some Demagogues in American History," *American Historical Review*, LVII (1951), 45. Bilbo's career is summarized in A. Wigfall Green, *The Man Bilbo* (Baton Rouge, 1963). His support for the New Deal is discussed in Chester M. Morgan, *Redneck Liberal: Theodore G. Bilbo and the New Deal* (Baton Rouge, 1985). The viciousness of Bilbo's racism may be seen in his characterization of a political opponent as "begotten in a nigger graveyard at midnight, suckled by a sow, educated by a fool." Quotation taken from R. J. Zorn, "Theodore G. Bilbo," in *Public Men in and out of Office*, ed. John Salter (Chapel Hill, 1946), 284. Also see Theodore G. Bilbo, "The Vardaman Idea Brought Up to Date," in *The South Since Reconstruction*, ed. Thomas D. Clark (Indianapolis, 1973), 442–48.

transformation, marking his political campaigns with racial and religious hatred. Watson's venomous attacks on Jews undoubtedly contributed to the lynching of Leo Frank for the 1913 rape and murder of thirteen-year-old Mary Phagan. Watson's characterization of Frank as a "typical libertine Jew" helped arouse the passions of the mob that stormed the Georgia prison in 1915 so it could drag Frank outside to a "hanging tree."[43]

A second consistent theme of demagogic oratory was sectional rivalry. In their stump appearances, the demagogues often pitted the South against the North and made "Yankees" and "carpetbaggers" scapegoats for many of the South's problems. By stirring up sectional animosities, the demagogues generated a kind of regional xenophobia that attracted much sympathy from their audiences. Closely related was their invocation of the "Lost Cause" romanticism so commonly found in postbellum southern literature and journalism. Tom Watson, for example, exploited his friendship with Alexander Stephens, the former Confederate vice-president, and with Robert Toombs, a former Confederate cabinet member and general, to win popular support in his early campaigns.[44] By extolling the virtues of Johnny Reb, the demagogues gave their rural supporters a nostalgic and idealized vision of their region's past. This emphasis on sectionalism also manifested itself in the demagogues' repeated attacks on the Republican Party, the party of "niggers and Yankees," as Cole Blease declared.[45]

A third constant theme of demagogic oratory came in the form of rural chauvinism. Appreciating the harshness and drudgery of the daily life of the tenant farmer and sharecropper, the demagogues deftly juxtaposed the supposed virtues of agrarian existence to the alleged sordid materialism of urban life. They exposed the vices of modern industrial society by comparing the innocence of the farm with the corruption of the city. Corporations, industries, the capitalistic system itself became natural targets for much of the invective heard in demagogic stump appeals. Tom Watson exploited this rural-urban hostility in a typical stump speech when he re-

43. Woodward, *Tom Watson*, 135–66, 332–27, 366–67, 435–39; Grantham, *Southern Progressivism*, 52.

44. Woodward, *Tom Watson*, 47–51.

45. Quoted in Daniel W. Hollis, "Cole Blease: The Years Between the Governorship and the Senate, 1915–1924" (Paper delivered at the annual meeting of the Southern Historical Association, Atlanta, 1976). A revised version of the paper was published as Daniel W. Hollis, "Cole Blease: The Years Between the Governorship and the Senate, 1915–1924," *South Carolina Historical Magazine*, LXXX (1979), 1–17.

ferred to Atlanta: "If the devil himself were to come to this town in a palace car and propose to haul the balance of the state to his infernal kingdom, and to allow Atlanta capitalists the profits on the transaction, they would cry, 'Hurrah for the devil. He's going to build up Atlanta!'" It is instructive that Watson's attacks on Atlanta led the city's power structure to brand him as a "demagogue" in the early 1890s.[46]

Class antagonisms became the most common recurring theme in demagogic oratory. In a host of lively harangues, the demagogues mocked and scorned the hypocrisy and pomposity of the upper classes, and they made railroad magnates, rural landlords, industrial entrepreneurs, and bankers the objects of many of their most scathing attacks. Simultaneously, they turned the impoverished masses into subjects of praise. Because the Horatio Alger "rags to riches" story so popular in the contemporary industrialized North and Midwest had little relevance in the agrarian South, the demagogues devised a kind of reverse Social Darwinism in which they employed biblical aphorisms ("Blessed are the poor, for they shall inherit the earth"; "It is harder for a rich man to enter the kingdom of heaven than it is for a camel to pass through the eye of a needle") to preach the ultimate spiritual victory of the plain folk.

Jeff Davis of Arkansas effectively used these class divisions to appeal to the plain folk in his state. He frequently made corporations and trusts objects of derision. In one speech, he said: "Mr. Corporation, if you are a member of ANY, a-n-y pool or trust, you cannot do business in Arkansas." Uniting the plain folk of Arkansas, who encompassed everyone from people living in the mountains in the north to dirt farmers in the southern flatlands, Davis declared that "we are all united by a community of interests binding us together, that comes down from the great White Throne of God himself." He called for these plain folk to join him in his great crusade to clean up the state government, which he asserted was thoroughly riddled with corruption engendered by the moneyed interests: "There is no great reformation on the earth that did not come from the ranks of the humble and lowly of the land."[47]

To communicate these themes with maximum effectiveness, the demagogues transformed southern politics into a form of mass entertainment.

46. Woodward, *Tom Watson*, 168–77, 179 (quotation).

47. Annette Shelby, "Jeff Davis of Arkansas: 'Professional Man of the People,'" in *Oratory of Southern Demagogues*, ed. Logue and Dorgan, 42–43.

In their travels through rural areas, they instinctively knew how to attract large audiences by offering food and music and how to hold their attention by engaging in an assortment of buffoonery to enliven traditional platform rhetoric. Some donned flashy clothing; others regaled their listeners with humorous anecdotes. One classic tale related countless times by Earl Long of Louisiana illustrates a common demagogic tactic:

> I know many fine rich people, but most of them are like the mean ol' rich feller who died in Plaquemines Parish. Before he was sentenced to Hell, he took an appeal to St. Peter: "One day in 1923, I gave a nickel to a blind man." St. Peter's clerk looked up the entry, and after 386 pages of how that ol' stump wormer cheated the poor, he found the record. "That ain't enough," said St. Peter. "Wait," said the ol' codger. "In 1939, I gave a nickel to a widow." After 579 more pages of lying and cheating, the clerk found that entry. "That ain't neither enough," said St. Peter. "DON'T sentence me yet!" screamed the hateful ol' thing. "In 1952, I gave a nickel to the Red Cross." After 1,235 more pages, the clerk found that entry, so he said to St. Peter, "Your Honor, what are we going to do?" St. Peter said, "Give him back his fifteen cents and tell him to go to Hell!"[48]

To the southern rural masses, accustomed to a highly isolated existence that effectively distanced them from the mainstream of society, such antics gave them a temporary and fun-filled release from their daily grind. Through their magnetic personalities and in their fiery stump appearances, the demagogues took southern politics off its aristocratic pedestal and placed it squarely on egalitarian grounds. Their campaigns featured a considerable amount of personal contact between themselves and the voters, with the demagogues mingling with the plain folk, often eating, sleeping, and tilling the fields with them.

In summary, the demagogue proved a unique character in southern history. Often maligned, almost always misunderstood, he gave the white plain folk of the South a voice in the region's political system. To be sure, he exploited their ignorance and bigotry, often enriching himself while ignoring their genuine needs, but if the plain folk had not suffered generations of neglect of those needs, the demagogue would never have arisen. His populist rhetoric and progressive platforms addressed legiti-

48. Author's collection of Long political humor; for a slightly different version, see A. J. Liebling, *The Earl of Louisiana* (New York, 1961), 75–76.

mate grievances that the South's traditional political leadership had not addressed. The demagogue did at least address those grievances and in so doing, became the political incarnation of the plain folk of the South.[49]

49. A sampling of other comments on southern demagogues may be found in James Bryce, *The American Commonwealth* (2 vols.; New York, 1904), II, 578–80; Allan Michie and Frank Rhylick, *Dixie Demagogues* (New York, 1939); Clarence Cason, *Ninety Degrees in the Shade* (Chapel Hill, 1935), 88–89; Francis Butler Simkins, *A History of the South* (New York, 1953), 538–44; William B. Hesseltine and David L. Smiley, *The South in American History* (3d ed.; Englewood Cliffs, N.J., 1960), 486–89; John S. Ezell, *The South Since 1865* (New York, 1963), 372–82; Monroe Lee Billington, *The Political South in the Twentieth Century* (New York, 1965), 320–24; William J. Cooper, Jr., and Thomas E. Terrill, *The American South: A History* (2d ed.; New York, 1996), 544–49; John R. Boles, *The South Through Time: A History of an American Region* (Englewood Cliffs, N.J., 1995), 406–407; Clement Eaton, *The Freedom-of-Thought Struggle in the Old South* (New York, 1964), 181–84, 259–61; W. J. Cash, *The Mind of the South* (New York, 1941), 250–59; Robert Sherrill, *Gothic Politics in the Deep South* (New York, 1969), 203; Albert D. Kirwan, *Revolt of the Rednecks: Mississippi Politics, 1876–1925* (Lexington, Ky., 1951), 162–77; Stetson Kennedy, *Southern Exposure* (Garden City, N.Y., 1946), 127–31; Henry Savage, Jr., *The Seeds of Time: The Background of Southern Thinking* (New York, 1959), 221; Robert C. Cotner, *James Stephen Hogg: A Biography* (Austin, 1959); Daniel M. Robison, *Bob Taylor and the Agrarian Revolt in Tennessee* (Chapel Hill, 1935); Roger L. Hart, *Redeemers, Bourbons, and Populists: Tennessee, 1870–1896* (Baton Rouge, 1975), 84–107; Robert A. Caro, *Means of Ascent* (New York, 1982), 289–90, Vol. I of Caro, *The Years of Lyndon Johnson*, 2 vols.; David R. Colburn and Richard K. Scher, *Florida's Gubernatorial Politics in the Twentieth Century* (Tallahassee, 1980), 66–69, 280–81; William Anderson, *The Wild Man from Sugar Creek: The Political Career of Eugene Talmadge* (Baton Rouge, 1975); Raymond O. Arsenault, *The Wild Ass of the Ozarks: Jeff Davis and the Social Bases of Southern Politics* (Knoxville, 1988); Frank H. Kent, "Our Political Monstrosities," *Atlantic Monthly*, April 1935, pp. 407–11; Alva Johnston, "Political Showmen," *Forum*, July 1932, pp. 21–25; William A. Mabry, "Ben Tillman Disfranchised the Negro," *South Atlantic Quarterly*, XXXVII (1938), 170–83; Herbert A. Ladner, "James Kimble Vardaman: Governor of Mississippi," *Journal of Mississippi History*, II (1940), 185–95; Sarah M. Lemmon, "The Ideology of Eugene Talmadge," *Georgia Historical Quarterly*, XXXVIII (1964), 226–48; John W. Owens, "Tom Heflin," *American Mercury*, November 1932, pp. 272–79; Clarence N. Stone, "Bleasism and the 1912 Election in South Carolina," *North Carolina Historical Review*, XL (1963), 54–74; J. Wayne Flynt, "Sidney J. Catts: The Road to Power," *Florida Historical Quarterly*, XLIX (1970), 107–28; Richard L. Niswonger, "A Study in Southern Demagoguery: Jeff Davis of Arkansas," *American Historical Review*, LXXXIV (1979), 970–92; Leah R. Atkins, "Felix Grundy McConnell: Old South Demagogue," *Alabama Review*, XXX (1977), 83–100; Michael L. Kurtz, "Demagoguery," in *The Encyclopedia of Southern History*, ed. David C. Roller and Robert W. Twyman (Baton Rouge, 1979), 354; and Hugh Davis Graham, "Demagogues," in *Encyclopedia of Southern Culture*, ed. Charles Reagan Wilson and William Ferris (Chapel Hill, 1989), 1163–64.

CONTRIBUTORS

JOHN B. BOLES is professor of history at Rice University, managing editor of the journal *Southern History*, author of numerous works, and coeditor of *Interpreting Southern History: Historiographical Essays in Honor of Sanford W. Higginbotham*.

BRADLEY BOND is assistant professor of history at the University of Southern Mississippi. He is the author of *Political Culture in the Nineteenth Century South: Mississippi, 1830–1860*.

LACY K. FORD is associate professor of history at the University of South Carolina. Among his many publications is *Origins of Southern Radicalism: The South Carolina Upcountry, 1800–1860*.

J. WILLIAM HARRIS is associate professor of history at the University of New Hampshire. Perhaps the most notable of his publications is *Plain Folk and Gentry in a Slaveholding Society: White Liberty and Black Slavery in Augusta's Hinterlands*.

SAMUEL C. HYDE, JR., is assistant professor of history at Southeastern Louisiana University. He is the author of *Pistols and Politics: The Dilemma of Democracy in Louisiana's Florida Parishes, 1810–1899*.

JERAH JOHNSON is a professor and coordinator of graduate studies in the History Department at the University of New Orleans. He is the author of multiple articles on southern history and culture.

MICHAEL KURTZ is professor of history and director of graduate studies at Southeastern Louisiana University. Among his many publications is *Louisiana: A History*.

BILL MALONE recently retired from his position as professor of history at Tulane University. His most recent book is *Singing Cowboys and Musical Mountaineers: Southern Culture and the Roots of Country Music*.

SALLY G. McMILLEN is associate professor of history at Davidson College. Among her many notable publications is *Motherhood in the Old South: Pregnancy, Childbirth, and Infant Rearing*.

GRADY McWHINEY recently retired from his position as Lyndon B. Johnson Professor of History at Texas Christian University. Perhaps the most notable of his many publications is *Cracker Culture: Celtic Ways in the Old South*.

GARY MILLS is professor of history at the University of Alabama. He is author of *The Forgotten People: Cane River's Creoles of Color*.

INDEX

	DATE DUE	